For Steph and Ethan, and they know why.

About the Authors

Debra and Brad Schepp have blended their interests in technology and pop culture throughout their careers as journalists and authors. For more than 20 years they've written about cutting-edge technologies and how those technologies are changing our lives. Their work has been featured in publications such as *Newsweek, The Chicago Tribune,* and *U.S. News and World Report*. Together Brad and Deb have written nine books from *The Complete Guide to CompuServe* (McGraw-Hill, 1991) to *Kidnet: The Kid's Guide to Surfing Through Cyberspace* (HarperCollins, 1995). They have been buying and selling on eBay since 1999.

Contents at a Glance

Contents

Acknowledgments

This book is the result of the countless hours we spent researching the lives of PowerSellers and writing about those lives. Although it sometimes seemed we'd spend the rest of our days here in our offices, the effort we put into the pages you hold would have gone for nothing if not for the generosity, creativity, and intelligence of the scores of PowerSellers who spoke with us, wrote to us, and let us into their business lives. It would be too much to ask of our readers if we called out each seller by name. They know who they are, and we've tried to show them throughout the life of this project just how much we appreciated the treasures they shared with us. It is very humbling to try to return the debt owed to people who have answered our endless questions promptly and with grace, good humor, and wisdom. We'd like to offer them a collective thanks and more admiration than they'll ever know for all they've achieved.

Among that group of PowerSellers, there is a core of people who offered us even more. These are the sellers who agreed to be the subjects of our profiles. We'd like to thank them each individually. To Andy and Deb Mowry, you taught us so much and you made us laugh, too. Adam Nollmeyer was generous with his talents both as a PowerSeller and a professional photographer. Tony Cicalese has more heart and more smarts than most people can even imagine. Katrina and Jeffrey Hess shared a wealth of knowledge about selling precious items and protecting both those items and the customers who buy them from fraud and theft. Christina Carr brings creativity and common sense to the art of forging an eBay lifestyle. Dan Glasure, Nick Boyd, Glen and Diane Turner, and Lou DiDona are all collectibles dealers on eBay who gave us great insight into that niche of the eBay world. Gary Neubert shared his perspective about branching out from his family's business; and finally, to our anonymous Square Trade mediator, a silent thanks.

Other people who contributed valuable pieces of information were not necessarily PowerSellers, but people who were very savvy about the world of eBay and e-commerce. We'd like to thank Joe Cortese of the eBay elite and a PowerSeller. Ina Steiner of AuctionBytes was a wonderful resource about all types of eBay matters. Scott Samuel of Auction Ethics taught us a great deal about auction management software. Win Bent of Bent Sound Research allowed us to feature his eBay Negative Feedback locator. David Kay, a PowerSeller, shared his packaging expertise with us. Jerry Weinstein taught us a great deal about providing excellent customer service. Zhe Wang of Novato Technology helped us with the Appendix, and Scott D. Prock of The PowerSeller Report was generous with his work. Terry Lanier shared his expertise in QuickBooks, and Larra Clark of the American Library Association helped up gather a great deal of information.

Of course, it takes a whole group of people to create any book, and we'd like to thank the talented people who helped us create this one. Our agent, Margot Maley, was the first one who thought this book was a great idea. Margot was followed closely by Margie McAneny, our Acquisitions Editor, who agreed. Other people at McGraw-Hill/Osborne Media who deserve thanks include Scott Rogers, who made all the details work out. Agatha Kim got more e-mails from us than any human should have to suffer. Jenny Malnick paid great attention to us, and often made us hungry with her descriptions of her other job as a pastry cook. Michael Kaiser and David Alexander were our Technical Editors who made sure we were both correct and accurate, and Bob Campbell was a great copyeditor.

On a personal note, we'd like to thank our family, who endured our long absences and tremendous preoccupation with all things eBay. Thanks for the phone calls that kept us connected when visiting just wasn't possible. Thank you to Stephanie and Ethan, who made do without us more than we wanted them to. Finally, to Skippy for chasing the DHL man away every time he came to the door. To Max and Mollie, thanks for keeping our desks and monitors warm. Thanks to their diligence, not a single mouse ran across either of our desks throughout this entire project!

Introduction

Have you sold a few things on eBay, enjoyed the whole process, and wondered how you could make eBay selling a full-time job? We have too, and that's why we wrote this book. We love eBay. We love the satisfaction that comes with selling things and making good money in the process. We also love providing people with things they may not be able to get anyplace else.

In many ways, running your own eBay business is a new version of the American dream that tugs at so many of us: the dream to be your own boss; to no longer be subject to the forever changing corporate winds; to captain your own ship. Thanks to eBay, that dream is more possible now than it ever has been. Never before has starting your own business been so easy and inexpensive. Selling on eBay can begin as a hobby that supplements your income while you work toward building your dream of independence. Once you've achieved a steady cash flow, you will never again be required to dress a certain way for work, be at work at a certain time every day, or sit in that rush hour traffic.

You may be one of the millions of people who have sold items on eBay, but only a fraction of eBay sellers have made eBay selling their fulltime jobs. Only a fraction of those sellers have reached the top tier of eBay sellers: the PowerSellers. These are the most successful sellers on eBay. To become a PowerSeller, you must maintain at least $1,000 per month in sales for a period of three consecutive months. Many PowerSellers have consistently achieved far more than that, and some maintain more than $150,000 in monthly sales. The question is, how can you become one of them? We're here to tell you.

Now you may be wondering who we are and what makes us such eBay authorities. We're old hands at being online; in fact, we've been online since 1983, when most people didn't even know there was such a thing! Brad was an Editorial Director for America Online. We've written books about working from home and guides for using the Internet. Finally, we've been collecting things and shopping at garage sales and flea markets for more years than we care to admit, and we've bought and sold things on eBay since 1999. But none of those things qualified us to write this book. It only qualified us to ask the questions.

To *answer* those many questions, we went right to the source. We interviewed scores of current eBay PowerSellers to get their advice and to learn their secrets about how they achieved their status. This book is the culmination of our research.

As a book of secrets for people who are already comfortable on eBay, *eBay Powerseller Secrets* will not provide you basic information about registering yourself as a seller, or learning the basics of buying and selling on eBay. That information is readily available on eBay, and there are many fine eBay primers that cover all that. We didn't think the world needed another one. If you're new to eBay, go ahead and buy one of those basic primers. If you're ready to move beyond the basic, and you hope to become a PowerSeller yourself, buy this book, then pull up a chair. We're here to help.

It used to be that you could sell pretty much anything and everything on eBay. In the early days, the site gained the reputation as the "yard sale" of the Internet. While it's still true that you can sell almost anything at all on eBay, selling stuff on eBay and working toward building a full-time eBay business as a PowerSeller—a business that will support your family and sustain a comfortable standard of living—are two entirely different things. PowerSellers have shown us that today eBay is way more than a "yard sale" of any type. Be prepared to find a niche for yourself amid a world of commerce that spans the globe and crosses into every type of commodity you can think to buy and sell. The possibilities are almost boundless, and we'll show you how to think beyond the old sports equipment, outgrown clothes, and other cast-offs that once defined eBay's content.

We've organized this book based on what we believe you'll need to know as you make your eBay business grow. The early chapters will help you define your business goals, begin to locate those all-important sources of inventory, and equip your new business for processing volume orders. Without a constant and steady flow of inventory, you'll be able to sell on eBay as a hobby, but you'll have a hard time achieving PowerSeller status. Without a well-planned business setup, you'll soon be swamped with work that you can't quite keep up with. Rather than having your business thrive, it will actually falter.

Then we'll show you how to create effective, attractive, and successful auction listings. You'll learn how to maximize your every effort to build not only your sales, but also the customer base that will keep your sales strong. You'll learn all the ins-and-outs of processing your customers' payments, shipping out your merchandise, and providing the kind of customer service that distinguishes the PowerSellers. Finally, we'll take a look at what you'll need to do to keep proper business records, and we'll explore whether or not you should have your own eBay store.

In each chapter you'll learn inside tips and advice from the PowerSellers who have already achieved your goal. They once stood right where you are and dreamed the same dream. Now that they've achieved that dream, they've been generous enough to share some of what they've learned with the rest of us.

You'll find the PowerSellers to be a fascinating group of people. They are smart, they work hard, but they also live lives they've fashioned for themselves. While reading this book, you'll find that many of the sellers we interviewed live in Florida. One after another told us the same thing, "Since I can work and live anywhere, why shouldn't I live where it's beautiful all the time!" Other sellers have found ways to bring old family businesses into the 21st Century. They work in a new branch of a long-held family business that held no real appeal to them before they could do it on eBay. Still others have been able to reorganize their lives to better meet the needs of aging parents and young children, staying close to home where they're needed most.

They *are* a fascinating group, which has allowed us to write a book that we believe is fascinating, too. (You'll have to trust us on this. If you think it's awful to read a boring book, just imagine how it must feel to have to write one!) We've shared a wealth of knowledge with you, but we've also made it fun to learn about eBay and the art of the PowerSeller. We've used a lot of wisdom from the PowerSellers, and we've told you stories about who they are and how they work to illustrate the advice they've given us. Each chapter ends with a PowerSeller's profile, including a photo so you can see the real people behind the user IDs that identify them on eBay. We wanted to remove some of the mystique that surrounds this group, and show you that they are no different from anyone else.

Except that they are PowerSellers, of course. And you can be one, too. We, along with the scores of PowerSellers whose strategies and secrets are documented here, will show you how.

Chapter 1

Know Your Business/ Grow Your Business

So, you have decided to run your own eBay business. You are in excellent company, as nearly 200,000 eBay users are already earning their livings this way. With the proper planning, dedication, and hard work, there is no reason you should not be able to join them. Here's the good news: You don't have to invent this whole thing for yourself. You can learn from others who have gone before. Reality check: You don't have an open field either. Among those 200,000 users are people who are selling exactly what you want to sell. You'll need to figure out your own place in the eBay world and claim your own piece of it. Don't let that discourage you. Not only do you have all of the power of your own imagination, you also have a community of people who are willing to help you learn your way around. You are not just signing on to a web site when you log on to eBay, you are joining a community of business people.

In that respect, owning your eBay business is not really different from owning a brick-and-mortar store. You will have all of the same concerns that any business owner must endure. You'll need to plan for inventory. You'll have to develop customer service policies. Cash flow, as with all businesses, will be a concern. You will also have all of the same rewards that owning your own store can bring. You decide what to sell and how you want your business to operate. And, of course, your boss is someone you can be sure to get along with. PowerSellers will tell you that in many ways, you can consider your eBay business as a little shop in an enormous mall. That's just how much running an eBay business resembles operating a regular store.

On the other hand, eBay makes your business unlike any other store humans have ever known. For one thing, your store never closes. Whether you are actively working or not, people from all over the world are conceivably shopping with you at any moment of the day or night. Your customers come from all over the globe, and it is not very likely that you will ever meet a single one of them. Nearly all of your interactions will occur through your computer, creating new challenges in communication and customer service. That's not to say you won't know and care about your customers, because you surely will. After all, people are still the driving force behind every business. And, although you can't easily stop in at the shop next door and talk business with your neighbor, you can certainly become a part of a vibrant business community and find support, advice, and friendship just on the other side of your computer screen.

Know Yourself

Before you can begin to know your business, take some time to be sure you know yourself. Running an eBay business is not right for everyone, and even if you want to give it a try, you may find out that your personality is not really suited to the realities of life as an eBay PowerSeller. Operating your own business requires enormous energy and commitment. There are certainly easier ways to earn a paycheck, and you must be sure you are being realistic about the challenges that lie ahead.

Make Sure Your Personality Is Well-Suited to Sitting in Front of Your Computer

You will spend countless hours day after day listing your products, answering e-mail, tracking your auctions, preparing your shipping, keeping your records, and communicating with other sellers on discussion boards. Know in advance that your work life will be spent intimately connected to a computer. If you require more physicality in your job, you should recognize that before you go too much further. TraderNick told us how his brother teases him every time he steps into his work area, asking him how he can possibly stand sitting there all day long. eBay is a computer-based universe, and you cannot conduct your eBay business without putting in endless hours at the computer. Many of us don't mind, but you might, and it's important to know if you're more like TraderNick or his brother from the very beginning.

» Be a good time manager

Be honest with yourself. If left alone, will you devote the time you need to your eBay business, or will you find yourself tempted to get out into the garden on a nice day, play catch with the kids, or take the dog for a walk? Once you become your own boss, it's up to you to determine your work schedule. Only self-motivated people work successfully from home, and answering this question for yourself is vital to your future success.

On the other hand, do you have a tendency to work way too hard? Will you know when it's time to stop and go spend time with your family and friends? Your eBay store never closes, but you have to be able to shut the door on your time there. TraderNick decided he had to have a storefront in addition to

Be a good time manager

his eBay business for just this reason. He said it became obvious to him that he wasn't being a good dad or husband, because he was so focused on his eBay business. Now he has a distinct time each day that work ends and family time begins. That's not to say you have to go to the extreme of taking on a storefront in addition to your eBay business, but you do have to be able to close up shop for the day and get back to the rest of your life.

Selling on eBay Is As Much a Way to Live As It Is a Way to Earn a Living

PowerSellers live a life that is different in many ways from the lives other workers know. They work very long hours, but they choose which hours they work. They work hard to find and list the products they sell, but they get to immerse themselves every day in items they know and care about. There is no such thing as a PowerSeller who is lukewarm about his business. There are many people who sell on eBay as a hobby or to bring in a little money, but if your goal is to become a PowerSeller, accept that you will live, breathe, eat, and sleep eBay every day.

PowerSellers often report that they have no vacation days. They can't interrupt the flow of their operations long enough to have a stretch of time away from home and work. Sure, they have the flexibility to take the morning off to see their kids participate in the assembly at the elementary school, but you can be sure they'll work later that night to make up the time they missed. E-mail must be answered every day. Products must be packaged and shipped. Listings must be posted. Any day that is missing these activities is a day that cuts into the profits of a PowerSeller's business. You can be sure PowerSellers don't miss too many days!

On the other hand, this is a business that can still operate when you don't feel well enough to go into an office among other people. You can work in your pajamas if you choose. You can catch up on work during a patch of insomnia. Your freedom is as real as your responsibility and commitment are. That's part of the joy of owning your own business, especially on eBay.

Know eBay

The business you are planning now will exist in a virtual world. This virtual world is inhabited by millions of other people, including thousands of others who are earning their livings

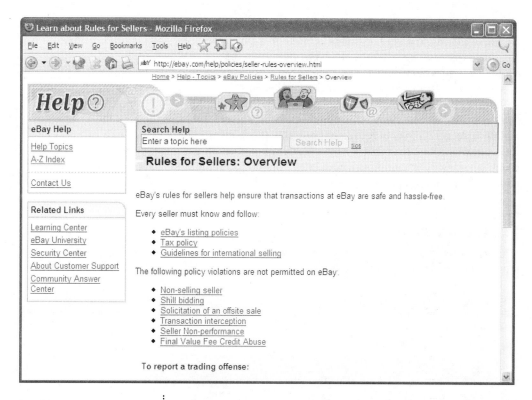

FIGURE 1-1 The eBay sellers' rules screen is a good place to start exploring all of eBay's rules.

If you list an item for sale and someone bids on it, you have to sell it. You have entered into a binding contract at that point—a contract that's binding for *both* parties. If you refuse to sell an item you've listed, the buyer has a legitimate complaint, and when your failure is reported to eBay, you will be warned and/or disciplined. eBay will consider you a Non-Selling Seller for that transaction. Now you may wonder, why on earth would I refuse to sell something after I've listed it? But, it's not inconceivable that you might feel you haven't received enough money for the item, or you might just regret having listed it once you've done it. This may be especially true in the beginning when you may be listing things from your own personal collection of items. So be sure you really want to sell anything you list!

You may not artificially inflate the bidding on your item by "shilling" it. In other words, you cannot bid on your own item under another screen name, or have a family member or friend do this to drive up the cost of your auction and generate interest in your sale. That's not to say no seller on eBay has ever done it, but it is against the rules, and you will be disciplined if you are caught.

Use the site map

Remember that you are in this now for the long haul. You are not just trying to sell a few things here and there. You are creating a business. Use good business practices from the beginning to set yourself on a solid footing, and know the rules of the community you are working in.

eBay operates on a basic set of values. Most of these are similar to the ones we learned as children, including "Treat other people as you wish to be treated yourself." It's familiar, wouldn't you agree? To set the tone for your eBay business, check out eBay's community values at http://pages.ebay.com/community/people/values.html shown in Figure 1-2.

» Use the site map

You can always spot the tourists in any large city by the friendly tour-guide maps sticking out from their back pockets. The

FIGURE 1-2 eBay's community values page

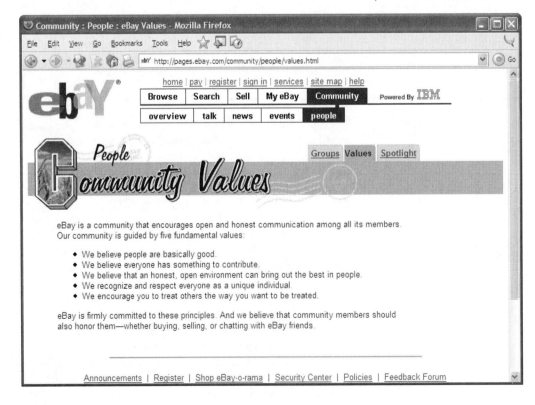

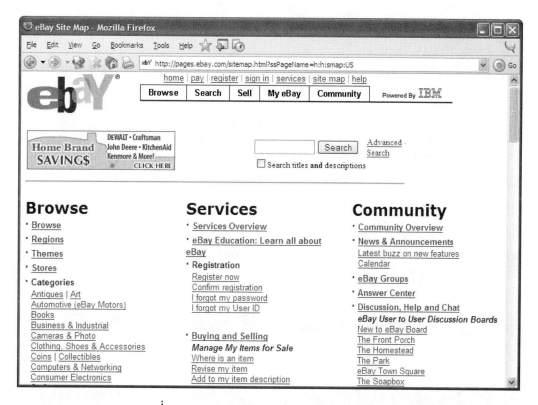

FIGURE 1-3 The opening screen of eBay's Site Map

virtual city of eBay also has such a convenient tool, and luckily for you, it is a lot less conspicuous. You've probably been getting by on eBay without much need to navigate too deeply into the site. You know how to find items to bid on and how to do basic listings to sell items too. You probably also have a My eBay page set up to get quick access to everything you're doing on eBay. Now's the time to learn all about eBay, and the way to start is by using the Site Map. When you click the Site Map button from any eBay screen, you will see the screen shown in Figure 1-3. The people at eBay couldn't have made it easier for you to find your way around and turn up the many little corners of eBay designed to help you learn more and become a more effective eBay user. "My first step when I'm wondering how to do something new on eBay is to start with the Site Map," reports Baronart. Keep it simple and use this great tool eBay provides for you.

Keep Educating Yourself, Because eBay Changes Every Day

You will have to work to keep current with eBay, because it is an ever-evolving entity. Once you are familiar with all of the basic rules, stay up to date on the changes that come about routinely. Fortunately, eBay makes that easy for you. Go to http://www2.ebay.com/aw/marketing.shtml, shown in Figure 1-4, for the latest announcements and news features.

❯❯ Subscribe to AuctionBytes

If you're like most online veterans, you subscribe to lots of free newsletters, most of which you just delete because you don't have the time to read them. Well, AuctionBytes newsletters at www.auctionbytes.com/ really deliver the goods! They claim to

FIGURE 1-4 eBay's news and general announcement board

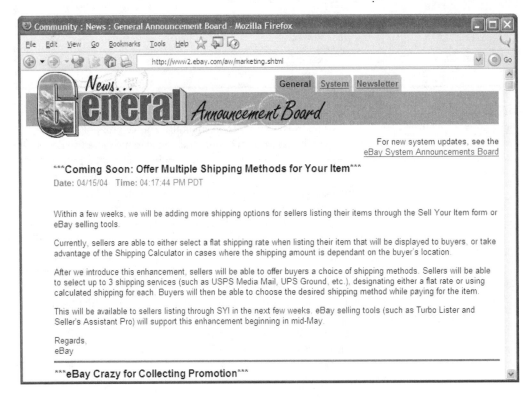

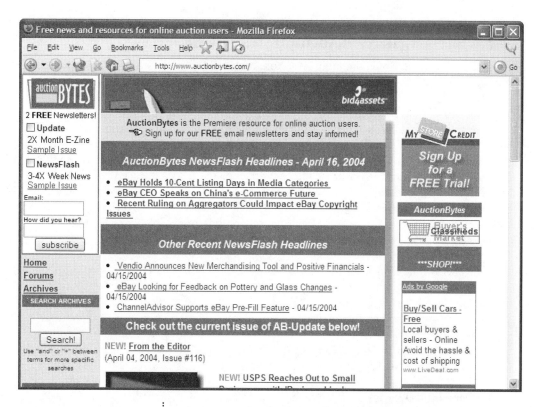

FIGURE 1-5 AuctionBytes newsletter

be the number one source of news on the online auction world, and there's no reason to doubt them. AuctionBytes' NewsFlash newsletters, electronically published three or four times a week, are worth every second you spend reading them. They feature insightful news about eBay with no hype. They also include product reviews, a letters section, and a whole lot more. Through the AuctionBytes home page, you can also access "Cool Tools." These include photography tips, a classified section, and reviews of auction-related books. They don't limit their news coverage to just eBay but include information about other online auctions and auction sites, too. Of course, right now all of your energy is devoted to learning about eBay, but it doesn't hurt to keep an eye on the rest of the online auction world when news is delivered with your e-mail automatically. Subscriptions to the newsletter are free, so you have nothing to lose. Figure 1-5 shows you an example of an AuctionBytes issue.

A Sample Article from AuctionBytes Newsletter

eBay Elite Sellers to Hold Summit in New York May 1–2
By Ina Steiner
AuctionBytes.com
April 7, 2004

A group of high-revenue, high-volume eBay sellers will gather in New York on May 1 and 2 with the goal of creating an ongoing problem-solving mechanism between eBay and its top performers. The group, calling itself the "eBay Elite," will discuss issues they feel are critical to their continued business success. Topics on the agenda include Fraud, eBay's Feedback Mechanism, Non-Paying Bidders, Buyer/Seller initiatives, Fees and PayPal Policies.

PayPal and SquareTrade representatives and analysts from Merrill Lynch and Prudential will speak at the Summit as well as eBay Elite sellers Joe Cortese (Noblespirit); Jonathan Garriss (Gothamcityonline); Alexander Zacke; and John Kincaid (Jayhawkks). eBay declined to send a representative to the Summit.

Members of the eBay Elite currently hold discussions online on eBay Groups, a place eBay has set up on its site for members to create public or private meeting areas. eBay Platinum PowerSeller Joe Cortese is a wholesale supplier of coins, stamps and paper money and also operates Meridian auction management service for eBay sellers.

"The ultimate goal is to support and insure eBay's continued global success," Cortese wrote on the welcome page of the eBay Elite discussion group. The group is private and is limited to top sellers and specially invited guests. There are 525 eBay Elite members, including the Automotive Elite, and Cortese said he expects 125 members from as far away as California and Germany to attend the Summit in New York.

Cortese said the group felt an offline summit was important to help members reach resolutions regarding the group going forward. "We will explore opportunities that are both open to us and those that we will identify as worth pursuing," he said. "Once the group has consolidated its mission statement and outlined a course of action, it will take steps to act upon those convictions."

When asked about the eBay Elite Summit, eBay spokesperson Hani Durzy said, "We are always happy to see people get together to share best practices, to talk about what works and what doesn't." Durzy stressed that the group is no different from any other group of eBay members. "We believe in a level playing field," he said. "eBay welcomes feedback, but changes must benefit the community as a whole."

As for the name of eBay Elite, Cortese said the following:

It conveys a commitment to being part of a like-minded group of top sellers dedicated to improving business practices on eBay. eBay Elite members are professionals who are concerned with growing their businesses and maximizing their profits. "eBay Elite" conveys a desire to engage in meaningful dialogue to increase knowledge and learn from each other. We recognize that the unique concerns, problems and challenges of full time sellers are areas best understood by other veterans like ourselves.

Cortese said that the eBay Elite is in the process of arranging a significant presence at eBay Live!, the auction site's third user conference that will take place in June in New Orleans.

» Tune in to eBay radio

Broadcast by wsRadio, the "worldwide leader in Internet talk," eBay Radio is a fun, easy-on-the-eyes way to get up to speed on eBay topics and stay current with important developments within the community. A new show is broadcast every Tuesday from 11:00 A.M. to 12:00 noon Pacific Standard Time. It's easy to find at www.wsradio.com/ebayradio/. This link leads you to wsRadio's eBay Radio page, shown in Figure 1-6. If you can't be available during the broadcast time, don't worry. You can easily access recently archived shows or search the entire archives for shows dedicated to subjects that will interest you.

Once you find a show you're interested in, just click the link for it, and click the type of media player you have, for example, RealPlayer. You can also listen to a show by clicking the icon that allows you to download the show as an mp3 file. Once you click this icon, the radio show begins playing thanks to streaming media technology. There you have it, good solid information available for you to learn more about eBay any hour of any day, simply by listening to the expert guests and their call-in questioners.

FIGURE 1-6 wsRadio's eBay radio home page

» Sign up for eBay's Seller Newsflash

eBay makes it easy for you to get the news sellers need to stay competitive. Go to Seller Central and click News & Updates. You'll be able to sign up for e-mail notification of upcoming eBay specials and features. You'll learn when eBay is planning to have free listing days and feature discounts, and you'll learn about upcoming educational events from eBay University. It's easy to get registered for these e-mail updates, and eBay assures all users that the company will not rent or sell their personal information to third parties for marketing purposes. If you miss out on the news flash, your competitors might just scoop you.

» Attend eBay University and stop by eBay's learning center

eBay University is a college that comes to you. Its instructors travel from city to city to bring their wisdom to eBay buyers and sellers across the country. Courses are available for both buyers and sellers. There are two course levels, for beginning and advanced students. The advanced course for sellers ("Beyond the Basics") is perfect for readers of this book. It's designed to help sellers build their businesses and move up the success ladder. The cost for attending eBay University is $39 for a full one-day seminar. You can also attend online courses or buy the course on CD-ROM. Each is available for $19.95. eBay University's Welcome screen is shown in Figure 1-7.

eBay University is only a small part of the eBay Learning Center. You will find the center at http://pages.ebay.com/education/. In addition to the eBay University courses, you can come here to listen to or view brief tutorials on basic and more advanced eBay buying and selling topics. The Learning Center also includes links to other resources, such as Sellers Central and information about eBay fees and PayPal.

Feedback Is Everything

In the world of eBay, nothing is more important to a seller than a stellar Member Profile. This consists of your total feedback score and the level of positive feedback you've received. Think of it as the face you show the world. It is the only way buyers and sellers know about each other's trustworthiness, and it keeps eBay from being totally anonymous. Sellers with relatively poor Profiles are

Attend eBay University and stop by eBay's learning center

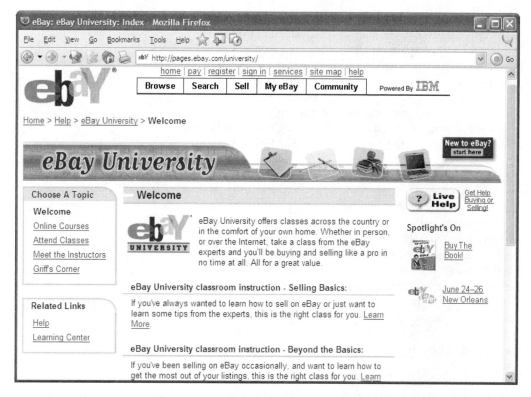

FIGURE 1-7 eBay University's Welcome screen

at a real disadvantage on eBay. Some buyers won't take the risk in doing business with you until you've proved yourself in the community. With a low feedback score, you are even limited to the number of postings you can make on eBay message boards. Until your feedback score exceeds 10, you are limited to no more than 10 postings a day.

As you already know, PowerSellers must maintain at least 98 percent positive feedback. Here's how that works: For every transaction that happens on eBay, both the buyer and the seller may leave feedback for each other. Your feedback "score" consists of the number of distinct trading partners who have left feedback for you. The percentage of this feedback that is positive is also part of your Member Profile. (Note that an individual user can only impact your rating by one point either positively or negatively, regardless of how many transactions you have with that person.) Unlike in school, an "A" rating is nothing less than 97 to 98 percent. Anything below that means that shoppers need to examine the feedback comments for this seller carefully and shop very cautiously.

You must begin to build and safeguard your Member Profile from the very first day you start your business. For every transaction you complete on eBay, complete a feedback report as the final step. If you have been casual in leaving feedback, vow to change your ways as of right now. PowerSellers unanimously say that they guard their Member Profiles as preciously as they guard their greatest treasure.

The first thing you can do to build your feedback rating is to buy more things on eBay. Now, that may seem like odd advice to someone who wants to sell, sell, sell. But, think of your eBay purchases as part of your startup business costs. You don't have to purchase expensive items. You can also tailor all of your purchases to things you're going to need for your eBay business so that you can get the tax advantages of business expenses. Surprisingly, feedback you receive as a buyer is completely valid in building your Profile. Most people checking on this don't bother to notice whether you earned praise as a buyer or a seller. They just want to know that you legitimately completed your transactions, you were true to your word, and you conducted yourself as an honorable member of the eBay community. To ensure you receive positive feedback as a buyer is simple. Pay quickly and follow the seller's rules for calculating your shipping and handling.

» Don't use your e-mail address as your username

If you use your address as your username, eBay will notify you immediately and tell you to change your username. You might as well save yourself the trouble and create a separate eBay username for yourself right from the beginning. This bit of advice is strictly for your own protection. You will find that sellers report all types of scams and schemes dishonest people use for gaining access to sellers' accounts. We'll discuss specific buyers' scams in Chapter 7, and you'll learn about protecting your computer in Chapter 3, but one simple step you can take now is to separate your e-mail address from your username. While you're creating a new username, why not make it one that speaks directly to your business? Making your username specific and memorable helps your customers remember your business and find you more easily for repeat visits. For example, it's hard for customers of Wegotthebeats to forget this seller or that he sells music CDs.

Don't Be a Stranger

Remember our comparison of your eBay business to a small shop in an enormous mall? Well, it's time to meet your neighbors. You are not just beginning a new business venture, you're joining a new community. As in any other neighborhood, you'll meet people who rub you the wrong way, people you'll want to befriend, and people you'll simply do business with. The amazing thing about eBay is the community that forms around the globe, across cultural barriers, and beyond the limits of the physical world. People who earn their livings on eBay share certain values and aspirations. They are kindred spirits in their search for better ways of earning a living. They may be all different, and they are, but they also share a common bond. They come to this virtual marketplace to make a life for themselves that previous generations couldn't possibly dream about. Don't be shy, go on out and meet your fellow sellers. The place to get started doing this is at the Community tab from eBay's home page. Click here and you'll find the screen shown in Figure 1-8. It includes four

FIGURE 1-8 eBay Community's welcome screen

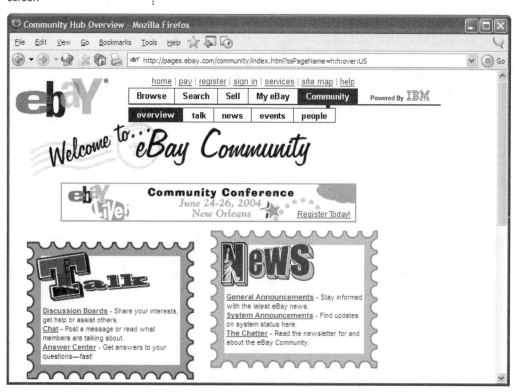

options: Talk, News, Events, and People. You are standing at the gateway to the eBay community. Go on ahead and jump right in.

» Get involved in the discussion boards

One of the best ways to join the community is to get involved in the discussion boards. At first, you may feel that you should spend all of your time strictly listing and selling your products, but becoming part of the community will help you build your business because it will put you in touch with hundreds, if not thousands, of people who have been where you are right now. It is only smart to learn from them. From the Community page described in the preceding section you'll click Discussion Boards. Here you'll see a screen listing all of eBay's boards, shown in Figure 1-9. There are boards for Community Help, Category Specific Discussions, General Discussion, Workshops, and Giving Works, eBay's charitable fundraising.

Seller Center is one eBay discussion board you'll want to visit early and often. Find it from the discussion boards screen,

FIGURE 1-9 eBay's Talk boards

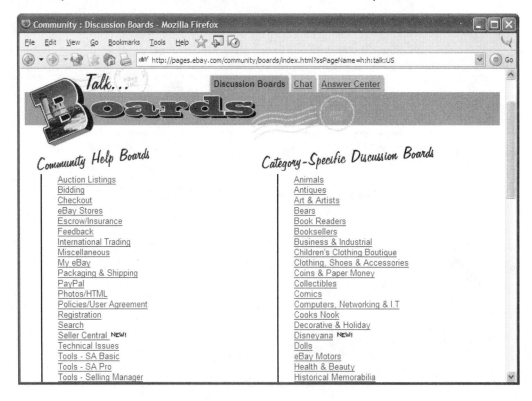

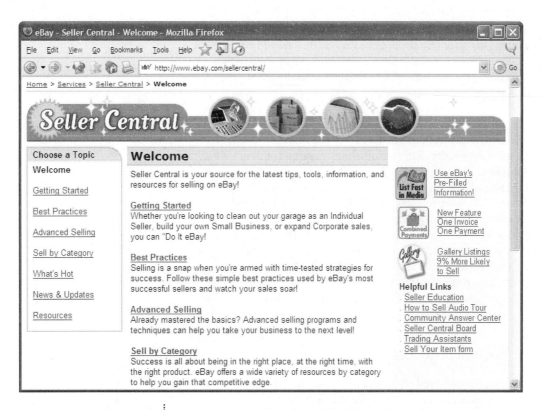

FIGURE 1-10 eBay's Seller Central discussion board

or you can go directly to Seller Central by typing www.ebay.com/sellercentral into your browser. Once you're there, click Seller Central Board under Helpful Links on the right side of the screen, shown in Figure 1-10. You'll see a long list of topics under discussion. You can just browse the topic listings and click whatever topic interests you. When we stopped in today, the liveliest topic was Seller Tips & Tricks of the Trade, with more than 500 postings. If you don't have the time to browse, you can find specific topics you're researching. Just go to the end of the List of Topics, and click the Search button. All of eBay's boards work this way.

» Get involved in groups

Groups are distinct from discussion boards in the types of information they offer. You will still find discussions in the groups, but you will also find posted newsletters, photos, and polls. Groups are more focused than the boards. Different groups are dedicated

Get involved in groups

to specific topics. You can reach all of the groups from the main Community screen by clicking the People tab. This will take you to Group Center, shown in Figure 1-11. Notice that some of the groups are private. Unlike the discussion boards, which are open to everyone, groups can be designated as "public" or "private." If you wish to join a private group, you must request membership and meet the criteria for joining. Go to http://groups.ebay.com/index.jspa?categoryID=35 to see a complete listing of groups devoted just to sellers. Or, from the Group Center screen, click View All (just to the right of seller groups). The screen shown in Figure 1-12 will appear. As of this writing there are more than 400 seller groups! That's not counting any of the groups meant specifically for PowerSellers and PowerSeller wannabees. There are additional groups for you. To join a private group (private groups are labeled *private* next to the group name), you'll need to send an e-mail to the moderator explaining why you qualify for membership. To get you started, there are also some groups for aspiring PowerSellers that are open to the public and full of useful information for people like you who are trying to reach PowerSeller status.

Know Your Products

Now, you've explored your personality and found it suitable to an eBay business. You've explored the eBay community with the eyes of a serious seller, and you've begun to learn your way

FIGURE 1-11 eBay's Group Center screen

FIGURE 1-12 The Seller Groups screen

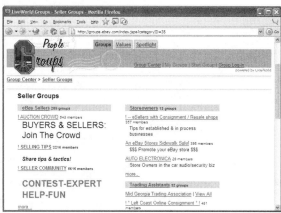

around the neighborhood. Next you must decide what you are going to sell on eBay. No single decision you make will alter your early experiences quite as much as this one will. Fortunately, many sellers who have gone before you have offered you some profound advice.

» Start with what you know

This is the single, most universal bit of advice PowerSellers offer to those who want to follow in their wake. It may seem obvious, but there are practical reasons to follow this piece of advice. "If you sell what you know, you'll start your business with a knowledge base that would ultimately take years to build otherwise," says Dan's Train Depot. You won't have to be learning the ins and outs of a product area at the same time that you're learning the ins and outs of an eBay business. You give yourself an added advantage right from the beginning.

If you start by selling things you know about, you also gain the added advantage of knowing that you can trust your gut. "Being able to trust yourself to take a risk early on is very important," says Wegotthebeats. You won't do that if you're dealing in a product area that is unfamiliar to you.

» Don't sell things you don't know about

Now, this may seem like an obvious counterpoint to the preceding tip, but there are reasons to be specific in calling it to your attention. You are not just trying to sell a few things on eBay, you are trying to create a whole new business. You must appear to be in control of your business even if you don't feel terribly confident about what you're doing. Your spouse, your family, and your friends can lend their support to your shaky self-image as an eBay seller, but your customers must not doubt your professionalism for a moment. If you're dealing in items that you don't know, you will never be able to project the self-assurance necessary to create the public image you are seeking.

From a very practical viewpoint, selling items you know nothing about makes you vulnerable to taking losses on valuable items. Many sellers will tell you that items rise to their own market value on eBay. To a degree that's true, but if you don't know what you have, you are likely to place it in the wrong category. This may cut the amount of action you'll get from

Don't sell things you don't know about

your auction. You will also be less able to write the kind of powerful item description that brings you top dollar for your item. Don't sacrifice an item out of a lack of education. It's too easy to do the research necessary to learn about what you have. Until you're sure, hold on to it and list things you know about.

Research What You Sell

Fortunately, researching your items could not be easier. You can start by searching for your item in completed auctions. To do this, go to the Search feature on eBay's toolbar and enter your keywords and other search options. Check the box for completed auctions. Figure 1-13 shows you what your search screen should look like. This will pull up all of the items similar to yours that have sold on eBay within the last 15 days. With this search, you will be able to see what the going price was for items similar to yours and if those items actually sold. You will also be able to

FIGURE 1-13 A search screen to find completed auctions for comparing your items to those already listed and sold on eBay

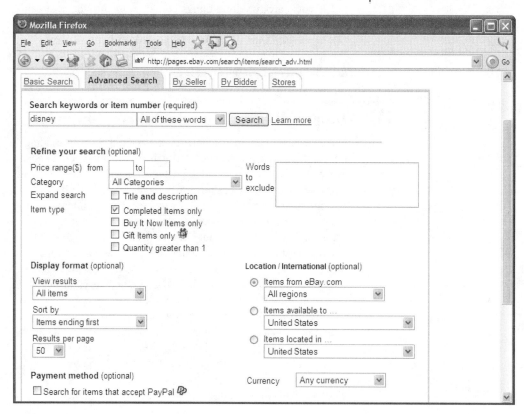

compare the condition of your item to items that have competed directly with what you want to sell. Open individual auction listings, and you can get a look at the different methods other sellers have used to describe the item you have. Look at these descriptions with an eye toward the ones that sold for the most. You'll surely get some tips about what to include in your own descriptions! For an even fuller look at auctions similar to yours, search current auctions as you're searching completed ones. Just open each search (completed, current) in its own screen, and you can easily switch back and forth.

In many ways, eBay has helped cut into the publishing market for collectible guides. Instead of having to purchase a new book every year to reflect changing values, many sellers who deal in antiques and collectibles use eBay searches as their buying guides. Not only is the market value up to date, it is also more realistic. Ultimately an item is only worth that which a buyer is willing to pay for it. What better place to see what the market will bear than the world's largest marketplace?

» Seek out marginalized niches for your product

Keep the view of the world's marketplace in mind when you are considering what products to sell. Once you open an eBay business, your customers are just as likely to come from across the ocean as they are to come from across town. "I look for things that aren't so popular in the United States as they are in Japan and Germany," says Wegotthebeats. This seller specializes in CDs, and he knows his market well enough to know what products are hot in foreign markets. Not only does this allow him to buy his inventory knowing that he'll have customers for his items, it makes it possible for him to scoop up music that isn't commercially successful here for pennies and sell it overseas for, sometimes, hundreds of U.S. dollars. Now, you can't expect to have that kind of experience right out of the starting gate, but you can expect to ultimately know your product area well enough to identify niches that will be just as profitable to your business.

» Research your own customers

Once you start selling on eBay, check to see what your customers are buying. This is simple enough to do. From the main search

Stay away from contentious items while you're just getting started

menu, click to search by bidder. You'll get a screen that allows you to specify that you want to see everything a specific bidder has made bids on in both current and completed auctions. Figure 1-14 shows you a completed search for one particular bidder. Now you know absolutely everything your customer has been interested in during the last 30 days. When you gather your inventory for future sales, you'll know exactly what your customers are shopping for.

» Stay away from contentious items while you're just getting started

It's very important to remember that not only are you beginning a business, but you are also building your reputation. Don't start off by selling items the condition of which can be contested. "We built our feedback rating selling vintage postcards," says Debnroo. "Our customers were nice, mostly older retired

FIGURE 1-14 A completed search for a specific bidder's history

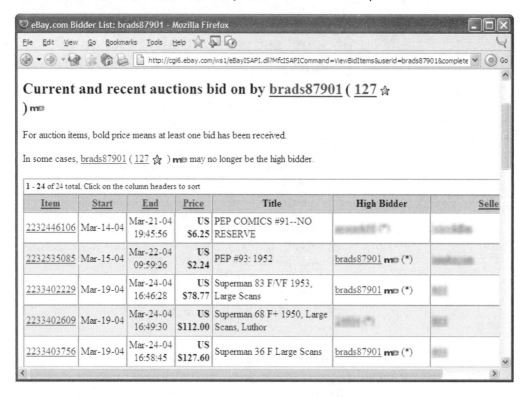

people, who honored their bids and paid their bills." Debnroo quickly built a strong positive feedback rating even though selling postcards was not ever going to make the couple rich. "Don't start out trying to build your feedback rating by selling china, for example," they explained. "The grading of this item is very subjective. Even if you know a lot about china, buyers and sellers are bound to disagree about the condition of pieces. You want your early sales to be without question so that you can build strong feedback. So, stay away from anything that can be interpreted too loosely." By the time this couple branched out into other product areas, they were well-established and well-respected eBay sellers.

» Sell what you love, but don't be blinded by your emotions

Of course, you must love your product line, but don't let your own feelings and opinions get in your way. "If it were up to me, everything I sell would be green," says Christina's Crafts. But, this seller was savvy enough to recognize that her customers did not necessarily share this passion. Ultimately, you are not shopping for items for yourself, you are shopping for items your customers will want to buy. Christina's Crafts stocks far more blue items than green, because she knows that blue is the best-selling color of items in the United States.

To learn what sells best, simply use Google to search for "best-selling." Then you can enter whichever item or descriptor you are working with. Best-selling color, best-selling scent, best-selling fabric, for example, will all show you what most shoppers are looking for. The search results for best-selling software are shown in Figure 1-15.

You will also find that you can do research everywhere you go, as long as you keep your eyes open. When you are going about your daily business, notice what items people seem to be using, wearing, or buying. Keep in mind which of these may be good for you to add to your stock. The owner of Christina's Crafts took some extra yoga and meditation classes, because she knew those were the types of activities her clients would be interested in pursuing. She said that with each class, she noticed the clothes, scents, and jewelry her classmates were wearing, and she made it a point to include similar items in her inventory.

Sell quality items

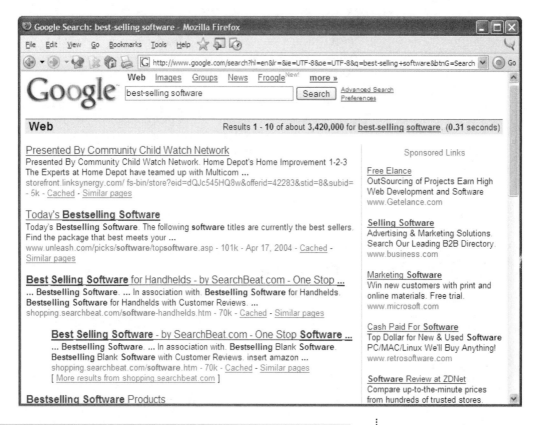

FIGURE 1-15 Google search results for best-selling software

» Sell quality items

When you are shopping for inventory, ask yourself, "Would I be proud to give this to my best friend?" recommends Christina's Crafts. If the answer is no, don't sell it. Many people go on eBay to sell off the same items they'd sell in a garage sale. They can be very successful in getting rid of unwanted things this way, to be sure. But, this is not the attitude to take when setting out to build a whole business on eBay. Your goal is not to be a one-shot seller or a twice-a-year-clean-out-the-kids'-rooms seller. You're shooting for PowerSeller status, and that's a whole different thing. Your challenge will be to build a renewable and reliable source of inventory that you can sell repeatedly to a customer base you will build over time. Start from the beginning by stocking high-quality merchandise. It is impossible to effectively sell products you don't believe in, so don't even start with them.

A good part of building any business is building loyal, repeat customers, and that is more likely to happen when your customers know you sell quality goods. Keep this larger goal of building a customer base in mind and you won't even be tempted to scrimp on product. The last thing you want is for someone to open an eagerly awaited item purchased from you and feel disappointed. Disappointment creates a customer you can never get back, plus it is likely to leave you with disappointing feedback, too. In Chapter 2 you'll learn a lot more about identifying product areas and researching sources of products to sell.

» Don't forget practical considerations

Your new life as an eBay PowerSeller will change many things you can't even foresee from where you stand now, but certain things won't change, and you need to consider them. Don't set yourself up for failure and frustration by choosing items that simply won't work with the life you currently have. For example, when you're deciding what to sell, don't decide to stock and sell large items if you live in a small space. You're bringing your job home, and no one will be happy if the kitchen is given up to boxes that you have to climb over every time you want to get to the fridge. Consider all of the practical elements of combining business with home. Will you have a dedicated computer for your eBay business? Do you have a place you can devote to photographing your items? Life is easier if you don't have to keep setting up photo shoots every time you want to create a new listing. Remember all the incidentals that are vital to your business. Where will you store packing material? Where will you do your shipping? Are you equipped to package fragile items for shipping? If not, you may want to rethink what you'll be selling. None of these considerations is insurmountable unless, of course, you don't bother to consider them. So think long and hard. Decide carefully, and be willing to stay flexible enough to change your mind if you need to.

Know What Not to Sell

There are some things that are illegal to sell on eBay, and there are other things that may be legal but don't make for good, consistent business dealings. On your way to making PowerSeller status, don't step outside the boundaries of the law or the boundaries of common sense. Some items may not be totally banned, but they are restricted, and you must meet certain criteria in order to sell them. eBay is a socially conscious company and

Don't forget practical considerations

has banned some items that may be technically legal but not
honorable to trade. eBay bans, for example, the sale of items
related to the World Trade Center post 9-11. That makes some
sellers feel better about the marketplace as a whole. "I'm glad to
know eBay won't allow such morally questionable things to sell.
It makes me feel better about conducting my business with them,"
says Bidnow5. For a complete list of prohibited and restricted
items, go to http://pages.ebay.com/help/policies/items-ov.html.
You'll find the screen shown in Figure 1-16.

Don't Break Any Laws

If it's against the law to sell it in the real world, you won't
get away with selling it on eBay either. This may seem like
plain common sense, but you'd be surprised how uncommon
a commodity that can be in the rush to get ahead. Don't break
any copyright laws either. You may be tempted to record a
popular show that has not yet been released to video or DVD

FIGURE 1-16 eBay's
prohibited and restricted
items overview screen

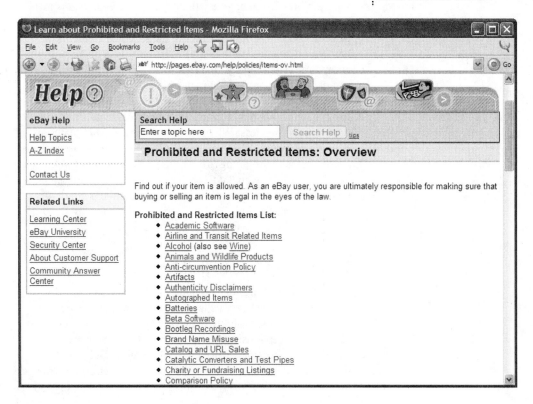

and make a quick sale, but don't do it. You'll lose your chance to build a solid eBay business, and you could easily leave yourself open for prosecution on criminal offenses, too.

» Don't sell homemade food or body items

There are very strict guidelines for selling food on eBay, but sellers are allowed to trade in food items as long as they respect the restrictions and follow the guidelines. Every year, especially around the time of the holidays, you'll find homemade goodies and treats for sale. Now, this may seem like a great way to supplement your income, especially if you have a specialty that makes you a favorite among your friends and family. Whether it's fudge, flavored oils, or a favorite body lotion, it's a bad idea. Don't do it. You are likely to leave yourself open for all kinds of trouble, ranging from disgruntled customers to liability lawsuits.

» Include disclaimers and allergy warnings for all consumable items you sell

If you sell items meant for human consumption, don't forget to state very plainly in every listing that you are not recommending the item for medicinal purposes or making any claims about what the item can do to treat or heal any medical condition. Also, be sure to warn potential allergy suffers not to bid without first checking with you about all of the product's ingredients to be sure they do not include anything that will cause allergic reactions. For example, Christina's Crafts sells herbal teas and Burt's Bees skincare products. Every listing includes these warnings, not only to prevent her customers from having unrealistic expectations about the items and their efficacy, but also to protect her from anyone who might buy a nice chamomile tea expecting relief from a stomach ulcer. Be very clear that your items are being sold strictly for the purpose of recreation, relaxation, and enjoyment.

Mind Your Business

Not to sound rude, but stay focused on your business and start thinking like a business owner from the very beginning. Now is not too soon. Let's get a little philosophical here. eBay has made it possible for people who may never have once considered operating their own businesses to have them. That is incredibly empowering, and you must start harnessing that power from the very beginning. It has never been easier to start a business with very little capital risk and watch it grow. Minding your business, there is almost no limit to what you and your new eBay business can do together.

» Start small, start slowly, and don't quit your job

Throughout this book you will read stories of people who discovered eBay one evening and by the next morning they had their first item listed, and they never looked back. Some people almost accidentally stumble upon the right product at the right time and off they go. You are under no pressure to join them. Spend time doing your research. Decide what you want to sell. Learn your way around eBay. Develop policies and procedures for managing your business, and get yourself started.

Unlike the favorite children's method for getting used to the water, your best bet here is probably not to just dive right into the lake. "If you work as a lawyer, you can't expect to quit your job, start an eBay business, and make up for your salary," says TraderNick. It's good advice to remember. That's not to say you won't ultimately be able to quit your job and make up your salary, but starting a business is stressful enough. Why would you want to add risking your family's security to the stress? You'll know by reason of your cash flow when your business has grown enough to support your lifestyle. In the meantime, don't quit your day job!

Every Time You Learn Something New, You Add Another Brick to Your Invisible Store

Christina's Crafts offered this bit of advice to eBay sellers hoping to build their businesses. Keeping this in mind helps you to focus on the task of building your eBay business in a very concrete way. If you were building a brick-and-mortar store, you'd have to spend time physically creating, decorating, and preparing the space. For your eBay business, most of this planning stage is going to happen intellectually as you build your knowledge and competence in a virtual marketplace. You would give yourself the time and devote the energy necessary to physically building your store if you were opening one on Main Street. You must also allow yourself the time and devote the energy necessary to the intellectual pursuit of learning your way around the eBay marketplace. This is not time wasted in building your business, any more than choosing the right décor for your shop would be time wasted. Rather it is time invested in building your business.

Don't Be Discouraged If You Are Not a Business Person Now

That's the beauty of eBay—you don't have to be a business person to start an eBay business. "I was cleaning carpets when I discovered eBay," says Bidnow5. "I started selling on eBay, because my dad wanted to get rid of some stuff," noted Debnroo. Many people before you have come to eBay with little or no business experience. Don't let your lack of experience discourage you. You'll do just as they have done. You'll work hard. You'll learn quickly as you go. Next year at this time, you'll sit back in amazement at what you didn't know now. You have lots of advantages that those who have gone before you did not. You have much more help available to you on eBay than the pioneers to the site had. You also have this great book, which will offer you hundreds of tips PowerSellers took years learning. So, chin up, chest out, and no self-doubt allowed around here.

» Be Patient. Be aggressive. Be smart.

Be patient in giving yourself the time and freedom to learn about your business and set it growing strong. Be aggressive in sticking with your business plan, setting goals, and working hard to achieve them. Be smart in staying flexible with your product choices, acquisitions, and business practices. You'll be much more successful if you continue to question what you know, what you are learning, and what you are doing. Be ready to change and adapt. "They say it takes five years to build a business, and it can take just as long to build one on eBay. You are not necessarily going to step right into a success," advises Jeralinc.

Don't Be Surprised If Success Strikes Fast

On the other hand, dozens of PowerSellers tell tales of hitting one right out of the park on their first at-bat. "When I started, my goal was to sell ten wedding dresses a week," reports Bridewire. "Within a year I was selling 100 a week!" This kind of success brings its own set of challenges. No one ever said it was easy to ride a rocket. If this should happen to you, be prepared to work harder than you ever have in your life. Hang on tight, and enjoy the ride. You'll have quite a story to tell a year from now.

» Your eBay business will not work if you don't treat it like a business

You can have a great life selling stuff on eBay as a hobby and working at your regular job. There is nothing that says you ever have to strive to be an eBay PowerSeller. Except that something made you pick up this book, so you must have a drive of your own. Use that drive and make every listing you place on eBay from now on a step toward your PowerSeller status. You will never become a PowerSeller unless you take your business seriously and consider it to be as important as your full-time job. If what you want is to power-sell, then dedicate yourself right now to making every eBay interaction part of your plan to get from eBay user to PowerSeller. Even if you don't seem like a PowerSeller to the rest of the world, present yourself as one in your own head. It may be just a matter of your own perception now, but perception is a good place to start. In view of the first tip in this section, that means you'll be working two full-time jobs for a while, but no one said this was going to be easy.

» The money you earn from eBay isn't really yours

Very soon the checks will start coming in the mail and your products will start going out the door. Don't think for even a moment that those checks are your reward for what you're doing, and you should use them to go out to that favorite restaurant of yours to celebrate. Remind yourself with each new check you deposit that the money isn't yours. It belongs to your eBay business. "I've known lots of people who earn a little money, go out and spend it, then settle in to watch TV. They'll never have a business that way," says Dan's Train Depot. Dan couldn't be more correct. Folks like that may be perfectly happy selling a little here and there on eBay to earn a little extra cash, but that's not a PowerSeller frame of mind. In the beginning, absolutely everything you earn should be put right back into your business. There will be time enough to spend your earnings once you've built your business.

» Pay yourself a salary

When you have achieved a steady cash flow, start paying yourself a salary from your earnings. Just be sure to make it the smallest possible salary you can get by with. That's a legitimate business expense and perfectly acceptable as long as your budget can support it. This will also be a good way for you to determine when you can start scaling back on the job you have now. When your salary from your eBay business is approaching the total of your monthly living expenses, you may just be ready to make the leap.

» Know the value of every sale and go after it

In the beginning, every sale you make increases your feedback rating and builds a potentially loyal customer. Don't underestimate the value of even the smallest sale. Go after all of them. Many PowerSellers will tell you that they no longer feel it's worth their time to pursue the smaller sales. The volume they sell is too large for smaller sales to be profitable. You may someday feel the same way, but you are nowhere near that point now. You may find that you just don't want to be bothered responding to the customer who is sending you e-mail after e-mail to get more information about the item that's currently bidding at $4.99. Do it anyway! If you don't do it for the money, do if for the sake of building your business. You never know when that bothersome e-mailer will be the one who becomes your most loyal customer. Consider your profit margins, but don't live and die by them. There will be time for adjusting your business to those margins once it's a flourishing business.

Volunteer to Work and Learn

If, after reading this far, you're beginning to have second thoughts, here's a useful alternative. Find a PowerSeller in your area and volunteer to work for her. In return for your help with shipping, listing, or answering e-mails, she'll most likely be willing to teach you about the ins and outs of the life of a PowerSeller. You'll be

Know the value of every sale and go after it

investing nothing but a few hours of your time per week (she might even be willing to pay you a little). You'll get invaluable first-hand experience and a real taste for what this life is all about. Finding a local PowerSeller isn't too hard. Here's how you do it: Go to the basic search screen. Enter **PowerSeller** as your keyword. Be sure to check the box to search by both title and description. Leave the search designated to all categories. Now, in the box for Item Location, use the pull-down menu to find the geographic area closest to you. Figure 1-17 shows you an example of what the completed search screen should look like. Complete the search, and you can scroll through your results and find PowerSellers who both are near to you and sell products you are interested in.

Know Where to Find Help

Starting an eBay business now that eBay has matured gives you an advantage. You'll have some help available to you that

FIGURE 1-17 A sample search screen for PowerSellers by geographic location

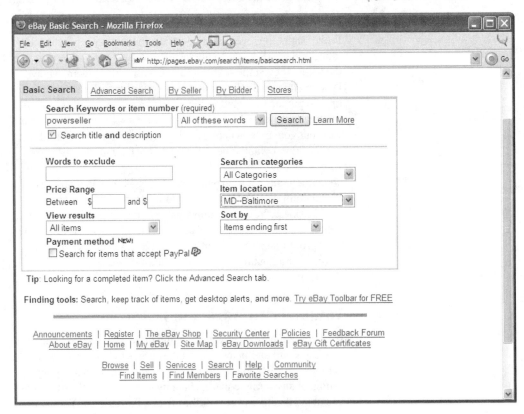

wasn't available to today's PowerSellers when they first began. With that said, know that, even now, you can't expect much help. The culture of eBay is a little like that of a family with a dozen kids. There are rules, there are people watching and policing the overall comings and goings, but when it comes to the details, you're better off figuring it out for yourself. eBay prides itself on providing a level playing field, and it's up to you to see how you're going to play on it. So, don't expect anyone from eBay to hold your hand, and you won't be disappointed or discouraged when no one does.

eBay has help pages that cover the rudimentary details of using the site. You'll find help at http://pages.ebay.com/help/index.html, shown in Figure 1-18. Since you are not a newcomer to eBay, you probably won't find much here that will help you. Still, the help pages are a place to start. You can also access Live Help, from prominentl eBay screens (e.g., the Home Page). You'll see a little Live Help button near the top of these screens. Clicking this button (shown here) will take you to a live chat with someone who can offer you help in real time. "Whenever I'm stumped on eBay, I just hit that Live Help button," says Baronart. "I always get good results from them." eBay's live help feature is definitely underused. Estimates suggest that most eBay users never press that button. Still, sometimes when you do press it, you receive a message stating that due to volume, you must expect a waiting time before anyone can address your question. Most sellers are too busy too spend much time on eBay's equivalent of "Hold." When you achieve Gold PowerSeller status, you will have your own Account Manager, and then you'll have better access to help. By then, the things you'll need help with will be much more complicated than the things that stump you now, so take heart, you will ultimately have some help. In the meantime, search for help in other places. Fortunately there's plenty to be found.

Most eBay Help Is Seller to Seller

Just like in that family with a dozen kids, if Mom and Dad are too busy to help you, you'll be better off going to a big brother or sister. The eBay community is famous for the friendly, helpful people who occupy it. Start with the Q & A discussion board and ask lots of questions. There is really no such thing as a

Get help from auction doctors

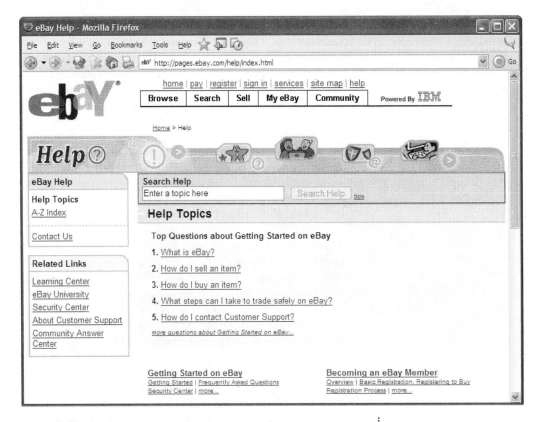

stupid question, and the people who populate these discussion boards do so because they like to help. It is only reasonable to assume that among all of the sellers who check in on the board, someone has already struggled with whatever issue is currently troubling you. Don't assume everything is brand new just because it's new to you. Ask, ask, ask, and the answers will flow back to you.

FIGURE 1-18 eBay's Help welcome screen

❯❯ Get help from auction doctors

Need expert help from seasoned eBayers? Sure you will, at first. Through eBay's Auction Doctors Group, you can find eBay veterans who will review your listings and suggest specific detailed improvements. Be sure to read the moderator's rules for the group (e.g., "When asking for a review, please just make a short list of initial relevant points that you would like our veterans to focus on"). This will ensure you get the help you need. Follow the advice here, become a successful PowerSeller, and then become an Auction Doctor yourself!

Don't Forget to Help Others, Too

As a community, eBay couldn't function if its members didn't help each other. In the beginning you'll be receiving a lot of help, support, and advice from sellers who have gone before you. When you get yourself established and start feeling like a pro, don't forget to pass it on. You don't even necessarily have to wait until you're an eBay veteran or a PowerSeller. Go directly to the discussion boards for your area of interest and start sharing your thoughts and ideas with others, even if you don't have a lot to say yet about eBay and its workings. Everyone has something to contribute, and you'll be a better community member if you remember to give back in kind what you have received. Don't allow yourself to feel too busy for this; after all, the people who helped you weren't too busy, were they?

» Search for help outside of eBay

Consider your product area and look for help there. Dan's Train Depot found that the hobbyists he knew offline were more than happy to help him in any way they could. Many of them knew something about eBay, and all of them knew plenty about his product area. Now that eBay is so much more mature, it's almost more likely that you will have trouble meeting people who don't know anything about eBay than you will meeting people who do know something. Don't hesitate to ask around in your particular field of interest for advice and help in getting started.

Work with a Friend

You don't have to do this alone. You may have a friend who is much more comfortable with computers than you are. Don't hesitate to ask for help getting started. You may even have a friend who is also interested in starting an eBay business. You can always work together and share your learning and success. That way, you double your experience level right from the beginning.

Dan Glasure

Dan Glasure is the Dan in Dan's Train Depot. You will find him on eBay under the username used.ho.trains. He's been selling on eBay since 1999, and today he carries more than 10,000 feedbacks, with a positive feedback rating of 99.9 percent. Not only does Dan have his eBay auctions and an eBay store, but his eBay business has also led him to open a brick-and-mortar store too. But that's getting ahead of the story.

When Dan first began exploring eBay, he was interested in another hobby, comic books. He had

only a small amount of eBay experience, and his real exposure to the site came when he decided to start selling. Since he knew a lot about comics, he started with those. He actually owned the first issue of Spiderman, a fact that would make many comic book fans drool. He explains that in his little home town of about 100,000 people, he may well have been the only one who owned this comic. He discovered when he came to eBay that his rare comic wasn't so rare in the eBay world. In a global marketplace, many others owned his treasure, and he decided not to sell it.

He also decided to branch out away from comics, and he turned to another of his hobbies, model trains. This is one of the cases when good fortune, good timing, and hard work all come together. Dan soon came upon a single huge collection of H.O. model trains that the collector was ready to pass on. With the financial help of his father, he bought the whole thing, and he and his dad got busy selling it on eBay. They soon sold the entire collection, and Dan began advertising locally to purchase more inventory. His inventory grew slowly from those early days, and today he advertises for products in national markets through train hobbyists' journals and magazines. He also buys the train stock of hobby shops around the country that are liquidating. Today he says that locating inventory is never a problem for him.

Dan's operation can be challenging because, since he sells hobby items, each item must be individually photographed and described. This makes listing his items very time consuming and, in order to manage his volume, he has hired good employees. He currently has seven employees between his brick-and-mortar store and his eBay business. One of his eBay staff members does nothing but photography for his listings. That explains why he currently has hundreds of auctions running. Dan recommends hiring staff as soon as you need them. "You can't do this all by yourself," he says, noting that a lot of new business owners hesitate to add the expense of staff. Dan reports that his staff makes his business far more productive and successful than he could make it alone.

He decided to open a store when he realized that it would be a reasonable complement to his eBay business. "I have $3.00 cars in my store. Nobody wants to be bothered with the shipping costs to buy such a small item on eBay. On my eBay auctions, I can sell the $1,000 brass collector's engine that no one in my little town would be willing to pay for." By having both outlets for his products, Dan has reached the local and global markets all at the same time.

Chapter 2

Power-Buy to Power-Sell: Building Your Inventory

We hope you're feeling sparked and energetic after reading Chapter 1. By considering all of the issues we discussed in that chapter, you've had the chance to reassess your commitment as a potential PowerSeller. It's wonderful that you've decided to keep going and join us here in Chapter 2, where we will address one of the greatest challenges PowerSellers face: where do you find all of the items you need to sell to achieve and maintain PowerSeller status? It's an excellent question, and you'll find many excellent answers suggested throughout this chapter.

Acquiring your inventory will vary greatly depending on what you decide to sell. If you're following our advice from the last chapter and starting with something you know about, you already have some ideas about where you can acquire products. That's yet another reason it's wise to start selling things you know about. But, gathering items for your own enjoyment and buying things in the quantities you'll need to stock your eBay business are not the same things. You'll have to work to come up with lots of new ideas about where you can get and maintain a steady stream of merchandise.

That little four-letter word, "work," is just what we mean. Many PowerSellers will tell you that they spend the bulk of their time finding, developing, maintaining, and servicing their supply lines. This work is not the kind of task you can do once and consider it finished. It's more like housework, always there, always needing your attention, no matter how much you seem to do. The tips you'll gain from this chapter will help you get started, and then you'll continue with your task as you work, learn, and make your eBay business grow. The good news—and this is encouraging—is that as you do this work, you'll hone your skills and your instincts will sharpen. Everything you learn will make you smarter, more effective, and more able to see the possibilities of new sources of product everywhere you look.

As your trusted tour guides, we wish we could tell you that by the end of this chapter, we will have given you the keys to the vault. You'll have zeroed in on all of the best sources of product, and you'll be well on your way to PowerSeller status. Well, it pains us to admit, but that's just not going to happen.

Don't despair. What we *will* give you is still going to empower you and get you on your way. First we'll help you clearly define your challenges, and that will help you plot your course. Then we'll stock your toolbox for the job ahead. We've spent countless hours researching sources of products and information to get you started. You'll still spend hours researching, but you'll be starting from the next level, not from the bottom wrung of the ladder. Finally, we'll help you learn how to distinguish what sources of products and information are valuable and what sources are not so valuable. At the end of this chapter, you will be initiated into the world of sourcing products for your eBay business, and that's a big step on your road to PowerSeller.

First Things First

Before we start down that road, let's set the course. The challenge you face in acquiring your inventory is really twofold. First you have to figure out what is marketable and selling well on eBay. Second, you have to figure out where to acquire these marketable goods in quantity and at a price that allows you to earn a profit when you sell them. Fortunately, we've gathered some excellent tools you can use for these tasks. But, first, you need to equip yourself with one thing that all PowerSellers must have, a tax ID number.

» Get a tax ID number, now

If your state has a sales tax, and most of them do, you will have to acquire a sales tax ID number before you can legitimately sell your products, even online. This process can take several weeks to complete, so go ahead and get it started now. By the time you're actually ready to be selling, you'll be registered and legitimately in business according to the laws of your state. You will need this number for reporting the sales tax you collect from the people who buy from you. For now, don't worry about that; we'll address it in much more detail in Chapter 10.

A tax ID number is often also called a *resale certificate.* Both of these terms prove that you are a legitimate business and registered with your state. Many wholesalers and manufacturers will not sell products to you if you don't have this documentation of your legitimacy. So, don't delay. It's the first thing to do as you go about acquiring your inventory.

Getting signed up is not so daunting a task as you might think. You can start by going to your search engine and entering a search for "Tax ID Number (your state)." You'll at least get some information about the tax ID program, and you may even gain access to forms you can complete online to get the process started.

Get a tax ID number, now

As an alternative, you can go to www.mtc.gov/txpyrsvs/
actualpage.htm, shown in Figure 2-1. From this site, you'll find
links to most of the states and the District of Columbia. The link
for our state actually allowed us to access the necessary forms
and get the process started.

What Are You Thinking of Selling?

Now's the time for you to look through your own ideas and
evaluate what you are thinking of selling. If your plan is to sell
new products, your road to inventory acquisition will take you
in a different direction from the path you'll take if you're
planning to resell used items. Either way, you'll have your work
cut out for you, but you'll definitely be approaching the tasks
from very different angles.

    Selling new products means that you need to identify
reliable sources of products. Reliable means that the products
are of a consistent quality and that the sources you find are

FIGURE 2-1 The Multistate
Tax Commission's home
page makes it easy to get
information about obtaining
a tax ID number.

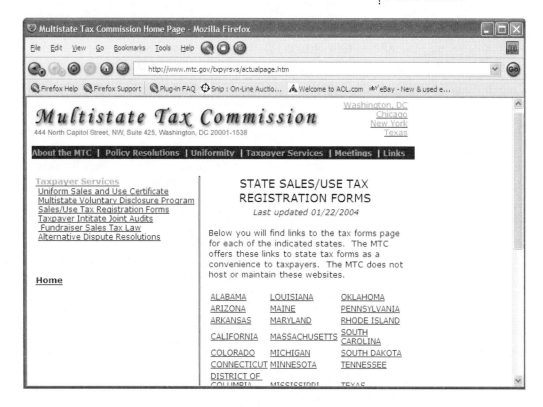

consistently able to provide them to you. You will also need to work to maintain a steady supply of products as the needs of your customers and the market for your items shift. You will be working to identify a group of specific sources, and then you'll work to keep them steady, while you continually keep your eyes peeled for more and even better sources of products.

Selling used products means that you will actually spend a great deal of your time going out to acquire products. Unlike when you research new products, which you can accomplish more readily at home, you'll have to physically visit the places where used items are sold. PowerSellers who resell used items claim that most of their weekly efforts are spent shopping for items to sell. Now, there are exceptions to this rule, which we will explore in a bit. But, being realistic, if you are going to resell used items, you should really love the thrill of the hunt and the joy of the chase.

» Think of your products as a total product line

As long as you're building an inventory anyway, consider the totality of your products and think of yourself as providing a *product line* to your customers. Instead of offering a variety of entirely different types of things you happen to come across, consider building a unity into your product line. Present your prospective customers with a body of products that go together. "The only way to differentiate yourself from other sellers is to give your customers a lifestyle," says a PowerSeller with a feedback number of nearly 5,000. "Combine your products. People want to belong to a group or club." She sells skin care products, but she also sells candles, incense, wind chimes, and decorative items to beautify a customer's space. All of these things can make a person feel pampered, and they are likely to all appeal to the person who would shop for any single one of them.

Not only does this strategy create a cohesive product line for you and your customers, it simplifies your shopping for inventory. You will find so many different products you might want to try, but sticking with a genre of products helps you focus your efforts. It keeps you from getting scattered by the temptations you'll come upon. Now, that's not to say you shouldn't keep your eyes open to a great source of new products for your line. That should always be your mindset, but stay focused, and don't chase after every new thing you see just because you've found a place to source it.

» Consider the needs of your products and your customers

When you're deciding what you'll sell, don't forget to consider the necessary items that go along with your products. If you decide to sell aromatherapy machines, you'll also want to sell the aromatherapy beads that go with them. If you sell cameras, also stock the batteries for the cameras. The same is true for any item that requires filters, bags, or any other consumable part. Make yourself the place your customers come to for their purchases and their repeat purchases.

Consider selling something that other eBay sellers may use. This goes beyond the usual packing supplies or shipping labels. As you build your business, see what items you find handy and then consider stocking them. Have you found a reliable scale for weighing your boxes? Do you have a favorite light for photographing your products? Can you provide a source of inexpensive, personalized stationery for sellers to include in their shipping? How about office products that you find especially useful? Anything you can identify that other eBay sellers might need and want gives you an automatic customer base to address.

» Calculate your budget

Before you start actually buying inventory items, calculate your total budget for your initial costs. Finding products to resell can be very exciting, and you can easily spend more than you should, because you're trying to buy a lot of items at one time. Knowing clearly what your budget is also allows you to allocate portions of it for specific product types. This enables you to spread your money across a variety of inventory items so that you can check on the return of your investment as you see what prices you get for different types of things.

» Always shop with a calculator

In time, you will be able to eyeball an item and know quickly if it will bring you enough money to make it worth your while. But, that time isn't now. When you consider how much you can spend on an item, a vital part of that equation is determining what you'll have to earn from it to make the process worth your while. Knowing the cost of the item includes knowing the true costs. For new items, those costs can include shipping the items to you, and possibly taxes and fees to the seller. For used items, those costs include your time in locating and transporting the item, how much work is required to get it ready to sell, and any supplies you might need to do that task. Calculate it all, and then see how much you'd need to earn from that item to give you a comfortable profit margin. Don't forget to include the value of your time, although you may not be able to recoup its full worth until your business is more established. Is that price realistic on eBay for this item?

Find Out What Sells

Answering that question of pricing is both art and science. The artistic part comes from the instincts you'll bring to the task. If you're dealing with items you already know and understand, you'll feel more confident in making this assessment. The science part comes with good old hard work. That means research, research, research, and more research. If only we could tell you that once you finish this research, you'll know everything you need to know. You *will* be smarter, but then you'll have to keep researching so that you can expand your product offerings and keep up with your inventory as it diverges into ever-new corners of your market. Researching will get easier as you find your favorite research tools and hone your research skills, but it will never be finished. Fortunately, we can help you get started.

» Use eBay's "Hot Items" by Category

eBay tracks the hottest selling items and publishes them monthly, in an easy-to-find location on the site. From any eBay screen, click the Services tab along the top. The right side of the Services screen that appears is devoted to sellers. Scroll down until you reach Selling Reference. There you'll find Seller Central. Click that hyperlink and you'll come to the Seller Central screen. About halfway down the page, you will see a hyperlink for What's Hot. Click that, and you'll come to the What's Hot page, shown in Figure 2-2. These two choices, Merchandise Calendar and Hot Items by Category, can provide some useful information as you begin your search for what's selling on eBay. We'll start with the Hot Items by Category list.

Use eBay's "Hot Items" by Category

The Hot Items list is a PDF file that you'll read using the Adobe Acrobat reader. You can't copy from it or manipulate the information that appears in the list, but you can study it and take notes. The first thing you should notice about the Hot Items list is its date. When we checked this in late May, the Hot Item list was reporting on March's activities. That's still fairly recent research, but you can assume that, in more than a month, some of the hottest items had changed a bit. Still, there's plenty of useful information to be found.

Within each of the eBay categories of products, the listings are studied for both the recent bidding activity and the new listing activity. Hot products are ones that show bidding growth that has significantly outpaced new listing growth. Also, these products have a higher bid-to-item ratio than other products in the same category. You can easily see that the traffic for these items has been good. The items are designated as Hot, Very Hot, and Super Hot. They then achieve Level 2, Level 3, and Level 4 designations. A Level 4 item in the Super Hot grouping

FIGURE 2-2 eBay's own What's Hot page makes it easy to find two valuable tools for researching hot product areas.

is the best-selling item in the whole product group. Let's take a look at the Home category as an example.

For the month of March 2004, a Super Hot item in the Home category was Baby Gear & Furnishings, as you can see in Figure 2-3. A Level 2 hot item would be anything in the general category of Baby Gear & Furnishings. Moving over to Level 3, you see that Bathing & Grooming products and general Nursery items were hotter than the average listing for the general category. Hottest of all the items in this grouping were the Level 4 items, Skin Care Products and Towels & Washcloths for babies. Now you know that Skin Care Products and Towels & Washcloths for babies had a spread of greater than 35 percentage points between the bid growth rate for those items and the listing growth rate for those items in the month of March. That's what it takes to be designated Level 4, Super Hot. You can see that, on eBay, the demand for these items outweighed the supply, and if you were selling those items in March, you probably would have done well.

FIGURE 2-3 Using eBay's Hot Items by Category list allowed us to zero in on the most popular items for babies under the Home category.

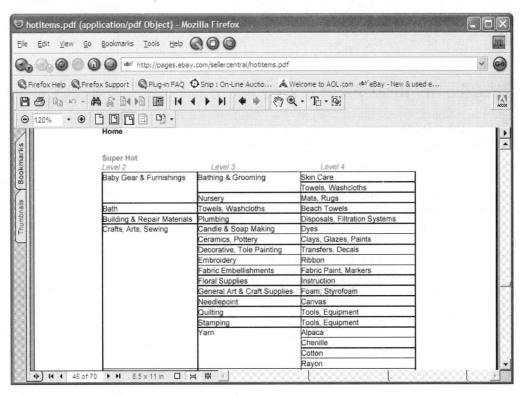

Keep the Hot Items list in perspective

The Hot Categories Report for March was 70 pages long!
You can see that there's a huge amount of available information.
You can toggle between the list and eBay searches to see how
much money the hottest items were bringing and what kind of
bidding action they were generating. Here's how: Let's stick
with the baby skin care item. With the Hot Items List minimized,
open a search page on eBay and do a Completed-Items search
for baby skin care products. Now you can see what prices
these items brought in the last two weeks. When we checked,
the highest priced item was sold at $13.50 with six bidders
participating in the auction. The starting price was $10.00. The
seller would have been satisfied to let the item go at $10.00,
but instead he earned an additional $3.50. That's a 35 percent
increase above the price he had designated as the lowest bid
he'd accept, so he's done well.

When evaluating the sale of an item, always consider the
starting price, the ending price, and the number of bids the listing
attracted. Combined, they provide the total history of the listing
and give you good insight into just how well the product did.

 *It is sometimes better to do a regular search and also have the current items screen up,
allowing you to toggle back and forth between the two screens.*

» Keep the Hot Items list in perspective

There is no doubt you can gain a huge amount of information
from the Hot Items list. It's free, it's easy to use, and you'll get
a good overview of everything that sells on eBay by using it.
It's a very worthy tool to begin with. But, remember, it's just a
beginning. Once you gather the information you can get from
the Hot Items list, continue on with your research, so that you
can put the information you gathered here into perspective.

First, remember that the information you got is likely to
be close to a month old, maybe even older, as our example
showed. That doesn't mean it's not valid, it just means it's not
the latest snapshot of what's going on. It's a capture of what
the market was, in this case, six weeks ago, not this week.
(Seasonality may also be a factor. Obviously, the demand for
mittens will surge during the winter months.) That's fine, as
long as you realize that it is almost guaranteed that there will
be some variation in the numbers since the information was
captured.

Next, remember that if you have such easy access to the Hot Items list, so do the 100 million other people who use eBay. If every seller on eBay used the Hot Items list alone to make decisions about what to sell, there would never be a single item on the Hot Items list twice. If researching what products are likely to sell well on eBay were really this easy, everyone would be a PowerSeller. Now that you know how to identify what has sold well on eBay, move on to finding products that you believe will sell well in the future.

Use eBay's Merchandise Calendar

The other choice from the What's Hot screen featured in Figure 2-2 is eBay's Merchandise Calendar, shown in Figure 2-4. This shows you what eBay will be promoting on the site for a three-month period. As you might expect, the calendar in Figure 2-4 features items for Mother's Day and gifts for Father's Day, as well as items for graduates for the months of May and June. As you can see, in the last week of April and the first week of May, the spotlight was on Mom. The usual types of Mother's Day gifts were scheduled to be in the spotlight. Piggyback on that, but think creatively too. Most people targeting this market will sell jewelry, perfume, and flowers for Mom. You might do well by featuring craft items, picture frames, or music for Mom instead. You can still gear your merchandise toward gifts mothers might like, but move yourself away from the crowd so that you can appeal to the customers who also look around the fringes of what's expected.

» Check out the numbers from Bid4Assets

In Chapter 1, we told you about a valuable tool, the AuctionBytes newsletter. Every week in AuctionBytes, you will find sell-through numbers, often provided by Bid4Assets.com. You can get the latest report by surfing to the AuctionBytes site (www.auctionbytes.com) and scrolling down to the link for Bid4Assets' report. Bid4Assets is a leading online auction site for government and private industry. It offers customized online, traditional, and webcast auctions plus storefront and private auction exchanges. The company focus is on high-end assets, including real estate, personal property, bankruptcy claims, and financial instruments.

Check out the numbers from Bid4Assets

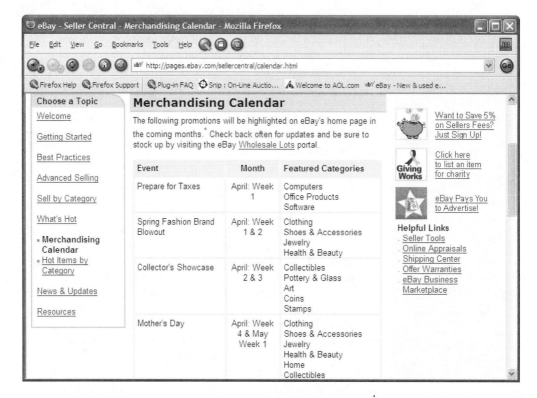

Sell-through data shows you the average percentage of the items put up for auction on the Bid4Assets.com site that actually sold. Because it's gathered weekly, the sell-through information you find published in AuctionBytes' newsletter is more up to date than the Hot Items list on eBay. But, it is also much less specific. Bid4Assets' sell-through reports are compiled 24 hours a day, 7 days a week, and tallied at the end of the week. They feature top-level and sub-level categories, and the data includes "BuyNow" items and items that sold in the final minutes of the auction. For the week ending April 3, 2004, sell-through rates included

FIGURE 2-4 eBay's Merchandise Calendar allows you to piggyback your products with eBay's promotional efforts and plan your offerings three months in advance.

- ■ **All categories** 73 percent
- ■ **Artwork** 76 percent
- ■ **Coins & Stamps** 100 percent
- ■ **Collectibles & Luxury items** 100 percent
- ■ **Computer Equipment** 33 percent

- **Furs** 100 percent
- **Jewelry** 70 percent
- **Sports Memorabilia** 100 percent
- **Technology Accessories** 60 percent
- **Tools** 57 percent
- **Toys and Games** 60 percent

Now you have a snapshot of what was selling at the Bid4Assets online auctions for one particular week. Remember, this is not a snapshot of what was selling on eBay, but watching this data weekly can help you spot trends and track product areas that consistently sell well online. The data arrives with your weekly issue of AuctionBytes, so it's free and easy to check.

» Use Price Finder and What's Hot from Andale

Andale provides tools and services for eBay users. You'll learn more about the counters Andale offers for your auction listings in subsequent chapters, but in addition to those, you'll also find some wonderful tools for evaluating potential inventory items directly on Andale's web site. Go to www.andale.com for a tour of everything the company offers. The Price Finder on Andale allows you to track the price and sell-through rate of specific items. Figure 2-5 shows you that between April 4 and May 3, 66 percent of the Brita Water Filter Smart Pitchers listed on eBay sold. The average selling price was $11.86, and the range of prices paid for the pitchers was $6.52 through $19.99. The Price Finder searched more than 56 million eBay listings to report back to us about the 50 listings for this specific item. Andale's information is recent, specific, and reliable. Using it to help you define your product line is an excellent choice. You can have a one-month free trial period for this tool. After that, the price for using it is $3.95 per month.

Andale's What's Hot tool provides detailed information about eBay's categories and the hottest items in those categories. You can use it to search for items you are thinking of selling, or you can browse categories to see which are doing well, and what items within those categories are selling. Figure 2-6 shows you just a sample of the information you'll find. The numbers to the

Use Price Finder and What's Hot from Andale

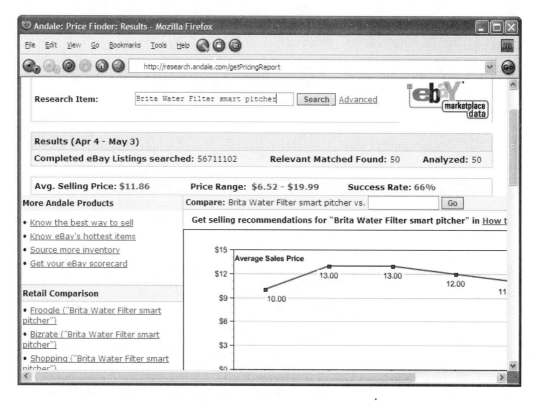

right of each category show you the number of hot auctions for each category. Now you can see which categories are generating the most traffic. You can study each category to find individual items that are selling well. You can also use a Smart Clustering tool that finds the hottest product groups.

Reports available to you through Andale's What's Hot tool rate how much demand there is for specific categories and items within those categories. You can also check individual products for average sale prices, auction successes, average hits, and the number of bids each auction attracted. All of this information can be exported to Excel for your own deeper analysis. The What's Hot tool costs $3.95 per month to use, but that price brings you unlimited use of the service. You can bundle What's Hot with Price Finder and three other Andale tools—How to Sell for researching eBay prices, Sales Analyzer for analyzing your own sales data, and Andale Counters for keeping track of traffic to your auctions—all for $9.95 per month.

FIGURE 2-5 The search results from Andale's Price Finder tool give you valuable insight into sell-through rate and pricing information for products you may be considering.

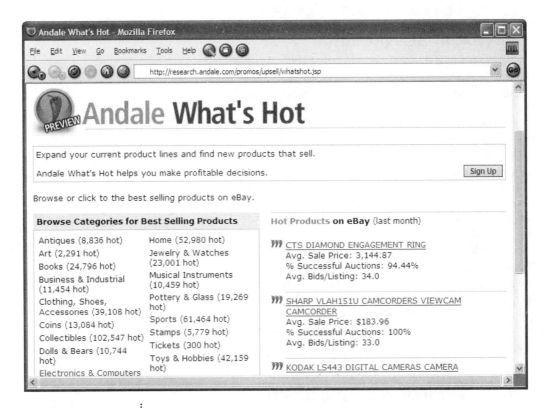

Andale What's Hot - Mozilla Firefox

http://research.andale.com/promos/upsell/whatshot.jsp

Andale **What's Hot**

Expand your current product lines and find new products that sell.

Andale What's Hot helps you make profitable decisions.

Sign Up

Browse or click to the best selling products on eBay.

Browse Categories for Best Selling Products

Antiques (8,836 hot)

Art (2,291 hot)

Books (24,796 hot)

Business & Industrial (11,454 hot)

Clothing, Shoes, Accessories (39,108 hot)

Coins (13,084 hot)

Collectibles (102,547 hot)

Dolls & Bears (10,744 hot)

Electronics & Computers

Home (52,980 hot)

Jewelry & Watches (23,001 hot)

Musical Instruments (10,459 hot)

Pottery & Glass (19,269 hot)

Sports (61,464 hot)

Stamps (5,779 hot)

Tickets (300 hot)

Toys & Hobbies (42,159 hot)

Hot Products on eBay (last month)

CTS DIAMOND ENGAGEMENT RING
Avg. Sale Price: 3,144.87
% Successful Auctions: 94.44%
Avg. Bids/Listing: 34.0

SHARP VLAH151U CAMCORDERS VIEWCAM CAMCORDER
Avg. Sale Price: $183.96
% Successful Auctions: 100%
Avg. Bids/Listing: 33.0

KODAK LS443 DIGITAL CAMERAS CAMERA

FIGURE 2-6 Andale's What's Hot tool allows you to see sales activity across eBay's categories and to evaluate sales within the categories too.

Where Will You Get Your Inventory?

Now that you've gathered some tools for determining what's selling well on eBay, where are you going to find those products at prices that will allow you to make a profit? Here we'll provide some ideas to get you started, and then you'll need to do your own research. At first, you'll find many different sources for your products, and then you'll begin to see which ones are the best. Where you'll find your inventory depends largely on whether you sell used merchandise or new merchandise. The channels and methods for acquiring each of these categories vary greatly, but you can use some basic strategies for learning about sources for both. Don't forget to keep your antennae up and your eyes open. You never know where a new source will appear, and you want to be ready to jump on it when it does.

❱❱ Think locally, sell globally

No matter where you live, there are things that are native to your location that other people in other places may never have heard about. If something is very popular close to home, consider it for sale to a global market. In our little part of the world, there is a wonderful, local producer of jellies and preserves. You'll find them at every tourist stop and attraction within 30 miles of our home. These might also prove to be favorites to people who don't live close enough to pick them up locally. Maybe your part of the world has a particular craft item, jewelry style, pottery line, or glass manufacturer. Start looking around for the things you may just take for granted and consider what appeal they may have to a wider audience.

You may also tap into local wholesalers, manufacturers, and liquidators. Once you locate these sources, you'll save money on shipping their products to you for resale. You'll also gain access to items that may not be readily available to others outside your geographic area. This not only provides you with sources of unique products, but it also lessens your competition once you get your product to market on eBay.

❱❱ Turn to your local reference librarian

If you need a jump-start on your research, don't overlook your reference librarian. Librarians are trained researchers, and most are more than happy to help you research a topic they may not often get called upon to explore. Stop by the library at an off-hour when your librarian may not be too busy with other patrons. Introduce yourself, and get to know each other. Tell him you are researching market trends and products. Ask him to help you locate wholesalers and manufacturers, and enlist his help in defining good search terms for Internet searches. Don't forget to ask him about local associations and organizations of businesses, auctioneers, and estate planners.

❱❱ Do it yourself on the Internet

"I spend hundreds of hours online searching for new sources," says a PowerSeller who sells only new products. Just as this PowerSeller devotes time every week to the search, you will too. We'll get you started with some sites to explore, but in the end you'll spend a lot of time tracking down sources for yourself. Be persistent, and don't allow yourself to get discouraged. Most of the PowerSellers who are now successful on eBay had to do this same thing for themselves. Your distribution channels won't appear overnight, and the task is never really ended. You'll continue to refine your sources and explore new opportunities just as long as you operate your business. In addition to the person-to-person opportunities for help we've already mentioned, many libraries offer online references via their web sites that include databases you won't be able to access from the Internet at large. Some larger libraries even offer live reference help 24 hours a day, 7 days a week.

» Don't expect to find help on eBay

Remember those friendly discussion boards we told you about in Chapter 1? Well, the sellers you find on those boards will be more than happy to lend you a shoulder to cry on and a sympathetic ear, but they will not give up their sources of products. Sellers guard their sources very carefully, and you can easily understand why. The hard work ahead of you was once ahead of them, too. They remember your pain, but they're not going to sacrifice their good, reliable sources of products to ease it. Will *you* when you've got your sources in place?

That's doesn't mean they won't answer questions about specific sources if you ask them. There are often lively discussions of sources that have fallen out of favor with sellers, and these discussions include valuable insight about why certain sources aren't what they once may have been. Just remember that asking other sellers overtly about a specific source of product puts you at the risk of revealing a potential jewel of a source you may have found for yourself. So, don't be too up front in your requests for information. It's better to hang back and read the discussions for educational purposes. The things you learn from them can help you in evaluating your own research.

There are other discussion areas you can visit outside of eBay for this type of research, too. AuctionBytes.com has forums that address sources. These are also good places to visit to help you eliminate some potentially weak sources. But, still look at these public forums as a way to avoid problematic sources rather than a way to identify solid, reliable ones.

» Hire a professional

Just because you can't expect PowerSellers to give up their sources, that doesn't mean you can't get help from a proven professional; a professional Information Broker, that is. Information Brokers are professional researchers who sell their services, usually on a per-hour basis. You can go to an Information Broker with virtually any request for information, and that person will do the research and provide you with a finished research report. You can start your search for an Information Broker by visiting the web site of the Association of Independent Information Professionals (AIIP), shown in Figure 2-7. Here you'll find a directory of Information Brokers, including their e-mail addresses and phone numbers. You can search the directory for specific brokers, or you can search geographically to find brokers who operate near you. You can also search by areas of expertise, businesses, and industries.

FIGURE 2-7 The Association of Independent Information Professionals is a good place to start if you're thinking of hiring an Information Broker to help with your research.

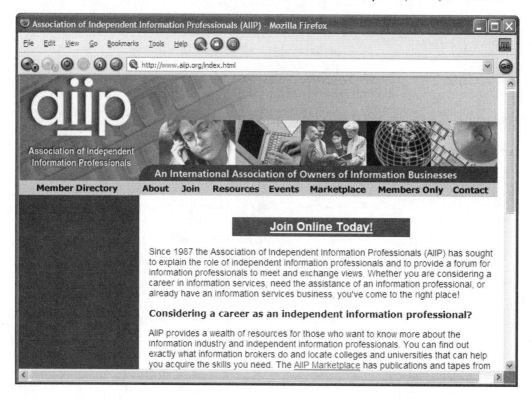

If you're considering hiring a specific broker, it's best to first make contact via e-mail. Explain what the scope of your research is and ask about the services she can provide. The next step is to speak on the phone. Don't hire a broker after only e-mail contact. You want to get to know this professional a bit, and clarify your needs in ways that are just not possible without directly communicating.

Information Brokers charge hourly rates that range from $75 to about $200. You can establish a "do not exceed" budget, and then your broker will provide you with the results of the research she was able to complete within the budgeted time. The deliverables you receive from the broker are also negotiable. They can range from simple lists of manufacturers to complete reports.

Why should you consider hiring an Information Broker rather than doing all of the research yourself? First of all, brokers know how to efficiently locate and use information, saving you hours of preliminary research. Second, Information Brokers have access to fee-based databases that are not available to the general public through the Internet. Not only *can* they use these databases on your behalf, but they also know *how* to use them to cherry-pick the best information available to you. Finally, aside from accessing electronic information sources, brokers also turn to printed sources, and as expert information sleuths, they'll actually pick up the phone too!

This is not to say, you'll hire an Information Broker and your research will be done for you. That's not going to happen. But, if you're feeling intimidated by starting this research, you should consider hiring a broker to help you on your way. Once you have some experience with the preliminary information you've paid for, you may be more confident to work on your own. Consider the fees you pay your Information Broker to be comparable to those you'll pay your accountant or lawyer when you find you're ready for those professionals, too.

Sourcing Used Items and Collectibles

If you've decided to sell used items, you'll have to get very specific. You don't want to start acquiring under the general category of "used," because you'll likely end up with no product consistency. You'll be too easily swept up into buying quantities of stuff that you simply can't sell on eBay. So how are you

Hire a professional

defining "used" for *your* eBay business? Will you sell high-quality children's dress clothes? Do you mean refurbished electronics? Are you thinking about kitchenware and gadgets? What about second-hand sports equipment? What you decide to sell will determine the places you should start looking for your inventory. As we've said before, be prepared to spend many hours shopping if you're going to sell used items. That means lots of driving, lots of hauling, and many early mornings getting the scoop on the best markets.

Garage and Yard Sales

In the early days, eBay was much like an electronic garage sale. This really isn't true anymore. As the site has matured, and the whole electronic commerce phenomenon, too, you are just as likely to find luxury items for sale on eBay as you are to find second-hand goods. It's impossible for you to stock your eBay business solely from garage sales and yard sales. You'll need to make these only a small portion of your shopping efforts. You can supplement your inventory this way, but you really mustn't count on this a source for building your inventory. For one thing, in most parts of the country, yard sales and garage sales are seasonal. You can't depend on any source of products that disappears for months at a time.

When you do go for the garage sale/yard sale method of inventory acquisitions, be prepared to start early. If you're not out driving by 7:30 on Saturday morning, you're late. Now, let's be a little crass. Start with the most affluent neighborhoods you can find. You're more likely to find items of higher value there. Move on to the less expensive neighborhoods when you're done with their wealthier counterparts. But before you do, go to the older neighborhoods, because there you're more likely to find older residents who have had years to gather and collect stuff they now consider junk. You're more likely to find a valuable collectible among the belongings of people who have been keeping house for 40 years than those who have been at it for 4.

Before you set out, read the ads, so you can plot your course. Often these ads list individual items or groups of items up for sale, and you'll be able to map your route to fit what looks promising. You don't want to lose valuable shopping time by wandering around aimlessly. If the ad lists lots of baby items and toys, you'll know you're dealing with a relatively young family that probably hasn't had the time or resources to gather enough valuable stuff to be able to sell it off at a garage sale. You can skip them altogether, unless, of course, you've decided to sell used baby items.

Moving Sales

Moving sales are more promising than garage and yard sales. First, people move throughout the year, so you don't lose whole seasons of shopping because of weather. Also, when people move, they're in a frame of mind that tells them to dump what they own rather than to move it. Moving is often the impetus to get rid of things they'd otherwise keep. So, not only are you likely to have a greater range of items to buy, but you're also likely to get a better price. When the option is dump it or pack it, people are often willing to dump it for less than they might otherwise expect to get for it.

Estate Sales

Estate sales can be even better than moving sales. Estate sales generally happen because a family is faced with divesting itself of the contents of an older relative's home. We know it seems a little ghoulish, but this presents you with the opportunity to buy a broad range of things that have probably been around for a good long while. Keep in mind that the cream of these things will most likely already be gone to family members as keepsakes and family heirlooms, but most estate sales still include lots of good, valuable items. Also remember that in some areas estate sales offer 20 to 50 percent discounts on the last day of the sale. So it sometimes pays to go back and see what's left over.

Professionals often run estate sales on behalf of the family, but not always. If a professional is involved, be prepared to pay slightly more for collectibles, because this person will likely recognize the value of the item almost to the extent you will.

Church Rummage Sales and Local Charity Fund-Raisers

Rummage sales and the like are not constant enough for you to count on them to stock your store, but at the same time, they are often great sources of things to use as supplements to your product line. Know the seasons for them in your area, and try not to miss them. Again, it's good to target the more affluent church communities if you can, but overall, you are often likely to find good items available at any church rummage sale. These events are usually planned within the church community well in advance so that the congregation members can plan for them and be prepared. Members are likely to save some of their nicer things to donate, because they are using these items to support a community that they truly care about. While you're acquiring your goods, you can also be doing good by supporting a charitable cause.

Local charity fund-raisers can include yard sale–like events or even much bigger events that resemble flea markets more than yard sales. Our local library has a wonderful book sale every year as part of our small town's Heritage Festival. We never miss this sale, and we get there early. All year long, the library accepts donations of books from its patrons. Dozens of volunteers sort, organize, and stack these books for the sale. On the first morning of the weekend-long event, we are always astonished at the wonderful books there are to buy. They range from hardcover bestsellers that were popular throughout the previous year to wonderful old collectible books that must have been Christmas presents in decades gone by. Nothing at the sale costs more than $1.00, and many of the books are in excellent condition. The library benefits from the proceeds, and we can scoop up some great items to be resold on eBay.

Auctions

Auctions are divided into two categories, private and government. These can each be divided again into online auctions and auctions that take place at physical locations. Auctions can be good sources of products, and indeed, some PowerSellers acquire almost all of their merchandise this way.

Private Auctions

Private auctions are generally operated by auction professionals. They may occur at the site of the property, much like an estate sale, or they can happen at the auctioneer's establishment. The ones that happen at the auctioneer's site are generally made up of goods gathered from many different estates or other sources. Check your local phone directory, or ask your librarian for local auction establishments, and get on their mailing lists. That way, you'll have advance notice of upcoming sales and you can prepare for them.

When you go to the auction, have in mind the types of items that you're shopping for. Don't go there with nothing specific in mind, because you're too likely to impulse-buy that way. On the other hand, don't close your mind to an unforeseen bonus item either. Just don't allow yourself to get carried away. The same is true when it comes time to bid. In the live auction setting it's easy to get caught up in the thrill of the bid and pay more than you should for an item.

We suggest getting a heads-up on the auction during the preview period, held either early on the day the auction actually begins or up to several days prior. This way, you can scope out all of the items up for bid.

Be sure you've registered with the auctioneer so that you'll be eligible to bid, and make sure you know if there are buying fees for the items you win. Make a clear list of the items you'll pursue, and designate your highest price for each. Then, do your best, but be prepared to let things go if you must.

Note *You don't always have to be present to win—you can leave bids and sometimes even bid by phone. Some auctions have catalogs, and some do not. Once you develop favorite houses, try to get on the mailing list for advance catalogs and review potential items and research prices before you go.*

At auctions, you're likely to find someone who simply wants the item more than you do. You must always bid with your potential resale price in mind, and don't chase an item someone else wants more. If you find this is a problem for you, enlist the help of a friend or partner who can help keep you in line, or pursue other sources of products. You can't stay in business long if you can't control your acquisition costs.

Government Auctions

Government entities ranging from the federal government to your local municipal government hold periodic auctions for all sorts of items, both at physical locations and online. Your local and state police may also have periodic auctions. You'll find different types of items at these auctions than the ones you'll find at public auctions. Radio equipment, office equipment, and electronics are commonly sold. You can often get great deals at these auctions, but you really have to know about the products being sold. Many of them will require some repair or refurbishing. Also, there are often seemingly slight differences in pieces of equipment of this kind that can dramatically alter their resale value.

Hire a professional

Items sold through these auctions are not always guaranteed to work, and there are no refunds or returns if you're not satisfied with what you've purchased.

Flea Markets

You'll know if your area has some good flea markets for you to explore. Flea markets can be good for second-hand items and collectibles, and some flea markets are targeted to these markets. In that case, you'll find many of the same types of items that you'd find at garage and yard sales, but you won't have as much driving around to do, since they'll all be in one place. At the same time, remember that flea markets are also seasonal in many parts of the country, so you can't depend on even the good ones to be consistent throughout the whole year.

We don't recommend that you pursue flea markets for new items, however. If you're going to sell new items, you want to be buying your inventory from the same people who sell it to the flea market dealers. Why should you pay the flea market person for acquiring it and dragging it to the market for you to buy? Cut out that middle person and keep the profits for yourself.

Thrift Stores

Thrift stores can be spotty places for finding inventory, but since selling used items on eBay means consistent and routine shopping, you're wise to add them to your list. Thrift shops often benefit from the goods that belonged to people who wanted to clear things out of their homes but didn't want to be bothered with a garage or yard sale. On the other hand, you'll also find they are the final resting place of things that were already offered at a garage sale and rejected.

Introduce yourself to the manager of the thrift store and get to know this person. Once the manager knows you and what you shop for, he may just be willing to call you when your type of item arrives. If he knows you stop in regularly, he may even hold it back for you when he sees it come in. Know when the truck arrives with new loads of goods for the thrift shop, and plan to be there soon after the staff has had enough time to sort through the delivery. Knowing the manager will go a long way toward your gaining this type of insider information.

Newspaper Advertising

Place ads in your local newspaper for items you want to buy. Don't overlook the little free supplement newspapers that serve nearly all communities. When you place your ad, be sure to include your e-mail address as well as your phone number. Your goal is to make it as easy as possible for people to get in touch with you. While you're checking on your ad in the paper, peruse the other listings of items in the "Wanted to buy" category. You may spot a competitor, or you may get some new ideas of the types of things people are shopping for. You may also get some copywriting ideas.

Collectors Are a Special Case

Collectors have a special home on eBay, so if you're coming to eBay to deal in collectibles, you'll be in good company. There are thousands of different categories of collectibles for sale on eBay, so as you might guess, you'll have a lot of competition. That shouldn't dissuade you, but just remind you that you'll need to work hard and stay focused to make dealing collectibles your path to power-selling.

The first thing you must decide is if you'll be selling collectibles or antiques. Antiques are legally defined by the U.S. Customs Department as any object that is more than 100 years old, according to Emyl Jenkins, author of *The Complete Idiot's Guide to Buying and Selling Antiques* (Alpha, 2000). Collectibles, on the other hand, are generally mass-produced items that are less than 100 years old. Collectibles can actually be anything that people like to collect, from 45 RPM records to Star Wars figures to Beanie Babies.

eBay owes its very existence to collectibles. In turn, eBay has changed the collectibles market. It is now so easy to trade in collectibles that collectors who may never have had the opportunity to complete a collection can do that through trading on eBay. Where it used to take a lifetime to gather the more esoteric parts of a collection by traveling locally and seeking out sources of collectibles through publications devoted to the genre, today's collectors can travel the world for their missing pieces and never leave home.

At the same time that eBay has opened up the world to collectors, it has also made the market for collectibles that much more challenging for sellers. Whereas sellers used to be able to operate in a regional field occupied mostly by people who came to know each other over the years of pursuing their collections, today's eBay sellers serve the world market. That means that they compete on a much larger scale for the same finite body of collectibles. At the same time, eBay has helped popularize collecting, and that has opened a whole new market for reproductions, which adds yet another challenge to the collectibles seller. "When people can pay $50 for a reproduction of a Fire King rolling pin, that depletes the market of my customers who are willing to pay $1,000 for the real thing," noted a collectibles PowerSeller from the Southeast.

Still, as anyone who has ever been bitten by a collector's bug can tell you, once you've got the itch, nothing can stop you. Plenty of PowerSellers deal in collectibles, and they wouldn't have it any other way, because by doing so they can immerse themselves full-time in something they truly love and enjoy. So, if you've got your heart set on power-selling collectibles, don't be discouraged. Just get ready to work.

Since you're already pursuing your collectibles hobby, you have a pretty good feel for where you can get items for sale. In addition to your own sources, you will pursue all of the venues we've already discussed for buying used items, and there are a few more you may not have already thought of. The challenge for you will be to create and maintain a steady enough stream to keep your inventory solid.

» Advertise in ways you may not have tried yet

In addition to advertising in newspapers and local supplements, consider advertising in national markets for your products. If your area of collecting has national journals, magazines, or newsletters, you may find you actually get a better return on your advertising money through these publications than you do by limiting yourself to local markets. You will also want to consider online bulletin boards where other collectors gather. Make yourself a presence on these and post your requests for products. You may be able to glean the doubles and extras from the collections of others. You probably won't find real bargains here, since you are shopping among people who know what they have, but you can still swap and trade items for resale with these educated partners.

» Search on eBay

Don't discount finding collectibles to resell on eBay. Search for your items under common misspellings, because those listings are likely to have been placed by someone who doesn't know much about your area of expertise. If you can scoop up something from a less savvy eBayer, you can make that seller happy, and you gain a bargain for yourself.

» Be prepared to travel

Every PowerSeller we spoke with who deals in collectibles travels, a lot. Know where and when your regional collectible shows are and be ready to go and build your inventory. You will most likely have to travel beyond your regional boundaries too, especially if your collectible area has big annual gatherings. Plan for these and adjust your budget so that you'll be prepared to spend money on inventory, knowing that as a collectibles dealer, you don't have the luxury of consistent shopping spread evenly throughout the year.

» Get to know your customers and what they buy

You can sharpen your collectibles sales by getting to know your customers. Then you can shop with them in mind. When you travel and uncover new product offerings, you can buy with the confidence that you know people who will be interested in your purchases. That's a huge benefit, not only because you can have quick turnover of your products that way, but also because it allows you to spend a little more, if you have to, in order to get the product. "I know which patterns of Roseville my customers shop for," said one PowerSeller from New Jersey who sells this art pottery. "I know if I find nice pieces in those patterns, that I've got customers who are likely to catch my auctions and bid." Once your customers get to know you and you get to know them, you'll start to recognize pieces that they may be specifically looking for to complete their collections. Now you can tailor your purchases even more.

You'll have to give yourself time to establish this type of presence, but the collectibles world, in spite of the numbers, is still a limited universe, and people can still carve parts of that universe out for themselves with good products and customer service.

Sourcing New Items for Sale on eBay

If your plan is to sell new products on eBay, your sourcing experiences will be very different from those of the sellers who deal in used products. Instead of spending much of your time driving around and scouring for great items to resell, you'll spend much of your time scouting around for reliable sources of products to resell, but you can do much of this scouting right from your home. The goal in finding products to resell is to get as close to the original source of those products as you possibly can. Every set of hands that pass the product from its creator to you takes a chunk of your profit margin for the effort.

When you're looking for sources, go for quality. Anyone can find and sell junk on eBay, but you won't build repeat business that way. The days of eBay as the world's electronic yard sale have passed. People come to eBay now for all types of purchases, from pet supplies to computer equipment, from baby strollers to fine jewelry. Your customers are likely to think of eBay first whenever they need to shop for a particular item, so use that market loyalty. Decide early on that you're not going to operate strictly by price. Figure what your profit goals are, and then go for exceptional customer service and great products. Together they will justify the price you need to get to earn your goals.

Avoid buying returns, damaged goods, and rejected products in lots. You will find so many items that are not fit for resale that what may have first appeared to be a good deal will prove more trouble than value. You don't want to have to sort through piles of junk so that you can glean the few items you can resell. Not only does that make those few items more expensive than you first thought, it's a big waste of your time and energy.

As you start your research, you'll find lists of sources for sale online, even on eBay, itself. Don't spend your time and money on these. If these sources are so easy to find that you can simply pay for them, don't you think the thousands of other people who want to sell on eBay can buy them too? Every story has a moral, and so does this one. If something really is a great, secret bargain, why is the person offering to tell you about it? If that list were really what the seller claimed it to be, he'd keep those secrets for himself and go on to make money by selling things more valuable than the list he's offering.

At the same time, don't forget to shop on eBay itself for new products to resell. Just as you might be able to scoop up deals on collectibles from less savvy eBay sellers, you might be able to find bargains on new items. You can also sometimes get good deals from sellers who only accept very limited payment options. Also, consider making some purchases from eBay sellers with no feedback or low feedback ratings. These new sellers—and you may be among them at first—often can't get as much for their products as more experienced sellers can, because people hesitate to risk shopping with them. Their auctions often don't generate the bid activity that drives their prices up. Here's an opportunity for you to scoop up something at a good price, and help a new eBayer at the same time. Just be careful. Try smaller purchases at first until you test the seller. Spend some extra time communicating with the seller before you bid so that you're sure both of you are clear on what the product is and what the terms of the sale are. Be sure you understand this inexperienced seller's shipping and return policies. Then, give it a try.

You should expect to try many different sourcing channels as you build your inventory. The more channels you open to yourself, the more likely you are to develop a good solid stream of inventory. You will eventually zero in on the ones that you like best, but in the beginning, be prepared to test out your different options. We'll help you not only learn where to find sources, but also how to protect yourself as you do your exploring.

» Buy at the end of the season

Not to sound too immodest, but we are two of the best shoppers we know. If it wasn't a deal, we simply don't own it. When our kids were small, we did all of their clothes shopping at the end-of-the season clearance sales. Watching the papers, we hit the finest department store in our area on the first day of their clearance. In February, when others were sick of the cold, nasty weather, we were scooping up snowsuits, sweaters, and corduroy overalls by the handfuls. In August, when others were thinking "back-to-school" we were thinking of next summer's trip to the beach, and we were gathering bathing suits, sun dresses, and little shorts. We made most of these purchases at 75 to 80 percent off the regular department store prices. At the beginning of the next season, when other parents were whining about the high cost of clothes and having to drag around to complete the

Buy at the end of the season

season's wardrobe, all we had to do was cut the tags and run the stored items through the wash. The kids looked great in clothes we simply could not afford at full price, and we saved a bundle.

This same shopping strategy works not only for children's clothing, but also for many other items. Just stick with things that are not too trendy or faddish. One season's hot item can easily be next season's reject, so shop for classic style and good quality as well as value. Also remember that you'll have to have a good place to store the things you buy in August that won't be sold until April or May. The basement isn't a good choice, because you don't want your merchandise to smell musty. You also can't use this strategy if you smoke, because even if you don't realize it, everything that comes out of your house will smell of smoke. Watch for pets too. You don't want to invest in new inventory that is no longer salable because it carries an odor. Ask a friend to be honest and let you know if your storage area has a smell. You can't usually detect the smell of your own place, in the same way an unbiased nose can. If you have to factor in off-site storage for your end-of-the-season's bargains, you'll take a chunk of your profits out of this sourcing option, and you may want to consider selling more "forgiving" items instead.

Safety Checks for Testing Sources

Whether you start working with liquidators, wholesalers, or manufacturers, you'll want to protect yourself from spending too much money on the wrong items. Don't expect to build your inventory sources without making mistakes. Every successful PowerSeller can tell you stories of deals that didn't work out as they'd hoped. You'll learn a lot from the mistakes you make, and that's okay. Just be careful not to get sucked into deals with dishonest, disreputable sources that are more interested in fleecing you than they are in selling you fleece.

Make sure the company you're working with actually exists. Get the physical address for the building that houses the company. Don't be satisfied with just a post office box as an address. If the company has nothing but a post office box, don't do business with them. They may be on the level, but they may also be nothing more than an individual who has nothing to sell you and only a box at the post office to collect your payment. Don't risk it, because there are too many other sources that can be documented to waste your time and money this way.

Get a telephone number for the company you're considering buying from and get in touch with a person there. Making contact with a human not only goes toward establishing a relationship with the source, it also allows you to clarify the company's product line, return policies, and shipping practices. You can tell a lot about a company by talking to an employee, especially when that employee is interacting with a potential customer. Evaluate how easy it is to get through to someone, how responsive this person is to your questions, and how enthusiastic this person is about doing business with you. It's information you can't gather without the human touch.

Now get information about how this company operates within its industry. Find out if the company belongs to its trade association. If they don't belong, find out why. Check with the Better Business Bureau to make sure there are no complaints filed against the company. That doesn't necessarily mean that you can count on the company to be reliable, but you will find a red flag if customers have been taken before. Don't stop with the Better Business Bureau. Go on to see what accreditation the company has. Look for backing from such sources as VeriSign, Dun & Bradstreet, Hoover, or other reputable companies that provide credit-checking services. This tells you that the company has met standards of operation that put them in reliable company.

Liquidation Sales

There are liquidation sales and then there are liquidators. Liquidation sales are one-time sales that go along with a business closing its doors, while liquidators are companies that sell off the inventories of other businesses. You will find liquidators both offline and online. When searching for liquidation sales, you can work locally. That makes it possible for you to actually inspect the merchandise personally, and you'll save shipping charges too. Just be sure that the liquidation sales offers are true. There is a great deal of misleading advertising here. When a business closes, it generally starts discounting merchandise at smaller percentages off, and the percentage increases as the last day of business approaches. Timing can be everything here. You want to strike when the percentages have increased so that you'll really get bargains, but you don't want to wait so long that all of the good things have been scooped up before you can buy.

If you learn of a pending store closing, consider approaching the owners with an offer early in their liquidation process.

Buy at the end of the season

If you offer to buy in bulk, they may be willing to shunt some of their merchandise to you and not include it in the general liquidation sale. Liquidation sales are tightly regulated by state and local business and tax laws, so be sure to know what those are for your area. Your local reference librarian can help you get this information and can also help you locate local liquidation companies.

Liquidation Companies

Don't be discouraged if there are no liquidation companies local to your area. You can easily find liquidators online. Buying liquidations online can be a little trickier than shopping locally, since you can't inspect the items you buy, but many PowerSellers use online liquidators for sourcing products. You just have to educate yourself and be careful about what you buy and which companies you shop with. Know in advance that the products you receive might include damaged goods mixed in with the salable items. This will alter the price point you pay for your merchandise. You may also find that what you ordered and what you got are not the same. But, those are some of the pitfalls of working with liquidators whose merchandise often includes items returned to stores by customers who were dissatisfied with them, items that have been damaged, and items that simply didn't strike a chord with their intended market.

When we did a Google search for liquidators, we got nearly 2,000,000 responses. At the top of the list was Liquidation.com. This means that you're not the only one who will stop by this site in your search for product sources. You're bound to hear about this site quickly, once you start using the discussion boards. Liquidation.com, whose home page is shown in Figure 2-8, is the online branch of Liquidity Services, Inc., and it's actually another online auction site. The merchandise offered for sale here ranges from clothing to electronics, and from building materials to cars. Liquidation.com doesn't actually own any of this. The site is for auctions that bring buyers and sellers together to swap products. So, the format is familiar to eBayers. Each auction listing includes details about payment and shipping and what the "buyer's premium" is. This is a percentage, often 5 to 10 percent of the purchase price, that the buyer must pay in order to complete the transaction.

FIGURE 2-8 Liquidation.com is a well-known auction site for sourcing liquidated items from a wide variety of sellers.

Sellers often complain that their Liquidation.com purchases come with very high shipping rates. They also have told us that, since Liquidation.com doesn't own the merchandise, there are some quality control issues associated with the products they've received. Stiff shipping charges and spotty quality are a dangerous one-two combination, and we urge you to use caution in buying products here. "I still use Liquidation.com," said a PowerSeller from South Carolina, "but not as much as I used to. I've found other sites I like better."

Another online source of liquidated products is Speedyliquidators.com, the home page of which is shown in Figure 2-9. This is a Canadian-based firm that specializes in selling off the undersold items from retailers. They accept only new products, never used ones, so you won't find any items here that have been returned or are defective. You also can't easily see what you're buying, because there are no images stored on the company's web site. You do have easy access to customer service and convenient hours for calling to get more information

Buy at the end of the season

about purchasing. It's a good alternative to try, and it's proof that there are plenty of other liquidation sites available to you online.

FIGURE 2-9 Speedy Liquidators is a Canadian-based source of liquidated products that are guaranteed to be new and never used. You will not find any damaged or defective products included in their shipments.

Wholesalers

When you buy wholesale to resell on eBay, you really have to watch your costs carefully. Not only will you pay more for wholesale items than you will for liquidated ones, but you have to add in the same costs whether you buy them wholesale or as liquidations. Those costs include shipping, storage, and sorting through the order to remove damaged goods. Wholesale goods often come in large volumes. Finally, you cannot shop with most wholesalers without a tax ID number, so aren't you glad you've already started that process?

eBay has a wholesale category right on its site, so stop by and check it out. The wholesale category is part of eBay's Business and Industry category. You can easily find it through browsing, or go directly to http://pages.ebay.com/catindex/catwholesale.html?ssPageName=BIhubMBlrglots1. You'll see the screen featured in Figure 2-10. As you can easily see, just about every category of wholesale item is for sale here. It's a good place to start your online wholesale search, but remember, everyone else on eBay has access to this same source. So stay focused on finding other sources, too.

For a directory of wholesalers, try Wholesale411.com, shown in Figure 2-11. Here you'll find lists of wholesalers, but you'll also find a lot more. The site lists wholesale trade shows where you can actually go and meet wholesalers in person. You'll also find very lively forums here where others discuss the wholesale industry. Look for forums with a lot of discussions, and you'll find some interesting views. Remember, some of these posters are there to push their own company's products or services, so don't take everything on face value. Usually, if you stop back often, you find others have posted messages that expose these blatant attempts at self promotion.

FIGURE 2-10 eBay has its own category for wholesale items.

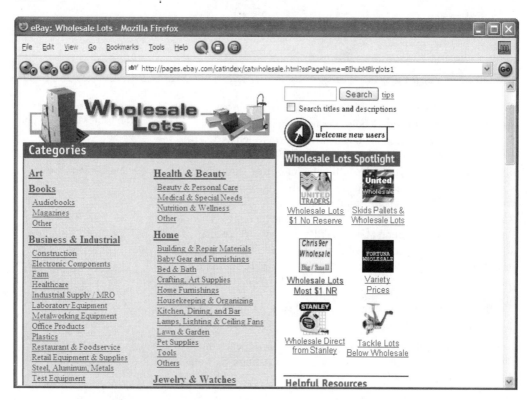

Buy at the end of the season

When you start searching for wholesalers online, use common search terms that wholesalers and their customers would use. Some of these include payment terms such as "Net 30 days" or "Net 60 days." Others to consider are "Purchase order" and "Letter of credit." You'll get a lot of hits from these, so be prepared to be patient. To get you started on your search, we've included a list of some wholesale sites and a description for each one of them. Many of these are sites gathered by The PowerSeller Report, found at www.TPRweb.com. We've also added some of our own. We'd like to thank Scott D. Prock, who produces The PowerSeller Report, for allowing us to share this information.

FIGURE 2-11 Using Wholesale411, you'll find sources of wholesale products and also information about the wholesale industry.

- **www.toydirectory.com/toytable.html**   A listing of toy manufacturers by category

- **www.wholesalehub.com**   Wholesale products from suppliers worldwide; a wide variety of listings, as well as message boards

Buy at the end of the season

- **www.wholesaleez.com**   A merchandise finder, broken down by category

- **www.greatrep.com**   "The premier Internet directory for the wholesale giftware, home furnishing, and furniture industries"

- **www.uk-trade-directory.com**   UK wholesalers, suppliers, importers, services, and product lines

- **www.buylink.com**   Helps retailers source products "that would normally be difficult to locate"

- **www.lightupchristmas.com**   B2B Christmas and holiday items

- **www.americanapparel.org/4col.cfm?pageID=103** Contacts for companies and suppliers in the apparel and footwear areas from the American Apparel and Footwear Association

- **www.diamondring.com/links/pages/Diamond_ Suppliers**   Diamond and jewelry suppliers—includes forums

- **www.globalsources.com**   Volume buyers will find product and trade information here

- **www.ebigchina.com**   Contact information for more than 120,000 companies, with over 180,000 products

- **www.ectradebiz.com/english/home.htm**   European site for B2B "trading"

- **www.wholesalecentral.com**   Claims to be the Internet's largest wholesaler, importer, manufacturer, and liquidator directory and marketplace

- **www.surplus.net**   Large and popular directory of surplus, salvage, and export dealers

- **www.wholesaleindex.com**   Another site linking wholesalers to retailers; this one focuses on the small retailer

- **www.baolink.com**   Bills itself as a "global trade show" bringing together wholesalers and retailers

- **www.suttondist.com**   Directories of *specialized* merchandise. Note: there's a charge for printing out records

Wholesale tricks to try

- ■ **www.nawca.org**   North American Wholesale Co-op Association, the place where wholesale buyers and suppliers meet
- ■ **www.cookbrothers.com**   A Chicago-based wholesaler in business since 1943

» Wholesale tricks to try

When you buy wholesale, you generally have to purchase in bulk. As you approach wholesalers, ask them about buying their fringe items. When a wholesaler fills a large order, there are often dribs and drabs of product left over. These lots are too small to make up another complete bulk order. Ask about buying them. You may be able to scoop up great products in the smaller quantities that are right for you anyway.

Here's one of our favorite tips. "Whenever I get a box of goods from a wholesaler, I peel back the label," revealed a PowerSeller who specializes in gift items. "Sometimes the wholesaler reuses boxes, just like I do, and some of these are from the manufacturers. Even if a manufacturer's label isn't complete, I've gotten enough of the manufacturer's name and address to find them online. Then I can approach them and try to buy from them directly. My family knows that every time this happens, we get to celebrate!" So, be vigilant, and never give up. You just don't know when a little tidbit can become a great new source.

Manufacturers

Manufacturers are a PowerSeller's cause for celebration, because buying from the manufacturer puts you directly at the source of your product. This reduces your acquisition costs and directly affects your profit margin. As you remember, this was your original goal, to get as close to the source of your product as you possibly can. Unfortunately, this is not that easy. Many manufacturers have distribution channels in place that do not include sales to individuals. They are selling in bulk directly to the wholesalers, who then sell to retailers and you. You can't expect to approach the biggest, most well-known manufacturers and have them welcome your individual business. You'll also need that tax ID number to work with manufacturers. You did start that process, right?

You should also expect to meet with some bias among manufacturers when it comes to eBay sellers. Unfortunately, some manufacturers consider it demeaning to see their products up for sale on eBay. It's all part of the eBay-as-garage-sale image. It's no longer true, and it's certainly not fair, but you will find that some manufacturers will refuse to sell to you once they know you're planning to sell on eBay. So, just to begin with, don't make it very obvious that you are an eBay seller. In the next chapter, you'll learn about why you'll want to have your own web site, and here's another reason you can add to that discussion. Once you have your own web site, you can simply say that you operate a web-based business. It's the truth, even if you only have your business on eBay, but with your own web site, you also have a domain name and an Internet address you can use to authenticate your claim. So, play it close to the vest while you're trying to get started with a new manufacturer.

Online Sources of Manufacturers

Searching for manufacturers online is not unlike searching for wholesalers. Some of the search terms you'll find useful for finding manufacturers include "manufacturer rep," "wholesale application," and "independent representatives and distributors." We have located two of the best sites for you to explore as you start your search.

Thomas Register of American Manufacturers

Thomas Register, shown in Figure 2-12, offers you direct access to 173,000 U.S. and Canadian manufacturers. Most of these companies sell industrial products for business-to-business sales, but with more than two million listings, you may just find something you'd like to source. Products include scales, halogen lamps, and even nails. Compare the items here to eBay's "Business & Industrial Category." You'll see that a lot of the same material is available in both places. If this is your line of interest, you've got a great source available right now.

Alibaba.com

Alibaba.com, shown in Figure 2-13, is a web-based marketplace through which you can search 700 product subcategories for sourcing everything from textiles to electronics. It was named by *Forbes* magazine as among the "Best of the Web: B2B" four

Try the Hong Kong Trade Development Council

years in a row. You can search the site by company to locate specific manufacturers, or you can search by country or territory. The site is home to many foreign manufacturers, especially those based in China.

FIGURE 2-12 Thomas Register of American Manufacturers is a good place to visit if you're thinking of selling industrial types of goods.

» Try the Hong Kong Trade Development Council

The Hong Kong Trade Development Council has a very useful web site you can find at www.hktdc.com. It's shown in Figure 2-14. Here you will find online sources of products and resources for contacting manufacturers and companies that operate not only in Hong Kong, but also in Mainland China and Taiwan. The site lists more than a dozen different categories of products available, ranging from jewelry to toys, from books to electronics, and from toiletries to transportation parts. Because the Council is based in Hong Kong, language is no barrier to English-speaking buyers, but services are also available in other languages,

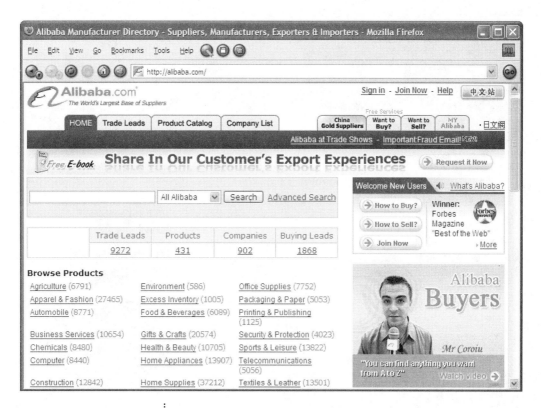

FIGURE 2-13 Alibaba.com is a well-respected online source of products, specializing in international trade.

including German, French, and Portuguese. You can set personalized bookmarks on the site so that you can easily return for more inventory when you need it. The site also has Hot Category listings and news alerts available. You can even set the browser on the site to track your buying history and recommend categories to you each time you sign on. "I use the HKTDC all the time," said one PowerSeller who specializes in apparel. "Not only is the site a great place to source my products, but I've used the Council to arrange escorted trips for me to China to visit and tour factories I'm thinking of working with. They take care of everything, making it possible for me to visit Mainland China and feel both secure and comfortable."

» Go to manufacturer's trade shows

Actually going to manufacturers' trade shows is a great way to make contacts directly with manufacturers. Get your reference librarian to help you find the dates and locations of shows that

Go to manufacturer's trade shows

will work for you. When you go, focus on the small- to medium-sized companies. These are companies that are just building their own reputations and establishing themselves in their marketplaces. You may find they are more eager to work with individuals, and they are not as likely to be able to afford any anti-eBay bias. You may just be able to help each other grow by providing them with a good distribution channel while they're too small to have established channels of their own. Also, you are more likely to meet a high-ranking employee of a smaller company, since owners of smaller firms are more likely doing much of this work for themselves.

While you focus on the small- to medium-sized manufacturers, don't discount the larger companies all together. You may find you're happier with the smaller firms, but if you're interested in something offered only by a larger company, don't be intimidated. Sometimes just making personal contact with someone and letting them see who you are is enough to get you through the gate with a

FIGURE 2-14 The Hong Kong Trade Development Council offers you sources of products and tools for developing your business through trade in Hong Kong, China, and Taiwan.

larger company. They may even be looking for an eBay distributor for their products, and you could provide that service. In doing so, you'll be establishing a new sales channel for them. You handle listing and sales, and they provide inventory, which can reduce your inventory costs.

Just be sure to have professional-looking business cards ready. Include your e-mail address and your web site, if you already have one, but don't mention eBay right away. Make a good impression and see where the conversation goes from there. You don't need to hide your eBay status, but your first meeting may not be the place to advertise it either.

» Tag-team the trade shows

PowerSellers Debnroo have come up with a great way to work trade shows. One of the partners goes to the trade show while the other stays home in the office. Using a cell phone and a portable communications device, in this case a T-Mobile Sidekick, they communicate about the items at the trade show. Partner Number 1 finds an interesting product and sends details about it back to the home office. Partner Number 2 is waiting and ready to search eBay for sell-through information. Together they work to determine not only what looks like an interesting product, but also how much they're likely to be able to get for it, and how well similar items are selling on eBay. By the end of the show, they have a good, clear idea of how well the items they chose are selling, and they have established clear sources for getting those products. No wonder these two have such a successful eBay business going. You'll learn more about them in the profile at the end of this chapter.

Don't Discount the Big Discount Houses

Sourcing your products through wholesalers and manufacturers will allow you to buy items for sale in bulk. That's how you can ensure a steady stream of products once you've focused on the items you want to sell. But once you have your distribution network in place, don't discount the chance to supplement it when an interesting opportunity comes along. Many PowerSellers do this through local shopping. You'll hear chatter about sourcing products through dollar stores on the discussion boards, but we don't recommend that. Generally, the items sold at dollar stores just won't generate high enough prices to warrant your time and energy pursuing them. The large discount houses and buying clubs in your area are a completely different story and often provide great supplemental sources of product. Just because you may have a Sam's Club or a Costco conveniently located near your home doesn't mean that everyone does. The same is true for sellers who live near outlet malls where many bargains can be found for reselling.

If you come across a great buy at stores like these, scoop it up and sell it to eBayers who are more geographically challenged than you are.

Are You a Special Case?

By now you've probably gotten the idea that sourcing your inventory will be a big part of the work that lies ahead of you as you build your eBay business. For most of us, that's entirely true. It will be the single most time-consuming, challenging part of operating your eBay business. You may be surprised to learn that some eBayers don't have this problem at all, and if you're lucky enough to be one of them, you begin with an automatic head start.

Do You Own a Store?

If you already own a store, you have absolutely no reason not to be selling on eBay. You already have your sources in place for finding your products, so selling on eBay just opens new markets for you, gives you a new revenue stream to tap, and allows you to broaden your customer base. Plus, you can use eBay to sell your own end-of-season clearance items or the items customers return. This is bound to be better than sending them to a liquidator or paying the overhead to store them for next year, when they may not sell any better than they did this year.

Does your merchandise lend itself to a trade-in/trade-up program? One North Carolina PowerSeller owns a store that sells youth sports equipment. This gets outgrown long before it wears out. He used eBay to start a trade-in/trade-up program for his customers and their parents. He buys back their used equipment and sells it exclusively on eBay. His manufacturers objected when he started selling their new products on eBay, but they don't have a problem with his selling their used products there. So, he actually earns money the first time he makes a new customer, the next time that person upgrades her child's equipment, and again when he resells the used equipment to another customer on eBay. This is a smart eBayer.

Are You a Wholesaler?

Just as store owners have no reason not to sell on eBay, the same is true for wholesalers and their families. One PowerSeller from Tennessee came to eBay to sell inventory from her father's wholesale shoe business. She claimed she never would have entered into her father's business as it was, but she was so fascinated by selling on eBay that she's gone on to train others in her area about selling on the site. In turn, her father's wholesale company has never been more successful now that a whole new world market has opened for him. If you're lucky enough to own a wholesale operation, or have a relative who does, you won't have any trouble getting all the items you need to become a successful PowerSeller.

Are You a Manufacturer?

Now it may seem obvious, but manufacturers also have opportunities as PowerSellers on eBay. Yeshosery is a manufacturer of socks for men, women, and children based in North Carolina. They started selling on eBay to eliminate their leftover inventory from their big orders. (In other words, their fringe items, as we talked about before!) They moved on to selling things they had left over from their production efforts. For example, they have auctioned huge bags of bows that they used on little girls' socks one season. Now crafters scoop them up as quickly as they get listed. Yeshosery moved on to producing their own items specifically for sale on eBay, and now they also source items from other manufacturers. Representatives of the company told us they had no idea when they started that their little effort to clean up the warehouse would explode for them into a whole new branch of their business.

Are You an Artist or a Craftsman?

If your life's work is producing beautiful things, you have a year-round business opportunity on eBay, and you'll never have to worry about finding sources for your products. You already search for markets to feature your items, so you have no reason not to turn to eBay as a new market just waiting to be tapped. eBay makes it possible for artists to be more independent than ever before, as they no longer have to depend on the middleman to help them market their creations.

It's All a Balancing Act

Okay, now that you've gotten all of this advice about finding great sources of items to sell on eBay, be careful. Your efforts are not over, because you're entering a very fluid business. Just when you think everything is in place, you have to be prepared to keep going and continue your searching. Remember those "Hot Items by Category" that we studied all those pages ago? Well, once your items start selling well, you'll end up helping to put them right into that same list that others are studying to learn what's selling well on eBay. Once other people see how well your items are doing, they'll start selling them too. Once that happens, the simple law of supply and demand will devalue your items.

Don't allow yourself to build your inventory to the point that you get stuck with a huge volume of devalued items when the market floods. While your product is doing well, keep researching and searching for the next great trends and products you'll pursue. That way, when the market drops for the items you already sell—and it most likely will—you'll be ready to move on to other more profitable products. Remember the sad tale of the Beanie Babies!

Debnroo—Andy and Deb Mowery

Debnroo, Inc., is a privately owned retail seller of home, garden, and pet products. With over $500,000 in sales for 2003, 200 percent annual growth, and over 6,000 positive feedbacks per year, we start to sound like the product of a good plan. Actually, it's more a mix of evolution, revolution, and survival. Ask eBayers about their past, present, and future and the answers will undoubtedly change year after year. You have to adapt. The products we were able to acquire defined our business better than our balance sheet. Our story is typical, yet unique.

Debbie and I met in 1987 as college students. After graduation, we took corporate jobs in Chicago. I left Chicago in early 1997 to ski and think in Telluride, Colorado. After three months, I was in love with both Colorado and freedom. Deb joined me in September after a surprise marriage proposal at the Bluegrass Festival, inspired by all its surrounding beauty.

By 1998, returning to a corporate lifestyle was impossible. A hemp macramé jewelry hobby became our first business. We sold at music festivals, which allowed us to meld our innate retail and marketing skills with a love of live music. We only made enough to survive, but enjoyed the travels and adventure.

In 1999, my dad Jim offered us an opportunity. He wanted to sell antiques on eBay from his store, but he was computer illiterate, and he wanted lessons. We started selling postcards, because Jim had a ton of inventory, and thousands sold on eBay every week. We planned to master the process and then sell higher-value items.

After three months, we realized: 1) eBay could fill the seasonal droughts of our jewelry business; 2) it was going to take *much* longer to teach Jim. In hindsight, we were simply hooked. We named our business "weauction4you.com," and planned to eventually open a retail store offering consignment services.

Our eBay and jewelry businesses ran parallel during 2000. We offered consignments locally, but postcards and other paper items were the mainstay. Our small condominium constrained inventory, but we could store 50,000 paper items on shelves. By mid-2000, eBay became our main focus. Selling paper collectibles was easy, and consignment was difficult. Product acquisition via consignment in a town so small it had no stoplights was not impossible, just difficult. And, shipping was an adventure.

We moved to Ft. Collins, Colorado, for its urban conveniences and access to the mountains we loved. Postcards offered good margins, stable sell-through rates, and nice customers who paid on time. However, every ad required a unique image and description. Through automation and software that automated e-mails, we developed processes to reduce the time consumed. To get ahead, we had to adapt.

We entered consumer products through a bad eBay buying experience—purchasing a digital scale. The seller shipped two weeks after payment. So, we found his manufacturer, opened an account, and became competitors. Within a few weeks, we matched that seller's volume. We compensated for low profit margins by eliminating the time it took to create unique ads. The time saved let us process more orders and give better customer service.

In late 2001, Deb found a pet fountain in a magazine and wanted it for our cat, Wilson. We found the manufacturer on the Internet and placed a six-unit minimum order. We sold the extra units the day after they arrived. Within two weeks, we were ordering 15 to 30 units per week. We became the top seller on eBay within two months.

During 2002, our path to product acquisition was a combination of Debbie's shopping skills, our combined analytical skills, and my negotiation skills. We would find products we wanted, see if they sold on eBay, and then test market one case at a time. In the worst case, we would buy something for ourselves wholesale. We soon had relationships with several suppliers of pet supply and home & garden products.

We also got our first taste of anti-eBay bias. Our business name (weauction4you) gave us away, and we often found it difficult to get our foot in the door with suppliers. We learned to avoid mentioning eBay until after the relationship was established.

We even had a supplier who faked running out of stock every six to eight weeks, hoping to discourage us. We caught him in numerous "inconsistencies," which only infuriated him. Eventually, he tried to put us out of business by not shipping two orders, weeks before Christmas. At 50 percent of our revenue, his products were crucial, yet he ended the relationship after I complained to his superiors. We got a letter canceling the relationship on Christmas Eve, after doing $75,000 worth of business that year!

A week later, we found local investors who started a new account with this supplier for a small percentage of our earnings. They purchased in greater volumes, which paid for their commission, and still gave us lower pricing. The crisis had created new opportunities.

By mid-2003, we gave up postcards for consumer products. Deb still shopped, but we also began attending trade shows. We identified ourselves as "Debnroo" to avoid the "weauction4you" bias, and found it easier to establish relationships.

By late 2003, our garage was packed to the rafters. We had to put up our festival tent to provide a dry packing area. We finally had to find more storage. We'd used a local shipping company for pack-and-ship services for our larger consignment items, and they had an under-utilized warehouse. UPS sent some technical people to help us create a system for remote shipping. Suddenly, we had a subcontracted pack-and-ship relationship.

By the end of 2003, we were selling over 250 products from 15 manufacturers, and processing 200 to 400 transactions per week. Simultaneously we were shipping from in-house, subcontracted, and drop-ship locations. Successful at product acquisition, we found that the new bottleneck was manually processing transactions. We worked 18 to 20 hours per day during the 2003 holiday season, with no employees.

Looking ahead, we are seeking new technologies and software to continue our revenue growth, automate as many functions as possible, and give us the security we need to hire employees. We look forward to when our garage is no longer a warehouse with a tent for an entrance, and we manage multiple shipping operations remotely. We plan to graduate from Platinum to Titanium PowerSellers, selling on International eBay sites in the local language, and creating wholesale eBay businesses. Our goal is to do it all from the swing in our backyard, enjoying every day with our cats Wilson and Sunshine.

Chapter 3

From Mom and Pop
to PowerShop

Automate from the very beginning

Before we get started building your PowerShop, let's take a quick survey. How many of you already have a computer with Internet access? How many of you are already registered eBay users? If we've done our market research correctly, everyone holding this book in their hands will answer "yes" to both these questions. Good. You have the foundation we'll need to build your new PowerShop. You've probably been doing just swell with your Mom-and-Pop setup, but now that you've set your sights on a genuine business, you're going to need to beef up your systems. No longer will you be able to get by with the basic tools that have let you buy and even sell a little on eBay. If you want to move up to PowerSeller, you simply must plan your PowerShop.

Fortunately, we've gathered a lot of help for you from PowerSellers. They've told us all about their computer hardware and software. We've learned how they manage their auctions, inventories, and communications. They've told us the best things they've learned about dealing with their photos and shipping their products. They've given us the benefit of their years of trial and error, so that you can build your PowerShop while avoiding some of the pitfalls they've experienced.

As you read through this chapter, don't allow yourself to be overcome with a sense that you are going to spend all of your time and money building your business before you can even earn a dime. You will find that we describe many different products, and most of them cost money. We're not suggesting that you purchase everything you learn about in this chapter. We're offering you a buffet of items from which to choose. Some of them are really not negotiable, such as a high-speed Internet connection. Others are going to be more useful to you once you've gained a bit more experience. Some you'll need right away, and others you can plan to add in the future. They are all tools that will make your eBay business more efficient and professional, but you don't need to purchase them all right away. Remember, PowerSellers are a creative lot. You'll find ways to tap into your own creativity as you build your PowerSeller's operation.

» Automate from the very beginning

You may be thinking that you just don't see yourself as needing too much automation right now. You may think you're doing just fine managing the sales you've had so far, and you'd rather spend your time making more money instead of building systems that seem too complicated for you. Don't allow yourself to be victimized by this shortsighted thinking. "Automate from the very beginning," advises a PowerSeller from Kentucky. "It's so much easier to build onto a system you have than it is to have to go back and retrofit your system to meet your needs when you're also busy." So, start your research, make your choices, and build your automation into your business. You'll be so glad you did once the sales start pouring in!

Your Computer

So, as a budding PowerSeller what sort of computer and peripherals do you need? This may come as a surprise, but unless your computer is something of a dinosaur, you probably already have in place just what you'll need to get started. PowerSellers told us that they started their businesses with the computers they already had in place, adding more computer power only when they needed it. Most people probably have all the horsepower they need in their current computer. It's the peripherals—especially a high-speed Internet connection and a digital camera—that you may have to buy.

Take into account what eBay sellers use their computers for. You'll be spending a lot of time doing the normal office tasks such as creating letters and documents, e-mailing, and running accounting software. Even when you add auction management software to the mix, you're not doing things that are especially system intensive. Most newer computers are more than up to the task.

We do have some recommendations though. (You knew we would, didn't you?) To make life easier, it's best to have a computer with USB ports right in the front, as shown in Figure 3-1. This makes connecting peripherals, such as a digital camera, as easy as possible. A large hard drive is important (this is no place to scrimp) for storing those big photo files, especially until you start using auction management software and image hosting services. Making sure you have a lot of memory (512MB is now the standard) is also smart. You'll especially appreciate that when you're multitasking, which as a PowerSeller you'll be doing a lot as you check on your auctions, evaluate your sales numbers, and respond to e-mail. If you have an IBM-compatible computer, it's also a good idea to be running an operating system at the Windows 98 SE level or better. This software will have built-in networking capabilities, which you'll need when connecting your computer to a home network.

Aside from these things, any newer computer has the processor speed you will need. If your computer is more than a couple of years old, you can always add memory if you need it, and even an external drive, etc., but new computers costing what they do, it may just make more sense to buy a new one. They're so inexpensive now that it almost doesn't pay to upgrade much anymore.

One thing you'll want to be sure your new computer has is a wireless network card. This will allow you to connect your computer, and the other computers in the house, to a router. That will enable you to share your high-speed Internet connection. You may think this technology is not necessary for you now, and you may be right. Wireless networks, while not difficult to create, are necessary only when you're trying to share resources among computers. But as your business grows and you add more computers, and maybe even employees, you'll want to keep your options for networking open. Purchasing your next computer with a wireless network card will ensure that.

Focusing on high-speed connections, unless you live in an area that doesn't offer cable or DSL service, there's no question about it; you must have one. You are spending too much of your time on the Internet to use dial-up. Uploading your pictures alone is reason enough to go with the high-speed connection. Once you do spring for it, you'll immediately see why we say that. It boils down to the simple question: what's your time worth? Does it make sense to sit and wait for web pages to load, or should you go from page to page as quickly as you can? Do you want to wait 5 seconds for a page to load or 50? (Actually, some cable companies claim their connections are a full 50 times faster than dial-up, although you will rarely achieve this kind of speed. Other factors such as the web site you're connecting to and how many others are using the service impact your speed.) Still, 10 times faster or 50, there's really nothing to decide here. If you're serious about your eBay business, you must have a high-speed Internet connection.

FIGURE 3-1 This computer is a Dell Dimension 2400, which includes USB ports at the bottom of the front panel of the computer. Courtesy of Dell, Inc.

» Buy the best technology you can afford

If you do upgrade your computer setup, buy the best technology you can afford. Not only will this give you extra speed and power, but it will help you put off the time when your new computer is obsolete. "We keep our eyes open for good deals, and add computers in clumps as we find a good buy," says a PowerSeller specializing in apparel. That's excellent advice. If you keep your eyes open, you'll find you can get the equipment you need on a non-emergency basis and actually acquire better equipment at a lesser cost. Start your search right on eBay.

» Build a network if you use more than one computer

As your eBay business grows, you are likely to add more computer power. When you do, network your computers. Not only will this allow you to share the high-speed connection, but it will also allow you to have ready access to all of your records and software, too. You don't want to have to keep switching back and forth between machines so that you can process different parts of your transactions. A network will keep your business operating smoothly. As an added bonus, when you add employees, you'll have your systems in place to allow them to be most efficient.

Stay Healthy to Get Wealthy

As a prospective eBay PowerSeller, know that your livelihood depends on your computer. You need for it not only to be operating, but also operating as close to its peak as possible. And you certainly don't want to let unsavory characters get the personal information about you that resides within it.

Of course, you want to protect your computer from viruses. You are probably already using a virus protection program; now you'll need to make sure it's operating automatically. It's no secret that an investment in a program such as Norton Antivirus, which you'll find at www.symantec.com/nav/nav_9xnt/, is better than money in the bank, especially these days. Buy it or a similar product, update it regularly, and keep those viruses at bay.

It used to be that all you had to worry about were viruses getting to your computer. But now there are other threats to your computer's health (and your own, if working to relieve your computer's sluggish performance gives you headaches). These new problems come from the Internet, specifically the broadband connections to the Internet that include cable or

Build a network if you use more than one computer

DSL. You need to have these high-speed services, but you also need to treat them with respect. The first thing to remember about them is that they're always on. As long as you're computer is turned on, you are connected to the Internet, whether or not you happen to be using it at the time. Not only does this give you the immediate access you desire, however, but it also lets other Internet users into your computer. What's worse, you may never even know they're there.

The first problem this creates involves potential hackers or other unauthorized people accessing your computer to nose around and wreak havoc or worse. The best way to protect yourself from these intruders is with a firewall, usually a software program that stands sentry between your computer and outside computers and creates a "wall" of protection. The firewall software filters the information that comes into your computer and goes out of it.

If you are using Windows XP, enabling its built-in firewall is as easy as can be. See the documentation that came with your computer or access the help files that are most likely available under your Start menu. If you use another operating system, you may want to buy a separate firewall program. There are shareware firewall programs, but we've never had much luck with them. The ones we have tried seem to keep *everything* from getting through, making accessing some web sites and web pages difficult. Two highly recommended commercial products are Norton Personal Firewall and McAfee Personal Firewall.

The second threat that comes from having a constant connection to the Internet is that web surfing leaves behind "spies" in your computer's operating system. These either track your web surfing (where you surf and for how long), or serve up annoying banner ads. These intruders can even hijack your browser and deliver sites that you had no intention of visiting. Even worse, while they're there, they can gather personal information about you from the keystrokes you enter when filling out online forms. Plus, they do this without your knowledge and permission. They just do. This can easily lead to that nightmare, Identity Theft. Finally, they are the cause of many computer crashes.

These programs are almost impossible to find and get rid of on your own. The only solution (and it's an easy one) is to install special programs that can sweep your computer's innards to find this stuff and get rid of it. Here aboveboard shareware comes to the rescue in the form of Ad-aware, which you'll find

Build a network if you use more than one computer

at www.lavasoftusa.com/software/adaware/, and Spy Sweeper, at www.spysweeper.com/. Download, install, and follow the simple instructions to run these programs. They'll unearth enough nasties to choke a horse or a computer. Ad-aware takes only a few minutes to run, whereas Spy Sweeper takes a bit longer and apparently does a more thorough job. The first time you run these programs, you may be amazed at what they turn up. Run them periodically to keep things humming.

Managing Your Business

Despite the fact that you probably have an adequate computer to start building your PowerSeller business, the same is likely not to be true of the systems you have in place for managing your auctions and operating your business. When you sell as a hobby, you can get by with the basics. You are surely using My eBay, and this will provide all the necessary management tools a casual seller might need. That changes quickly once you increase the volume of your listings and sales. The consensus is that once you've moved beyond 15–20 listings per week, you're ready to automate. You'll need much more power for storing your digital images, processing your orders, keeping your records, and running your operation.

Fortunately, there are a variety of tools and services available to you to support your business. We'll look at auction management software in Chapter 4. For now, we'll provide you with a shopping list of other tools you'll need. We'll introduce you to image hosting for your photos and tools for hosting your web site. We'll take a quick look at accounting software that will help you with your record keeping. (You'll get a more detailed tour of these products in Chapter 10.) Then we'll introduce you to tools that will help you analyze your sales and determine your best routes to higher profits. We'll help you determine which products you want to use now and which you might keep in mind for adding in the future. Let's get started with those images.

Image Hosting

Image hosting services provide one of the best ways to distinguish your auctions from those created by sellers without your PowerSeller aspirations. You can always tell the difference between an auction listing that has incorporated image hosting,

Build a network if you use more than one computer

and one that has not. The pictures are clearer and bigger, much bigger, so every detail is clear to your prospective buyers.

Using image hosting is simple. You just upload your pictures to the host's web server (there will be onscreen directions) where they are stored. When you're ready to incorporate your hosted picture within your listing, you simply enter the URL address for the picture(s), instead of the filename. You'll do this from the Sell Your Item form just where you previously entered your photos stored on your own computer. EBay will then snatch it off the web, as shown in Figure 3-2.

There are dedicated image hosting services that handle only this sort of thing. Some are even free to the user, because they are supported by advertisers. Figure 3-3 shows the home page of one such service, OneImageHost. You'll find them at www.oneimagehost.com. Keep in mind, this service is free, but you cannot keep your images here for very long. If you don't access them within 30 days, they'll simply disappear. You will

FIGURE 3-2 Input the URL address for your hosted pictures into this form, and eBay will automatically add your photo to your listing.

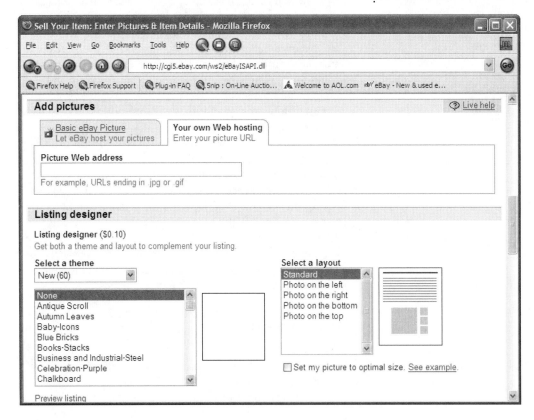

FIGURE 3-3 The home page of the image hosting service OneImageHost

also find that there is no customer service on this site. You are free to use it, but if you have questions about how to do that, you're on your own.

Auction management programs include image hosting among their features. Uploading your image is just as easy with auction management software as it is with the dedicated services. Plus you get the use of all the other features the software offers. In fact, one of the best reasons for using an auction management program is the image hosting. Once you upload your digital pictures to the company's computers, you can also use the auction management program to create your listing. Just browse your computer for the digital image, and the software will take it from there, assigning a URL and placing it within your auction. If you prefer to use your stored image with eBay's selling form, you can still do that. Just click the tab for Your Own Web Hosting on the Sell Your Item form's Enter

Use accounting software

Pictures & Details page. From there you can enter the "Picture Web address" (URL) in the box appearing on the next page.

Why would you prefer to use image hosting rather than to store your images on your own computer? There are several reasons:

- Even if you use eBay's "Supersize" feature, a hosted picture will still be much larger. Often this results in more bids, because buyers appreciate being able to more closely inspect your item.

- It's also cheaper this way, since you'll pay $0.75 extra for supersizing your images through eBay, but only a fraction of that in storage fees through your image hosting choice.

- You will free up valuable disk space on your own computer, leaving it for other tasks that can't be so easily put off to another storage area.

- Your pictures will load more quickly from an image host and save you valuable time when you're creating listings.

» Use accounting software

As you build your PowerShop, you'll need to give yourself the necessary tools for managing your records and keeping your books. Chapter 10 will give you all the information and advice you'll need to get started, but while you're gathering your tools, add accounting software to your shopping list. PowerSellers use accounting software in conjunction with their auction management software. The latter keeps track of their daily and weekly business transactions, and the former produces monthly, quarterly, and annual records that their accountants use to figure their taxes, profits, and losses.

QuickBooks

Many of the PowerSellers we spoke with use QuickBooks to manage their accounts. Intuit, Inc., the producer of QuickBooks, is accurate in describing their software as a full-featured accounting program that will easily meet the needs of your small business. We found, however, that not everyone agrees with Intuit that the program is "easy to use."

With QuickBooks, you can manage all of your basic accounting tasks, including printing checks, paying bills, and creating reports. You can produce reports that include standard profit and loss, balance sheet, cash flow, and sales reports. You can use the software to keep tax records, including records of income, payroll, and sales tax. QuickBooks also has a tax alerts feature to keep you informed about upcoming deadlines for quarterly, estimated, and monthly tax payments.

Seller after seller reported frustration in getting started with QuickBooks. Once you're up and running with the software, you won't have any trouble with it, but getting to that point can be a challenge. "QuickBooks setup can be tricky for a novice, but it's smooth sailing once that is done," says a seller based in Southern California. "You have to have a basic knowledge of double entry debit/credit systems to set up your files and to understand how to enter certain entries."

QuickBooks Basic 2004 costs $199.95. We recommend that when you buy the software you also buy *QuickBooks 2005: The Official Guide* by Kathy Ivens (McGraw-Hill/Osborne, 2004). It is the only official guide to the software, and it will be very helpful to you as you get started. Also, see Chapter 10 for more information about educating yourself in using the program.

Excel

Excel, from Microsoft Corporation, is a spreadsheet software program that many PowerSellers use to keep track of their expenses and earnings. A spreadsheet is a valuable tool because it allows you to input your data and then manipulate it to create and explore "what if" problems. Because changing the data in any one cell automatically changes all the relevant data in every other cell, you can quickly explore the ramifications of raising your starting price, changing your listing fees by adding listing upgrades, or lowering your product acquisition costs. Using Excel, you can create charts, tables, and graphs to visually represent your data for clearer analysis. Excel comes bundled with Microsoft's Office software suite, but you can also buy it separately for $229.00 (but discounted through many online retailers).

Analyzing Your Auction Data

Once you start gathering completed auctions, you also gather a wealth of data that you can use to judge the success of your selling and the areas of your operation that you can enhance for greater profits. You have tools available to you for analyzing the data you'll soon be collecting, and you should absolutely choose some of these tools as part of your PowerShop tool chest. Chapter

Use accounting software

6 will tell you more about using these tools to your best advantage, but we'll give you some advice right now about which tools you'll want to add while you're building your PowerShop.

Counters

You are, no doubt, already familiar with the most common and simplest auction analysis tool of all, auction counters. These little tracking devices are used in 89 to 90 percent of all eBay listings, according to former CEO and founder of Honesty.com, Scott Samuel (who created the first counters for online auctions). To understand how useful they can be and why it's important for you to add them to your listings, let's take a look at why Scott created them in the first place.

Like you, Scott sells on eBay, and he has for years. When he first got started, eBay was much different from what it is today. Then, there were only a fraction of the items listed for sale that there are now. I keep reading this last sentence, but it seems awkward to me. Just my reaction. eBay wasn't particularly well known then. Scott created counters because he wanted to be sure eBay was for real and that people were truly buying and selling things on the site. With a counter, you can track how many people have looked at your auction, and so you can tell how many people are viewing your items. If you're not getting many hits, you'll need to try to figure out why. Have you put your item in the wrong category? Does your title lack strong keywords?

Twenty percent of all people who use counters use hidden counters to keep buyers from knowing the level of attention their items are receiving. That keeps buyers at a slight disadvantage, because they can't easily judge how much competition they're facing. Also, from the seller's point of view, counters that show a lot of hits may discourage new customers from bidding. They may think the high numbers mean the item will sell for more than they want to spend, so they'll move on to someone else's listing. You can easily add free counters to your listings. To add a counter, just click the circle next to the counter you prefer at the bottom of the Enter Pictures & Item Details page, shown in Figure 3-4. Counters will provide you with only the most basic information. All of them will tell you how many people have viewed your auction listing, but other auction analysis products will give you much more information than that.

FIGURE 3-4 This section
of the Enter Pictures &
Item Details page on eBay
makes it simple to add
a counter to your listing.

» Use auction analysis tools

Auction analysis tools go farther along the path of tracking the data your bidders bring your way and analyzing it to your best advantage. These programs can give you a wealth of information about your bidders' shopping habits, their reactions to your product offerings, and the success of your operations. We'll review two of the most famous programs in this chapter. We've also saved one other review to be discussed in Chapter 6, where we share more details with you about using these tools to enhance your online auction business.

Andale

Scott Samuel says that Andale's research suite is their strongest offering. It's their core. Of that suite of tools, the best is Price Finder. Price Finder allows you to track the history of every transaction on eBay. It can give you a realistic idea of what

Use auction analysis tools

something is worth, much more so than any printed guide because the information is updated in real time.

Andale Price Finder uses data from completed eBay listings to provide you with price data for any eBay item. It's included with Andale Research Pro, a software application geared toward high-volume sellers. Here's what Research Pro can provide: average sale price, conversion rate, and the number of listings for multiple products at one time. You can use keywords, ISBNs, or UPC information to research thousands of your inventory items. A sample results page is shown in Figure 3-5.

One component of the software, "Andale Recommends," provides data on

- **Category** Find which category will yield the best price for your item.

- **Pricing** Learn the price at which you should start your auction.

FIGURE 3-5 Price Finder results from Andale's Research Pro tool help you to know how to price your item in order to stay competitive.

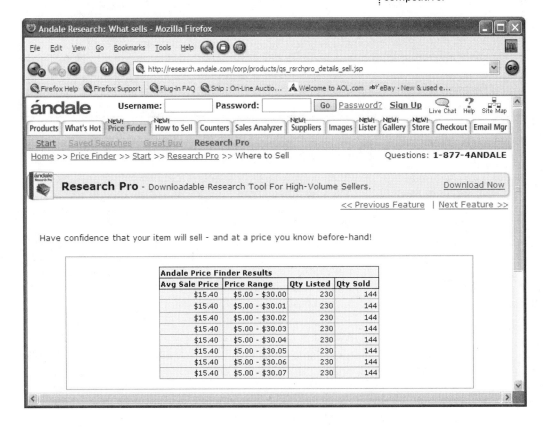

- **When to list**   Determine the best time of day and day of the week for getting the best price.

- **What features**   Learn which eBay listing upgrades, such as bold and highlight, work the best.

- **Recommend what to sell**   Learn what's selling on eBay.

- **Andale recommendations widget**   Plug in items to research using ISBN, UPC, or other data and get selling suggestions.

Andale Research Pro is not part of any other Andale package, so it must be purchased separately. It costs $49.95 per month for unlimited use, so it really is designed for high-volume users. It's a good thing to keep in mind for when your profits allow you to afford its many tools.

HammerTap

HammerTap is a division of Bright Builders, and you'll find them on the web at www.hammertap.com. The company offers a suite of auction analysis software as well as some other products to support online sales, including e-mail programs, bidder-blockers, and sniping software for buyers. We'll describe three of their software offerings here: DeepAnalysis, BayCheck Pro, and FeeFinder.

DeepAnalysis is the company's overall auction analysis product. With it, you can study any eBay market sector and produce detailed market research reports. You can choose to analyze eBay categories, sellers, search terms, and items.

In searching categories, DeepAnalysis will provide you with details about the total sales within the category, the sell-through rates of the auctions within the category, and Reserve auction statistics. When researching a specific seller, you'll be able to see

- The seller's sell-through rate

- The total sales the seller has

- The average bids per item

- The most successful sellers

You can use this data to see where you fit into the crowd. If you find you are consistently being outdone by other sellers within your own category, you have a real opportunity for

Use auction analysis tools

studying their auctions and learning what may be distinguishing them from your own.

You can also search by specific items. This can be invaluable information to have as you build your inventory and decide on your product line. You'll get information about items that includes

- The most popular items
- The total sales of an item
- The highest price the item received
- The average number of bids for the item
- The Reserve auction sell-through rate for the item

You can try DeepAnalysis for free, but then registration costs $179.00. You may want to wait a couple of months until you have enough data and experience to make your free trial period a good test of the value this software would bring to your business.

HammerTap's other offerings are less general than DeepAnalysis, and you'd use them for very specific types of analysis. BayCheck Pro gives you analysis information about individual eBay trading partners. Using it, you can research an eBayer's seller history to see what he's sold on the site, his bidder history to see what he buys, and both the feedback he leaves and the feedback he receives. You can also use it to send e-mail to any eBay user with just a single click. BayCheck Pro minimizes to a small toolbar that stands ready for you to input the username of any eBay user you may be curious about. Just copy that name into the ever-present toolbar and click for a history of that user's eBay activities. BayCheck Pro also offers you a free trial period, after which it will cost you $19.95 to register the software. A free version, BayCheck, is available that also allows you to check on details of other eBay users, but it tracks records for only the past 30 days, and it doesn't offer any e-mail links.

Finally, HammerTap offers you a FeeFinder tool. This tool provides you with exact calculations for all of your eBay and PayPal fees. It will automatically keep track of all the extra listing fees you may incur for special listing options. It is also linked to all the major shipping companies so that you can easily calculate and track your shipping costs. You can also try the FeeFinder for free, after which it will cost you $12.95 to register the product.

Your Web Site

These days it seems almost everyone has a web site. As someone who is building a web-based business, there's no question about it—you need a web site. Chapter 6 will give you more details about why this is so important in distinguishing your eBay business from so many others. Once you have a web site, you'll come up in the results of search engines such as Google and Yahoo. Just take the extra step and submit your URL online to the search engine company. (The Google online submission form is shown in Figure 3-6.) If, for instance, you're selling hula hoops and someone does a search for them, one of the search results he gets will be your web site, where he can view your products and go directly to your eBay listings. Eventually you'll use your web site for e-commerce operations that will allow your customers to buy directly from the site, but that's a long way in the future, so you mustn't concern yourself

FIGURE 3-6 Google's online submission form makes it easy to register your URL to turn up in more search results.

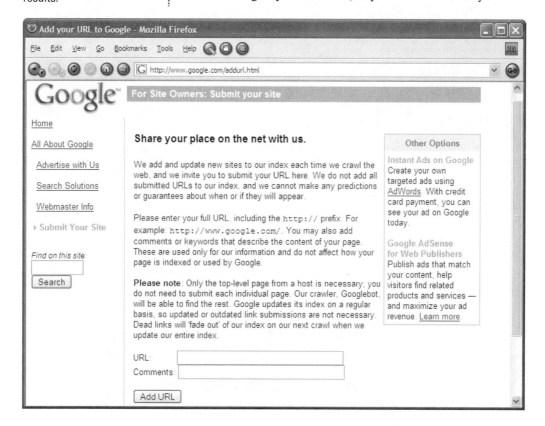

Pick your web address

with the details of that now. The
first thing you'll need is your own web address so that your
customers can find you!

Now, whole books have been written on the subject of
creating and maintaining your own web site. As you might
guess, we're not going to be able to provide you with all of the
information you'll need to accomplish this task. But, we can
give you some advice to get you started, and we're confident
you can take it from there.

›› Pick your web address

You'll need an Internet "address" for your web site so that
people can easily remember it and find it through Google and
other Internet search engines. It's no big deal to create your own
WWW address, or *domain* name. To illustrate, we'll discuss

FIGURE 3-7 Getting your
own domain name can
begin with a stop at Network
Solutions' home page.

how Network Solutions, a popular registrar of domain names, makes it an easy step-by-step process.

To start, you'll complete the following steps from their home page at www.networksolutions.com, shown in Figure 3-7:

1. Type in the domain name you would like.

2. Specify the extension you would like (probably .com for a commercial site).

3. Then search the database of domains to see if the one you want is available. If it isn't, try a name that's less likely to be taken, such as one that combines your last name and what you sell, or something a little offbeat. To keep with our example of hula hoops, you might want to consider something like www.loopyhoops.com, which was still available when we checked!

Next, Network Solutions asks if you want extra services such as adding e-mail addresses. Something sellers should consider is their Constant Contact feature, which lets you capture and review information about visitors to your site. You can try this feature for 60 days, at no charge.

The cost for just registering a domain through Network Solutions is $34.95 for one year. As you might imagine, the pricing is à la carte. Adding e-mail accounts sets you back $20.00 per year per e-mail address. You can also use their templates to create your own WWW site at $15.00 per page per year. You can see how quickly all this can add up.

This isn't an ad for Network Solutions! You can register a domain name and get other services similar to Network Solutions' through many other companies these days. For more information, including a list of companies, visit the InterNIC site at www.internic.net/index.html.

Once you've snatched your own address, you'll need to sign up with a web hosting company. These provide space on their computers for your web site. Typically, these companies offer 50MB to 100MB of storage and e-mail forwarding. Figure on spending about $8 to $12 a month "rent." This gives you space for your site and an interface for updating it.

When choosing a source for web hosting, pop **Web Hosting** into Google, and you'll be assaulted with a bewildering list of links, some of which are sponsored. Try another approach for finding the company that's right for you. CNET Network is an online media company that provides product reviews, features, news, interviews, and data services to the technology industry. Their goal is to empower technology users and allow them to make informed decisions. You'll find many reviews and recommendations about web hosting services through their web site at http://reviews.cnet.com/Hosting/2001-6540_7-0.html?tag=is.

» When looking for web design, think young

Hiring a professional web designer can be expensive. These professionals create awesome sites that offer all types of functions and options for the businesses who hire them. Those features are not cheap, and neither is the labor or expertise necessary to produce them. For your purpose, you need a clean, functional, attractive web site, but you don't need that site to be too fancy. For the more basic, yet attractive site you want, you can find a competent web designer much closer to home. Start with your local community college. Hundreds of students study web design at these schools. The instructors are sure to be able to recommend one of their students who would be glad to earn some extra money. If you don't have a community college nearby, consider the local high school. Many of these students, who have grown up using computers, are more than capable of helping you build the web site you're planning.

» Keep your search local

Another good way to find a web designer is to search for the web sites of local businesses, charities, and government offices. Look at the different sites and decide which ones you find most attractive and appealing. Then, search the site for the name of the web designer. It's usually there. Now, you can meet with this person and discuss your web design needs. If you decide to hire this professional, keeping your web designer local makes it easier for you to work together and customize your web site.

Photography

As you will see in Chapter 5, great photos are a vital part of your eBay listings. PowerSellers agree that the better your photos, the more likely you'll get bids, and the higher your final prices will go. That doesn't mean you need to become a professional photographer. It just means you need to plan for the supplies and equipment you'll need for taking good, clear, sharply detailed photos. Fortunately, that's never been easier or less expensive than it is today.

» Set up your studio

The size and type of area you'll need to set aside for photography depends on what you're selling and how large your items are. If you are planning to sell items that you can easily lift, you'll want to start with a solid platform, bench, or table for placing your items. It saves a lot of stress on your back if you can operate from waist level, and it makes it easier for you to focus directly on the item, too. Framing your shot is very important for featuring its details, and you want to be comfortable while you work. It's wise for you to push this flat surface against a wall or into a corner, if possible. That helps ground the surface and helps you with your photo backgrounds.

You'll want to use background drapes to highlight your items. You'll need two, one light and one dark. That way, you can create contrast to your items no matter what their colors are. That doesn't mean you must use stark white or deep black. Consider a soft pastel that will barely show, such as light blue or pale pink. Just make sure the color doesn't detract from the details of the item you are photographing. Using a piece of black velvet for your dark drape adds some texture and depth to the background of your photos, and that can be very pleasing to the eye. Just be sure you don't use a strong pattern in your drape. You want it to be a subtle stage for your item, and you don't want anything that will draw the viewer's attention away from the object you're selling. You don't have to spend a lot of money for your drapes, either. You may have some sheets or an old blanket that fits the bill just right. If you do decide to shop, go to your local fabric store and look through the bin of remnants. These bits of leftover fabric often sell for just a few dollars, and there's generally a large variety of pieces from which you can choose. Test a few to make sure they don't over-reflect your lighting and create bright spots in your pictures.

You may need some other accessories for your photos beyond just the drapes. If you're selling clothing, shop around for a mannequin. Clothing never looks as good on a hanger as it does on a body. If you can't use a human model, choose an artificial one. You can even purchase adjustable mannequins that allow you to adapt them to different sizes of clothing. If you can't find an adjustable one, just be sure to carefully and discreetly pin the item so that it doesn't look like a sack draped over the mannequin you have. Consider how you can best show the lines and features of the clothing, and adapt from there.

If you're selling jewelry, consider a stand to feature your necklaces or a model hand to show your rings. Think about your favorite stores and the things they use to display their products, and then try to re-create them in your own photography studio. Also, start to collect different-sized boxes and even cans to lift your drapery and support your items. You can do a lot to emphasize your products' details by featuring them as the center of a landscaped design of fabric and supports.

One last piece of equipment you'll want to consider is a tripod. It's very important that your pictures are sharp and clear. That clarity can be hard to achieve when you're holding the camera in your hand. You'll need to be very steady in your grip to ensure that you don't end up with fuzzy and muddled shots. If you've got a very steady hand, you may be able to get away without a tripod, but for most of us, it's a good piece of equipment to add. It allows you to frame the shot, set everything up, and snap your pictures quickly without having to reset the camera position from the start each time.

» Light up your listings

You'll learn a lot more about lighting your items for photographing them in Chapter 5, when we get down to the details of creating your auction listings. For now, while you're building your PowerShop, keep in mind you may need to buy some photography lights to show your items to their best advantage. Photographers' lighting includes spotlights on stands that allow the lights to be raised and lowered, and umbrellas that rest above the lights for diffusing the beam of light and making it softer. You can buy these items piece by piece, or you can purchase them in kits that usually include two spotlights and umbrellas. Prices for these kits range from about $150 to $300. Figure 3-8 shows you a sample kit we found listed for sale by a PowerSeller right on eBay.

You can also find less expensive and more ingenious ways to light your items for photographing them. Many of the

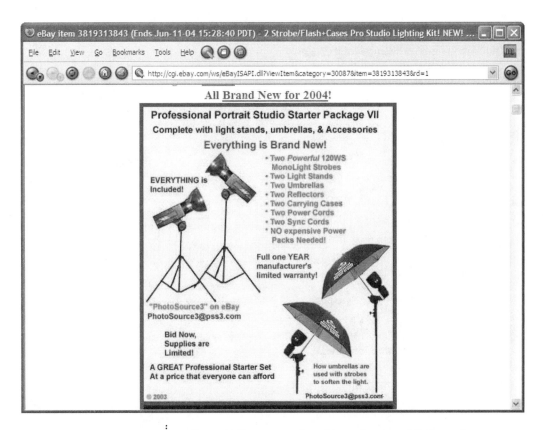

FIGURE 3-8 Light kits such as these are not inexpensive, but they do provide you with great versatility for lighting your items to be photographed.

PowerSellers we spoke with prefer natural light, so they prefer to create their photo area near a window, especially a north-facing one where the light is more diffused than the stronger southern exposure. Go to www.bulls2.com/indexb/lightinghelpfortakingpictures.html to view some ingenious ways to light your photos using very inexpensive equipment. Figure 3-9 shows you how you can use a plastic water jug to diffuse the light when shooting small objects. Seller NKTower, who sells model trains, created a tutorial that completely explains his clever technique. A pin is under the jug, and the top of the jug has been cut to allow the camera lens to poke through. NKTower uses the camera's flash and its self-timer so that he doesn't accidentally shake the camera. The plastic surrounding the pin diffuses the camera flash so that light comes at the object from every angle instead of striking it straight on. The softer light eliminates shadows and doesn't wash out the details of the pin. You can get more information about this technique

Get a digital camera

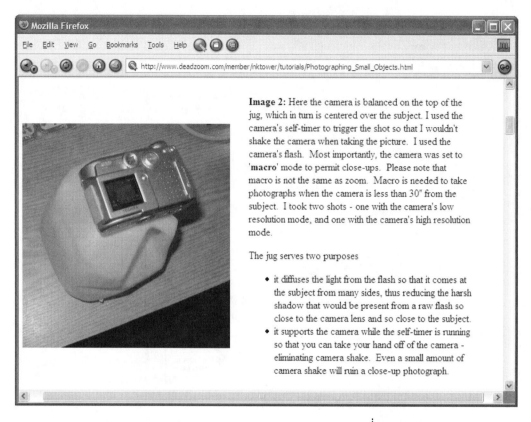

Image 2: Here the camera is balanced on the top of the jug, which in turn is centered over the subject. I used the camera's self-timer to trigger the shot so that I wouldn't shake the camera when taking the picture. I used the camera's flash. Most importantly, the camera was set to 'macro' mode to permit close-ups. Please note that macro is not the same as zoom. Macro is needed to take photographs when the camera is less than 30" from the subject. I took two shots - one with the camera's low resolution mode, and one with the camera's high resolution mode.

The jug serves two purposes

- it diffuses the light from the flash so that it comes at the subject from many sides, thus reducing the harsh shadow that would be present from a raw flash so close to the camera lens and so close to the subject.
- it supports the camera while the self-timer is running so that you can take your hand off of the camera - eliminating camera shake. Even a small amount of camera shake will ruin a close-up photograph.

from www.deadzoom.com/member/nktower/tutorials/ Photographing_Small_Objects.html.

FIGURE 3-9 This ingenious method for lighting small objects is both effective and inexpensive.

» Get a digital camera

This is the one piece of equipment (besides their computers, of course) that all PowerSellers agreed was absolutely essential to their eBay businesses. You may still be grabbing snapshots with the old film camera you've always used, and that's fine for your own personal use. If you're going to start taking photos for your eBay business, however, plan for a digital camera and soon. Since all of your eBay photos will be stored and transmitted digitally, it only makes sense for you to be capturing them that way too.

Digital cameras are simple to use. You can easily preview your image as soon as you've captured it. If you don't like what you see, you've wasted nothing but a moment's time. Even that wasn't a waste, since you can use your mistake to improve your next shot. You'll be able to ensure that you have exactly the

Inexpensive Lighting for Your Photos

Adam Nollmeyer, profiled in Chapter 6, is both a professional photographer and an eBay PowerSeller. Because he knows the ins and outs of photography, he's been able to create some excellent and inexpensive methods for lighting his photographs. He was kind enough to share his expertise with us.

Adam remarked that for the inexperienced photographer, using photographers' strobe lights can be difficult. He recommends using sunlight instead. Here's what Adam told us about using the sun for your strobe: "Do not shoot in direct sunlight. You need to diffuse the strength of the light, so look for an area where light is bouncing off of a building and into your nice, soft open shade area." Adam uses his patio to create the photo area shown at right. He creates the background niche for his products using white cardboard or foam-core.

"I use white for a background because it creates a nice 'high-key' image. These images really pop when you use the gallery feature on eBay and the user is viewing a small thumbnail photo." Adam also uses a "bounce card," shown next. This reflects the sunlight back onto your item centered in the white background. "This will make the shot less flat and give the product some dimension," advises Adam. "The bounce card throws light on the product, and then the white background bounces the light back onto the side away from your bounce card." Take a look at the fine example of the scanner Adam shot using this set up, as shown here. You'll see why following the advice of a professional can really pay.

Sun Bounce card for fill light

View from back of photo area

Get a digital camera

shots you want, and you'll do it instantly. Contrast that to your efforts with a film-based camera. You can carefully set up each of your shots; snap the pictures; finish up the roll with shots of the dog, cat, or baby; and trundle off to have the film developed. When you get it back, whether that's an hour later or a couple of days, you may just discover that you didn't quite catch the feature you were hoping to highlight. Then you'll have to start all over again. You have spent money on film and processing, plus the cost of your travel back and forth to the film processing spot. But, more importantly, you've lost valuable time. In the time it took you to go back and forth with the first roll of film, you could have finished your listings and have had your items up for sale! Now, days have passed, and you're no closer to profits than you were when you began.

So, obviously, you need a digital camera. Fortunately, the digital camera you need is nowhere near the fanciest, most expensive, and full-featured camera on the market. Many of the PowerSellers we spoke with didn't even know which brand of camera they owned, although all of them owned one. Only one PowerSeller could tell us, off the top of his head, which brand he used. He sells jewelry, and he chose the Sony Mavica, because he liked the sharp detail it captures for his smaller items. So, don't overload yourself with the whole concept of digital cameras. If you happen to have one already, that one should be just fine for your business. If you don't have one, keep it simple when you shop for one.

Digital images are made up of hundreds of thousands or even millions of tiny squares known as picture elements, or *pixels*. The more pixels captured within each image, the more detailed that image will be. Different cameras are capable of capturing different numbers of pixels. For your purpose, posting images to online auctions, you'll do just fine with a two- to three-megapixel camera. (A megapixel is 1,000,000 pixels.) This is currently at the low end of the scale of digital cameras, and it is quite possible to also purchase five-megapixel cameras. These will provide you with beautiful images, but you don't need that much power, and you don't need to spend that much money to get the camera you'll need for this task.

Lower-resolution cameras, those that provide fewer pixels, are actually preferable for web publishing, according to www.shortcourses.com (a fabulous source for more information about digital photography). That's because the higher the resolution, the greater the number of pixels in each file, and the longer it will take you to upload your images to your listings. If you keep your images near a resolution of 640 × 480 pixels, you'll achieve the clarity of detail you need and still have reasonable-sized files when it comes time to upload them and store them through your image-hosting service. If you're planning to use eBay's picture services, keep your photos near 400 × 400 pixels in size, if you're not planning to supersize them. When you choose your camera, be sure it has a Macro, or close-up function. This will be very important to you when you're trying to capture the detail of an item or when you're photographing smaller items. Most digital cameras offer this feature now, but some low-end cameras may not. Just one more warning: some lower-resolution cameras can also be more cheaply made. Although low resolution is fine for your purposes, low quality isn't. Be sure your camera is made well. Not only will that pay off in durability, but it will also show up in better image quality and color.

A Scanner? Well, Maybe

The whole subject of digital photography should not intimidate you in the least. The industry has grown very rapidly, and that's largely because digital cameras have come to be so simple to use. But if you have a scanner that you've grown very comfortable with, you may be able to get by with it alone for a while, depending on what you choose to sell. If you're dealing strictly in paper goods such as comic books, magazines, postcards, photographs, books, and sports cards, you may never need anything more than the scanner you've got, unless you want to sell a group of your items all at once. Your scanner will capture a digital image of any flat item as well as a digital camera will. It's just that using a scanner ties you to handling only flat items. PowerSellers generally like to give themselves more options than that. Of course, you could use your regular film-based camera to take your photos and then scan them on your scanner, but then we're back to the same disadvantages of operating with film as your capture medium. Take our advice and jump into the age of digital photography. You'll be very glad that you did.

Your Shipping Station

Before too long you'll be packaging and shipping dozens of items each week. Chapter 8 will provide you with everything you'll

Get a digital camera

need to know about efficiently packaging and shipping your products, no matter what their size, shape, or weight and no matter what their final destinations may be. For now, as you plan your PowerShop, you'll want to keep in mind some of the basic needs of this part of your operation. It's wise to plan a space for packaging your sold items and to plan for the materials you'll need to protect them, package them, label them, and get them on their way.

Just as you set aside a place to do your photography, you'll also want to set aside a place for packaging your sold merchandise. This space will probably be larger than your photography area, and you must also factor into it some storage space for your packing materials. You'll need a table or other platform large and sturdy enough to support the item you are packaging. If you're wrapping one or two items, most of us can comfortably operate on the floor, but when you're doing bulk packaging, you need to take your poor back into consideration. You'll be more comfortable working at the level of a table or counter.

Determine what types of packaging materials you'll need for your items while you're getting everything put into place and stock them in enough quantity to get you started. That way, you don't have to interrupt your flow to run around finding just the right boxes, packing materials, tapes, and labels while orders are coming in and e-mail is waiting for your attention.

Basic supplies include but are not necessarily limited to

- Boxes or mailing tubes
- Padded envelopes
- Bubble wrap
- Packing peanuts
- Tape, either clear or brown
- Labels
- Scale, preferably digital

In addition to these things, you'll need scissors, markers, and a utility knife is often handy. Plus, you'll need adequate storage to allow you to keep all these materials handy, but neatly tucked away too. Don't panic at the thought of acquiring and keeping all this. Chapter 8 is full of great tips about shipping your items, including a lot of suggestions for getting free or very inexpensive materials.

You'll Need a Digital Scale

A digital shipping scale is a must-have seller's tool, especially if you're planning to sell a variety of items. Couple a digital scale with a service such as Stamps.com, explained in Chapter 8, and you may never have to go to the post office again (well almost never). Newer models have large readouts, special slots for letters, and a hold feature that lets you remove your parcel and still view the weight. Figure on spending between $45.00 and $100.00 (price varies with features and capacity).

As you might guess, one of the best places to buy a digital scale is eBay itself. Type in **Postage Meters, Scales** as eBay search terms, and you're likely to get hundreds of products to choose from. Some have remote displays, can handle items that weigh hundreds of pounds, and can process hundreds of pieces of mail at one time. Your needs are likely more modest, and a simple scale with a capacity of 50 pounds or so is probably all you need, depending, of course, on what you're planning to sell.

» Consider a thermal printer for your labels

Just to whet your appetite, we'll share with you one great shipping tip now so you don't have to wait all the way till Chapter 8. Get yourself a thermal printer for your labels. You can either rent one of these from the USPS or UPS, or you can buy one. They often appear at dramatically reduced prices right on eBay. The real advantage to using a thermal printer for your labels is that you eliminate the need for toner, since the printers use heat to mark the labels. As an extra bonus, both UPS and the USPS will provide the labels to you without charge. Once you pay for the printer itself, you eliminate the costs of the consumables necessary for all your label printing tasks.

Miscellaneous Tools

You will certainly come up with your own tools and gadgets that you find useful to your individual business needs. All PowerSellers have their own little systems to make things work for them. One PowerSeller who operates high up in the Rockies needs a notebook computer. He simply has no high-speed access available except for a "hot-spot" at the closest Starbucks. He goes there to do all of his major uploading and downloading, so for him a notebook is a necessity of life. Another seller told us he uses a T-Mobile SideKick so that when he travels to buy inventory, he can easily stay in touch remotely with his home office. Still other PowerSellers told us they'd be lost without their cell phones. You'll find your own special loyalty to the devices you come across, and then you'll be able to give advice to less-experienced sellers, too.

» Pick up the phone

In the beginning, you'll probably find the phone line you have now is all you need. You may actually be able to eliminate a phone line, if you've had a separate one installed for your computer dial-up. Once you have high-speed access, that phone line will be obsolete, so close it out, or better yet, use it for your business phone line. Whether you use your family's phone line or keep a separate one for your business, you want to keep a business-like manner when you answer that phone. If a customer is trying to reach you, it makes a much better impression if you answer in a business-like manner. Likewise, if you're waiting to hear back from a potential supplier, you don't want your toddler to pick up the phone for you. It just doesn't make a good impression.

After working from home for decades, we've learned the best approach is to answer with a "business" voice and greeting. Not only does this send a clear signal to prospective business partners and customers, but it also lets your friends and family subtly know that you're working. It's much easier to get right to the point and then ask the caller if you can call back in a little while, if you've made it clear to them they've reached you while you're at work. Remember, as a PowerSeller, you'll be putting lots of hours into your job, and helping the other people in your life adjust to that in big ways and small will make life better for everyone.

Now it is almost difficult to remember when phone lines didn't include voice mail or answering machines. Once it was a big deal to be asked to leave a message, but now it's uncommon to find someone who doesn't have the ability to let the machine get the phone. If you don't have voice mail or an answering machine, get one. You'll have times when you're busy and just don't want to interrupt your concentration to pick up the phone. You'll also have messages you simply don't want to miss from suppliers and customers. Knowing that a message can still get to you while you run to the post office will reduce the stress in your daily life.

Pick up the phone

Finally, provide yourself with unlimited long-distance calling. These plans vary from area to area, so you may have to do a little research to find which one is best for you. But, you want the freedom and comfort of knowing you can pick up the phone and dial long-distance any time of the day or evening without worrying about how much each call is going to cost. You need to have this level of comfort, especially when you're researching suppliers. That's a part of your business that may require a great deal of phone time. You don't want to worry about the meter running, and you don't want to have to pay exorbitant long-distance charges either. Your best bet may be your long-distance provider, or you may actually do better with a cell phone company. Either way, do what you have to do to make it no problem at all for you to pick up the phone and dial.

Meet a PowerSeller

TraderNick—Nick Boyd

TraderNick was already a coin and collectibles dealer when he discovered eBay in 1995. He had a full-time job and pursued his business only as a sideline, when he started selling online. In 1997 he was able to begin working for himself, from home, selling his items exclusively on eBay. Within four years, he was ready to answer his "itch" and open a brick-and-mortar store of his own. Now he operates both his offline store and his online eBay business.

Nick calls eBay a "natural extension of what I already do for a living." By the time he opened his store, he was shipping about 30 packages per week. Today he has received nearly 6,000 feedbacks and has a positive rating of 99.9 percent!

Nick has been actively buying coin collections from all over the United States for more than ten years. He buys from private collections, estates, other dealers, and coin shows. He also visits coin shops and antique markets. He said he doesn't have much luck with garage and yard sales, so he doesn't use these as inventory sources. He travels throughout the Southeast a lot to buy his inventory, and he always drives so that he can stop along the way when he finds antique markets and coin shops. He said the biggest change he's seen in the last ten years of selling coins is the same problem that has befallen the hobby of coin collecting itself. When he began his business, he said, he had plenty of coins and too few buyers. Now he has the opposite trouble to contend with. He has plenty of buyers, but keeping his inventory fresh is a challenge. Fortunately, he enjoys both the hobby and the travel.

Nick has two computers networked together and was in the midst of adding a third when we spoke. He also uses a computer at home every evening to keep up with his e-mails. He emphasized that, although you don't need to be a computer expert to operate an eBay business, you should have a reliable base of computer understanding when you start out. That would include enough computer confidence to allow you to operate the software and add the peripherals you'll need. Nick chose Seller's Assistant Pro as his auction management software, and he's been using it for about two years. He emphasizes that you must use a digital camera and host your images on the Web. In addition, Nick uses the usual arrangement of office machines, including a copier. He called his cell phone "one of the most used pieces of technology I own." That's understandable, considering how much time he spends traveling.

When he began on eBay, Nick had a friend who showed him all about using the site. They worked together while Nick built his eBay skills. In return, he has happily helped other people come on to eBay as sellers. Today, Nick says that eBay itself is your best marketing tool for your eBay business. He attributes his marketing success to his descriptive auction listing titles and his accurate descriptions. His PowerSeller status and near-perfect positive feedback rating help assure his customers that they're in good hands and also provide good advertising and marketing for his business.

When asked about his goals, Nick said his dream is to have one or two employees to run his eBay business and one employee to run his shop. Then he could spend 100 percent of his time traveling to build his inventory. When we asked about what he's learned from his years on eBay, Nick said he really wishes he had started to integrate all of the aspects of his auction business much earlier than he did. He said his goal has been to make everything seamless, and that's not as easy as one might think. "I'm constantly working at trying to make the 'flow' a little smoother."

Nick is now living his life in beautiful central Florida with his wife and three children. He's earning his living by working at the thing he loves the most. He's a member of the American Numismatic Association and the Florida United Numismatists, and he's a well-respected member of the eBay PowerSeller's community. He enjoys his travels and has every reason to believe the goals he's defined for himself are achievable. It sounds like an excellent life to us!

Chapter 4

Automate Your Auctions for Smooth Selling

Know what's important when you go shopping

Now that you have your PowerShop ready to go, we've got one last tool to recommend, your auction automation software. Although you can live a whole lifetime using eBay for fun—and maybe even a little profit—without auction management software, once you've set your sights on PowerSeller status, you're going to need this tool. Trying to be a PowerSeller without it is almost like trying to be a carpenter without a level. You may be able to make it happen, but you'll be making life more difficult than it needs to be.

Auction management tools will provide the efficiencies you'll need to process your listings and sales in the volume you'll experience as a PowerSeller. Of all the PowerSellers we worked with, only two were not using an auction management program. Those two sold only very high-priced items. This allowed them to qualify as PowerSellers with only a few sales each month. If that describes your intended operation, go ahead to the next chapter. But if, like most PowerSellers, you'll be processing dozens if not hundreds of sales per month, you will very quickly need to get automated to stay on top of your work.

What can you expect from auction management software? You can expect the software to support you in every step of your transaction. From creating the listing and managing your images, to e-mail communications with your buyers, shipping support, and feedback services, all of these features should be part of any well-thought-out program. There are several dozen auction management offerings from which to choose, and finding the one that's right for you may require a bit of research on your part, but we'll help.

» ## Know what's important when you go shopping

Scott Samuel, the counters guy we introduced in the last chapter, has been online since 1980. In 2000, his company, Honesty.com, was sold to Andale, one of the largest providers of auction management services. Scott obviously knows what's important when you're shopping for an auction management product, since he's been so instrumental in creating that whole industry. He recommends that when you are evaluating an auction management program, these four things are the most important things to consider:

1. Simplicity

2. Learning curve

3. Problem resolution

4. Customer service

Which of these four is most important? Customer service. If your software freezes up, what are you going to do? Who are you going to call? When you deal with hundreds of transactions a day, maybe thousands per week, problems are going to occur, and you will need someone to stand behind you.

To test out the companies whose product you are considering, send test e-mails to them. See how quickly they respond. Look at the "About Us" page on their web sites. How many people are behind the company? Who are they? E-mail some of those people. Test out how quickly and how well they respond. "You have to have access to someone at the company who you can trust," says Scott.

What Should Your Auction Management Program Do for You?

The most basic requirement of your auction management tool is that it keeps all your information in one place and makes it simple for you to use and manipulate that information when you need to. Your goal in choosing auction management tools is to be able to have a system that allows you to input your data only once. Every keystroke you save equals time you can spend on more productive efforts in building your business. So, go for a system that allows you the power and flexibility to input your data and then make it work for you.

Auction management tools offer similar services, so what should you look for when you go shopping for your own

Know what's important when you go shopping

system? We'll step you through the features you'll be most likely to need and give you some tips for learning more about the tools that might be right for you.

Create Your Listings

The system you choose should make it simple for you to create your auction listings and do it quickly and in bulk. That means it should offer you templates for your listings that will allow you to create multiple auction listings without keying in every piece of information. A variety of templates will allow you to alter the look of your auction listings easily and without the need for you to know or use HTML. HTML, or Hypertext Markup Language, is the computer language in which web pages are written. We assume you're familiar with it, but if you're not, it sounds a lot more imposing than it really is. It isn't difficult to incorporate basic HTML instructions into your listings. They can be as simple as inputting <p> to indicate where a new paragraph should begin. Your auction management software will have a built-in HTML editor that allows you to incorporate the HTML codes using the equivalent of a word processing program.

The program you choose will allow you to import your already-existing auction listings into the new management tool, seamlessly so that you don't miss posting auction listings while you switch your system. You will want your program to offer you image hosting services or to make it simple for you to import your photo files from a separate image hosting service. Your auction management software should also allow you to schedule your listings to start when you determine you want your auctions to begin. This way, you can create all of your listings at one time and then have them automatically begin on a schedule that you determine.

Automate Your Communications

You will spend a good amount of time reading, sending, and answering your e-mail. Some of this work can be automated to cut down on the amount of time and energy you need to spend on this task. You cannot replace the good quality of customer service that responding individually to a customer's question will bring, but you can automate the more routine forms of e-mail that you must send for every transaction. Your auction management tool should allow you to automate your winning-bidder e-mails, your payment reminder e-mails, your "thank you" e-mails, and your feedback responses. The most flexible programs offer you choices of forms for these functions so that your e-mails and feedbacks don't become too robotic. In one case, five different positive feedback responses are available—the system will automatically rotate them to give your feedback a less automated feel.

Manage Your Inventory

Using your auction management tools, you should be able to quickly determine which of your items have sold and which have not. Then the software should make it simple for you to relist any items that haven't sold. You should also be able to see the status of all your sales to determine which ones have been paid, shipped, received, and noted in feedback. Some programs, but not all, will track your inventory and notify you when your supply of a particular item is running low. These may also help you track the expenses you incur for sourcing your products so that you can compare your sources for their cost-efficiencies.

Track Your Expenses

Your auction management software should allow you to quickly determine all of your operating fees, including your eBay fees and your PayPal expenses. You should also be able to export all of your accounting information to your accounting software, whether you choose QuickBooks, Quicken, or Excel. Further, the program should offer you graphic views and charts to help you see exactly how much money you are spending and earning.

Complete the Sale and Ship Your Item

Choose an auction automation system that will allow you to integrate with the USPS, UPS, and Fedex. This will make it easier for you to complete the transaction, calculate your customers' shipping charges, print shipping labels, and track shipping expenses.

How Do You Choose?

You will find that there is a great deal of competition among companies that provide auction management tools. There is also a wide range of features and functions available with these products, and pricing among the different products is very competitive. You may just find the program you like best here in the descriptions we'll offer you, but if you're still not sure, you should continue your own research.

» Start with Auction Software Review

One place to start your research is Auction Software Review at www.auctionsoftwarereview.com, shown in Figure 4-1. This site was created and is maintained by Andy Geldman of the United Kingdom. In researching auction management tools for his own

FIGURE 4-1 The Auction Software Review is a good place to start researching the auction management software that's right for you.

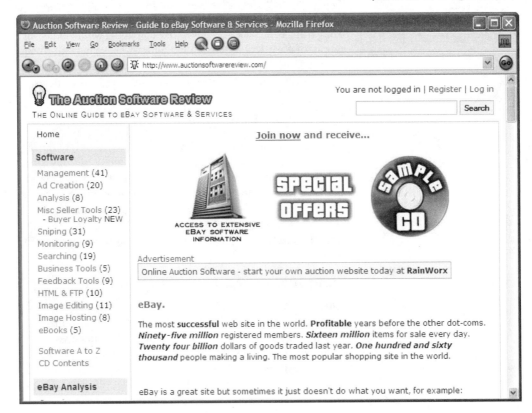

use, he realized there was no central source of information about these products. He set about creating one of his own. The site breaks eBay software down into 15 categories including management, promotion, analysis, business tools, image hosting, and ad creation.

In addition to auction management software, you'll find information about auction analysis software, sniping tools, feedback tools, and image hosting. In 2004, the site also added eBay analysis information to track and report on eBay sales across the many different categories of the site.

For a quick fix on what's available, program features, and company contact details, there's no better source of information. As we write this, Auction Software Review describes 200 products from more than 170 developers.

When you join the site for a one-time fee of $10.99 U.S. dollars plus $2.00 shipping and handling, you'll receive a CD with 22 completely functional software programs. In addition, you will receive 42 trial versions of eBay support software for you to explore. Finally, the CD includes 23 e-books on topics ranging from creating your listings, to selling on eBay, to sourcing your products. The product reviews on the site should not be taken at face value. (Who are the reviewers? Why aren't some popular programs getting more than a couple of reviews?) But, you can use the site to explore software you may not have thought of and to locate companies you may not be familiar with.

Unlike the reviews themselves perhaps, the icons that are part of the software reviews may be useful. The "verified" icon, for example, indicates the software company has met the criteria listed next. Some of these criteria are givens (has an e-mail address); others are important (no spyware). But if a company doesn't receive the appropriate icon, you are not told the reason why. And, that's important information to know.

Icons guarantee that the software company reviewed

- Has an active web site
- Has an e-mail address, feedback form, discussion forum, or other means of active user support
- Has functionality that can help users of eBay or other auction sites
- Does not include separate spyware, adware, or other software not integral to the program

Consider eBay's auction management tools

- Shows a minimum level of professionalism, e.g., no recurring errors, an intuitive interface, a clean install, and uninstall
- Has a trial version or is free for at least personal use

This site is a lot like Yahoo for auction software in that it categorizes everything (including some categories you may not have thought of) and provides hyperlinks so that you can get to the different sites quickly. Do your own evaluations of the software, or post and read relevant messages on eBay's discussion boards or the AuctionBytes boards. And, be sure to test the helpfulness of their customer service staff. That should give you all the background you need.

Some Suggestions to Get You Started

Because there are so many different auction management programs from which to choose, and because they can all seem so similar in their features, we've decided to give you a boost in your decision-making process. We've chosen nine different programs to describe to you here. You may be wondering why we chose the ones we did, so we'll briefly explain. First of all, in order to be included in our discussion, the program had to have been recommended to us by a PowerSeller. That's the only way we could begin to access a tool's efficiencies—by talking to someone who actually used it. Next, we chose the programs that came up again and again in our research. If more than a few PowerSellers were using it, we thought that was meaningful. Finally, we decided to start our discussion with the auction management tools eBay itself offers. Many of the PowerSellers we spoke with never went farther than eBay in finding a tool to manage their affairs. Sticking with eBay seemed easy and comfortable for them. Of course the sellers who ventured out to third-party providers were all glad they did, but we'll leave the final choice to you, the only one who really knows what it is you want.

» Consider eBay's auction management tools

eBay offers its own suite of auction management software. Many of the PowerSellers we spoke with have never migrated beyond these easy-to-find offerings. Not only do these tools tend to be less expensive than "outside" solutions, they are also guaranteed to work seamlessly with eBay. There are four different tools you can choose from: Seller's Assistant, Seller's Assistant Pro, Selling Manager, or Selling Manager Pro. We'll focus only on Seller's Assistant Pro and Selling Manager Pro, because these two offer the most power and are most suitable for the PowerSeller you will soon be. Seller's Assistant Pro, shown in Figure 4-2, is a desktop-based tool, while Selling Manager Pro is web-based. Both of these tools offer

- Listing creation and scheduling
- Inventory management
- Sales information tracking
- Post-sale information and management
- Monthly reporting

FIGURE 4-2 eBay's own Seller's Assistant Pro auction management software offers a desktop solution to your auction management needs.

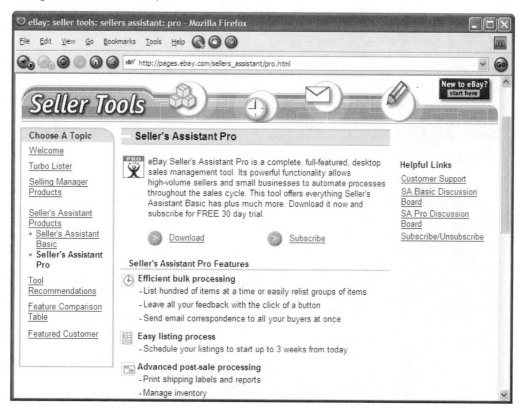

Consider eBay's auction management tools

Selling Manager Pro, shown in Figure 4-3, offers more features for automating your customer communications and more monthly reporting features. With Selling Manager Pro, you will have

- Automatic notification e-mail for both payments received and items shipped

- Automatic feedback left when buyer pays

- Printer-friendly views for printing your records

- Tracking of your buyer communication and whether your items have been paid or shipped in bulk

- Records of all your buyer communication to help you process Non-Paying Bidder reports

Selling Manager Pro seems to offer more features than Seller's Assistant Pro, but there are also some disadvantages of

FIGURE 4-3 Selling Manager Pro is eBay's web-based auction management software.

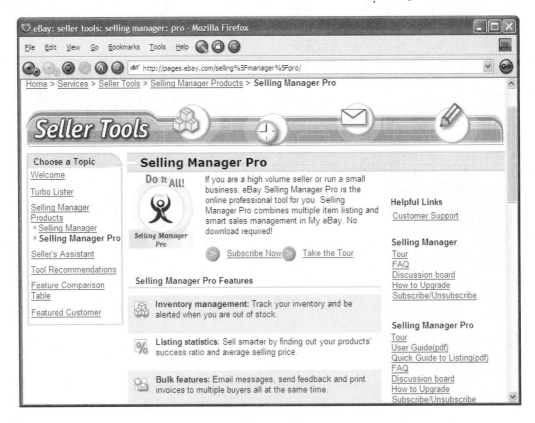

choosing the tool with more features. For one thing, Selling Manager Pro does not allow you to create your auction listings offline. If you want to create your listings without being connected to the web, you'll have to also use eBay's Turbo Lister as shown in Figure 4-4. Turbo Lister is free, and the sellers we spoke with who use Selling Manager Pro couple it with Turbo Lister. They claim to want the convenience of creating their listings offline and then just going online to upload them. They also find the Turbo Lister tool to be a more efficient way to create their listings. Some PowerSellers never move beyond the combination of using Turbo Lister and Selling Manager Pro.

Keep in mind Selling Manager Pro will store your data for only 120 days, after which you can no longer access your records. You can work around that by downloading your records monthly, which is a good plan anyway, but if you're not always conscientious, you could lose some of your older data. Seller's Assistant Pro, because it stores all of your data on your own

FIGURE 4-4 If you choose eBay's Selling Manager Pro, you'll also want to add eBay's free Turbo Lister so that you can create your auction listings offline.

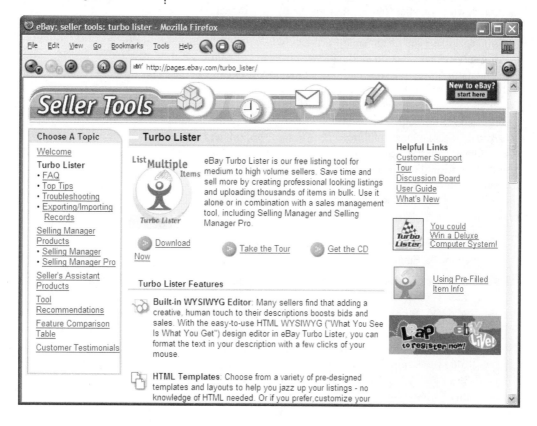

computer, maintains files indefinitely. You'll still have to purge your files and move them into storage, but you don't run the same risk of accidentally losing your data. Seller's Assistant Pro costs $24.99 per month. Selling Manager Pro costs $15.99 per month.

» Andale

Andale is famous for its auction counters, but it is also a giant in auction management and analysis software. Andale offers you a complete, one-stop approach to all of the management tools you'll need for your auction business. Andale's services are sold on an à la carte basis, which potentially makes them more expensive than some of their competitors, but on the other hand, they also offer bundled services through a variety of Quick Packs. These allow you to purchase only the tools you will actually need and offer users a discount over the individually priced modules. Andale also has a supplier service that will link their users with potential sources of products to sell. This service is available for $3.95 per month.

Andale prides itself on its "smart" services, which are decision-making services and auction automation tools, some of which are shown in Figure 4-5. They claim to be the only provider of truly "smart" services that help Andale users make the best possible decisions concerning pricing, sourcing, listing creation, cross-selling, and sell-through data.

Andale offers all users unlimited free e-mail support, and the company also has a premium support service that offers you two additional levels of support. These provide you with a number of telephone "incidents" per month to answer any questions you may have about any aspect of Andale's services or selling on eBay in general.

- **Programs** Lister, Gallery, Images, Checkout, Feedback, Email Manager.
- **Platform** Web-based, except for Email Manager, which is desktop.
- **Listing capabilities** Lister is for creating eBay auctions and for inventory management. It offers more than 100 layouts and templates. Lister allows scheduled listing times and dates. A separate Gallery feature allows you to highlight up to 50 live items from your other listings within each auction you create.

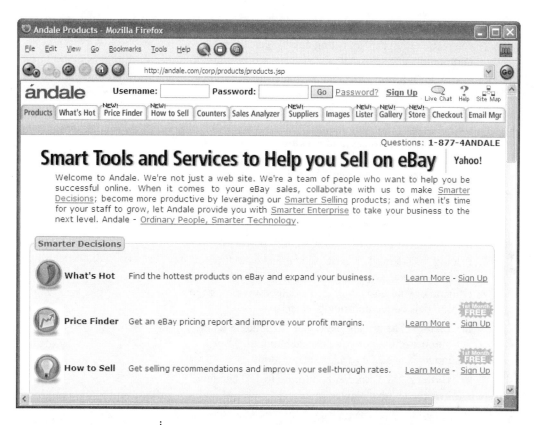

FIGURE 4-5 Andale offers a very complete set of software solutions to manage and support your eBay sales.

Image hosting Andale Images allows you to crop, resize, and auto-fix your images. With it, you can add photos to your listings with a single click. Image hosting space depends on the pricing plan you choose. It begins with 3MB, and you can purchase up to 20MB and more.

Inventory management Lister includes real-time inventory management. It automatically tracks your items and updates your inventory records as they sell or fail to sell. It features UPC/ISBN-based tracking. You can keep track of your out-of-stock inventory for reordering purposes. You can easily track your suppliers so that you can compare costs for similar items.

E-mail handling Email Manager allows you to organize and manage buyer communication. It offers you auto-e-mail foldering, customer sales history, reusable e-mail templates, a spam manager, and a mailing list management tool. With every buyer e-mail you receive, you can get listing details, customer information, and sales status.

■ **Post-sale features**   Andale Checkout allows you to send custom e-mails for winning-bidder notification. It also offers PayPal integrated checkout and USPS and UPS integration for automatically calculating shipping costs, printable invoices, and packing slips. Andale's Feedback automates leaving feedback for your buyers. You can receive an automatic e-mail alert when a buyer leaves you neutral or negative feedback. Andale Feedback is free.

■ **Customer service/education**   Andale Help Central provides all customer service and support.

■ **Pricing**   Andale's à la carte pricing makes it difficult to offer you precise pricing information. To get the best estimate of your costs in using Andale's services, go to www.andale.com/corp/pricing_corp.jsp.

   ■ **Lister**   The pricing plans vary, depending on the number of listings you post each month. They range from $2.00 to $225.00 per month.

   ■ **Gallery** $2.95 per month for up to 100 auctions launched within a given month.

   ■ **Images**   Plans range from $2.00 to $65.00 per month depending on how many MB of storage you require.

   ■ **Checkout**   From $2.00 per month for 10 checkouts or fewer, to $225.00 per month for up to 5,600 checkouts.

   ■ **Email Manager**   One flat monthly fee of $5.95 brings you the Email Manager.

■ **Additional features**   Live chat is available; tutorials to help you use Andale products are also on the web site. A premium support plan offers telephone support. Plans for this service begin at $5.95 per month.

■ **Further information**   www.andale.com.

❯❯ AuctionHawk

AuctionHawk, shown in Figure 4-6, claims that with the same effort you'd expend to manually list 10–20 listings per week,

FIGURE 4-6 The AuctionHawk home page features their tools for eBay PowerSellers.

you can feature 10 to 20 times that number of auctions using their AuctionHawk offerings. What's more, your listings will look better. AuctionHawk is one of the few services that charges a flat fee, and fees are not based on usage or volume. This leads them to claim that their services cost 50 to 80 percent less than competitive products. You would expect it, as a smaller company, to offer better customer service, and that seems to be true.

When we spoke with them, the company was planning to start specifically tailoring their software to PowerSellers and "Shooting Stars," the top tier among PowerSellers. They will be doing this by adding more integration with services such as UPS, the USPS, and PayPal. Their idea is to have a dashboard from which you can control everything about your auctions.

Knowing that competition against Andale and Vendio is not a reasonable goal, AuctionHawk instead targets a specific niche of eBay sellers that includes PowerSellers and Shooting Stars.

AuctionHawk

One of the real advantages of AuctionHawk is that the company keeps their services simple to use.

- **Program**   EZ-Lister online auction management service.
- **Platform**   Web-based.
- **Listing capabilities**   EZ-Lister offers one-click listings. You can schedule your listings, create bulk listings, and manage repeatable listings. With 300 template designs for your listings, you have a broad variety of looks to choose from.
- **Image hosting**   AuctionHawk allows easy integration of images into your listings. With EZ-Lister, you can crop and edit your images. It also includes watermarking, to safeguard your photos from being lifted by other sellers. The different pricing plans for EZ-Lister offer you between 20MB and 50MB of storage, depending on the plan you choose. Either is enough so that you don't have to worry about running out of space.
- **Inventory management**   The At-a-Glance inventory list page lets you see how many listings are pending, current, sold, or unsold. You can also list items separately and not have them put into your general inventory.
- **E-mail handling**   Track e-mail sent. Automated winning-bidder e-mail is sent immediately at auction end.
- **Post-sale features**   With AuctionHawk, you'll get automatic invoices sent, bulk feedback delivery, feedback monitoring to track the status of all your feedback, and feedback alerts to be notified of unfavorable feedback received. The program also offers bulk-relist support, and lifetime archiving for all your listings.
- **Customer service/education**   A free monthly e-mail newsletter for eBay PowerSellers features tips, tricks, and tactics for business management. Discussion boards provide help from other users, and e-mail support brings you customer service help from the company.
- **Pricing**   AuctionHawk features flat fees with no extra listing fees or percentage charges. The Basic plan is for posting up to 50 listings per month, and you have up to 20MB of image space for $12.99. The Preferred plan

offers up to 250 listings per month and 40MB of image space for $24.99 per month. The Unlimited plan offers unlimited listings per month and 50MB of image space for $44.99 per month.

■ **Further information** www.auctionhawk.com.

» Auctiva Pro

Jeff Schlicht, the founder of Auctiva Pro, was once an avid online auction seller himself. In the course of trying to create hundreds of auction listings, including lumps of coal from the wreck of the Titanic, he realized that there had to be a way to automate the process and make it easier to complete. That's when he created Auction Poster (Auctiva Pro's predecessor), which allowed him to triple his listings.

Auctiva Pro, shown in Figure 4-7, targets small businesses and individuals selling to consumers. They've been featured in many publications and have won many awards for their software. The company has received kudos for Auctiva Showcase, specifically. This tool offers users a "virtual storefront" that allows them to feature all auctions, both from within eBay and outside of eBay including Amazon and Yahoo. Auctiva Pro claims this is valuable because most sellers have their offerings scattered in several online auction sites. With the Showcase product, you can collect all of your auctions into one unified storefront offering. Once you sign up for Showcase, an Auctiva Showcase link is appended to all of your auction listings, automatically. Clicking this link takes your customers to a separate web page featuring all of your listings. This web-based service is free. The company also produces a weekly e-mail newsletter.

■ **Program** Auctiva Pro.

■ **Platform** Suite of desktop software tools and web-based services.

■ **Listing capabilities** Auctiva Poster offers unlimited postings, professional listing templates, batch uploads, auction scheduling, and a showcase link to allow you to cross-market your listings, featuring pictures of other products for sale in each of your listings.

■ **Image hosting** Two picture hosting services are offered. Auctiva Picture Hosting Pro is paid for

Auctiva Pro

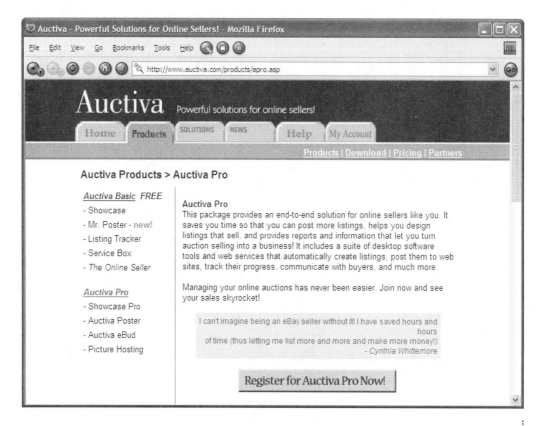

Auctiva - Powerful Solutions for Online Sellers! - Mozilla Firefox

File   Edit   View   Go   Bookmarks   Tools   Help

http://www.auctiva.com/products/apro.asp

Auctiva   Powerful solutions for online sellers!

Home   Products   SOLUTIONS   NEWS   Help   My Account

Products | Download | Pricing | Partners

Auctiva Products > Auctiva Pro

Auctiva Basic FREE
- Showcase
- Mr. Poster - new!
- Listing Tracker
- Service Box
- *The Online Seller*

Auctiva Pro
- Showcase Pro
- Auctiva Poster
- Auctiva eBud
- Picture Hosting

Auctiva Pro
This package provides an end-to-end solution for online sellers like you. It saves you time so that you can post more listings, helps you design listings that sell, and provides reports and information that let you turn auction selling into a business! It includes a suite of desktop software tools and web services that automatically create listings, post them to web sites, track their progress, communicate with buyers, and much more.

Managing your online auctions has never been easier. Join now and see your sales skyrocket!

I can't imagine being an eBay seller without it! I have saved hours and hours
of time (thus letting me list more and more and make more money!)
- *Cynthia Whittemore*

Register for Auctiva Pro Now!

with picture credits. You receive 20 credits per month included in your subscription. A picture credit will give you up to 250,000 bytes of image hosting space. A typical auction picture is 30 to 50 thousand bytes, so on average you can include six images per picture credit. This means you'll get approximately 120 images included in your monthly charge. Picture editing and slide show creation are possible.

- **Inventory management**   Auctiva eBud is the tool for tracking and managing your auctions. It allows you to check the status of all open and closed auctions in a spreadsheet format. You can display a "stock ticker" scrolling marquee of all your auctions on your desktop while you do other work. You can keep records of old auctions that include complete histories. The

FIGURE 4-7 Auctiva Pro's home page targets small businesses and individuals.

database features allow you to quickly see who your repeat buyers are.

■ **E-mail handling**   Automatically send a "thank-you" e-mail to everyone who leaves you positive feedback. You can track all of your customer correspondence with eBud. It includes customizable form letter e-mails for every step of the auction process. You can combine e-mails for multiple auctions won by the same bidder.

■ **Post-sale features**   Supports multiple payment options. Feedback Manager automates the process of leaving feedback. It automatically leaves feedback to everyone who leaves you positive feedback. You can preset your feedback messages and store those that you use most frequently.

■ **Customer service/education**   Auctiva Pro offers community forums where users can share advice. The company also offers online product tours to help familiarize users with product features, and e-mail support.

■ **Pricing**   Auctiva Pro has seven pricing plans ranging from a Starter Plan to the Unlimited Plan. Each plan features a variety of software tools and services. The Starter Plan is $9.95 per month. The Unlimited Plan is $109.95 per month. There is also a PowerSeller Plan for $74.95 per month. All the services and products are also available on an à la carte basis.

■ **Further information**   www.auctiva.com.

» ChannelAdvisor

ChannelAdvisor provides both auction and "market management" software. Its clients range from mid-level eBay sellers all the way to Fortune 500 companies, including IBM and Motorola. ChannelAdvisor is also eBay's largest supplier of liquidation auction services for companies such as Best Buy and Sharper Image. ChannelAdvisor offers three levels of auction management products. The smallest level is the one the company recommends for eBay sellers, including most PowerSellers. The products include ChannelAdvisor Pro for small businesses and eBay PowerSellers. Then there is ChannelAdvisor Merchant for

ChannelAdvisor

medium-sized businesses and the "top tier" eBay PowerSellers. Finally, ChannelAdvisor Enterprise is for large business. Our discussion will feature ChannelAdvisor Pro, shown in Figure 4-8.

- ■ **Program** ChannelAdvisor Pro.
- ■ **Platform** Web-based.
- ■ **Listing capabilities** Standard templates and layout themes are available, or you can design and use your own. The *edit multiple ads* feature enables you to update information for several different listings at once. You can post your listings immediately, but you can also schedule them to post when you choose. You can use the product for a one-time listing or set a listing to upload on a recurring schedule.

FIGURE 4-8 ChannelAdvisor Pro is designed for small businesses and eBay PowerSellers.

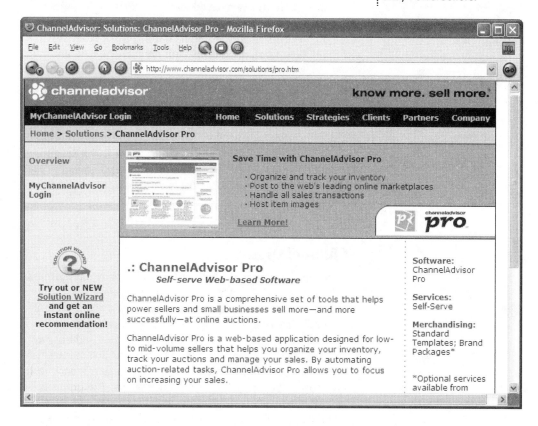

- **Image hosting**   Image hosting is integrated into the listing creation component of ChannelAdvisor's software. You receive 250MB of free image storage, and you can buy more in 250MB increments. You can upload up to four images at once, and you can upload a larger number in bulk via File Transfer Protocol (FTP). You can also organize and manage an image library.

- **Inventory management**   You can add an item from your inventory directly to an invoice. With the *create item* feature, you create a record that then tracks your available stock. You can also assign items to item classes that you define. There's an Excel template that lets you create files offline and then upload them into your ChannelAdvisor Pro account. If a buyer contacts you and asks to buy something in addition to what was in the auction, you can create a new invoice right from an inventory item. ChannelAdvisor Pro automatically updates your inventory.

- **E-mail handling**   As part of your ChannelAdvisor Pro menu, there are customer management settings. These settings determine what sort of communication you will send and when you will send it. You can choose to send automatic winning-bidder notifications. You can automatically send an e-mail when you receive payment and when an item has been shipped. Software includes e-mail templates, or you may create your own.

- **Post-sale features**   ChannelAdvisor Pro has a customer checkout feature. You can select shipping and insurance options as well as payment options. A customer feedback option simplifies the process of leaving feedback. You can choose to automate feedback or keep it a manual function. You can also send bulk feedback if you'd like.

- **Customer service/education**   A member newsletter includes product news and auction tips. Active discussion boards give you access to advice from other users. E-mail support is stressed as "personalized."

- **Pricing**   ChannelAdvisor Pro offers three types of monthly plans. Pricing is based on the number of "closings" per month. A closing is any listing you create and post, whether it sells or not. Additionally, a closing includes any inventory added to an existing invoice. For example, if your customer buys one blue widget and then asks if he can add two more to the invoice, that's two closings; quantity for identical items doesn't matter. If he buys a thousand yellow widgets, that's one closing, but if he then adds a hundred green widgets, two blue widgets, and a red widget, that's four closings. Fortunately, you can see your current closing count in your summary statement.

- **Standard plan** $29.95 includes 500 closings per month. Each additional closing will cost $0.10.

- **Gold plan** $54.95 includes 1,000 closings. Additional closings are $0.08.

- **Platinum plan** $99.95 includes 2,000 closings. Additional closings are $0.06.

Annual plans are also available. You can learn more about them on the ChannelAdvisor web site.

- **Further information**   www.channeladvisor.com.

» inkFrog

An important focus of inkFrog's business is image hosting. The company prides itself on having the most reliable and fastest-loading images on eBay. Image hosting is as important to them as their auction tools. Targeting both small- and large-volume eBay sellers, the company's marketing displays a sense of fun, as shown by their home page featured in Figure 4-9. Their frog-based logo is both appealing and omnipresent on their site and in their materials. You can even get your own inkFrog T-shirt or polo shirt if you wish. inkFrog advises buyers to expect questions such as, "What the heck is inkFrog?" when they wear their shirts. More importantly, the company also prides itself on its low fees.

Greg Sisung founded BayPal, an online auction management service that then became inkFrog. The company claims that it is now growing by leaps and bounds. This group seems to have created a great sense of customer loyalty as expressed by the enthusiasm customers bring to inkFrog's message boards and the excitement they expressed when inkFrog's T-shirts were first introduced.

■ **Program** inkFrog.

■ **Platform** Web-based.

■ **Listing capabilities** My Lister options and settings are listed on a single page. You can schedule, launch, track, and manage your eBay listings from this page. Flash previewer is automatically added to each listing to allow you to highlight your other listings. inkFrog's Sonny tool allows you to create your own templates.

FIGURE 4-9 inkFrog brings a sense of fun to their auction management software and their home page.

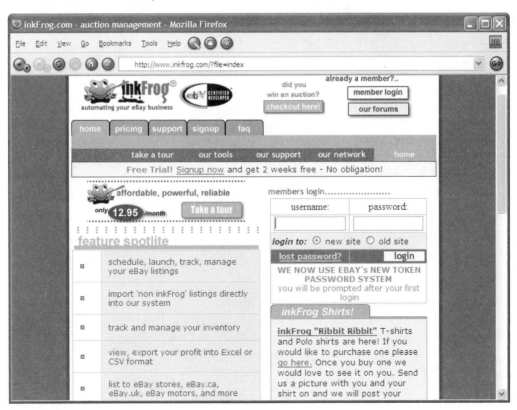

inkFrog

- **Image hosting** photoFrog provides picture storage and picture sharing services. Just upload your photos to their servers, where they're stored in your account. From there, you can view and edit them with inkFrog's "image magician" tools. This service is separate from inkFrog auction management and requires a separate account. The standard is 20MB of storage, with more available at an additional cost.

- **Inventory management** With inkFrog, you can track and manage your inventory. You can resubmit, relist, and bulk-relist unsold items. View your profits and export your data to accounting or spreadsheet software, specifically Excel or CSV format.

- **E-mail handling** Manage winning-bidder e-mails, create auto-e-mails, and send payment reminders with inkFrog.

- **Post-sale features** With inkFrog Checkout, you can create a checkout profile that includes name and address information, payment and shipping terms, and default shipping method. You can also manage both the feedback you leave and the feedback you receive through inkFrog. The software lets you track the item status to determine whether you've received payment, shipped the item, or closed the transaction.

- **Customer service/education** Forums allow you to interact with other inkFrog users. Online tutorials and e-mail assistance help you learn to use the tools and solve any problems that surface.

- **Pricing** Three pricing plans are available for inkFrog products. The Image Hosting Only plan is for people who use eBay's listing programs or a third-party lister and who only need image hosting. The cost for this service is $4.95 per month. The Premium plan includes image hosting of up to 400 images, My Lister provides for the use of prebuilt templates, or you create and save your own with Sonny. You can view and manage your current eBay listings, archive your auctions, and add images to existing auctions, but this plan does not offer scheduling and does not allow you to relist or resubmit your closed auctions. The cost for this plan is $7.95 per month. The Pro plan is for people who list 20 auctions a week or more. It offers image hosting of up to 1,000 images and use of the "image magician" tool; using it, you can schedule your auctions and bulk-list them at intervals, manage your closed auctions, automatically relist unsold auctions, and resubmit duplicate or edited closed auctions. It will also permit automatic winning-bidder e-mails, inventory tracking, and automatic feedback. This plan is $12.95 per month. Two plan add-ons can be added to both the Premium and Pro plans. The first is Gallery Showcase, which allows you to include the previewer in each of your current auctions so that customers can see your other items up for sale. This also includes a web page that shows all of your current auctions with a thumbnail picture next to each. This add-on is an extra $4.95 per month. The second add-on is inkFrog Checkout, which enables you to build a personalized checkout page for your buyers and allows them to pay immediately through PayPal or through other methods you approve. It lets you invoice, track, and monitor your sold auctions as well as send invoices and payment reminders to buyers. It is integrated with the USPS and UPS, and it has a feedback manager that lets you monitor your feedback and send feedback reminders, as well as leave feedback in bulk. The Checkout add-on costs an additional $2.95 per month.

■ **Further information** www.inkfrog.com.

» Marketworks

Marketworks claims to be the leading provider of online marketplace management software and services for high-volume eBay sellers. The company, whose home page is shown in Figure 4-10, is proud of the fact that they became one of the first companies to achieve the level of eBay Preferred Solutions Provider (PSP). They claim to have more than 100 eBay Shooting Stars as customers.

Not only does Marketworks target the top-tier eBay sellers, but they also offer services to Fortune 1000 companies including the Home Depot, Olympus cameras, and Disney Auctions LLC.

Marketworks

Soon after Marketworks was founded, they gathered a group of 28 of the top 50 eBay sellers to create their Founders Club. They used this group to determine some of the most important features and functionality now found in their product. They turned to experienced eBayers to base their offerings on what these pros needed and wanted in auction management tools.

FIGURE 4-10 The Marketworks home page features products for eBay PowerSellers and such giants of commerce as Toshiba and Home Depot.

- ■ **Program** Marketplace management software.
- ■ **Platform** Web-based.
- ■ **Listing capabilities** Marketworks offers single- and bulk-item launching, scheduled launching, and customizable templates for creating listings. Thumbnail ad previews are available for bulk listings, and one-click relaunching of unsold items is possible.

- **Image hosting**   You may choose from 100MB to 1,000MB of image hosting space. You can do bulk image uploads of up to 15 images at a time. Services also include automatic image resizing and thumbnail views.

- **Inventory management**   Marketworks includes database import utilities, bulk-inventory upload, customizable folder organization, an inventory monitor, and real-time sales activity.

- **E-mail handling**   Automated customer notifications that include winning-bidder notifications, item shipped, payment received, and thank you notification messages are possible with Marketworks.

- **Post-sale features**   Included in Marketworks post-sale features are Non-Paying Bidder notices, final value refund requests, and reciprocal feedback posting that automatically posts feedback once it's been left for you. Shipping label printing and automated invoicing with shipping and taxes calculated are also included.

- **Customer service/education**   Toll-free phone support, e-mail support, and online tutorials are available for helping you learn and navigate Marketworks.

- **Pricing**   You pay 2 percent of the closing price of each transaction that has a winning bidder. There's a $0.10 minimum and a $3.00 maximum for each successful listing. Marketworks also has minimum monthly charges of $14.95 for up to 100MB of image hosting; $24.95 for up to 250MB; $49.95 for up to 500MB; $99.95 for 1GB. If your total monthly transaction fees don't meet or exceed the monthly minimum service charge, you will be billed only the monthly fee and no per-listing fee.

- **Further information**   www.Marketworks.com.

» Vendio

Vendio (see Figure 4-11) is one of the largest third-party suppliers of seller services on eBay, enabling sales of $50 million of merchandise each month. They began in July 1998 under the name AuctionWatch, a message board for auction users. They

Vendio

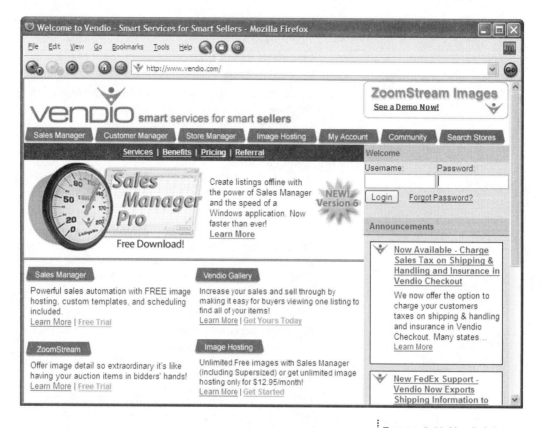

FIGURE 4-11 Vendio's home page features the company's Sales Manager Pro auction management software.

received funding from private investors that allowed them to enhance their message center and develop services including image hosting and auction launching. The company changed its name to Vendio Services, Inc., in 2003.

Vendio's web site features case studies of customers who use their services. These allow you to gain insight and experience from sellers who have gone ahead of you. Vendio also allows you to create and maintain your own online store directly on their web site. They've teamed with Froogle.com, Google's shopping search engine, so that items from Vendio stores will appear in the results of Froogle searches. Vendio claims to have nearly 100,000 successful merchants worldwide, nearly twice as many as any other service.

- **Program**   Vendio Services include Sales Manager (web-based) and Sales Manager Pro (desktop-based). Separate modules are available for e-mail management (Customer Manager).

- **Platform**   Web-based or desktop.

- **Listing capabilities**   Vendio offers automated auction scheduling and features a variety of templates.

- **Image hosting**   Free unlimited image hosting is included with your Vendio products. Vendio also offers a separate image-hosting-only service that is available on a flat fee or a per-image pay-as-you-go basis.

- **Inventory management**   Sales Manager Inventory is an inventory management service that allows you to track your inventory. You can designate your listing to be an inventory profile. This automatically tracks that item as it either moves out of your inventory when the sale is complete or remains in your inventory if the item doesn't sell. You can include UPC, SKU, or ISBN information for each inventory item if you choose, but these are not required fields for inventory tracking.

- **E-mail handling:** Vendio e-mail services include automated invoicing, Final Value Fee refunds, and Non-Paying Bidder alerts. Through the separate Customer Manager service, you can reduce e-mail management by 50 percent, according to the company. Customer Manager features response templates and built-in message filtering and prioritization. Customer Manager allows you to maintain a customer database. You can track your customers' histories to see how much and what they've bought from you. You can even track all the e-mail messages you've received from each customer. Every listing you close automatically gets imported into Customer Manager. Customer Manager pricing starts at $14.95 per month.

- **Post-sale features**   A post-sale link from Sales Manager takes you to the Post-Sale Summary home page. A row of action keys allows you to send winning-bidder notifications and reminders. You can mark an auction as paid, leave feedback and send a feedback reminder to your buyer, print invoices, and mark items shipped, to mention just a few of the actions possible from this page.

■ **Customer service/education**   Vendio Education Center offers Vendio users free online courses covering tips for using their various products. Also, you will find forums to discuss issues with other Vendio users. Two categories of courses include free courses and premium courses. The premium courses touch on subjects that people would be eager to spend money to learn about. For example, for $97 you can take a course about how to become an eBay PowerSeller.

■ **Pricing**   Pricing for Vendio products falls into two major categories: Flat Rate pricing or Variable Rate pricing. If the average selling price per listing is above $30, Vendio suggests you go with the Flat Rate pricing plan. For an average selling price of under $30, you're better off with the Variable Rate plan.

The Flat Rate Premium plan is recommended for sellers with fewer than 300 listings per month. For this plan, you'll pay $12.95 per month and $0.20 per listing. The Flat Rate Power plan is $39.95 per month and $0.10 per listing; it is recommended for sellers with more than 300 monthly listings.

The Variable Rate Power Plan, for sellers with 300 or more monthly listings, is $29.95 per month, and you pay a 1.25 percent Final Value Fee. You pay a maximum of $4.95 per item. The Variable Rate Premium Plan, for sellers with fewer than 300 listings per month, costs $12.95 per month, $0.05 per listing, and a 1 percent Final Value Fee with $4.95 maximum per item.

Vendio offers a pay-as-you-go plan and an annual listing plan. For more information about these programs, visit Vendio's web site.

All Sales Manager plans include

■ Support for eBay, eBay stores, and eBay Motors
■ Scheduled listings
■ Unlimited image hosting

■ Custom templates

■ "Branded" shopping-cart checkout

■ Non-Paying Bidder and Final Value Fee credit submittals

■ UPS, Fedex, and USPS integration

■ Bulk feedback submissions

■ **Further information**   www.vendio.com.

» Consider customized auction management software

Some PowerSellers have worked with software developers to create auction management software that is tailored to their own particular businesses. This ensures that the software they use can handle everything they need for it to do. It also allows them to design the program so that it works intuitively with the structure of their own operation.

One advantage to doing this is that once you incur the initial expense of developing the software there are no ongoing expenses—you don't have to pay monthly fees to an outside company. You may, however, have additional costs down the road as you revise your software to keep it current and in synch with the changes eBay rolls out. Plus, according to John Mueller, author of *Mining eBay Web Services* (Sybex, 2004), there's also some expense involved in having eBay certify your custom application, which must happen in order for you to use it.

There are companies that specialize in creating custom applications for eBay PowerSellers. To learn more, try plugging these search terms into Google: **eBay API custom "auction management"**. You may also consider hiring a recent college graduate for less than you'd have to pay an established company.

Finally, once you've got your customized auction management software up and running, you'll be able to decide if you want to sell it to other eBay sellers who are shopping for auction management software. You wouldn't be the first eBay PowerSeller to venture into the software market simply by having had the experience of developing an auction management program.

beer_auctions—Louis DiDona

Louis DiDona began selling through online auctions on America Online before there even was an eBay. He came to eBay in 1997 and specializes in Breweriana collectibles, which he both buys and sells. He sells other advertising memorabilia items as well. In addition, he is a Trading Assistant and does a great deal of his business on consignment.

Lou uses Seller's Assistant Pro (SAP) from eBay for his auction management software. He chose this product because he prefers a desktop solution to his auction management challenges. He says that the only real disadvantage of using a desktop tool is that you may not have easy access to your records when you travel. He works around that by using GoToMyPC.com. Once you download the software at this site, you can access your home computer from any remote location as long as you have Internet access. The advantage to using his own computer is that he never suffers any downtime, which is common for people who use web-based programs.

Using SAP, Lou keeps track of his sales, which range between $3,000 and $5,000 per month. He finds the program especially useful to track his consignment sales, because it has a built-in consignment feature that automatically tracks the commissions for each sale. He also appreciates the automatic sales tax feature. The program will automatically add 6 percent sales tax for his state to any item that is being shipped within the state, as well as create reports for filing.

Lou appreciates the reports he's able to get with SAP. He can print profit and loss reports that include his Final Value Fees, shipping costs, and inventory costs. SAP also allows him to do profit ratios. He can enter the costs of his items and then determine the margins he'll need for each sale. SAP also helps Lou manage his inventory. The software automatically tracks the remaining inventory Lou has after each sale. When he creates his auction listings in SAP, the program will not allow him to list an item that is no longer in stock. Finally, using SAP allows Lou to use eBay's own Checkout system, which is free. Other programs, including some of those featured in this chapter, charge for this service, as each part of the software requires a separate purchase.

Lou does use QuickBooks in addition to SAP. He uses QuickBooks to track his income and expenses, and to track all of the information he needs for filing his federal taxes. With QuickBooks he can print quarterly and year-end reports for tax purposes.

Lou recommends that the best way for you to learn to use an auction automation program is to just start using it. If you choose SAP, he recommends that you browse the message boards for help and suggestions. You'll find both there. "It takes a smart person to be a success on eBay," says Lou. That probably doesn't come as a surprise to you, but it shouldn't intimidate you either. People like Lou are there and willing to help.

Chapter 5

Get Your Auctions Going!

Congratulations, you're ready to start listing your auctions and earning some real money. You can be proud of yourself for all of the preliminary work that's brought you this far. You've researched your product line. You've got your "PowerShop" up and running. You've got enough inventory to get started, and you know where you can get more. Look at all you have accomplished. Now, let's make these auctions scream!

Chapter 5 will give you all of the ins and outs of listing your auctions. We know, you've created auction listings before, so you may be tempted to skip this chapter and move on to Chapter 6, where you'll learn to power-charge your eBay business. Please return to your seat and fasten your safety belt. You may have listed dozens of auctions already, but you haven't done it with the PowerSellers' secrets in mind. We'll skip the basics, but you've still got a lot to learn about choosing the best keywords for your titles, timing your auctions, writing strong descriptions, and strategically pricing your items.

Before we begin, here's a little word of warning. PowerSellers have very strong opinions. They didn't get to be successful without more than a little self-confidence. As you read this chapter, you'll see some conflicting tips. No, we haven't lost our minds by recommending one course of action in one tip and the opposite in the next. Different approaches work differently for PowerSellers, depending on such things as the items they handle and their personal preferences for how they operate their businesses. We decided to give you all of the options suggested to us and let you decide which of those options makes the most sense for your particular business. We're not trying to confuse you, just show you the many different ways there are to be successful eBay sellers.

Your eBay Image

The eBay world is only going to know you through the image you present. Your auction listings speak volumes about your competence as a seller. Your member profile is your permanent record, and precious as gold. Your customer service and shipping policies will be invaluable to keeping your eBay reputation solid. But, there are still some other things you can do to create the kind of eBay image that will keep customers coming back and earn you a respected place in the eBay community. When all of your communication is via your computer, it's important to consider your image every time you send an e-mail or write an item description.

Your About Me Page

People tend to shop more regularly with merchants they know and trust. Your every action on eBay will contribute to your being a trustworthy business owner, but you can help your customers get to know you very easily by creating an About Me page. You'll use this page to create a "face" that you want the eBay world to see, so get this up and running right from the start. If you already have one, you'll want to consider changing it to include some of the tips PowerSellers have shared with us. Editing your About Me page is relatively simple. You can either edit the HTML code that's behind your current page, or you can create an entirely new one. You learned about HTML in Chapter 4, so you're already equipped to make this decision. It's a good idea to check back in from time to time just to keep everything looking fresh and current.

» Include a picture on your About Me page. Show a little personality

Yes, your eBay business is serious, but here's a good place to let a little bit of the real you show. Remember, this is about image, and you want your customers to feel that they've learned a little bit about the person behind the auctions when they've read your About Me page. So, put a picture of yourself on the page. Don't hesitate to include some of your family members, pets, products, hobbies, or favorite possessions in the photo. Everyone loves a picture, and you become real to your customers through a visual image in a way that words simply can't match.

Have a little fun with the things you want customers to know about you. If you support a favorite cause, or if you have a special interest, tell the world about it. One seller included all of her pets as "employees" complete with descriptions of each one's job, personality, and special skills. The page was the subject of a discussion thread because it was so much fun to read. You don't have to go to quite this extreme, but reward your customers' curiosity by giving them something to smile about.

» Put your About Me page to work

Have some fun, but all play and no work isn't your goal. Make your About Me page earn its way. Use it to describe your business and products. Explain why you are the person your customers should trust. Toot your horn about your expertise and even give

Put your About Me page to work

them some information that will prove you know what you're doing. Figure 5-1 shows you the About Me page for PowerSeller Sharonscollectibles. You'll see why Sharon is someone with trustworthy collectibles knowledge and why her son Shane would know about medical supplies. Then you get to see Sharon and Shane together.

Your About Me page is also the place to clearly state your policies and terms. Be sure your customers know how you handle payments, shipping, and returns. That's not to say you won't have to deal with customers who will still claim not to know your terms, but at least you'll know you're doing everything you can to minimize misunderstandings.

Link your About Me page to your web site. You'll learn more about creating a web site and why you'll want to do that in Chapter 6, but when you do, be sure to add a link to your site from your About Me page. eBay does not permit you to link any of your auction listings to outside web sites, but you are allowed to include links to your favorite web sites within your About Me page. Just make your own web site one of your favorites.

Set Your Rules

Of course, you'll need to establish rules for operating your business. Only you can decide what payment options you'll consider (Chapter 7 will help), what your refund policies will be, how much time passes between the end of your auctions and the time you expect to be paid, and how you'll handle shipping your

FIGURE 5-1 PowerSellers Sharonscollectibles use their About Me page to give you good information and a little personality, too.

products. All of these things are up to you, and you are well within your rights to make rules that your customers are expected to follow and then stick to the rules. You'd be foolish not to do this. You're here to make a profit, and you have reason to protect your business with good business practices and policies. That said, here are some tips for striking a balance between letting your customers know the rules and sounding like a martinet.

» Decide on your rules and make them clear

You made sure your policies and procedures were clear on your About Me page, and you have room to state them in every auction listing, too. Not every buyer will bother checking out your About Me page, although we always do before we bid. You owe it to both yourself and your customers to be clear about how your business operates. For example, if you plan to hold shipment of an item for ten business days while a personal check clears—and you should in some cases—say so in your listing. If you offer a discount on shipping for multiple purchases, be clear about it. Your goal in every listing is to sell the item with a minimum of e-mail exchanged between you and the buyer and a minimum of room for misunderstanding. Don't hesitate to make rules you expect your buyers to shop by. Notice in Figure 5-2 that Bridewire is very clear about her return policy. Customers know right away how soon the merchandise must be returned and in what condition. They also know what the fees will be for returning the dress. At the same time, this PowerSeller makes sure her customers know that she understands how hard it is to buy a dress this way, and the whole tone of her statement says she's on the customer's side.

» Don't threaten. Don't scold. Keep it friendly.

With your rules in place, remember you set the tone for your business with words and pictures alone. No one can see the smile on your face as you share the rules with them. We've all had the experience of going into a shop owned by a crotchety character. You feel like that owner is just waiting for you to break something. Who wants to do business with someone who's just looking for an excuse to be ugly? Figure 5-3 shows

Don't threaten. Don't scold. Keep it friendly.

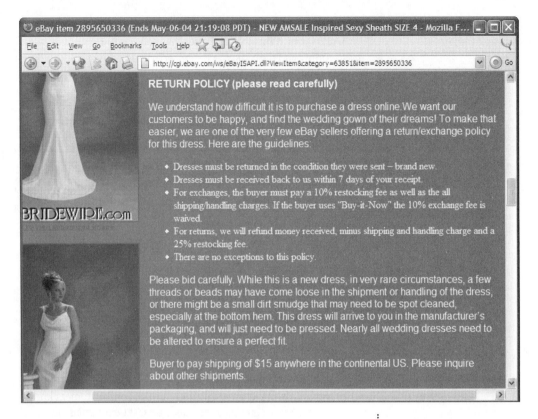

RETURN POLICY (please read carefully)

We understand how difficult it is to purchase a dress online. We want our customers to be happy, and find the wedding gown of their dreams! To make that easier, we are one of the very few eBay sellers offering a return/exchange policy for this dress. Here are the guidelines:

- Dresses must be returned in the condition they were sent – brand new.
- Dresses must be received back to us within 7 days of your receipt.
- For exchanges, the buyer must pay a 10% restocking fee as well as the all shipping/handling charges. If the buyer uses "Buy-it-Now" the 10% exchange fee is waived.
- For returns, we will refund money received, minus shipping and handling charge and a 25% restocking fee.
- There are no exceptions to this policy.

Please bid carefully. While this is a new dress, in very rare circumstances, a few threads or beads may have come loose in the shipment or handling of the dress, or there might be a small dirt smudge that may need to be spot cleaned, especially at the bottom hem. This dress will arrive to you in the manufacturer's packaging, and will just need to be pressed. Nearly all wedding dresses need to be altered to ensure a perfect fit.

Buyer to pay shipping of $15 anywhere in the continental US. Please inquire about other shipments.

FIGURE 5-2 PowerSeller Bridewire's policies are stated both clearly and in a friendly way.

an example of some reasonable policies set in an unpleasant tone. Here the seller is saying that the customer cannot ask for more specific details about measurements for a special event garment. Don't even bother to ask, because this seller won't open the manufacturer's packaging to answer the basic question. Which seller in these two examples would you rather buy your formal wear from?

Even if that's not your intention, words posted online can seem much harsher than you intend them to be. So, here are some things you might want to keep in mind:

- ■ **Don't threaten.** It sets a nasty tone. Don't say, "If you leave negative feedback for me, I'll leave negative feedback for you." That's too simplistic. You have a long way to go between a customer service problem

Don't threaten. Don't scold. Keep it friendly.

and a negative feedback, so don't make the leap before there's even a problem.

- **Don't scold.** Don't say things like, "non-paying bidders will be reported." Of course, you'll file a non-paying bidder report, but all of the people who plan to pay for their bids don't need to think of you as so eager to snap.

- **Don't yell.** Turn off the Caps Lock. Saying anything in all capital letters makes people online feel like you're yelling at them. If you want to say your item is FANTASTIC!, okay, use the capitals, but if you want to state a policy, set it off with a line space instead of yelling it at people.

FIGURE 5-3 This PowerSeller has the right to set these policies, but could be friendlier in presenting them to customers.

- **Don't use red type to state your policies.** It sets the wrong tone. If your goal is to make them pop, change the font or box them.

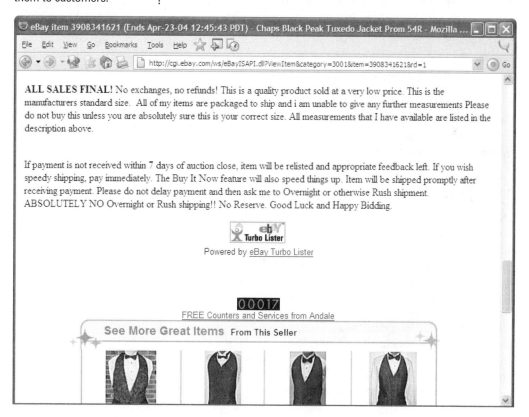

›› Make sure it's fun to shop with you

Don't underestimate the fun value of eBay. If it weren't fun to shop on eBay, 100 million people wouldn't be doing it. You want your customers to think that stopping by your auctions will be an enjoyable way to spend their time. If they don't, there are lots of other auctions they can explore instead. When you were a kid, didn't you love the shoe store that gave you a balloon with each purchase? Well, you don't have to give away a balloon, but you can set a friendly tone. And, if your customers return whenever they need the product you sell, so much the better. You can't actually smile at your customers as they walk through your door, but you can certainly make sure they think of you warmly. Wish them "Good Luck." Tell them "Happy Bidding." Thank them for stopping by your auction. Tell them you answer all e-mail inquiries. Make sure they know you're glad they're there.

You're One of the Crowd Now

Now that you've had some opportunity to think about and plan the face you'll show eBay, take it out for a test drive. We talked in Chapter 1 about becoming part of the eBay community, but it's hard to talk about your eBay image without revisiting the subject. You build your eBay image with every interaction you have on the service. Make yourself an active member of the community, and you'll reap benefits that far exceed the effort you will expend.

›› Spend time on the Q & A boards

The question and answer boards are fascinating places to explore. You will find Q & A boards for such a wide variety of subjects that your challenge will be to limit yourself to just a few or spend way too much time exploring everything. Figure 5-4 shows the opening screen of the Q & A boards. You can get here by choosing Talk from the eBay Community screen. Within the Talk section, the Answer Center is the last choice on the menu. These particular boards are deeply educational, because people come here with every type of question and problem you can imagine and many you can't even begin to imagine. With every question come answers that will lead you to ever more knowledge, facts, and understanding of eBay.

This is a good first stop if you're having a particular problem. For example, one day we were checking out auctions for a group of PowerSellers we'd been working with. Every username entered

FIGURE 5-4 The opening screen of eBay's Question and Answer boards

resulted in a response that said, "No auctions listed for this username." Now, since these are PowerSellers we were looking for, that seemed a little unlikely. Stopping by the Q & A boards revealed that many users were having trouble that day, both searching eBay and completing their listings. It took only a few minutes to realize the problem was not ours, and it was a little bigger than our individual frustration. That let us redirect our energies to other, more productive pursuits, and sure enough, the next morning, everything was back to normal.

You have other, even more self-serving reasons to make yourself a presence on the Q & A board. Every time you leave an answer—and trust us, you'll feel confident enough to do that very soon—you leave not only your username, but also a link that allows others to view your auctions. It's a great way to get traffic to your auctions, and if you participate in a friendly, helpful way, others are bound to be curious about what you do. They'll stop by to take a look. One PowerSeller who asked to remain anonymous says, "I try to spend at least three hours a week on the Q & A boards. It's time well spent."

» Don't be too quick to pick a fight

As you explore eBay with the mindset of someone aiming for PowerSeller status, you're likely to find other sellers who are violating eBay rules. Some of these sellers might even compete directly with you. If the violations are egregious, illegal, or directly harmful to your business, you'll have to take the problem to eBay. This is certainly the case for such serious violations as shill-bidding or providing links to off-eBay web sites within your auction. These actions potentially threaten the community at large, and as a good citizen of that community, you should act on them immediately. But, if the violations could possibly be accidental or simply based on a misunderstanding of eBay policy, don't be the first to go screaming to eBay about it. Whenever you report a violation against another seller to eBay, they not only explore the violation you're reporting, but they also take a look at all of your listings at the same time. That's only fair. After all, one competitor could make a claim against another just to cause trouble, so eBay is right to try to get a look at both sides of every story.

Take your concern to the Q & A board instead and ask other sellers for opinions about what you should do. Another solution in a case like this might be to contact the offending seller via e-mail and take care of it as one seller to another. Running to the teacher as a tattletale made us unpopular as kids, and it doesn't serve us well as eBayers either.

Your Listing Strategies

Your auction title, your description, and your photos combine to form each listing you will put on the eBay web site. We'll explore each of these facets of your listing in just a bit, but first let's cover some strategic issues that will affect all the listings you create. We'll strategize about some best practices before we get to the more specific aspects of creating listings. You'll have a good, solid background then for dealing with the details.

How Much Is This Going to Cost?

You already know that eBay charges everyone who lists an item for sale on the site. When you were selling a few items here and there, these fees were negligible. When you become a PowerSeller, that's no longer true. "I paid more than $10,000 last month in eBay fees," reported a PowerSeller from the western United States. Now, that, like having to pay a lot in income tax, is the kind of problem most of us would be happy to have. eBay fees are a fact of life. It's simply the cost of doing business, and you must consider it equivalent to the overhead expenses you would pay if you opened a brick-and-mortar store. In view of this comparison, it's certainly less expensive, but keeping track of your fees helps you set the price of your items and figure your profit margins when determining new products to introduce to your customers.

eBay's listing fees fall into two basic categories: Insertion Fees and Final Value Fees. Insertion Fees are based on the opening value of the item you list. You can see the cost of inserting an item in Figure 5-5. This fee is non-refundable, and you pay it even if your item doesn't sell. The other fee

FIGURE 5-5 eBay's Insertion Fees screen

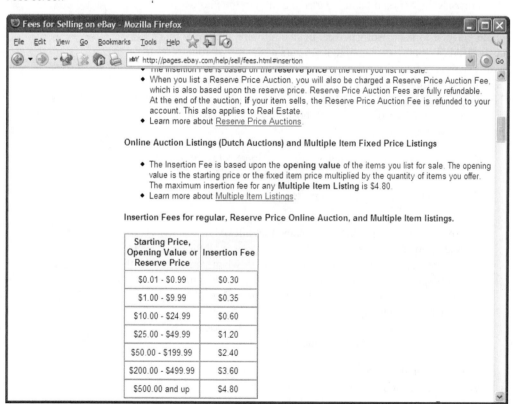

CHAPTER 5 • Get Your Auctions Going! **163**

Don't be too quick to pick a fight

is the Final Value Fee. This is a percentage of the final price your item brings when your auction ends. The Final Value Fee is based on a sliding scale, and here's how that works:

- If your item sells for $0 to $25, you pay 5.25 percent of the closing value.

- If your item sells for between $25 and $1,000, you pay 5.25 percent of the initial $25 (or $1.31) plus 2.75 percent of the remaining closing value balance ($25.01 to $1,000).

- If your item sells for over $1,000, you pay 5.25 percent of the initial $25, plus 2.75 percent of the amount between $25 and $1,000, plus 1.50 percent of the remaining value above $1,000.

In addition to these two basic listing fees, eBay charges for listing upgrades and for extra photos you add to your listings. We'll discuss the optional listing extras in a bit, but the photos are a necessary expense, so we'll cover them here. The first photo you add to your listing is free. Each additional picture costs $0.15. The preview photo that appears at the top of your listing is free, but it will be the same shot you use in the main part of your listing. Other photo options and their prices follow. These options are available to you only if you host your pictures directly on eBay rather than on a web hosting service such as those discussed in Chapter 3.

- You can create a slide show of up to six images that blink in succession, creating an animated effect for $0.75.

- You can supersize your images to up to 800×600 pixels for $0.75 each.

- You can choose the Picture Package that allows you to add up to six pictures to your listing, supersize all the pictures, and display a photo in the gallery when your listing pops up in the search results screen for a single price of $1.00, as opposed to buying each of these features individually for the cost of $1.75. (Note that for supersizing to work, pictures must be at least 440×330 pixels when uploaded.)

For a complete list of all of eBay's current fees, go to http://pages.ebay.com/help/sell/questions/seller-fees.html.

» Watch for eBay listing sales

eBay periodically offers listing sales. These sales may be for reduced rates for whole listings or for reduced rates for special features added to your listings. Watch for the announcements of these special sales events. Signing up for eBay's Newsflash newsletter, discussed in Chapter 1, will allow you to receive advanced notification of these special listing days.

eBay doesn't usually give you much advance warning. Generally, the offers last for just a very short time, between one and three days. Be prepared to work overtime to take advantage of them. Also, be prepared to have some technical challenges, because the volume of new listings on these days often makes eBay quirky, and it slows the whole system down.

Appearance, Appearance, Appearance

It may be location in the world of brick-and-mortar stores, but on eBay, it's the appearance of your listings and how well your items are featured in those listings. You're working now to build a professional business image, so we're going to help you put the garage-sale approach behind you. It may work to slap up a card table in your driveway and dump the kids' outgrown snow boots to a neighborhood family with kids just a little younger. But you're not in the garage sale world anymore, so let's look at your listings the way you'd look at the display strategies of your favorite store in the world.

» Neatness counts

Your mother was right about this one. Neatness really matters to your listings. Here are some points that can make your listings speak well for you from the very beginning. You'll be doing all the work to create the listings anyway, so you might as well maximize their effectiveness by considering these PowerSeller-proven bits of advice.

- Listings should be well organized so that all of the information is clear to see.
- They should be clean without a lot of extras that can distract your buyer.

Neatness counts

- They should be complete so that all of the relevant information about size, color, material, condition, and use are easy to find.

- They should be professional so that your buyer can trust he's found a competent eBay seller. That means they should not have a single typo or misspelled word. Be certain of this.

- They should include some details such as border, background color, or a small icon you create to remind shoppers you're an established seller who can be trusted to have long-term eBay goals.

You can see an example of a well-produced and professional-looking listing in Figure 5-6. Professional doesn't mean stuffy or stodgy. This listing is quite pleasant and appealing to the eye. It includes a quick list on the left to detail the specifications of the

FIGURE 5-6 A clear, professional, and attractive listing

item. It includes the background information about the crafter who made it on the right. Then it adds a little personality about who might like this. The rest of the listing that follows is full of details about shopping with this PowerSeller, including payment options, shipping details, and customer service policies. As a buyer, you will view this listing and feel confident that you know all you need to know about this particular item. The seller has also made it clear what doing business together will be like. You can feel secure that you have little to risk here.

» Don't be too cute

Clever, yes; cute, no. You want to appear smart, clever, competent, and capable. But, you don't want to cross the line into cute, and please, we're begging you, guard yourself at all costs from cutesy! Suppose you decide to sell teddy bears. You get the sweet idea of adding background music to your listings; the Teddy Bears' Picnic seems a good choice. Now, I'll be the shopper who has a houseful of teddy bears and still can't get enough. I know every teddy bear seller on eBay, so I'm thrilled to see you sign on. The first time I stop in to look at your listings, I may very well think, oh how cute. This person knows her way around a computer. How clever to have added this little bit of music to her listing. The next time I stop in, I'll notice it, but not be surprised. The third time, it's going to start bugging me. It won't take me too long to decide that I just can't stand that stupid song one more time, so I'll go back to all the other people who sell teddy bears on eBay.

Now, maybe you were never thinking of adding music to your listings anyway, but what about a little flashy character who runs back and forth across the screen? Or maybe a scrolling text line that does the same. Stop and reconsider. Your goal here is to get people to stop in to view your auctions frequently. You want them not only to check one auction out, but be willing to browse your other auctions too. What seems cute to you on one listing can very quickly grate on the nerves of someone who wants to follow your auctions several times during the week and track your inventory regularly. Especially since this buyer is going to many auctions as part of her eBay shopping trip.

Aside from distracting and, worse, annoying your customers, these extras work against you in another way. Consider the many eBay members who still use dial-up services rather than

Don't list more auctions than you can process

broadband. All of these extras slow down how quickly your auctions will load. Many online shoppers simply won't wait. They'll move on to the next listing instead. Don't give shoppers any reason to close out their screens on your auctions. Don't give them any reason to choose one of your competitors over you.

›› Don't list more auctions than you can process

Sure, you want to list and list and list so that you can sell and sell and sell, but let's not get ahead of ourselves here. There's more to your eBay business than just listing items for sale. Every item that sells requires multiple e-mail interactions, payment issues, packaging, and shipping. You don't want to get so far ahead of yourself that you're not able to process your orders in a timely manner that will lead to positive feedback. (Remember, that goal is just as important at this early stage as earning money is.) Pace your listings so that you can manage the workflow.

When handling auctions manually, three to five auctions per day are manageable for a seller working alone. At seven, it starts to get stressful, and ten is stretching the capabilities of the average seller, recommends Nick Sevino, a PowerSeller who writes for AuctionBytes under this pseudonym. Remember, it's not just the listing, it's also the order processing, the payment, the packing, the shipping, and all those e-mails. Before you get to the breaking point, you'll need to enlist help or move to an automated auction management system as discussed in Chapter 4.

›› Automate from the start

In Chapter 4 you learned all about auction automation software and why you must use it to become a PowerSeller. By now, we hope you've decided on your favorite and are familiar with all of its features. Good. Now, work to automate absolutely everything you do from the very start of your business. Every keystroke you can enter once and use multiple times builds your business. Every template that you can design to get your information where it needs to be is money in the bank. It does not take anything away from the look of your listings to use automation. Take a look at Figure 5-7 to see a great example of an automated listing. This PowerSeller, Shoetime, had more than 1,900 items listed the day we took this screenshot. Notice the grid that gives all of the information you'd need to know

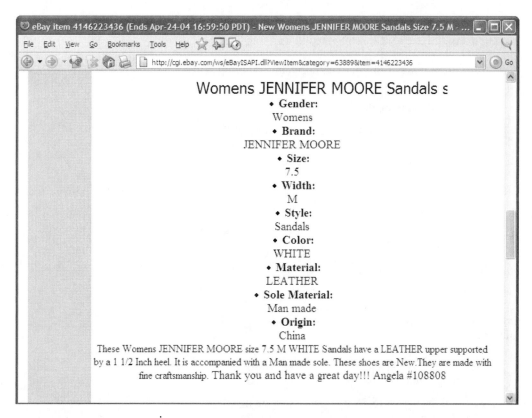

FIGURE 5-7 An excellent example of a listing created using an automated system

before buying these shoes. That grid doesn't change from listing to listing, only the item-specific information that gets input for each pair of shoes changes.

Other types of information perfect for automating include payment options, shipping information, and customer service policies. Even if you're just using eBay's own Sell Your Item screen, it's easy enough to store this basic material as templates that load into each listing you create. Not only does this save you time and keystrokes, but it makes it possible for you to control your spelling and grammar. You input it once, make sure it's perfect, and use it over and over again.

» eBay automates some listings for you

eBay's new Pre-filled Item Information option is an incredible timesaver, and therefore, a money maker too. You can use this feature to speed-list books, movies, music, video games, digital

eBay automates some listings for you

cameras, PDAs, and cell phones. Let's use a sample book listing for comparison. Here's what listing the old way was like:

1. Scan the cover (2 to 5 minutes depending on equipment).

2. Laboriously fill in eBay's forms to select the right category and write the title (2 minutes).

3. Review the book carefully. Find the specs (e.g., page count, author, edition) and selling points (description, reviewers' comments). Note the condition. Draft and then polish your copy so that you will have the most compelling description possible. Carefully enter all that information into the form (15 minutes).

4. Review your pricing, payment, and shipping information (1 minute).

5. Sign off on the listing, and have eBay post it (1 minute).

6. Total time: 20+ minutes per listing.

Now, here's what that same process is like using the new automation from eBay:

1. Choose your category (books) and subcategory (1 to 2 minutes).

2. Fill in the book's ISBN number (easily found on the back cover, or on the copyright page) (1 minute).

3. Indicate whether your item is new or used.

4. Watch in amazement as eBay automatically fills in a stock photo of the book, a complete description including loads of great cover copy, and details including year published, edition, author, reviews if available, and much more (1 minute).

5. Check your shipping information and pricing (1 minute).

6. Sign off on the listing, and have eBay post it (1 minute).

7. Gloat at how smart you are (varies with the person).

8. Total time: 5 minutes per listing.

Even if you're a speed typist with fast scanning equipment, and professional copywriting skills, using Pre-filled Item Information saves 50 to 75 percent of your listing time. And in the end, the

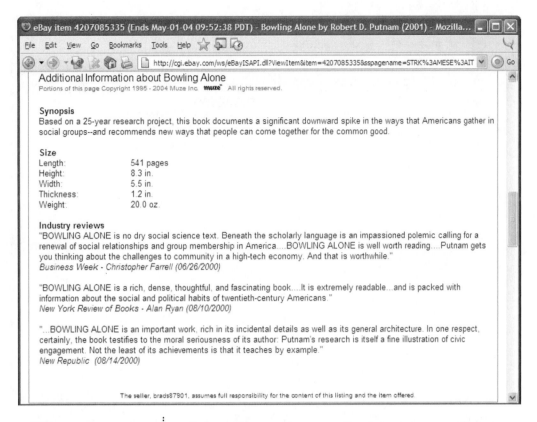

FIGURE 5-8 A listing created with eBay's Pre-filled Item Information option

listing will be much more complete than one you were likely to create. Figure 5-8 shows you one of our listings created using this new eBay feature. Aren't computers wonderful?

For movies and the other items for which you can use this option, you may need to enter other information such as the UPC code or the title. But the result is the same.

This listing option appears on the regular "Sell Your Item" screen, if you've previously indicated you're listing a book, DVD, or other item for which this feature is available. You'll see you now have two choices. These are

- List with Pre-filled Item Information
- List the Standard Way

As Figure 5-9 shows, because "Books" was chosen prior to this screen as the selling category, the screen includes an explanation of ISBNs, and where to find them on books.

eBay automates some listings for you

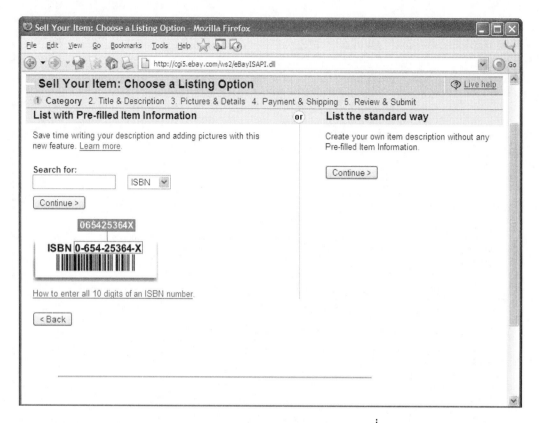

Just a reminder: The feature cannot fill in detailed product condition for you. You select either New or Used from the pull-down menu. Those choices might be okay in many cases, but other times you'll want to provide more detail (e.g., used, but only read once, with a flawless dust jacket). Also, be sure to check the pre–filled-in information, as on rare occasions details such as publication date may be off.

But don't let these concerns keep you from trying this feature. You're guaranteed to love it. And, if in using the pre-filled form you find that for some reason your book, movie, etc., is not included in eBay's database, you can always list it "the old way." But you'll miss the speed of the new system big time.

FIGURE 5-9 eBay's Pre-filled Item Information option makes it easy to find the information you need to complete your listings.

Grading and Placing Your Items

With an understanding of some good practices in creating your listings, we're still not ready to study a listing by examining its three parts: title, description, and photo. There are yet two details to consider before we get started. These two have as much to do with what you're selling as they do with how you list them. You must grade your item to give your customers a clear idea of what condition it's in. That might be as easy as saying it's new, but in most cases that's not enough. You must also choose under which category your item will appear. That's a lot more complicated than you might first think, and making the right choice here definitely affects the success of your listing.

» Grade your item below what you think it's worth

Depending on the items you'll sell, grading an item can be very simple or simply impossible. If you're dealing in new merchandise, you have no worries. Everything you sell can be listed as new, in manufacturer's packaging, or new with tags. Problem solved, skip to the next paragraph. If you, like most PowerSellers, sell a combination of new and used items, you'll need to think this through a little more carefully.

Grading items for sale is purely subjective. What looks like excellent condition to one may be very good condition to another. "Always err on the side of a lesser value," says Carrocel-restorations, a dealer and restorer of fine antique furniture. "Grade them lower than you think they really are," agreed Wegotthebeats, a CD seller. Both of these PowerSellers say it's better for your customer to get something and be delighted that it's better than they expected, than it is to get it and be disappointed. This may seem counter-intuitive. It may seem you should be proud of your items and try to get the most you can for them. Won't you get a lesser bid if your excellent item is listed as very good? You'll soon see how to use photos and descriptions to make your customers want your items. Giving them the thrill of receiving something that's even better than they thought it was going to be, turns a one-time shopper into a return customer and, hopefully, a customer who thinks of you first whenever he's shopping for your type of item.

There is an exception to this grade-your-item-lesser-rule. That is if your item has been objectively graded by a third party. Items like this might include fine jewelry and art. For example, if you deal in comic books, you know about a company that is well known and respected in the comic book industry, Comics

Grade your item below what you think it's worth

Guaranty, LLC (CGC). For a fee, CGC will professionally grade your comic book and check to see if it's been restored. They will then seal it between two slabs of acrylic, adding the grade and other details (e.g., off-white pages) on its official label. As long as the seal is in place, that comic book is guaranteed to be accurately graded by the well-established grading system CGC uses. It's an industry standard and widely respected among comic book collectors and dealers. In selling rare comics, there is a great price difference between a book rated Good and one rated Fine. If your comic has been objectively graded as Fine, there's no reason to list it as graded lesser than that.

Generally, without a guarantee from an objective third party, as long as you are the only one making the decision, you should stick with a lesser grade for your item. (We say "generally," because other areas such as coins, stamps, and trading cards have established grading standards commonly used by experienced collectors. If these are adhered to very closely, they can approach the legitimacy of a third-party grader.) That means, you'll never use "mint" condition, if the item has been opened even once. Mint would mean this product is now exactly as it was when it came from the manufacturer. Mint condition becomes "excellent" or even "excellent condition, never used." But, only if you're certain that it's never been used. If you can't vouch for that without a doubt, stick with excellent condition.

Choose Your Category

Choosing the right category for your item is like finding the right spot for it on a shelf in a brick-and-mortar store. eBay offers you hundreds of categories to choose from. When you consider all of the subcategories that fall within these main categories, you'll see how challenging this decision can be. It is an important decision, too. Your goal in placing your item in the correct category is to increase the traffic to your auction and thereby increase the likelihood that your auction will receive bids. Placing your item correctly can mean you'll get enough traffic to really start a bidding contest, and that can drastically affect your final price. On the other hand, if you misplace your item, you are likely to miss potential customers, and maybe not receive any bids at all. And intentionally putting your item in the wrong category to increase its exposure violates eBay rules.

Fortunately, choosing the right category is a manageable task, with a little help from the PowerSellers, and a lot of research.

» Know the categories

Your first job is to browse the categories so that you can become familiar with your choices. Clicking the Browse button from any eBay screen brings up the main categories. If you scroll to the bottom of this list, you'll see the choice See All Categories. Click this link and you'll see a much more detailed list of the categories. Figure 5-10 shows part of the list of thousands of different categories and subcategories. Be sure you've chosen the feature Show Number Of Items In Category. This will let you see which areas have the most listings.

Now you can study the different subcategories and select the one that seems most suitable for your item. Base this selection on which subcategories get the most action. A PowerSeller, who is

FIGURE 5-10 A partial glimpse of the All Categories screen that lets you see eBay's categories and the number of items in each category

Search for your item across categories

also an eBay educator, says this is the best strategy because it increases the likelihood that shoppers will see your auction. Any subcategory that has more than about 4,000 items is active. If you get above 10,000, you are in very popular territory.

Don't hesitate to place your items in very competitive categories. Those are the categories that are getting the most action, and the most shoppers. Place your item in an inactive category only if it's very specific and meant for a very targeted audience.

» Search for your item across categories

Once you're familiar with the different categories, determine which ones might be right for your item and then study which of those different categories seems to be the most profitable. Now you'll see exactly what your competition is. You will also see where other sellers have decided to place items similar to yours, and you'll have the opportunity to check out competitive listings. The best way to do this is to, once again, search completed auctions for items similar to yours. Sort them by highest price, and check on the different categories other sellers used to place the items. Place your items in categories that brought the most money and had the most activity.

Listing Extras

Are listing upgrades worth it? Before we attempt to answer that question, let's review the available upgrades. As Figure 5-11 shows, you can upgrade your listing by spending anywhere from an extra $0.05 for adding the "Buy it Now" designation, to $79.95 for having two or more of your listings rotate on and off eBay's Home page. (They cycle on and off. They don't remain there as a banner ad would.)

eBay reports that the following upgrades will boost your sales, or increase your bids by the amount shown.

- **Bolding and Highlighting** When your item appears as part of a list within search results, you can make yours stand out by bolding it ($1.00), or highlighting it via a colored band ($5.00). This increases the final price by 7 percent for bolding and 15 percent for highlighting.

- **Gallery Picture** For $0.25, this adds a thumbnail photo (usually the first photo you upload as part of your

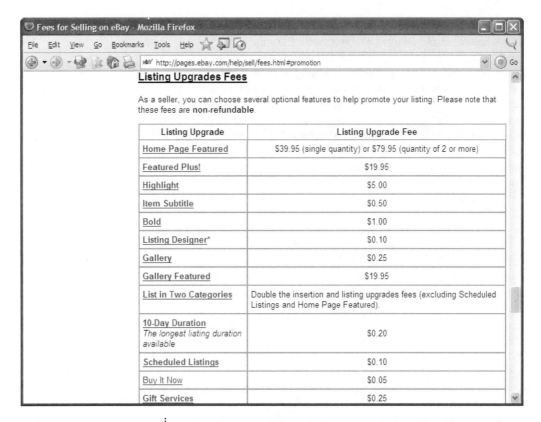

Listing Upgrades Fees

As a seller, you can choose several optional features to help promote your listing. Please note that these fees are **non-refundable**.

Listing Upgrade	Listing Upgrade Fee
Home Page Featured	$39.95 (single quantity) or $79.95 (quantity of 2 or more)
Featured Plus!	$19.95
Highlight	$5.00
Item Subtitle	$0.50
Bold	$1.00
Listing Designer*	$0.10
Gallery	$0.25
Gallery Featured	$19.95
List in Two Categories	Double the insertion and listing upgrades fees (excluding Scheduled Listings and Home Page Featured).
10-Day Duration *The longest listing duration available*	$0.20
Scheduled Listings	$0.10
Buy It Now	$0.05
Gift Services	$0.25

FIGURE 5-11 eBay's Listing Upgrades Fees screen

listing) next to your item title as it appears in searches and listings. It increases the final price by 11 percent.

- **Featured Plus!** For $19.95, this places your listing in the top Featured area of search and listing results. This means when buyers search for a particular item, yours appears before all the regular (non-featured) items. It increases the final price by 76 percent, the number of bids by 69 percent, and your chance of selling your item by 23 percent.

- **Home Page Featured** For $39.95 for one listing or $79.95 for two or more, this places your item in the Featured area of eBay's Home page, on a rotating basis. It increases bids by 58 percent.

 There are no statistics yet regarding the effectiveness of adding subtitles, a promising new listing enhancement. The addition of a subtitle costs $0.50.

Search for your item across categories

Now we'll offer you the necessary caveats. The percentages eBay cites are based on only one month's sales (for most of the percentages just cited, that's January 2004). So, as the mutual fund companies would say, past performance is no guarantee of future results. eBay's own lawyers say it this way: *No representation is made that a seller's final price, bids, and conversion rate on a specific item will increase by the average percentages noted above.* What about the priciest upgrade of all, the Home Page Featured placement? eBay doesn't guarantee where your item will appear on its Home Page, or even that it will appear for certain on its Home Page. It may wind up on the main Browse page instead. Further, there is no guarantee when your item will rotate on and off the Home Page. That could very well happen in the middle of the night when few people are there to view it.

Now, back to our original question. Are these upgrades worth the money? Knowing their costs and what eBay has to say about their results, start by looking at listings in a category that interests you. See if the bold ones, for example, really do catch your eye more. Try keeping track of some by bookmarking them, or adding them to the items you're watching through your My eBay page. Check to see if they really do have more bids or higher current prices, thereby justifying their cost. And once again, review Completed Listings for insights. The upgrades such as bolding and highlighting still appear for these auctions, so you can gauge their effectiveness. You'll have to go by the information eBay provides for the Home Page featured items, as there is no way for you to check on those as completed auctions.

PowerSellers who list hundreds, if not thousands, of items per month pay steep eBay fees to begin with. They are reluctant to add to their costs by upgrading their listings. That's understandable. Adding something as simple as bolding will add $1.00 to each listing. Multiply that by 100 or 1,000 and, well, you get the point. But if you list only a few items and you have starting prices of $50 or greater, try gallery view, bolding, or highlighting and test these yourself. Run similar listings at the same time without the features and see how they compare. "Adding bolding or highlighting does seem to increase the traffic to a listing, but I wouldn't use it if the item was worth less than $50," said one PowerSeller who asked not to be named.

Creating Your Listings

Now that we've explored the strategies behind creating your listings, you're ready to get on with the real work. Your title, description, and photos will combine to place you among all of the other eBay sellers, and we'll help you see how to make yourself stand out. Each of these three elements plays a vital role in selling your products. We'll help you understand the purpose of each part of the listing at the same time you learn great ways to distinguish yourself and your products.

Titling Your Listings

People are not likely to ever see your auctions if you don't title them properly. All of the work you do to take your photos and describe your item will go for nothing, if shoppers don't find your listings. The most likely way for them to find you is through the eBay Search feature. Sure, in the recent section devoted to choosing a category, we focused on eBay's Browse features, but although browsing was a great way for you to learn about the different eBay categories, it is not the most popular way for users to find what they're looking for on eBay. It's just too time consuming.

Most eBay shoppers use the Search feature and look for specific items. The default for this search is a Titles Only search. It is possible for shoppers to specify the search is to include title *and* description, but many won't do that if it's likely it would yield an unmanageable number of auctions to review. So, if you want your item to come up in the search results of your prospective customers, you have to carefully consider what words to use to create your most searchable titles.

eBay's search engine is really quite a simple one. You enter certain keywords and it spits back the listings that include those keywords in their titles. Unlike some more sophisticated search engines, eBay's does not try to match your requested keywords with others that might also be similar. There's no "artificial intelligence" at play here. It's up to you! Your results will reflect only the keywords you specify. The secret to creating keywords that will pull up your auctions is to think like a buyer. What kinds of words would a buyer use to find the item you sell? When you can adequately answer this question, we can start working with the reality that you'll get only 55 characters to use in your title. We're going to set out to get you the proverbial bang-for-the-buck, and we've got some ideas that will make that happen.

» Turn the key with your keywords

To determine which keywords to include in your title, put your buyer's cap on. Ask yourself, if I wanted this, how would I search for it? When you have a few ideas in mind, let's go back to the seller's side of the equation. (You can leave the buyer's cap on if you like it!) Do some searches with the words you've come up with and see what you get. How close to your item have you come with the words you first thought to try? How can you alter those words to get even closer?

Once you start getting results that look like the item you're selling, take some time to go back to those completed listing searches. Use the completed listings to see which items sold for the most and which auctions generated the most bids. (Or again, for a full picture, toggle back and forth between current and completed listings from any search.) Check the bottom of the listing pages to see if the seller included a counter. This is a great way to judge how many people stopped by to take a look. At this early stage, you aren't considering any of the other aspects of these listings. You are thinking of just the keywords. It won't take you long to determine which keywords were effective in getting people to stop by for a look.

» Don't confuse keywords with adjectives

It's very easy to think of snappy words that you'd like to include in your auction titles; fantastic, beautiful, one-of-a-kind, for example. But let's work on the distinction between a keyword and an adjective. A keyword might be a good adjective, but not all adjectives are good keywords. Some keywords have to be nouns. Where should you start? Let's start, as always, by exploring listings already up on eBay.

Let's begin with "shoes," a respectable keyword. If you enter a title search for shoes, you'll get so many responses that the search won't be useful to you. Our attempt brought more than 90,000 responses, far too many for us to deal with. So we'll add an adjective. Let's choose "women's." "Women's shoes" will still get you way too many hits, but we're down to just over 12,600 pairs of shoes, so it's getting a little better. Now, let's move to a more specific adjective and indicate size. The next title search will be for "women's shoes 7." Ahh, now we have only 2,774 possible matches to our search. Let's think how else we can distinguish the pair we're looking for. Let's think clogs (hey, I'm co-authoring the book, and they're my favorites). Now, we'll search "women's shoes 7 clogs" for a result of 89 pairs. To distinguish this search even more, let's enter a particular brand of clogs, Born. Okay, now our search is for "women's shoes 7 clogs Born" and we get 9 matching results. Now we can look at each individual title and choose a pair. Oh sorry, back to work. Let's look at the words we chose to get us this far.

"Shoes" turned out to be an ineffective keyword. We can eliminate it by choosing to do our search in the category of Clothing, Shoes, and Accessories. So, let's eliminate it. If we searched for just "clogs," we'd get some cute little ones for kids, and some very large ones for men, so "women's" is an effective choice. The size kept us from wading through items that wouldn't fit, and specifying our favorite brand increased the chances we'd see something we like.

So, if you wanted to sell a pair of size 7 Born clogs, you can clearly see which words are worthy of your precious limited title space. By narrowing down the keywords to just a few, you have some room left for descriptive adjectives. Always choose your keywords first and then add the descriptors as space allows. No buyer is going to enter as a keyword "new" and hit the shoes category. When we did that, we got more than 38,000 items of every type. New is important information to a buyer, but only after that buyer has found the kind of product she's looking for. So, using our example, let's add some good descriptors.

Your basic title for this item would start "Women's Seven 7 clogs Born." (By including the number as a numeral *and* spelled out you can account for both methods of searching.) Someone shopping for a pair of clogs would get this result even without the word Born. But someone who was only shopping for Born clogs wouldn't miss it because you've included the manufacturer's name. The manufacturer's name is a very important descriptive keyword. You could also add the color of the clog, or any distinctive features such as buckles, suede, buck, or trim.

Think also of other words that your buyer may use to describe the item. For example, some shoppers might think of "clogs" as a type of "mule" or even a "slide." If room allows, include these keywords also, not because you think of the shoes that way, but because one of your customers might. In that respect, they are actually more important keywords than adjectives such as black or brown. This is the case even though, from your point of view, they aren't that descriptive of this particular pair of shoes.

Remember when titling, keywords are your hook. Adjectives and descriptors are nice, but only after your hooks are as sharp as you can make them.

» Don't let your titles L@@K like this!

Surprisingly, a search for L@@K brought more than 75,000 results. Many of them were for expensive cars, real estate, and other fine items. This is a ridiculous convention and uniformly scorned by PowerSellers. It looks cheesy, and it suggests that you couldn't think of anything more valuable to do with the precious 55 characters you had to work with. It reminds buyers of walking down the main row of carnival hawkers at the last carnival they attended. It might be fun for a warm summer evening, but it doesn't serve you well on your way to PowerSeller status. You've got other, better ways to attract attention to your auctions, mostly through careful planning, careful placement, and careful titling techniques. Please, we're begging you, as one of our readers, don't create even one auction that includes this feature.

» Don't be redundant and repeat yourself

To help make every one of those 55 characters count, keep careful check on your redundancies. For example, don't use "antique" and "old." By definition, antique is old. If you're not really sure it's antique (generally considered 100 years old), then just call it old. You'll use the description to make it clear just how old this item is. Old comes in handy when you're dealing with items that have been reproduced. For example, FiestaWare dishes are highly collectible from the 1930s through the 1950s. They were reissued in the 1990s and grew to be very popular again. If you have the older ones for sale, by all means, title them old to distinguish them from the reproductions that are now much more prevalent and less expensive.

Avoid "rare" as a descriptor. It wastes space, and it also can backfire against you. It may be rare in your neck of the woods, or it may seem rare because you haven't seen many. But eBay shoppers come from all over, and in some other areas, it may not be rare at all. If it's not rare and you say it is, you lose your credibility. If it is rare, your buyers will know about it. It's not worth any of your 55 characters.

"Vintage" is another one that you can skip. It means something different to just about everyone who uses it. It simply has no bang for the seven characters it takes away from your title.

» Ways to get around that 55 limit

It may seem like 55 characters is a lot. For our example of the Born clogs, it was perfectly adequate. But, what if you're selling books? Some titles take up almost that many characters and will leave you very little room for other types of information, such as condition, edition, dust jacket. As with everything else, titling your items will depend largely on what it is you're selling. Fortunately, eBay and its users have come up with some handy acronyms. They create a shorthand language that lets you add valuable details to your titles without chewing up too much of your 55 character limit. The list that follows gives you just an example of some of the most common ones:

- **BIN**   Buy it now
- **COA**   Certificate of authenticity
- **COL**   Collection
- **GBP**   Great Britain Pounds
- **HTF**   Hard to find
- **LTD**   Limited edition
- **MIB**   Mint in box
- **MIJ**   Made in Japan
- **MOC**   Mint on card
- **NBW**   Never been worn
- **NIB**   New in box
- **NM**   Near mint
- **NOS**   New old stock
- **NR**   No reserve
- **NWOT**   New without tags

- ■ **NWT** New with tags
- ■ **OEM** Original equipment manufacturer
- ■ **OOAK** One of a kind
- ■ **SH** Shipping and handling
- ■ **VHTF** Very hard to find

This list, of course, is by no means complete. There are many acronyms unique or commonly used within particular categories. Book auctions, for example, may well include these additional acronyms:

- ■ **1st** First edition
- ■ **ANTH** Anthology
- ■ **AUTO** Autographed
- ■ **BOMC** Book of the Month Club edition
- ■ **EXLIB** Ex library book
- ■ **HB** Hardbound
- ■ **HB/DJ** Hardbound book with dust jacket
- ■ **HIST** Historical
- ■ **NC** No cover
- ■ **OOP** Out of print
- ■ **PB** Paperback

For more information on acronyms commonly used on eBay, go to the Community Frequently Used Terms page at http://pages.ebay.com/help/basics/community-terms.html.

» Make your titles precise and perfect

Deb's dad was an air traffic controller. He was very serious about precision in language, because he said when directing air traffic, imprecise language could lead to tragedy. She learned as a small kid never to ask, "Do you know what time it is?" That would elicit a yes or no answer, depending on whether he was wearing a watch or standing near a clock. Then would come the lesson entitled, "Mean what you say and say what you mean." Dad could have had no way to know how relevant this advice is for titling eBay auctions.

Make your titles precise and perfect

As you know, the search engine eBay uses does not have any artificial intelligence capabilities, so it can't make any assumptions about what you mean. While eBay is rolling out some functionality to address common misspellings, for now it will only return your search results to you exactly as you enter your keywords. When creating your titles, don't allow any accidental misspellings, because if you do, you will be left out of all searches for the item you are selling. For example, if a typo lists your Sassoon hairdryer as a Sasson hairdryer, you are out of luck. Your only hope is that someone else will make the same typo and accidentally find your hairdryer in a field of one. In that case, you won't have much competition, but more likely, your item will go unsold.

On the other hand, when titling your auctions, it's smart to consider misspellings and typos the average buyer might make. Purposely include those in your title along with the correct spellings, and you'll scoop up more buyers than your less savvy competitors. Here are two common examples: Little Tikes is a line of popular and durable children's toys. If you are listing a Little Tikes items, write the title like this, "Little Tikes/Tykes sand toys." That way, the common mistake of calling the company Little Tykes is already accounted for in your title. Or if you are selling a Canon camera, include "Cannon" in the title. You know it's wrong, but the search engine will still pop up your listing for the customer who just happened to make a mistake.

Writing Your Item Descriptions

After you've decided on your best title, it's time to work on the item description. This vital element of your eBay listing not only contributes directly to how well your item sells, but it also goes a long way to determining how smoothly your eBay business operates. Your goal with every description is to provide your customers with enough information about the product to make them decide they want to buy it. You want to be clear about all of the item's features and characteristics, and you want to give your customers all of the information they'll need to complete the transaction with you. Ideally, your customers will be able to read your listing and complete the transaction without any further communication. Cutting down on the time you need to respond to e-mail gives you more time to work on listing, processing your orders, and shipping. Realistically, you'll still get lots of e-mail questions from your customers. The number of people who don't actually read your entire listing but then send you e-mail asking you for information you know you've included may surprise you. You have no choice but to smile to yourself and answer politely, but making your listings complete can help reduce the number of these e-mails, even if it won't eliminate them.

» Use templates if you can

Just because you have to create item descriptions, that doesn't mean you have to write each one individually, starting fresh each time. If you are selling repeatable items, for example shoes, clothes, or CDs, create a template that will allow you to fill in the item fields for each listing. Figure 5-12 shows another Bridewire listing. Because this PowerSeller sells 100 wedding dresses a week, she couldn't possibly write new copy for each listing. Instead, she has created a template that allows her to input specifics for each dress by using single-word descriptors. In addition, she has created paragraphs that relate specifically to this group of gowns, explaining where she purchased them and giving some background detail about the manufacturer. Further down the listing, but not featured in Figure 5-12, is a sizing grid that will let the shopper estimate her correct size. This is also repeatable from listing to listing. As you can see, this PowerSeller provides great amounts of information without the need to keystroke hundreds of individual listings.

FIGURE 5-12 These two views demonstrate how templates help list both an item's specifications and the background of the item's origins.

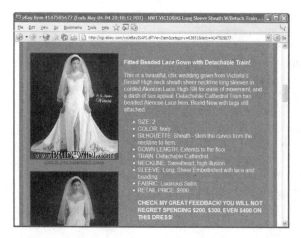

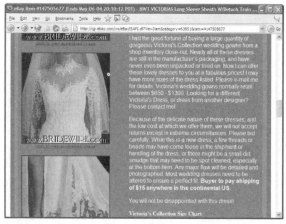

Look to the right to see our description for this item!---------->

This vintage ad is not a later reprint, photocopy or any kind of reproduction (most print ads were published at one time only, and were likely never commercially reproduced). A scarce and distinctive piece for your frame!

If you are looking for an ad that we are not currently listing, please email us at

item-request@237.com and we'll email you once we have your item available!

If the picture does not show up fast, please let us know and we'll email you a scan, and thanks for your patience.

FIGURE 5-13 A PowerSeller's listing that includes valuable background history of the item for sale

Your descriptions give you a chance to shine

If you are selling items that require you to write each description, don't despair. Consider this your opportunity to shine and show off a little bit with some of the information you've gathered over all the years you've been pursuing your interests. Figure 5-13 shows you how this PowerSeller from Denver lists his movie promotional advertisement. Notice, he gives all the information necessary to evaluate the item, but he also puts in a little history about how this particular ad was used in the promotion of movies from the 1940s. Not only does this help his customers learn more about the item, but it also gives them confidence that he knows what he's talking about. If you've followed our advice from Chapter 1, you're selling things you know and care about. Don't hesitate to let your customers know your areas of expertise.

» Don't just repeat your title

Your title was your hook to get people to open your auction listing. Now that they've done that, give them more than they expected. You don't need to repeat what you've said in your title, because you've already told them that. Tell them as much about the item as you can. Give them the color, dimensions, style, and manufacturer's information. If you've acquired this item through an estate sale, tell them something about the person whose estate was being sold. Give them a little history of the item and how it was used in the past. Add value to the description of the item by sharing information about it and its place in history. That way, even if the shopper doesn't make a bid, you'll leave a good impression. This particular item may not be what they're shopping for, but you could become a favorite seller who they'll stop back to visit for other auctions.

» Be accurate and completely honest

Your descriptions are your chance to shine, but not in the fiction-writing category. Tell your customers the exact truth about the item. Play up its positive features, of course, but don't suggest that it may be something it's not. If it has flaws, not only mention them, but highlight them. Make sure your customers know exactly what they're bidding on. Just because something may have a flaw, crack, or defect, that doesn't mean it won't find a buyer on eBay. Many collectors expect to have their items come to them with common forms of wear and signs of age. It's not necessarily a disadvantage, unless you're not honest about it. Then you not only risk having the item returned to you, but you also risk losing a customer for good and damaging your feedback rating.

» Be professional and positive

From the moment your customers open your listings, you want them to feel that they are in the company of a competent seller. Even before you attain PowerSeller status, you can make that happen through your listings. Remember that every communication you have with your customers gives them the opportunity to judge your professionalism, and don't waste a single chance to impress them.

As you describe your items, suggest alternative uses for what your customers are seeing. Show them your creativity by giving them some new ways to look at the item you're selling. If you've used the item before, give them some ideas of how you used it and what you liked about it. Help them to see themselves using what you're selling, and you'll make them want to have it or give it as a gift. Make yourself a consultant to your shoppers, not just a source of goods.

Don't allow a single negative to enter your listings. For example, never make statements that disparage yourself or your item. If you don't really know much about the particular thing you're selling, never say so. Hold on to it until you've educated yourself about it, and then list it when you can speak with authority. Even the flaws of the item can be called out without a negative. For example, in describing a collectible composite doll, you can say "the worn paint on her face reflects years of having been loved so well." You're making it clear that she's not perfect, but you're presenting her imperfections in a positive light. Compare that with "paint worn on face." The latter is shorter and required fewer keystrokes, but the former created a better impression of your doll.

» Don't violate anyone's trademark

When you're writing your titles and your descriptions, be careful not to violate anyone's trademark or copyright. eBay's Verified Rights Owner (VeRO) Program protects the owners of trademarks and copyrights from having their product names used inappropriately. For example, if a seller wants to list a purse that is very much in the style of one sold by Chanel, he cannot include "Chanel-like" or "Chanel look" or any other form of the trademark Chanel. (In fact, to include Chanel in the *title* merely to draw in hapless bidders would be considered title keyword spamming under eBay's rules.) More than 5,000 property rights owners are registered with eBay, and they will go after sellers using their product names or logos. All they have to do is file a Notice of Claimed Infringement (NOCI) form with eBay and your auction will be removed. Repeat offenders will be suspended. To learn more about the VeRO program, do a search from the Help screen. You can also visit the About Me pages of hundreds of registered VeRO partners to see what the companies have to say about fair use of their names.

» Make your descriptions neat and tidy

Once again, neatness counts. Your descriptions should be complete and descriptive, but they also must be neat and tidy. Spell-check and proofread every listing, recommends a Platinum PowerSeller from New York. You don't want to make small mistakes that detract from the overall feel of your listing. If writing isn't your favorite thing, develop some standard descriptive phrases and reuse them. Just make sure they are spelled correctly and don't contain any grammatical errors. Also, avoid using slang. You don't care if your customers think you're cool, just that they think you know what you're talking about. Nothing shakes a buyer's confidence faster than dealing with a seller who doesn't sound professional.

Tip *Here's an old proofreader's tip: Read your copy backward. By taking each word out of context, you see it only for itself, and you are more likely to catch the common typo or misspelling that way.*

» Remember you're writing for an online audience

Writing text for a computer screen is different from writing for paper. People using computers process their information better if it comes to them in short bursts. So, keep your sentences short. Don't use long paragraphs. Put line spaces between your paragraphs. By creating more white space on the screen, you'll help your customers move their eyes across the screen, and your information will be easier to absorb. You'll also increase the likelihood that people will actually read all of your listing, and that's very important, since you'll pack so much useful information into your descriptions.

» Give them a little style

Just because your description has to be professional, complete, accurate, honest, and neat, that doesn't mean you can't have a little style and fun with it. Don't hesitate to use some small design elements to spice up your descriptions. For example, create a little icon that can represent your business—a stylized shoe, a little bunch of flowers, a train engine. Something that suggests your business will stick in your customers' minds and help build your image as a professional.

Backgrounds also add pleasant design touches to your listings. Most of the auction management software packages discussed in Chapter 4 offer design element choices, but you can find others on the Web. Go to www.grsites.com/textures for more than 5,000 different backgrounds you can add to your listings, and they're free. Figure 5-14 shows the Absolute Background Textures Archives' welcome screen.

Photos That Sell

When we asked PowerSellers for secrets about successful selling on eBay, the nearly unanimous advice offered was, "great photos." Nothing showcases your items like good, clear, detailed photos. In Chapter 3, we discussed the equipment you'll need to take great shots. You also learned why you

FIGURE 5-14 Visit Absolute Background Textures Archives for free backgrounds for your listings.

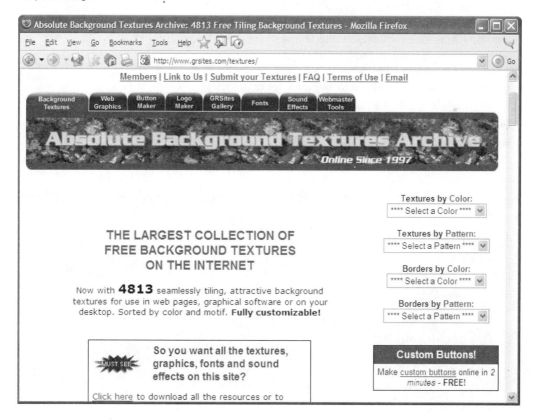

should have a single area set up and dedicated to photographing your items. Here, you'll learn how to make the most of the equipment and photo setup you create. You'll also learn some great strategies for making the most of your pictures.

» Use great photos and lots of them

Even if you don't start out as a great photographer, practice can help you develop great techniques for showcasing your items. When capturing your images, make sure your photos are clear, big, and detailed. Focus your camera carefully so that the image is sharp. The first photo you show for each listing is free. Additional photos cost $0.15 each, but this is one case where paying extra is definitely worth the investment. One PowerSeller from Florida told us that the more photos you show, the more bids you'll receive. You want your shopper to be able to view the item almost as closely as he would if he were viewing it in person. Figure 5-15 shows multiple images of a Roseville vase listed by a PowerSeller from the Midwest. Notice that the background contrasts with the item but doesn't interfere with the view. Also notice the multiple shots that show every angle of the vase, so prospective buyers can be certain they are seeing every detail. So, use great photos and provide lots of them for each listing. Here are some tips to help you.

■ Use multiple shots and capture them from different angles. That way, your customers can see the entire item as though they were holding it in their hands and rotating it.

FIGURE 5-15 Here you can see every side and angle of this beautiful Roseville vase.

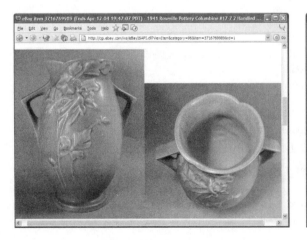

- Don't forget shots from above, and show the bottom of the item, too. Focus on details that make your item unique, such as signatures and manufacturers' markings.

- Capture the image from an angle to showcase the depth of the item and make best use of its shadows.

- Specifically photograph every flaw and make sure the flaws are visible in the photo. You don't want to cover anything up that will later reveal itself to be trouble for both you and the buyer.

- Use a tripod if your hand is shaky. You want every detail to count.

» Use good lighting

When capturing images, use good lighting to best show the details. The best light for photos is natural, so try to place your photo area near a window. If you want to shoot your pictures outside, do it out of the direct sun. Too much sunlight directly on your item will wash it out rather than highlight features. Direct light can also cause hot spots (glare and reflections).

When using artificial light, try to light the item from two directions at once to reduce shadows. Using light from two sources also reduces the glare from your flash. Some sellers swear by fluorescent lighting. They claim it gives a whiter light and truer color reproduction than the more yellow incandescent light from regular light bulbs.

» Make your item stand out

In order to make your item stand out, use a neutral but contrasting background. That means you'll need to have at least two backdrops, one light and one dark. Avoid patterns on the background because they can be busy distractions to the item itself. That doesn't mean you should feel stuck with using a white sheet or a black one. Rich color can add elegance to the photo, so consider using an eye-pleasing royal blue or deep violet for the dark background and a pale blue or pink for the light one.

Some of your items might benefit from being scaled for size. Consider placing a ruler next to the item. Another option is to photograph it next to something commonly recognized, such as a quarter or a penny. At a glance, your customers will know exactly what the size of your item is.

» Protect your photos

It may surprise you, but sellers have been known to swipe each other's photos for use in their own auctions. That may seem a little silly and petty, but it's serious to the seller who loses his photos. That's part of your intellectual property. It's time-consuming for you to produce your best images, and no one else should have the right to use your work without your permission. It's very difficult for eBay to police this type of seller-to-seller problem. Consider adding an identifier to your photos. If you look back at Figure 5-2, you'll see the web address for Bridewire stamped along the bottom of the photo. Even if another seller took this image, it wouldn't do much good for his auction. It's plain to see who owns the image, and it adds a little advertising pop at the same time.

» It's not necessarily all up to you

Resourceful PowerSellers find other sources of photo images for their listings, besides capturing every image themselves. If you're dealing in new merchandise, check with the manufacturer for stock images of the items you sell. That means all you do is upload the image that already exists, and you bypass the whole problem of taking photos.

If you sell books, CDs, DVDs, or videos, you can take advantage of eBay's automated listing service (discussed earlier) that includes a good many stock images of the items in these categories. When using stock photos, it's especially important to be up-front about your item's condition. Otherwise, some buyers may assume it's in the same condition as the one in the stock photo, and they'll be disappointed if it's not.

If you are selling paper goods such as postcards, sports cards, books, or comics, you can directly scan your items on a flatbed scanner. You'll still want to capture multiple shots, but you won't have to work with a camera to do it. Lighting and background won't be considerations, and you'll be able to address the size and features of each item in the description. Of course, you should still provide specific scans of any flaws or defects.

» Hire some help

If you are really intimidated by the thought of doing the photography, consider hiring someone to help you. Before too long, you'll be looking for help with your eBay business, anyway (see Chapter 6), so why not choose an employee who can also do photography? Most high schools and community colleges offer photography classes, and a young photo-bug, just starting out, would be delighted to gain some experience, build a portfolio, and get paid a little something at the same time.

» Store your images via web hosting

One of the best reasons for using an auction management program is that it likely includes image storage (or "hosting") of your pictures. This feature lets you upload your digital pictures to the auction management company's computers. From there, if you are also using the auction management program to create your listing, you'll be able just to browse your computer for the digital image, and the software will take it from there (assigning a URL, placing it within your auction). If you prefer, you can still use your stored image when using eBay's selling form. Just click the tab for your own Web hosting on the Sell Your Item form's Pictures & Details page.

Why do this? Even if you use eBay's "Supersize" feature, a "hosted" picture will still be much larger, allowing buyers to be able to more closely inspect your item. It's also cheaper this way, since you'll pay $0.75 extra per supersized image through eBay, but only a fraction of that in fees for additional pictures and in storage fees from the auction management software company.

Timing Your Auctions

Timing your auctions can seem a little like trying to time the stock market. No one can say for sure, and there are no guarantees. The glib response to the question "When should my auction end?" is when the bidding has reached its highest price. Fortunately, unlike the stock market, it's possible to apply a little common sense to the question of timing your auctions. You can't be guaranteed you'll hit the best time every time, but you can use some tips from the PowerSellers to increase the chance that you'll at least time them well.

Timing Tidbits

The first thing to remember when setting your auction ending times is that eBay operates on Pacific Time. If you're an early bird who lives back East, don't bother to get a jump on your listings and post them by 6:00 A.M. local time. You'll risk missing all of the potential customers out West who prefer to sleep at 3:00 A.M.

That's important to consider, because as with any auction, the real action happens within the last hours of your listing. "In a seven-day listing, the first six days and 23 hours is the viewing time. The real auction happens at the very end," says PowerSeller Jeralinc, and many others agreed. You want to try to end your auctions when most people are likely to be paying attention.

Keep in mind that your auction ends at the exact time of day that it started. Your auction begins when you complete your listing. No matter how long you choose to run your auction— and you'll learn more about that soon—the hour it starts is the same hour it ends. You can create your auctions, store them, and schedule them to start at a designated time. eBay offers this feature at an added cost, but your auction management software will do it for free.

» Consider your audience

Here is yet another example of how your research can pay off in real profits. Know who your audience is, and you'll have a better idea of when those people will be on eBay. "My audience is mostly women, ages 30 to 60," reported a PowerSeller from New Jersey. "When I first started, I was ending my auctions in the afternoon, because that was the most convenient time for me to list them. Soon, I realized that the people most likely to buy my products weren't even home in the middle of the afternoon, let alone on their computers. I switched my ending times to the evening and saw a big improvement almost immediately." If your audience is most likely to be made up of working people, follow this PowerSeller's advice. If, on the other hand, your audience is more likely to be stay-at-home moms, afternoon might work to coincide with naptime. Retirees may be more active in the morning than they are late at night. Experiment a bit, but do it with your audience in mind.

» Statistics favor certain times

Luckily for you, we have some statistics to turn to in determining the best day and time to end auctions. Your actual results may vary depending on many factors, including the products you sell, the time of the year, the weather conditions across the United States, and what's currently hot on TV, but statistics are a good place to start. Every year for the last five years, AuctionBytes.com has completed a survey of eBay sellers to determine the best time to end an auction. Consistently, over all these years, Sunday evening has proven to be the most popular time to end your auctions. Overall, the evening hours, between 6:00 P.M. and Midnight, have fared the best. This year the survey included nearly 1,000 respondents. Of those, 76 percent reported those hours to be the most successful.

AuctionBytes.com was kind enough to allow us to include their research. Table 5-1 shows the best day to end an auction, with results going back to 1999. You may notice that this year's results don't equal 100 percent. That's because, for the first time, AuctionBytes.com included the category "Doesn't Matter" in their possible response choices. Approximately 8 percent of those who responded chose this answer. Table 5-2 shows this year's results for the best time of day to end auctions.

2/04	3/03	1/02	2/01	12/99
Sun 57.5%	Sun 64%	Sun 60%	Sun 54%	Sun 41%
Mon 9.5%	Mon 11%	Thu 10%	Mon 18%	Sat 18%
Sat 7%	Sat 8%	Sat 9%	Sat 11%	Mon 15%
Thu 7%	Thu 7%	Mon 9%	Thu 8%	Fri 11%
Tue 5%	Tue 4%	Wed 4%	Wed 5%	Tue 6%
Wed 4%	Fri 3%	Tue 4%	Fri 3%	Thu 5%
Fri 2%	Wed 3%	Fri 3%	Tue 1%	Wed 4%

TABLE 5-1   Best Day to End an Auction

It's clearly Sunday, except when it's not

Respondents	Time of Day
54%	6:00 P.M. to 9:00 P.M.
22%	9:00 P.M. to Midnight
13%	3:00 P.M. to 6:00 P.M.
3%	Noon to 3:00 P.M.
2%	9:00 A.M. to Noon

TABLE 5-2   Best Time of Day to End an Auction

» It's clearly Sunday, except when it's not

Sunday has consistently been the favored time to end your auctions, but don't forget, there are exceptions to this rule. Super Bowl Sunday is clearly one of them. If the Sunday in question falls in the middle of a three-day weekend, you'll have less traffic. People travel and socialize more on holiday weekends than on regular weekends, and you'll feel their absence online. For long weekends, Monday evening may prove to be better.

Seasonal changes affect listing traffic, too. PowerSeller Jrgolfwarehouse had no listings posted at all one week late in March. When we spoke, he said the market for junior golf equipment would pick up in April when the weather improved and until then, he was concentrating on other parts of his business and holding back on his listings. Overall, PowerSellers remind newcomers that all businesses have seasonal ups and downs, and an eBay business is no exception. The important thing is to figure what your seasons are, and prepare for them.

Seasons, like the weather, come and go. Some PowerSellers watch for changing weather across the greater part of the United States. When the forecast calls for snow, more people will be stuck at home and likely looking for diversion. That's potentially a good time to up your listings. Of course, the weather, like most predictions, is questionable. You don't want to choose a huge blizzard to list, because people who lose electricity are usually not online!

Armed with statistics, common sense, and the experience of PowerSellers, you can experiment with your products and customer base to find your best listing times. As with all other aspects of running an eBay business, be willing to stay flexible and try new things.

How Long Should Your Auctions Last?

Although you have fewer choices for the duration of your auctions than for when you should start and end them, it's still one that brings varying answers from PowerSellers. You can choose to run your auctions on eBay for one, three, five, seven, or ten days. If you choose ten-day auctions, you'll have to pay $0.20 per listing for the extended time. The default listing is seven days, and certainly, this is a very popular choice among all sellers, including PowerSellers. Ten-day auctions are the next most popular choice, and three-day auctions have a special place in a PowerSeller's arsenal. Our discussion will focus on these three choices.

One-day listings are not generally useful to PowerSellers because they don't last long enough to generate strong competition, and they end so quickly that it's too difficult to keep up with processing them in large numbers. Five-day auctions don't share these drawbacks, but there's also not much point in ending the auction after five days when leaving it up for two more doesn't cost anything in extra fees. PowerSellers who use five-day auctions often tend to want to do it strategically to turn inventory over more quickly.

» A seven-day auction may be a week, but it's strong

Seven days seems to be the charmed length of most auctions. "I never, ever, run an auction for less than seven days. It costs me the same amount of money (listing fees) to run a seven-day auction as it does for me to run a three-day auction. I want all the exposure I can get for my 35 cents," says PowerSeller Bargain-Hunters-Dream. Seven-day auctions will give shoppers ample time to watch the action and still check back in for bidding. They are also easy for PowerSellers to track. If you designate Sundays, Tuesdays, and Thursdays as your listing days, and you use seven-day auctions, you'll always know when your auctions are scheduled to end. This can simplify your workflow.

» Ten-day auctions; more time for more money

"If I believe an item will sell for more than $200, I run it for ten days in an attempt to get more exposure and, hopefully, a higher final bid amount," says Bargain-Hunters-Dream. PowerSellers of large-ticket items share this opinion. Baronart deals in fine paintings and never runs auctions for less than ten days. She feels it takes this long for potential shoppers to find her items and decide on these big purchases. If you are dealing in very expensive merchandise, the extra listing fees for an extended auction won't matter.

Combining ten-day auctions with seven-day auctions is a popular technique for Wegotthebeats. He posts most of his auctions on Sunday evenings, but for some less-common CDs, he'll give them a ten-day run by starting them on Thursday. This way, all of his auctions still end on Sunday evenings, which is his preference.

» The one-two punch of the three-day sale

Most PowerSellers frown upon the three-day sale, but not all of them do. Acmeresale sprinkles his listings with some three-day auctions. According to this PowerSeller, the most active times in any auction are the first day, when the listing is new, and the last day, when the auction is about to end. If you run a three-day auction, you have good activity throughout almost the entire auction.

Acmeresale also described a brilliant strategy for combining three-day auctions with five-day auctions. "If I have five pieces of the same item, I'll list three of them as five-day auctions, and two as three-day auctions. I know I'll sacrifice price on the three-day auctions, but all the bidders who miss out on those items and lose the auctions, automatically get e-mails from eBay directing them to my active five-day auctions. It actually generates much more traffic for the remaining auctions and higher final bids on the other items still for sale. It's worth sacrificing the lower-priced auction just for that."

» Do more research

We know, we sound like a broken record, but research is the key to your learning about your own niche on eBay, and deciding for yourself about the length of your auctions is yet another part of that learning. So, it's back to research once again.

As before, a good place to start is with completed auctions for competitive items. Look for the ones that sold for the highest price and see how long they lasted and when they ended. Then, experiment on your own. Try some of each of the different auction lengths to see which ones appeal to you the most. Your choice will be based on the price you can get for your sales, but it will also be based on how you feel about the flow of your work for each of the various auction lengths. You might find that sticking to a schedule is better for you, or you may prefer to mix it up so that auctions end throughout the week rather than on particular days only. As with everything else in your eBay business, you're the boss.

Pricing Strategies

There are basically two schools of thought about pricing. "Start it low and let it go," says Acmeresale. Many PowerSellers start all of their auctions at $0.99. They believe this is the best way to generate early interest in their items and build the pool of people looking at the auctions. Others say, list an item for the least amount of money you are willing to take for it, even if you don't sell it the first time and have to relist it. That way, you can't take a loss on something that doesn't recoup its acquisition costs. We'll explore both of these strategies more fully, but before we do, let's consider the different pricing options available to you through eBay.

Choose Your Format

eBay gives you choices in determining what pricing scheme you want to pursue. Most PowerSellers choose from among three variations: a standard auction format, an auction with a Buy It Now (BIN) feature, or a Fixed Price listing.

A standard auction is probably the type of sale you've already conducted on eBay. You choose the duration of the auction and the starting price. The rest is up to the customers you're able to attract, and the auction proceeds to its conclusion with the final price determined by whoever bids the most.

Adding a Buy It Now feature to your auction costs an additional $0.05 per listing. Your BIN price is just that, the price you would be satisfied receiving for your item if it were to sell immediately. When you list with a Buy It Now feature, your auction continues for the duration or until someone offers you the BIN price. As soon as someone does, the auction closes and your sale is complete. When someone bids on your item, your

BIN figure disappears and the auction continues as any other auction would. So, a BIN price is not a guaranteed final price; it's just a way to end the auction early for a price that will satisfy you. PowerSellers use the BIN feature when they want to give customers the option of not having to wait for the auction to be completed. If you have a clear profit margin in mind, you can choose BIN for a price that will bring you the earnings you're looking for, and move along to other auctions.

The preceding discussion refers to a BIN auction without a reserve. You can also combine BIN with a reserve auction. In that case, the BIN remains until the reserve is met. The BIN price must be higher than the reserve (if only by a penny).

Fixed Price listings are a relatively new format for eBay. In just a brief time they've become so popular they represent a substantial percentage of eBay sales dollars. They are actually not auctions at all. When you create your listing, you establish a price and someone either pays that price or your item doesn't sell. Fixed Price listings can be for multiple items, so listing once you can specify that you have up to a quantity of ten identical items for sale. In the actual listing, the price will appear as a BIN, but the difference here is that the price will not disappear when someone makes a purchase. It will remain until the end of the auction, which is either when time runs out or when all of your items are sold. There is no additional fee for listing your merchandise as a Fixed Price sale. Very often, PowerSellers who use Fixed Price sales deal with new merchandise. They know what the item costs to acquire. They have a regular and repeatable source of inventory. They know the retail value of the item. They have a clear idea of their expected profit margin, and they establish a fixed price based on these factors. Operating your eBay business on a fixed-price basis is the option most like operating a brick-and-mortar store.

Now that you understand your pricing options, let's take a look at the two main strategies PowerSellers follow for pricing their items. We'll also consider the option of using a Reserve price, and we'll look at some strategies for bumping up your final prices.

» Start it low and let it go

Starting all of your auctions at the lowest price has some real strategic advantages. It is a sign of a veteran eBay seller who feels the thrill of starting an item at $0.99 and watching it climb to its final value. Aside from the thrill of the ride, starting your auctions low keeps your listing fees in line. Listing fees are linked to the starting price you set. Check back to Figure 5-5 to see the progression of fees as your starting price increases. You may not think there's much difference between listing an item at $9.99 for $0.35 and listing that item closer to your expected final price of $25 for $1.20. For a single item, you're correct. But when you multiply a single item by the hundreds you'll be listing every month in order to become a PowerSeller, that $0.85 difference matters. If you sold 300 items this month, you'd pay $255 in additional fees for the sake of listing your item at $25. That's money coming directly out of your profits. Even if your final value for some of these items never reaches your target of $25, you'll still be ahead.

Starting your items low has other strategic advantages. When you start low, your item comes to the top of the list of any search sorted by lowest price. Many shoppers sort their search results this way, and with low prices you're guaranteed a spot at the top, at least for a while until the price escalates. With your item at the top of the search list, you'll get a lot of attention early in the auction. This builds momentum. Once people bid on your auction, others tend to be more willing to place bids too. It's human nature for people to want what others have already shown they want, too. Building momentum early in your auction actually increases the demand for your item and, therefore, your final value price.

Experienced PowerSellers report that the items they start low rarely, if ever, sell so low that they regret the sale. For the few times that might happen, they feel the trade-off of added attention, improved momentum, and lower fees is worth it.

» Find its worth and stick to it

As we mentioned, this approach is to establish the lowest price you'd be satisfied with and start your auction there. To control your fees, you may decide that price is going to be $24.99 or less. At this rate, you'll only be adding a modest increase in your listing fees, and this strategy may give you the peace of mind you need as you get started. Keep in mind, you may not get as many bids, and with decreased competition your final price may actually not be as high as it could be. But, you also won't be taking risks before you're ready.

If you find your item doesn't sell at all, you can relist it for another try. A simple click of a button allows the item to be

Find its worth and stick to it

automatically relisted. eBay will even credit you with the cost of relisting your auction if you meet the following criteria:

- You must relist the item within 90 days of the closing date of the original auction.
- Both the original listing and the relisting must be in the auction format or in the fixed price format, so you can't use this with an eBay store.
- You may relist only single-quantity items.
- The starting price for the relisted item cannot be greater than the price in the original listing.
- You cannot add a reserve price to the relisting if one was not in the original listing.
- The relisting must end with a winning bid for you to qualify for a refund.

Clearly the choice is yours in terms of which pricing strategy feels right for you. Again, since you're the boss, why not try some auction listings in both strategies and see which ones bring you the best results?

Reservations about Reserves

Many new sellers seek comfort in adding reserve prices to their auctions. As you may know, a reserve is the absolute lowest price your auction must achieve before the item sells. You set your reserve price at the time you create your listing, and your listing shows that there is a reserve on the item. If the reserve price is never met, your item doesn't sell, and your auction just runs its course to the end, with no winning bidders. Believe us, we understand the security you have when you know your item has a rock-bottom price below which it simply can't be sacrificed. The fees for adding reserves to your auctions range from $1.00 for items priced $49.99 and below; $2.00 for items ranging between $50.00 and $199.99; and 1 percent of the reserve price (up to $100) for items priced at $200 or above. As a new seller, you may think this fee is well worth the security it buys. PowerSellers nearly unanimously disagree.

Most PowerSellers recommend that you never use a reserve. The reason they state, again and again, is that it puts buyers off to your auctions. They report that some buyers won't even look at your listing if it has a reserve. With such strong buyer aversion to the reserve, it actually reduces the likelihood that your item will sell. The fees may not seem so steep, but when you factor in what a reserve does to your traffic, you find it actually costs you a great deal more than it seems to on the surface.

Is there ever a time when you'll use a reserve? Probably. You'll most likely want a reserve price if you're selling an item for someone else as a Trading Assistant. (Chapter 6 will tell you more.) In this case, you have not only your investment to consider, but someone else's too. You might also use a reserve if your item is in the category of rare or fine art. Baronart uses reserves because her items sell for thousands of dollars each. She also has a much smaller, more specialized, target audience than other PowerSellers, and her customers are less likely to be put off by the reserve.

One last tip about reserves: PoweSellers agree, if you're going to use one, state what it is in the listing description. People generally don't, but that's really silly, in the long run. As one PowerSeller asked, "What's the big secret?" If you clearly state what your reserve is, you get the comfort and protection you seek, but your customers also get to see how much money they'd have to spend in order to get your item. It seems a reasonable compromise, doesn't it?

» Combine pricing and timing for smart selling

A combination of pricing and timing strategies can really boost your sales, and here are a few ideas to get you started. As we discussed in Chapter 2, building your inventory is a delicate balance between finding a popular item and overexposing your popular item in the marketplace. As a pricing strategy, don't flood your own market. You'll drive the price of your items down quickly. If you come upon a group of items, list them a few at a time across weeks so that you keep demand steady, but don't overdo the supply.

» Research and act fast

Here we go again. Go back for more research, but this time, don't just learn, move. Find competitive auctions that are doing very well and time yours to end right after them with a low starting price, recommends Acmeresale. Your auction will come up along with the successful one in any search that lists results by auction ending times. You'll catch the momentum of someone else's successful auction, and your low starting price will heat your auction up from the very beginning.

Christina

Hello, I'm Christina! I began selling on eBay about four and a half years ago as a joke. Today, I am proud to say that I am an eBay PowerSeller with an eBay store of my very own. My business provides me with not only a steady income and pride of accomplishment, but also a rosy vision of future growth. As far as I am concerned, the stars are the limit!

All of this began with a "smart" comment from a good friend. One day while visiting, she pointed out that my hobby of collecting recipes had grown to proportions rivaling Martha Stewart herself!

"You should try and sell them on eBay!" she laughed. Little did she know what a "smart" suggestion this would become.

Being a florist by trade, I've always felt that there might be room for improvement in the income department. So, I sat at our home computer and typed up a couple of collections of my favorite family-tested recipes, and then posted them on eBay as Dutch auctions at $2.00 apiece. They required no

picture and could be e-mailed to the bidders upon receipt of their payments. Soon the first bidders discovered me and began bidding, and bidding, and bidding! I tasted the first of many exciting experiences eBay would provide!

By the end of my first year on eBay, I was already fantasizing about the possibility of turning my "hobby" into a real business. I began to save the seed money from the sales of the recipe collections to purchase items wholesale that I could use to build a store.

I spent many hours pouring through the other sellers' auctions and stores to see what worked for them. What I realized was that they all seemed so similar to me. What could I offer my customers that would be different and help me to stand out from the others? I looked around my own home and decided that I could best sell the things that I knew most about! I would create a store that catered to a lifestyle . . . my lifestyle! I love to browse through New Age stores for unique items and interesting books. I enjoy fine teas and little "luxuries" and treats. I am also unable to pass by a bath products store without going in just to "sniff around" at the wonderful fragrances! My target audience of women between 30 and 80 would also love these same items . . . and they do!

But that is now . . . . Over the past few years I have made many fundamental mistakes. I'm sure by now you understand the importance of a clear picture of your item, and an even clearer description! But, did you know that most bids are placed in the hour just prior to the auctions' close? I used to spend most of my day off from my floral design job fussing over the best possible descriptions for my items, and carefully editing their photos. Then, after I felt everything was just right, I would launch them. This usually occurred between 1:00 and 3:00 P.M.

Had I but looked up from my ardent typing for a moment, I might have had time to realize that seven days later, when these auctions were about to close, my target audience would be nowhere near their computers, much less online and poised to bid on them! Always be sure that your auctions will close when the people you want to bid on them will be available! Be aware of when the "hot" shows are on TV, special events such as the Super Bowl, and major holidays. No one will be shopping your auctions during these slow times.

Each new idea or tip was like a coin dropped into a piggy bank, and luckily, there was plenty to learn. Here was a forum where I could learn and grow *along with* my business at my own pace! eBay has been a unique opportunity in these unique times! Where else could the average Joe, or Josephine, begin a business with such a small investment and reach such a wide and varied audience? This is the place to give that "niche" business that has been on your mind a try, or retail your own hand-made delights and adornments with very little risk.

Don't ever be discouraged out of a great idea even if you find that other people are already selling that very item! There are only so many different items on the market. Your job is to make your presentation as uniquely your own as possible. Give it a new and exciting title, or describe the item's various uses! Be creative!

I would wish you all the best of luck, but success is not luck . . . it's knowledge! I hope my experiences will contribute to knowledge upon which your success is built. Then, coin by shiny coin, your piggy bank will become a treasure chest! See you online!

Chapter 6

Power-Charge Your eBay Business

Now that you've learned what the PowerSellers know about creating great auction listings, it's time to start thinking of your whole eBay business from a PowerSeller point of view. It's not enough to create great auction listings; you need to understand the many ways there are to make the most of these listings. Power-charging your auction sales will get you thinking of your eBay business in its totality. In the last chapter, you had to concentrate on each individual listing, but now it's time to put them all together and see what your eBay business looks like as a whole. Then you'll be ready to pump up your auctions, your sales, and your profits.

In power-charging your auctions, you'll consider the needs of your customers, along with the effectiveness of your auction strategies, advertising options, and business practices. You are already moving from eBay hobbyist to potential PowerSeller, and the issues you'll explore in this chapter will take you even further along this journey. This journey will take you along a toll road, and the price you must pay is time in the form of trial and error. You'll have to stay flexible, use common sense, try what seems right to you, and be willing to move on if it doesn't work out. You will notice that many of the options we present to you here come with a price tag. We're not recommending that you spend your money by trying everything we offer. We're just showing you what's out there and what the benefits of many different choices are. Which options you choose and how you allocate your resources will be up to you.

Your Business and Your Customers

Your business success depends on your success in attracting and retaining customers. That statement is incredibly simple, and yet at the same time it is terribly important. Without your customers, you can't succeed in business. Staging your business on eBay presents you with a set of challenges that you would not have to consider if you were operating a brick-and-mortar store. Not the least of these challenges is the fact that you most likely will never meet a single one of your customers in person. On the other hand, you'll have a pool of 100 million potential customers to draw from. But, you don't want to have to go back to that huge pool every time you make a sale. Your goal is to have a subset of those customers return regularly to shop with you. You want to build business relationships with your customers that will make them want to come back to you every time they need or want the products you sell. Let's take a look at some of the ways you can start building your customer base right now.

Court Your Customers

Every sale you make gives you the opportunity to make a customer for life. Think of your every interaction with a new customer as a chance to court a new friend. Your auction listings are already helping, because you're working to make them neat, accurate, and friendly, but there are still more things you can do to be sure your customers will remember who you are and think of you the next time they shop on eBay.

» Maintain an e-mail database

Every e-mail you receive from a buyer becomes a point of contact with your customer. Once a customer sends you an e-mail to ask you a question about an item listed or gets in touch with you at the end of an auction, you are free to capture that customer's e-mail address and add it to your database. In the database, include details about the sale, including what the person bought, how much he spent, and any reactions you might have had to the sale. You can use this information if you need to contact the buyer again.

Now, you don't want to make a pest of yourself or get in trouble for spamming anyone, but you can put a link in your auctions to ask if your customers would like to receive e-mail about future products and auctions. You should include a line that makes it clear you will not use the person's e-mail for any other purpose but to offer them more opportunities to shop, if they'd like. But many customers will be delighted to find another item up for auction and will be happy to take a look. You've already proved yourself to this buyer as a good seller, so you can think of this e-mail as a service to your customer.

» Use an e-mail signature

A few lines that serve as a signature at the end of every e-mail can be a wonderful way for you to add value to every correspondence you send. Adding an e-mail signature is an option in nearly all

Use an e-mail signature

e-mail programs. It is easy to set up and becomes a part of every e-mail you send. Some of the items of information you might want to consider including are

- Contact information for reaching you
- A few tips for safe eBay shopping
- A little information about yourself and your business
- A hyperlink to a current auction or to your About Me page

The tips you offer prove you are an experienced seller. The links you provide bring this already interested customer back to your auctions. Here's one that didn't get away.

How about a Monthly Newsletter?

Because you're selling products you know about, you can provide valuable information and suggestions to your customers. Consider a monthly e-mail newsletter to be distributed to your customers. A PowerSeller on the East Coast loves to write, so this is a great opportunity for her to practice her hobby and keep her customers up to date with her business. Your first step is to include a link in your auction listings that will allow your customers to sign up to receive a free, monthly online newsletter. Once a customer agrees, add him to your newsletter e-mail list.

Every month you can send along a piece of news relevant to your products. You can offer advice for using the product or include a brief case study of a customer who is using the product in an interesting way. You can review a different product each month and perhaps include a brief review of a book your customers might be interested in. You can even have a joke corner, as long as it's tasteful. Your imagination is your only limit. It only takes a couple of hours a month to create it, and it puts you in front of your best customers every few weeks.

Reassure Your Customers

Just for a moment, put yourself in your customer's place. Every time you buy something from an unproven eBay seller, you take a risk. No matter how well produced the listing is. No matter how clear the policy statements are. Even in view of a good, solid feedback rating, there comes a moment when you simply have to trust that the person selling what you want is going to live up to the promises he makes in his auction listing. That's one of the main reasons so many people stick with PowerSellers: they've proved themselves in this marketplace. Until you've achieved PowerSeller status of your own, you have a variety of programs available to you, both inside and outside of eBay, to give your customers some peace of mind in doing business with you. You certainly will not choose all of the programs we'll describe here, but some of them will seem right to you.

Of course, the first place to look for reassurance is eBay itself. eBay's SafeHarbor is the resource center for all of eBay's user safety features. You'll find it at www.pages.ebay.com/help/confidence/problems-support.html. Figure 6-1 shows the welcome screen for SafeHarbor. You will find all of the community values and resources listed from here, and so will your customers. In addition to this resource area, eBay also offers buyers a level of

FIGURE 6-1 eBay's SafeHarbor welcome screen, the first stop in exploring eBay's buyer protection offerings

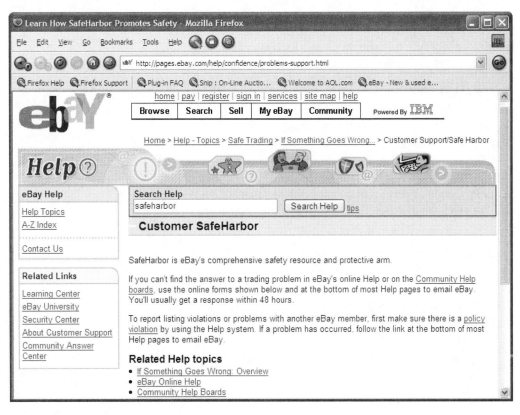

protection against seller fraud. If a buyer makes a purchase and the seller either never delivers the product or delivers something that is significantly different from the item description, the buyer can pursue a claim against the seller. After completing the claim procedure and attempting to resolve the dispute, the buyer can file for a reimbursement of up to $200 minus a $25 processing fee directly from eBay. If the buyer used a credit card to pay for the item, the claim must first be submitted to the credit card company.

» Use PayPal

We'll be spending a lot more time with PayPal in Chapter 7, when we discuss payment options for your sales, but PayPal is an excellent way to reassure your buyers that they have some protection in doing business with you. PayPal is owned by eBay and, as such, is part of the eBay dynasty. Settling disputes via PayPal is like keeping the problem in the family.

As a seller using PayPal, you offer your PayPal-member buyers the option of paying for their items with a major credit card. This not only gives them the charge-back assurance from their credit card companies, but it also provides them with two different types of PayPal buyer protection. The standard Buyer Protection program offers buyers up to $500, in U.S. dollars, of protection when purchasing a PayPal-backed item. The Buyer Complaint Process is the other option available to PayPal buyers. Each is described in the sections that follow.

PayPal Buyer Protection Program

Buyer Protection offers buyers the chance to be refunded the full cost of an item purchased, up to $500. Request for refunds must meet the following criteria:

- Items must be paid for through PayPal directly to the e-mail address the seller has specified on his PayPal account.

- Protection is offered for items that are never delivered or are significantly different from what was described in the listing.

- Items must have been purchased on eBay, rather than another online auction site.

- The items must be tangible. Services and items that are intangible are not covered.

- Only one claim per PayPal payment is permitted.

- You have 30 days from the date of the payment to file a claim.

- No more than two PayPal Buyer Protection refunds will be issued in a calendar year. If you exceed this limit, PayPal does not guarantee that you will receive a full refund; rather, you will be awarded only what can be recovered from the seller.

- You must be willing to participate in the investigation by providing PayPal with all the necessary information to resolve the matter.

The Buyer Complaint Process

The Buyer Complaint process differs from the Buyer Protection program in that no refund is guaranteed in this case. PayPal agrees to investigate a complaint made through this process, but damages are subject to the successful recovery of funds that are owed to you. PayPal attempts to complete the investigation and reimburse the buyer within 30 days of the date the complaint is filed, but this is also not guaranteed. To file a Buyer Complaint, the following criteria must be met:

- The buyer must have used PayPal.

- The complaint must be filed within 30 days of the payment.

- The purchase must be for a tangible item.

- The item you purchased was never received. Unlike the Buyer Protection program, there is no coverage under the Buyer complaint process for items that were not what the buyer expected. Complaints of that nature appear against the seller's record but are not reimbursed.

The PayPal protection programs are skewed in the buyer's favor. There are no equivalent seller protections available. Unscrupulous buyers can conceivably charge back the cost of their item to their credit card, get a refund from PayPal, and never return the item to the seller. This frustrates some PowerSellers, but the system was designed to protect only the buyer. The seller gains from participating with PayPal in having a safe, secure way for customers to use credit card payments for eBay auction items, and in offering buyers the protection that paying with PayPal brings. Every auction you list with PayPal as a payment

Use PayPal

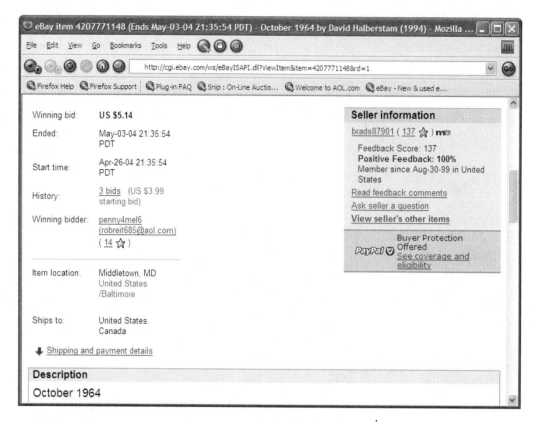

FIGURE 6-2 The PayPal Buyer Protection statement as it appears in a listing

option includes the PayPal Buyer Protection statement shown in Figure 6-2. It may seem an unfair system to sellers, but offering your buyers the option of paying through PayPal does give them a level of assurance that you cannot match without PayPal.

To qualify as a PayPal seller, you must meet the following requirements:

- You have to have received feedback comments from at least 50 distinct trading partners.

- You must carry at least a 98 percent positive feedback rating.

- You must be a verified member of PayPal.

- You must hold a Premier or Business PayPal account (see Chapter 7 for details).

- You must have a U.S., U.K., or Canadian PayPal account.

- Your PayPal account must be in good standing.

So, by all means, go ahead and sign up for PayPal as soon as you are eligible. Don't concern yourself too much about the fear of being taken by unscrupulous buyers. Most disputes between buyers and sellers can be resolved long before they reach this point, as you'll see in Chapter 9. Plus, keep reading—in Chapter 7 we have some other PowerSeller advice to protect you from buyers you may not want participating in your auctions.

» Try Square Trade

Square Trade is a privately held company that offers protection services to online buyers for eBay and other online merchant sites. You will find Square Trade's web site at www.Squaretrade.com. When you sign up with Square Trade, the company verifies your address and contact information and does a check of your feedback rating and past history of settling customer service disputes on eBay. If you qualify, you will become a registered Square Trade member, and you will have the Square Trade Seal added to all your auction listings as verification that you are an approved seller. The seal tells buyers that you've met the verification standards and that your merchandise may be eligible for Square Trade's buyer protection services. It also guarantees that you agree to participate in Square Trade's Online Dispute Resolution service should the buyer need to resolve a problem purchase.

Let's start with the idea that merchandise *may* be eligible for the buyer protection services. Why would some items be eligible and others not be? For an item to qualify for buyer protection, the transaction must have met the following requirements:

- The seller displayed an active and valid Square Trade Seal at the time the winning bid was placed.

- The Member Profile page showed a specific level of Buyer Protection for that specific transaction.

- The transaction happened on eBay and had a valid eBay item number.

- The transaction was for a tangible product.

- The listing was not for multiple items. No Dutch auctions can be honored with Buyer Protection.

- The issue to be resolved was a matter of fraud, according to Square Trade's definition.

Try Square Trade

- The party making the claim was the actual buyer.
- The buyer has a positive feedback rating or no feedback rating at all.
- The buyer has paid for the item and can provide proof of payment.
- The item was not damaged or lost in shipping.
- The item was not in violation of eBay's restricted and prohibited items policy.
- Your claim under eBay's own protection program was granted.

A buyer will know what level of protection you offer, because the Square Trade Seal includes a hyperlink to your own profile page for each auction you list. That profile page lists your payment, shipping, and customer service policies. It also lists

FIGURE 6-3 Square Trade's buyer protection coverage statement for a particular listing

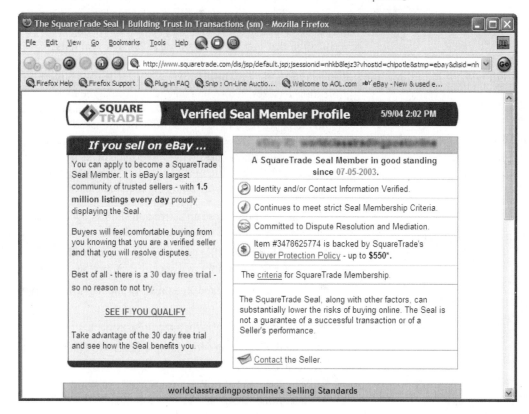

the amount of buyer protection coverage available for that specific item number. Figure 6-3 shows just what that page looks like for a particular PowerSeller's listing.

In addition to the Square Trade verification process, Square Trade also offers a Dispute Resolution service. Dispute Resolution is a two-part program. The first is a free direct resolution attempt that helps the buyer and seller resolve their differences on their own. If this fails, the parties can turn to the Mediation branch of Square Trade's services. Square Trade maintains a network of over 250 mediators who will step in to resolve an issue between the buyer and the seller. The person who files the case agrees to pay a fee of $20. Both seller and buyer must submit copies of all e-mails relevant to the disputed sale. Square Trade does not guarantee the problem will be resolved through meditation, but the company does claims a 90 percent success rate for completed cases, and those cases number more than 150,000 per year. Chapter 9 includes a profile of a Square Trade mediator.

Square Trade costs $7.50 per month, with the first month free as a trial. You can also choose to sign up for the Preferred Plan. The Preferred Plan costs an annual fee of $67.50 and offers the following benefits:

- A 25 percent discount on monthly fees for the first year
- An additional $300 of buyer protection
- Eligibility to participate in Square Trade's promotion "Featured Seal Member" program on their web site
- Discounts on requests for mediation and feedback removal
- Full access to 20 business reports

Square Trade's seal activity reports analyze your listings to report back to you how often buyers visit them and when those visits take place. You can also view reports updated daily that track your sales for month-to-month comparison and competitive analysis to other sellers in your categories.

One final service Square Trade offers is a negative feedback notification process. If a seller receives negative feedback, Square Trade will notify her immediately and offer to negotiate a settlement with the buyer and a possible removal of the negative statement. This process carries the same mediation fee of $20 and no guarantee that the negative can be removed.

Have your ID verified

PowerSellers are not terribly supportive of this program. One PowerSeller noted that this seems to hit a person at his most vulnerable moment. When the negative feedback is fresh, the seller is often so angry that he will agree to pay the $20 fee just out of an emotional reflex. In view of eBay's new Mutual Feedback Withdrawal program, discussed in detail in Chapter 9, some PowerSellers view this service as obsolete. Some even suggest that keeping this program going is Square Trade's attempt to capitalize on a seller's devotion to a spotless feedback rating.

Much like PayPal, Square Trade's protection services are heavily weighted toward the buyer. The benefit that sellers gain from participating with Square Trade is the affirmation with their buyers that they have met Square Trade's standards and have agreed to abide by Square Trade's programs. This is not negligible. Square Trade does not offer a perfect set of tools for sellers, but it does offer a level of assurance to buyers that sellers are not able to offer on their own. So, go ahead and sign up for Square Trade. You'll find it a valuable tool as you build buyer confidence in your services.

» Have your ID verified

eBay's ID Verify program proves your identity to your potential customers. For a $5.00 fee, eBay will use your personal information to verify that you can prove you are who you say you are. You submit personal information such as your address, phone number, date of birth, and certain installment and credit accounts with their associated monthly payments. This information is not a credit check, and the credit account information is used only for verification purposes and is never stored permanently on eBay. Only your contact information and date of birth are kept on file. Once you pass the verification process, the fee will be added to your eBay bill, and you will remain ID verified until your name, home address, or telephone number changes. You will then receive an ID Verified icon that will appear in all of your auctions. ID Verify helps you prove yourself to potential customers and helps assure them that you are a valid eBay seller.

Unlike other buyer assurance programs, ID Verify also offers real advantages to the seller. Once you are verified, you are eligible to use the Buy It Now feature on any eBay listing, you are able to bid in an amount above $15,000, and you can sell in eBay's Mature Audiences category. Currently, ID Verify is only available to residents of the United States and U.S. territories (Puerto Rico, U.S. Virgin Islands, and Guam). Keep in mind that once you request ID verification, you will not be able to alter your contact information for 30 days, but with this in mind, the program is definitely worth the small investment it requires. You'll find the ID Verify program from eBay's Services menu, or you can go directly to the ID Verify screen by entering http://pages.ebay.com/services/buyandsell/idverify-login.html.

» Consider a warranty

You can go a long way toward reassuring your customers by offering some form of warranty. As PowerSellers described them to us, their warranty policies ranged from "100 percent satisfaction guaranteed, no questions asked" to "refunds offered for merchandise that is significantly different from the listing description, please ask questions before bidding." Many PowerSellers offer a limited-time return policy, but almost all PowerSellers offer their customers some means of finding satisfaction in the face of disappointment. The last thing you want is for a customer to close a deal with you and feel that he didn't get what was coming to him. We'll cover these issues in much greater detail in Chapter 9, but for now, no discussion of customer assurance can be complete without at least a brief mention of warranty offers.

eBay offers a Service Plan that buyers can add to their computer and electronics purchases. The plans are offered by a third-party company, N.E.W. Customer Service Companies, Inc., a leading provider of extended service plans. Your buyer can choose either a Service Plan or an Extended Service Plan. The standard plan is for products that don't come with a manufacturer's warranty. The coverage on these products begins 30 days after the end date of the auction or beyond the Buy It Now date of the transaction. The extended service plan allows your buyer to extend a 90-day, 6-month, or 1-year manufacturer's warranty. Both new and used items are eligible for coverage, but if a product is used, it must be less than five years old. All products must be fully functional at the time of the sale. These plans are not available to customers living in Maine, Alaska, Guam, or Puerto Rico, because of local statutes against the sale

Consider a warranty

or purchase of extended service plans in those areas. In other areas, the service plans are available for products including

- Computers
- Consumer electronics
- Cameras and photography equipment
- Video games
- Musical instruments

For the seller, there is very little risk in offering a buyer an extended service plan. From eBay's Services menu, scroll down the list of Seller's Services until you find the hyperlink for Warranty Program. You'll come to a screen that provides an overview of the Service Plan offers. At the bottom of that screen is a link to a service plan overview for sellers, shown in Figure 6-4. From this page, you will find links to the HTML code that you can copy

FIGURE 6-4 The overview screen of eBay's Warranty Program

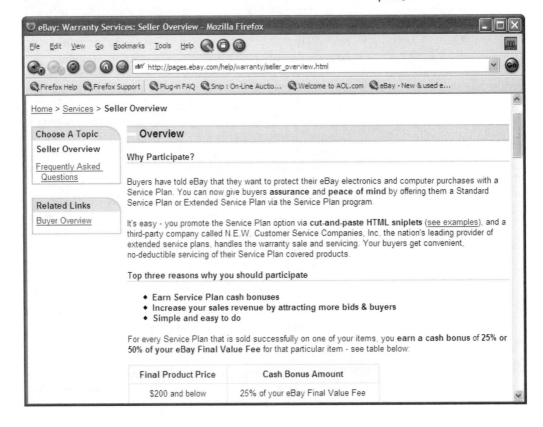

directly into your item descriptions. You can choose to use a graphic and text or text-only link. You are obligated to use the HTML in both your listing and your e-mail to the customer who purchases the item, but that's where your obligation ends. If the customer decides she wants the service plan, clicking that link in your listing or e-mail takes her directly to NEW, where she completes her service plan purchase. The good news for you is that, just like the salesperson in the big-box chain stores, you earn a little kickback for every service plan your customer purchases. If the item you sell costs less than $200, you get a 25 percent refund of your final value fees. If the item sells for more than $200, you get a 50 percent refund. That savings can range from a mere few pennies to as much as $21.56.

Now, we personally never buy the extended warranty, but then we enjoy living life on the edge. Even if you only sell one warranty every few months, any little savings on your eBay fees goes toward improving your profit margins. With no investment and no risk to you, why not add a warranty?

» Don't bother with buySAFE

As you move along among the world of PowerSellers, you most likely will come upon a seal program known as buySAFE. buySAFE, Inc., in conjunction with The Hartford Financial Services Group, offers bonding services for people who sell at online auctions. Sellers bonded by buySAFE go through a qualification process that validates them as dependable, reliable sellers of good reputation. Once a seller is bonded, she receives a buySAFE logo to include in her auction listings. This seal not only proves that she has met the necessary requirements of the bonding process, but it also offers the buyer financial protection against fraud and default, backed by Hartford Financial. In exchange for the program's vouching for your decency as a seller, you pay buySAFE 1 percent of your final transaction price. If your item doesn't sell, you pay nothing. Now, at first blush, this doesn't seem like a bad plan. But, here's the catch. To qualify for bonding through buySAFE, you must be based in the United States and meet the following requirements:

- $1,000 in monthly eBay sales
- 100 eBay feedbacks
- 98 percent positive eBay feedback rating

Offer a coupon

Sound familiar? Of course it does! These are the standards for becoming a PowerSeller! So, to be bonded by buySAFE, you must already be a PowerSeller. But if you're already a PowerSeller, you've proved yourself to be a reliable, dependable seller, so why do you need to pay a percentage of your final transaction fee to a company that will verify you are a reliable, dependable seller?

Reward Your Customers

You will reward your customers by providing them with quality products and great customer service. In addition to those two necessary elements, you can also reward them with little bonuses and treats. Every time you please a customer, you increase the likelihood that he will return for more shopping. PowerSellers have come up with ways to reward their customers, and some of these ways may seem just right for you, too.

» Offer a coupon

Most of us love getting a little bit off the price of a purchase, and a coupon is a great way to do this. When you ship your item, include a coupon for dollars off the customer's next purchase. Or, you can offer a percentage off, if that seems a better choice to you. Spend a little time creating a coupon that says, thanks for shopping, and here's a little incentive to come back and shop again. "When shipping my product, I randomly include a coupon for $10.00 off," says a PowerSeller with more than 33,000 positive feedbacks. That customer is bound to feel like a winner and return to use the cash-back offer. Figure out your price point and your profit margin, and then decide what type of offer makes the most sense to you, but consider offering an incentive to stop by again.

» How about a little "Thank You" gift?

PowerSellers have devised lots of creative ways to send a little love out to their buyers. A coupon is only one way to look at this. You may keep it as simple as printing little thank-you business cards that get popped into every package. Of course, these include your username and some graphic representation of your business. You may include a favorite recipe with every shipment. Try to choose something that will make a connection between the bonus and your business. One DVD-selling PowerSeller includes a bag of microwave popcorn with every shipment. Until you can afford that added expense, there are many creative ideas you can use. Just remember that you can't advertise your bonus gift in your listings without violating eBay's rules, but you can certainly slip it into your shipping boxes as an added surprise. Maximize the value of your little gift by making sure it includes your web site address and your eBay username on every piece. Here are just a few of the creative ideas PowerSellers shared:

- Magnets
- Pens
- Key chains
- Candles
- Calendars
- Flower seeds
- Cell phone antenna boosters
- Gift boxes
- Infrared transceivers for wireless transfer of data from a notebook to a desktop computer!

» Try eBay's Anything Points

eBay offers a program for sellers that offer PayPal as a payment option. Using PayPal, you can choose to participate in the Anything Points program. Once you sign up, you designate the listings you want to offer Anything Points with and how many of these points you wish to offer. Any buyer who pays with PayPal becomes eligible to receive the Anything Points. This is a little like the online equivalent of the old Green Stamps program, and here's how it works.

As a seller, you sign up to participate in the Anything Points program. An Anything Point has a value of $0.01, and you can choose to offer from one to five points per dollar. For example, if you offer two points on an item that sells for $50, your buyer would earn $1.00 in Anything Points, if she paid with PayPal. If she is not an Anything Points participant at the time of the sale, eBay will store her points for her and add them to her account when she signs up. You pay for her Anything Points as a line item on your monthly

Try eBay's Anything Points

eBay statement. Obviously, Anything Points are not worth a great deal alone, but just like those Green Stamps, they can add up.

Sellers can use Anything Points also, to pay for goods they buy on eBay or to pay their monthly eBay fees. There are other good reasons for sellers to try them. When you designate which of your listings include the points and how many points are included for each sale, eBay automatically updates the listings, explaining the offer to your customers. Now, your listing will come up in any title and description search that includes "Anything Points" as a keyword.

Anything Points can be used to pay for the complete eBay purchase, including taxes, shipping, and insurance. In order for a listing to qualify to earn Anything Points for buyers, it must meet the following requirements:

- It must be paid for through PayPal.
- The item must be originally priced on eBay in one of these currencies: U.S. dollars, Canadian dollars, Pounds Sterling, or Euros.
- The item must be paid for within ten days of the auction ending.
- The item must have been purchased on eBay using the same eBay account that was used to register for Anything Points.

Sellers must ensure that the item was originally listed on eBay.com (U.S. only) and that the billing currency is U.S. dollars, Canadian dollars, Pounds Sterling, Euros, or Yen.

eBay has also come up with additional ways to earn Anything Points for both buyers and sellers. If you hold an eBay-sponsored credit card, you can earn one point per dollar of the purchases you charge. Partners have also joined eBay in offering these points. At the time of this writing, some of those partners included FTD.com, Priceline.com, and U.S. Airways. For a complete list of partners currently participating, go to http://anythingpoints.ebay.com/getpoints.html.

Your Business and Your Auctions

Let's turn away from your customers now and take a look at your auctions to see how you can maximize them to your best advantage. PowerSellers have advice for linking your auctions, advertising your business, and making the most of your space on eBay. Once you've read about the different ways PowerSellers manage their listings, you'll have many ideas for how you can get your auctions power-charged too.

» Keep the traffic flowing

"I constantly run 10 to 12 fixed-price listings of my most popular items, all linked to my other auction listings," says a Florida-based PowerSeller. He knows these listings will sell, and his constant presence on eBay not only keeps him available to his return customers but also drives traffic to his other listings, allowing him to expand his product offerings and try new markets.

» Relist your unsold items

When you have an item that doesn't sell the first time you list it, go ahead and relist it to try again. Just do it within 90 days of the closing of your first auction. If it sells during that second listing, eBay will refund the second listing fee, so your cost will not be greater than if it had sold the first time. To qualify for this refund, you must relist the item at the same original price or less. You also may not add a reserve if the first listing did not have one, and if it did, you can't increase the reserve. Before you relist, consider changing the title, improving the photo, or reworking the item description. See if you can come up with something to freshen the listing for its second time around. Relisting an item is a simple process. From the My eBay page, click the listing that didn't sell. Figure 6-5 shows you the Relist link in an unsold item listing. Just click that link and get the sale going again. Unfortunately, if the item doesn't sell the second time, you'll be charged for the second listing fee as well as the first, so do your best to make it move when you relist it. Now's the time you may want to move it over to your eBay store, where it will remain active for 30 days. We'll explore your eBay store options in much greater detail in Chapter 11.

Give Your Bidders a Second Chance

You will certainly have an opportunity to offer your bidders a second chance to purchase something you've listed. If your winning bidder does not pay for the item, you are free to get in

Relist your unsold items

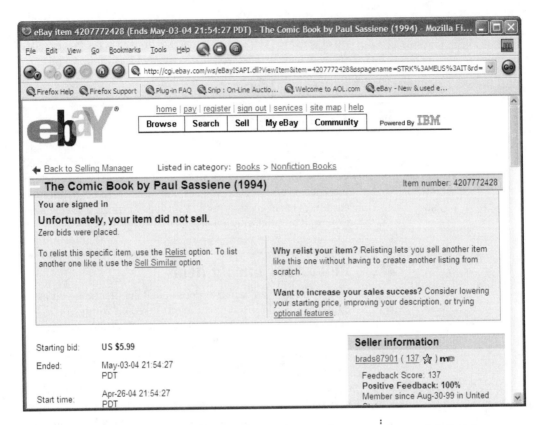

FIGURE 6-5 Relisting an unsold item is as simple as pressing a button.

touch with the next highest bidder and offer him the chance to buy it. You can also contact the highest bidder in an auction that does not meet your reserve price if you decide that you are willing to sell the item for that price after all. Finally, if you have multiple items, but you only list a single one in an auction, you are free to contact the other bidders and offer those items for sale. None of these actions will violate eBay policy, and they all make good business sense. It's just a matter of turning a nibble into a good catch!

Here's what you'll do to create a second-chance offer. From the Bid History page, the My eBay page, the item page for a closed listing, or the Non-Paying Buyer program, you can access the second chance feature. Your first offer will be to the next-highest bidder for the item. If that bidder is still interested in the purchase, you will create a pre-approved bidder auction that will result in this bidder being the only one who can bid on your item, and the price will be listed as the price of his highest bid. (You'll learn all you need to know about pre-approved bidders in Chapter

7.) If, for some reason, that new bidder decides not to complete the purchase, you can then offer a second chance to the next bidder on your list, offering the opportunity, to one bidder at a time, until all prospective bidders have been notified or one of them makes the purchase.

Advertising Your Business

Advertising is a business expense that any business owner must consider. Your eBay business will draw upon different forms of advertising, but it's wise for you to plan to spend some time and money promoting your new business. We've already given you some advice from the PowerSellers in recommending that you send out little reminders and gifts to the people who buy from you. That's sharply targeted advertising directed to people you already know are interested. You've also seen that keeping a steady stream of auctions listed at all times helps direct a flow of traffic to all of your listings. But there are still some additional advertising investments that you'll want to try. As you might expect, most of your advertising will happen right on eBay, but you'll also see some ways you can branch out to the rest of the Internet to entice new customers.

» Keywords for sale

The eBay Keyword program is a simple way for sellers to increase traffic to their listings. Here's how it works: You "purchase" a number of keywords or "keyword phrases" that match items you're selling. When someone enters one of the keywords you've bought into the eBay search box, a banner ad appears on the screen above the search results. Sometimes it will be yours. (We say sometimes, because these ads cycle on and off, and there's lots of competition.) Each banner for each keyword is shown a maximum of three times every 24 hours so that shoppers can get a variety of offers. Clicking your ad takes prospective buyers to your auctions or your store, whichever you specify. You can easily create your own banner ad through the service itself, or you can upload one of your own.

The cost works this way. You specify a total budget for your current campaign, for example $50. You then select keywords that match the items you have for sale. Be specific when you do this. The more closely you match the keywords to the items you

Keywords for sale

sell, the more likely you are to attract shoppers who will actually buy your item once it pops up in the search. Then you enter the maximum bid you are willing to pay for each keyword every time someone clicks your banner ad. This ranges from $0.10 to about $2.00. You only pay that cost-per-click amount when your ad appears *and* when someone clicks it. How often will your ad appear? It depends on the popularity of the keyword and how much you were willing to bid per click. Those sellers who name the highest bids get the highest priority. When you are setting your bid price, you will immediately see where you rank in terms of getting the top spot for the banner ad. You can also view your competition to see how high you'll have to go to be the top bidder.

Although this service is relatively expensive, the banner ads are very attractive and the targeted keywords increase the chance that the person searching is going to want to purchase. Figure 6-6 shows a banner ad that popped up when we searched for cat toys. As you can see, this is an attractive link. The secret to using this

FIGURE 6-6 A banner ad appears above the search results list when the right keywords are entered.

service is to choose your keywords carefully. You want them to be specific so that your item will be well represented, yet at the same time you want to include other words that might also appeal to people shopping for your item. For example, if we sold cat toys, we'd also consider buying keywords for "cat beds" or "cat grooming," since people shopping for those products might also want to take a look at cat toys. Then our banner ad would appear for any of those keyword searches. It may seem to you that this is an expensive form of advertising, but many PowerSellers use it, and it might be worth a try for you, too.

» Shoot for eBay's Co-op Advertising program

Once you become a PowerSeller, you will be eligible to participate with eBay in a co-op advertising program. This will allow you to create advertisements for print publications that combine your business with eBay. You must complete the registration process and use eBay's Ad Creation Wizard to create your advertisement. Then you must submit your ad for pre-approval by eBay before you can use it. Once your ad has been approved and is actually running in the publication you've selected, you can submit a form to eBay for a reimbursement of 25 percent of your advertising fee. In order to be reimbursed, you must provide eBay with the following information:

- A completed Co-op Reimbursement Form
- An original tear sheet of the advertisement as it appeared in the publication that includes the entire page, not just your ad
- A copy of the invoice for the ad
- A published rate card including the publication's circulation numbers, which must exceed 10,000.

This type of advertising can be very expensive, and you're not ready for it anyway. But, it gives you something to shoot for now, and to consider when you do become a PowerSeller. By then you may feel ready to take this next step.

» Use your own web site

As you saw in Chapter 3, having a business on eBay makes it very important for you also to have your own web site. Fortunately, now you know how to go about getting one. Using

Use your own web site

that web site to advertise your eBay business couldn't be easier. You already own a domain name, and since you followed our advice, you chose one that reflects your eBay business. Now, every time someone does an Internet search relevant to your products or business, your domain name will pop up in the search results. No search engine will ever find your auctions or your eBay store, but your own web site is another story. You'll simply include a link to your eBay store and auctions from your web site, and all the visitors who stop by there can easily see what you have to offer for sale on eBay. "I don't even let my customers get into the main part of eBay. I link all my advertising directly to my eBay store, that way I bypass all the competition," said a PowerSeller with a 99.99 percent positive feedback rating.

Taking Care of Your Business

Having an eBay business allows you to learn as you go, and you must keep doing both right from the start. Learn your lessons, incorporate what works, move on from what doesn't, and don't be afraid to cut your losses. There is no magic formula for your eBay business or any other business. Operating on eBay makes it easier for you to be flexible. You should use that flexibility to your advantage. Never miss an opportunity to learn something new about a better way to take care of your business. Here are a few tips from PowerSellers that should help.

Study Your Sell-Through

In Chapter 2, you learned about identifying potential sources of good products to sell on eBay, and now it's time for you to test your theories. Use a practical formula for determining your sell-through rate. For a period of time, let's say one month, take the number of sold auctions you have and divide that number by the number of ended items you have. Suppose you listed 120 items in the month of June. As of July 1, you have sold 60 items. Your sell-through rate would be 60 percent, which is an amazing number and a sign that you're on to some good products.

Your sell-through rate is important because it reflects what your actual cost is to do business. If your sell-through rate is 50 percent, you are actually paying more than the going rate for all your listing fees because you're paying for all of the auctions that don't result in sales as well as the auctions that do. That adds to your listing fees for the successful auctions. So, you want to keep a careful eye on your sell-through rate. By studying your sell-through carefully, you'll be able to identify the most profitable parts of your business, and you'll see new business opportunities. At the same time, you'll see what isn't selling well and you'll learn what not to pursue any further.

Use Your Auction Management Software

As you learned in Chapter 4, most PowerSellers use auction management software and you should be using it too. Every auction management program includes data for studying your sell-through. You can print monthly reports that show all of your listings and all of your items that sold. These will help you calculate what percentage of your listings is actually selling. You will also find these monthly reports invaluable to your record keeping when we get to Chapter 10.

» Use your counters creatively

You learned in Chapter 3 about why you should be using a counter on your auction listings and you saw the many choices you have, including some free counters from Andale. Now, it's time for you to use those counters to study the results of your efforts. Here are some good ways to do that:

- **Run listings in different categories.**   Double-check your category choices by running listings for similar items in more than one category. Then, watch your counters carefully to see the results. This will allow you to keep refining your category choices for increased traffic.

- **Run listings with different titles.**   By using different titles for similar items, you can check on your keyword choices. This will help you see which keywords are generating the most hits and the greatest traffic to your listings.

- **Use counters to refine your auction timing.**   Watch your counters carefully to see when your auctions are getting the most traffic. Then you can change your auction ending strategies to take advantage of your greatest number of visitors.

Consider Sellathon ViewTracker

■ **See what other eBayers are saying about you.** One little tip to remember is that if your auction is getting a lot of traffic, but no bids, people are talking about you on the discussion boards! It may seem like a huge universe, but it's not that enormous that gossip doesn't travel. Just consider the listing featured in Figure 6-7. Not only did he have more than six million viewers before his auction ended, he made it onto eBay radio and national television!

» Consider Sellathon ViewTracker

As your business grows, you may find you want more exact data than you can gather from either your auction management software or your counters alone. That's when you may be ready to turn to Sellathon and their ViewTracker product. ViewTracker not only keeps track of all your auction visitors, but it also tells you how they found your auction, if they saved your auction to their My eBay pages, how many times they've checked in, and much more too. You will find the Sellathon home page at www.sellathon.com.

Here's how it works. When you are a Sellathon user, every time you create an auction listing, you add a little code to the bottom of your auction. Once this code is added, two things happen. First, you get a little Sellathon banner that appears in your listing. Second, every time that banner loads on your auction page, it sends a huge amount of data from the viewer's

FIGURE 6-7 These two views show an unusual eBay listing and the counter recording of how many people viewed this auction, even after the item was sold!

computer to Sellathon's computers. When you check on your Sellathon listing pages, you'll find the following information for each visitor:

- The sequential number of that visitor, whether he was the fifteenth or the fiftieth to view your listing

- The date and time the visitor arrived

- The visitor's IP address, the numbers that are unique to each computer

- The visitor's geographical region

- If the item already had a bid

- If the visitor is watching the auction in My eBay

- Whether the visitor browsed a category, searched a category, searched all of eBay, used eBay's Product Finder utility, came to the auction through your "See Seller's Other Items" link, or found your item in some other way

- The category this visitor was either browsing or searching in when your auction was found

- The search terms the visitor used if he was searching

- Whether the search was for "Titles Only" or "Titles and Descriptions"

- Did your visitor choose to view Auctions Only, Buy It Now, or both?

- Which search preferences and options your visitor chose. For example, show/hide pictures, sellers that accept PayPal, etc.

- The visitor's method for sorting results. For example, high price, low price, auctions ending first

Sellathon users can also view their own auctions for information about the traffic they receive. That information includes the following:

- The most active time of day for each auction

- The most popular ways visitors are finding the auction

- The most popular search terms used

- The type of search, Titles only or Title and Description

Use Medved's eBay Auction Counts

- The preferred sorting method used to view the auction
- The total number of visitors to the auction
- The busiest day
- The most frequent IP address for this auction
- The page number visitors are finding your auction on most frequently
- The current high bid for the auction

At this point, you probably don't need as much information as Sellathon provides. You've got too many other things to concentrate on now before you'll be ready to use this much information. When you've built a solid business, you might want to invest some money and give this program a try as you fine-tune your business. You'll be able to check your keywords, timing strategies, and category placements on the basis of solid data. Sellathon ViewTracker is not inexpensive, but it does provide a lot of value for the money. You can buy the licensing rights for one year for $49.00. That allows you to track 25 simultaneous auctions. If you list more than 25 auctions, you'll receive an e-mail offering you to upgrade to the next licensing level for a fee if $89.00 per year. You don't have to upgrade, but then only the first 25 auctions will be tracked. The highest level of licensing will cost $199.00, but that is far more than an individual user is likely to need.

» Use Medved's eBay Auction Counts

If you took our advice in Chapter 1 and subscribed to the free monthly online newsletter AuctionBytes, you are already familiar with the services of Medved eBay Auction Counts. (If you didn't take our advice, shame on you! What are you waiting for? Put this book down and go sign up for AuctionBytes, then come back.)

Every week AuctionBytes publishes the weekly sell-through rates for eBay's top-selling categories. The data are often gathered by Medved Auction Counts. Medved gathers statistics from eBay every 1.5 hours, 24 hours a day, 7 days a week. They study completed auctions so that they can capture the data from both last-minute bidders and buyers who used the Buy It Now feature. By studying their percentages every week, you can calculate how your listings compare to the others in your same categories.

Medved's web site provides users with graphs of daily, weekly, monthly, and yearly data. You can also see the sum total of all the data they've collected in a single graph. To view the graphs, go to www.medved.net/cgi-bin/cal.exe?EIND. Let's take a look at just a couple of these graphs so that you can see how valuable they are to you in gathering information about your business.

The weekly chart shown in Figure 6-8 shows that sales were highest on Sunday. That's not surprising, given what we know about the popularity of Sunday evening auctions. Sales bottomed out on Tuesday morning and then, for this week, steadily increased toward the next weekend. Thursday evening proved to be a good time to shop, just as we saw in Chapter 5, but surprisingly in this particular week, Friday during the day was just as successful. By checking other weeks in comparison, you'll see that the standard advice of Sunday nights and Thursday nights for ending auctions, while generally reliable, is not cut in stone. Take a look at this chart for just a few weeks earlier, shown in Figure 6-9, and you'll see that sales were just all over the place. Carefully studying the weekly charts can help you determine the best times for you to list and end your auctions.

The monthly charts Medved provides are also useful. You can use these to track slow and busy seasons for you and other eBay sellers. You can determine if your slow month corresponds with months that are just slow for you, or slow for other eBay sellers too. This might help you determine if you'll need to

FIGURE 6-8 The weekly chart from Medved shows a typical weekly flow of traffic on eBay.

FIGURE 6-9 This weekly Medved chart shows just how unpredictable eBay traffic can be.

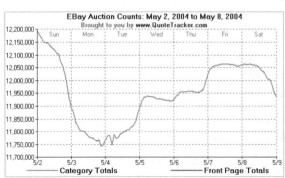

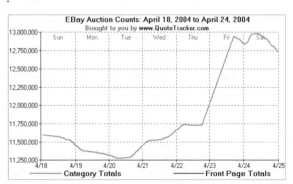

broaden your product offerings to get you through those slow months by targeting things that might sell better in the months that are slow for your standard product line. Just as PowerSeller Jrgolfwarehouse, mentioned in Chapter 5, knew to plan for a slow month in March, armed with that information you'll be able to plan for your slow months too. If you find your slow months are also slow for most other sellers, you may decide those are the months you'll use to plan your vacation.

Manage Your Business

You're the boss now, so it all comes down to you. Here are a few suggestions for you to keep in mind as you go about your business. PowerSellers learned most of these things the hard way. Aren't you glad you don't have to?

» Turn over your inventory

Your goal is to move inventory into your business and out of your business. That's where the profits lie. But, suppose you buy a load of items and in studying your sell-through, you can see they really aren't going to earn what you hoped they would. Get them going. Even if it means you only make your costs or even if you occasionally have to take a loss, it's more important to get some money out of that inventory so that you can put it in more profitable items. "Rapid turnover and reinvesting your money for more products is one of the keys to long-term success on eBay," a PowerSeller from New York told us. "Turning over your inventory is the key to high profits," agrees a Florida-based PowerSeller. No one likes to settle for no profit, but sometimes it's the best alternative you have.

» Automate everything

"Work constantly to automate and streamline your process. Listing, e-mail, shipping, everything that can be automated makes your sell-through better, and gives you time for building your inventory. It's not as easy as you'd think," said a PowerSeller who specializes in coins and collectibles and maintains a 99.9 percent positive feedback rating. "I wish I'd started earlier trying to integrate all aspects of my auction business, to make everything seamless. I'm constantly trying to make the 'flow' a little smoother," he added. He had to retrofit his operation, but thanks to his willingness to share his experiences, you don't. You can build these systems into your operation as you go, giving you an advantage from the very start.

You need to think and work like a PowerSeller. Use every tool you have, from your auction management software, to your web-hosted photos, to your automatic feedback procedures. These tools should work to replace your effort in some of the day-to-day details of the task with an automated process that you can manage.

» Hire help

"Hire help early on. Look at the end result of what you want. If you want high volume, you have to have help," advises PowerSeller Cultureandthrills. This is a difficult thing for new sellers to do. First there is the money to consider. Then you have to be willing to trust something you're just starting to build to someone else's work habits. It's difficult to give up control and allow someone else to do what you're just getting used to doing yourself. Do it anyway.

Look at it from a different perspective. By bringing someone in to help you early on, you'll be able to have that person train along with you. You'll be perfecting your systems while you're teaching them to your employee. This will give you, not only you own perspective, but someone else's too. You'll be learning the process with two brains instead of just one.

"My energies must go to acquiring inventory and properly cataloging what I have. I can't possibly be successful if I have to do all the listing and shipping myself, too," added our PowerSeller. Know what you must do as the boss, and find parts of your business you can turn over to a trusted employee.

Remember you don't need to hire full-time help. You certainly are not ready for that. You don't have the volume, you don't have the money, and you don't have the need. Instead hire part-time helpers. Perhaps start with someone who comes in two afternoons a week for a couple of hours to do all your shipping. Maybe you'll then move on to train that person in listing auctions, leaving you to do all of the e-mail responses along with the inventory management. You'll find your own way to make use of help once you have it.

Now, where will you find a trusted employee? There are many places to look. The local high school is full of reliable, worthy, and capable students. Get in touch with the principal for some recommendations. You will most likely find a pool of potential helpers who would so much rather work for you than

Hire help

flip burgers for spending money. Plus, these people are very likely to be completely at home in front of a computer. They can probably teach you a thing or two about HTML also! The next step would be the local community college. You're bound to find students here who need some extra cash, and they'll be even more likely to come to you with computer skills you'll find useful.

For many of your tasks, don't overlook the stay-at-home mom. By the time moms have kids in school, many are looking for a little diversion during the day that can also help supplement the family income. You can provide them with a little work on a flexible schedule that could easily integrate with the demands of their families. Plus, you could be helping them to learn a business they'll then want to pursue for themselves. Or, consider a retiree. They can be the most reliable employees of all.

Don't look at the expense of hiring help as a draw against your bottom line. Look at it instead as a way to maximize your effort. "When my helper comes in for the afternoon, and I'm free to do listings and plan inventory, I'm always so surprised at the end of the day to see how many things I also have packed and ready to be shipped," crowed a PowerSeller from New Jersey. You don't have to offer a huge salary for these part-time workers either. If you stick with minimum wage, and you pay for four to six hours of work per week, your employee wages will be no more than many people spend per week on babysitting fees. Chapter 10 will tell you more about the record-keeping issues and concerns for hiring help. The return on your expense will be well worth the investment.

Become a Trading Assistant

Once you've gained some experience and feel confident with your ability to list and sell on eBay, you may want to leverage this confidence into another branch of your business. Trading Assistants sell products on eBay for people who don't want to do it themselves. Often these are people who are intimidated by computers or who don't feel confident in their abilities to successfully navigate in eBay's waters. Their intimidation can translate into profits for you. We spoke with many PowerSellers who are also Trading Assistants, and it's a good match. As you build your business, you will already be putting all of your systems in place. You'll have all of the equipment and expertise necessary to create excellent auctions, so you might just find that you enjoy offering this expertise to others.

» Get listed in eBay's Trading Assistant Directory

Becoming a Trading Assistant on eBay couldn't be easier. You must meet some basic requirements, but these are not difficult to achieve. You must have sold at least four items in the last 30 days. You must have a feedback rating of at least 50, with a positive rating of at least 97 percent. Once you've met these requirements, registering with eBay as a Trading Assistant is easy. You can use the Site Map to go directly to the Trading Assistant discussion board in eBay's Answer Center, as shown in Figure 6-10. On the right side of this screen, you'll see a menu of choices that will let you learn more about becoming a Trading Assistant or sign up to become a Trading Assistant. From a hyperlink in the introduction to the board, you'll be able to go directly to the Trading Assistant directory to search geographically for other Trading Assistants. Trading Assistants in the directory are listed according to their

FIGURE 6-10 The Trading Assistant discussion board in eBay's Answer Center is a tremendous resource.

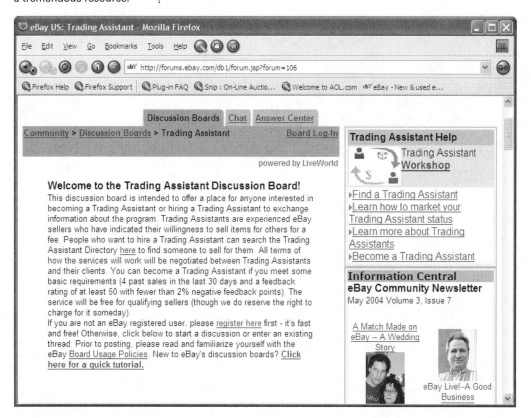

Decide on your policies up front

level of experience and the volume of transactions they've completed. The more experienced ones are listed first.

When you click the link to Become a Trading Assistant, you'll get the blank form to complete for being listed in eBay's Trading Assistant directory that is shown in Figure 6-11. Simply complete and submit this form and you'll be listed as an eBay Trading Assistant in the Trading Assistant directory.

» Decide on your policies up front

In order to decide on your policies, you have to complete the only part of becoming a Trading Assistant that is complicated. That is deciding how you will charge your customers and what your policies for operating your Trading Assistant business will be. As the Trading Assistant, you will be billed for all eBay listing fees whether or not you sell the item you list. That's a point of negotiation between you and your customer. Will you cover these fees as an expense of doing business, or will you

FIGURE 6-11 The registration form to join the Trading Assistant's directory makes signing up simple.

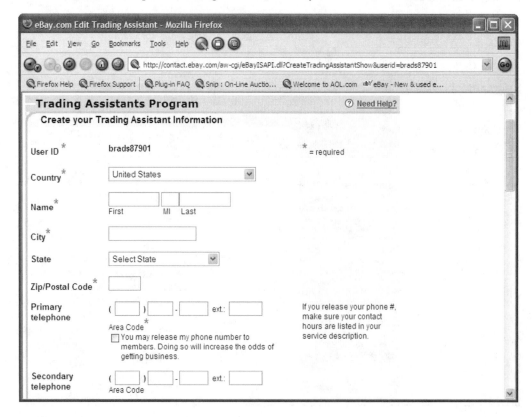

charge a base fee that will include that charge no matter what the outcome of the auction is? Will you charge a base fee for picking up the item? Will you earn nothing at all if the item doesn't sell, or will you charge a fee for your services in processing the auction? Will you establish a base value below which you will not take an item on consignment? There's not much profit to be made on selling something for $15, when you only get a commission from the sale. You must decide for yourself before you complete your directory listing so that you can clearly state your policies to prospective consigners.

» Know your competition

Using the Trading Assistant directory, search by your zip code to see who your competition is. Then you can see if your competitors specialize in particular categories, and you can see what their areas of expertise are. Now, you can tailor your own marketing efforts to areas they may be missing. You'll be able to distinguish yourself from the crowd in your own niche.

» Market yourself as a Trading Assistant

eBay encourages you as a registered Trading Assistant to promote your services in your auction listings, your About Me page, and your local home town. You can include a link to your Trading Assistant directory listing from all of your auctions, your eBay store, and your About Me page. eBay also has some materials you are free to download to use as advertisements you can post in the local grocery store or other local bulletin boards. Go to http://pages.ebay.com/tradingassistants/collateral/index.html for examples.

Search for Possible Consignments

Marketing yourself as a Trading Assistant will help drum up business for you, but there are some other things you can also do to get the consignments coming your way. Talk to everyone you know about your new venture. Make yourself the local eBay guru. Here are just a few suggestions to help get you started:

■ You'll find that many older people who may be considering a downsizing move might be more than happy to let you take some unwanted items for them.

Prepare a standard contract

- Go to successful small brick-and-mortar businesses and offer them your services. They have very little to lose in allowing you to open up a whole new market for them.

- If you go to yard sales, ask if there are any items the sellers might not have included in the sale but might want to sell in a more profitable venue.

- Approach your religious community to see if there are any items just stored away in the building that could be turned into needed cash.

» Prepare a standard contract

When you enter into an agreement with a prospective client, be prepared with a standard contract that clearly states your services, fees, and responsibilities. You can find contracts such as these by searching the listings on the Trading Assistant discussion board of eBay's Answer Center. Make sure you include all possible charges, including listing enhancements the client might want. It is a good idea to include a chart of eBay's listing options so that your client can see very clearly how the fees add up. Make sure your client also understands that in addition to the listing fees, he'll have to pay the Final Value Fees from his proceeds as well.

Make your standard contract as comprehensive and clear as possible to prevent any misunderstandings that might arise in dealing with someone who is not experienced on eBay. You are well within your rights, for example, to charge a flat fee for listing the item whether it sells or not. If this fee is modest, your client shouldn't complain about it. After all, it will take you time to research the item and prepare it for the auction, and you deserve to be paid for that time. Just make sure your client understands that this fee will be assessed whether or not the item sells. And, of course, reassure him with your excellent eBay reputation that you are likely to get his item sold because you are a proven, successful eBay seller.

Include some basic eBay operating rules in your contract. For example, make sure your client knows that he can't go onto eBay and bid on his own item in order to bump up the price. Make sure he understands that once the item is listed, he cannot easily back out of the agreement. Be sure he knows the item will sell to the highest bidder even if he thinks it hasn't earned quite enough money. A reserve is not a bad idea when you're working with an inexperienced client, because it offers a level of reassurance that a newcomer might need.

» Trading Assistants pricing advice

Most Trading Assistants agree that a sliding scale is the best way to charge your customers. With a sliding scale, you'll begin with a significant percentage of the sale price as a fee and move to a smaller percentage as the price of the sale item increases. For example, you may charge a rate of 30 percent for an item that sells for $100. That rate will steadily decrease as the price of the item increases. You may even go as far as only 2 percent of an item that sells for $20,000 or more.

Most Trading Assistant/PowerSellers we spoke with agreed that in order for the percentages to work out favorably, you should not accept items for consignment that bring less than $100 as a final value. Of course, as you're just starting out, you may be willing to work at a slightly lesser profit margin, adjusting your needs as your business grows and you attain PowerSeller status.

» You're a professional, so make a professional impression

Part of the joy of having your own eBay business is that you are free to operate it in your own style. If you want to work all day in your pajamas, who's to stop you? But, this is no longer true if you're trying to branch out as a Trading Assistant. Now, you'll need to exude competence and professionalism. Always make sure you look professional when you meet a prospective client. Remember how important image is on eBay? Well, it's just as important when you're courting prospective Trading Assistant clients too. Why should someone entrust you with something she considers valuable if you don't make her feel that you know just what you're doing.

So, dress the part. Have nice business cards printed so that you can leave one behind for further contact. Send all correspondence to prospective clients on your own letterhead. When you present your contract, make sure it's printed neatly and is clear and easily understood. Putting some money into these tools will pay back in a professional image for your Trading Assistant business.

Adam Nollmeyer

Adam Nollmeyer is a PowerSeller and a Trading Assistant who started on eBay in 2000. You will find him there under the username Acmeresale. Reselling items is his specialty. When Adam first began, he looked at eBay selling as mostly a hobby. He was a Ham radio operator, and he started to attend police auctions just so that he could add more radio equipment. Before too long, he realized that he'd acquired much more equipment than he could ever use, so he turned to eBay, just to see what it would be like to sell some of what he had.

Soon after he started selling on eBay, his car needed some repair work, and unfortunately it wasn't an inexpensive job. Adam realized he might be on to something with his eBay sales, when he actually had the cash to pay for the repairs, and it didn't come out of his usual budget! That was the jolt that showed him he might have discovered something more than just a hobby.

About this same time, Adam began working at a live auction house. This was where he learned

the ins and outs of auction selling. It was a perfect complement to his auction shopping, and it rounded out his experience for his own business. He even learned the basics of using the auction management software Seller's Assistant Pro, because that was the program the live auction house used. Working at the auction house also gave him the experience he needed to learn how to research prospective product areas.

With this experience, he went to the police auction prepared to shop for business. He was still ready to purchase the radio equipment he knew about, but he also took notes on other items up for auction. He'd go home to check them out on eBay to see the highest price and the average price they brought. Then he determined what he could spend and still make a profit. At the next auction, he was prepared to buy for reselling. Today Adam estimates that his average cost of acquiring an item is about $20, and his average sale for those items is $200. He still buys previously owned items for resale, but now his products often include two-way radio and communication equipment, police scanners, photography and camera equipment, and business and industrial supplies.

Adam offers some great advice for new eBay sellers. He is the one responsible for the phrase you've seen used in this book, "start it low and let it go." It's the philosophy he sells by, and it doesn't disappoint him. According to Adam, starting your item at a low price draws people into early bidding and that makes for a good auction. He told us of a group of ten battery packs he had. These are big battery packs that professional photographers use to power their strobe lights. He saw other sellers offering them on eBay for a starting price of $175. He started his for less than $10. Not only did this cut down on his listing fees, but it drove his auction prices, too. He sold all ten of them for closing prices that ranged from $200 to $225 each! His competition didn't come close to this. When he checked his counter and the counters of his competitors, he found that, on average, about 200 people had viewed each of his auctions while the others drew only about 30 prospective buyers.

In addition to being a PowerSeller and a Trading Assistant, Adam is also a professional photographer. He uses his professional experience well in photographing his items for his auction listings, but he also draws on it to decide what items to sell. Like other PowerSellers, Adam recommends sticking with things you know about. He reminded us that in the field of radio equipment, differences that are seemingly minor to the inexperienced eye can drastically affect the value among experienced shoppers. If you don't know radios, you simply won't know what to buy for reselling. The same is true for photography equipment.

As a Trading Assistant, Adam has about 15 regular clients. He says most of his business comes to him through word of mouth and good recommendations. Visit Adam's web site at www.acmeresale.com to learn more about this talented PowerSeller. On the web site, Adam shares a great story of how he sold one of Rock-and-Roll's most famous drum sets, owned by Neil Peart of the band, Rush. You'll see some examples of Adam's wonderful photographs, and you'll learn all about his experience selling this huge and valuable item on eBay for a client.

Chapter 7

Close the Auction and Collect the Cash

Here's the moment we've all been waiting for. You have a winning bidder and you're ready to get paid. It feels wonderful, don't you agree? This is the reason you started all this to begin with. Before we get too carried away with joy, let's not get ahead of ourselves. The celebration will have to wait until the details have been worked out, and there are plenty of those.

There is no part of the relationship between buyer and seller that requires more careful handling than the payment part. When it goes well, it's no issue at all, almost seamless. When it goes badly, it can lead to misunderstanding, hard feelings, negative feedback, and mediation. You can go a long way to prevent a bad outcome by understanding your payment options and how to make them work most effectively. You can also ensure a smooth experience by remembering that on eBay, communication is king.

When you created your auction listings, you carefully outlined your payment options to prospective customers. That, of course, does not mean that the winning bidder will have paid any attention to what you stated so carefully. When the auction ends, you will send an "end of auction" e-mail to the winner. Make sure your payment options are also clearly stated in this e-mail. You'll have the winner's complete attention for the moment, and now's the time to take advantage of that. Because so much trouble can be averted by clear communication between seller and buyer, you mustn't miss this opportunity.

That's not to say you should anticipate trouble from each transaction. Most of them will go through without a hitch. PowerSellers wouldn't be able to process hundreds of transactions a month if this weren't true. Most people on eBay, both buyers and sellers, are there to do business and are honest, trustworthy, decent people. Except for those who aren't. Just as in any other community, there is a small subset of people on eBay who are there for fraud, cheating, lying, and stealing. We'll show you some ways to protect yourself from them.

eBay payment options fall into two major camps: PayPal and everything else. PayPal is eBay's preferred method of payment, and that's easy to understand. eBay owns PayPal. When you sell something on eBay through PayPal, you'll pay your eBay fees, and then you'll likely also pay PayPal fees. That's a great way for eBay to get paid twice for the same transaction. In return, you and your buyer will both gain benefits from using PayPal. Your buyer will have all of the buyer protection services outlined in Chapter 6. She will also have the choice of using any one of

PayPal's multiple payment options, including credit cards, PayPal balances on her account, E-checks, and transfers from existing accounts. The flexibility of choice makes your auctions more attractive to your prospective customers. You will also enjoy the ease of using PayPal and the security it offers your buyers in knowing that they are backed by protection services. Much of this chapter will be devoted to discussing the ins and outs of PayPal, but first, let's take a look at everything else.

Payment Options That Are Not PayPal

You have a variety of options available for receiving funds from your buyers. Variety is the way for you to go. The more choices you give your buyers, the more likely they are to find one they like. You also establish yourself as a professional seller if you are able to offer your buyers a choice of payment methods. Remember, you are trying to get your customers to find it fun, easy, and secure to shop with you, so be flexible in choosing your payment options.

Just as with most other subjects, PowerSellers have a wide variety of opinions about what methods of payment they prefer. Much of this has to do with their personal experiences. Some sellers, once burned, will forever swear off a particular payment method. Other, more fortunate sellers may stay open to that same payment method and never have a problem. Don't be so afraid of being cheated that you close yourself off. Sometimes the risk is worth taking, and among the most successful PowerSellers, you'll find the widest variety of payment options.

Most people don't pay with cash on eBay, but it does occasionally happen. The risk in sending cash for payment is largely on the buyer. There is no paper trail to trace transactions, and we've all seen the statement on payment envelopes from bills that warns, "Don't send cash through the mail." Cash payments are a bad idea for the buyer, but some buyers will send them anyway. From the seller's point of view, cash can still be a problem. First of all, if you don't receive U.S. currency, you'll have the exchange rates to deal with, which will most likely cut into your profits. But your real problem with cash is if it gets "lost" in the mail. You've never received payment, and the buyer can't prove that he's paid, but he's out the money and the item, which you surely won't ship without payment. It's bound to cause bad feelings, and negative feedback is a possible result.

Accept personal checks

You can state in your auctions and end-of-auction e-mails that you don't accept cash payments, or you can tell your buyers who want to pay with cash that they must send it by registered mail. In the end, it won't happen often, but you'll still get cash through the mail, and you'll have to deal with it on a case-by-case basis.

⟫ Accept personal checks

PowerSellers have mixed feelings about personal checks. Some won't accept them as payment, but most do. The problem is, even if you say you won't accept personal checks, buyers are going to send them anyway. They require a little more effort on your part. You have to deposit them to your account and hold the item for ten business days to make sure the check clears the buyer's bank. The check may clear in fewer than ten days, but that's the default recommended by most banks. If the check doesn't clear, you have to do the paperwork necessary to return the check, and there are some bank hassles and possible bank fees to consider. But overall, most checks go through without a hitch. The real benefit to accepting checks is that buyers like to use them. They are easy. They don't build credit card debt. And they provide the buyer with a good, solid receipt. It's easy for a buyer to protect himself from a fraudulent seller if he has a canceled check to prove he's paid.

⟫ Don't always insist on holding the check

Your payment policy statement should make it clear that you will hold the item for ten business days while the check clears. That's your right, and it's a way to protect yourself from bad-check writers. No one can fault you for it. Once you've been clear about your policy, take it on a case-by-case basis. For the vast majority of checks you receive, make your buyers wait. But if you receive a check for a smaller purchase (you decide the amount, but less than $20.00 is a good sum for discussion purposes), check out the buyer's feedback. If this is a person with a high feedback number and a very clean feedback rating, don't make her wait for her check to clear. She's not a risk. Show her some respect for the fine reputation she's built on eBay and go ahead and ship her item to her. She's earned your confidence, and your consideration will go a long way toward encouraging her to come back and shop with you again. The same is true for your repeat buyers. Everyone likes to feel appreciated, and you will likely be rewarded with positive feedback.

Money Orders and Cashier's Checks Are Risk-Free Options

As a seller, you have no risk at all in accepting money orders or cashier's checks. These are guaranteed funds. They can't bounce, and they are just as good as cash. You can cash them easily. Money orders can even be cashed at the post office. They are a little more inconvenient for the buyer, because he'll have to actually go purchase one for a fee. It usually takes cash to buy a money order. Also, there is no paper trail for the buyer. He'll have a receipt, but he won't have any way to prove that the seller cashed the funds. If we were writing this from a buyer's point of view, we'd recommend that you send all money orders and cashier's checks with a delivery confirmation to prove that the seller received it. But since we're looking at the issue from your point of view, by all means, list money orders and cashier's checks as accepted payment options and hope your buyer uses them. They're instant cash, and they'll spare you the hassles of personal checks and the added expense of PayPal fees.

» Never use wire transfers

If your trading partner insists on using a wire transfer, walk away from the transaction and send a report to eBay. Any buyer or seller who wants to transfer funds should be happy to go through PayPal to do it. That's the secure route for transferring money between accounts. If someone is insisting that you do a wire transfer outside of PayPal, the chance you'll be entering into a fraudulent transaction is very high. Even if the person is legitimate, you simply can't allow yourself to take the chance. Wire transfers are one of the main sources of fraud in online auctions, and there's simply no reason to leave yourself open to risk here. Be very clear, it's either PayPal or nothing for transferring funds from one bank account to another.

» Register with Western Union's Auction Payments Service

Western Union's Auction Payments service (Auctionpayments .com) is a very nice compromise between a money order and a credit card sale. You get the money order: the buyer gets to pay with a credit card. Figure 7-1 is a graphic from the

Register with Western Union's Auction Payments Service

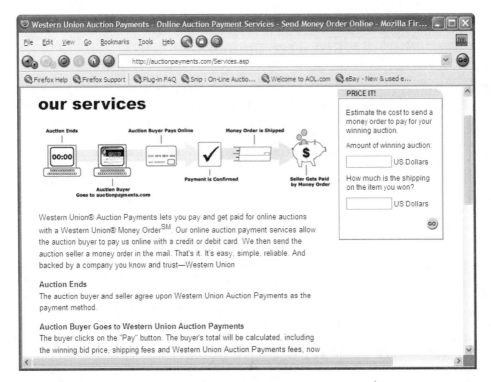

Auctionpayments.com web site to show you how it works. Best of all, the service is free to the seller. The *buyer* pays all the costs directly to Western Union.

You don't have to register to receive a Western Union money order, but you'll see there are advantages to doing so. To register as a seller, you can click the Get Paid link from any Western Union Auctionpayments.com's page. You will then establish a username and password for the system. Once you've done that, you will receive an activation e-mail from Western Union that includes a link to the pages that allow you to complete the account activation process. Now you are eligible to use the account management tools available only to registered sellers. By establishing your own account, you'll have access to data on past and present orders. By registering, you've also ensured that Western Union has your correct address. Registering is free; as a seller, you may incur a fee only if you choose a "payout method" other than a money order, such as a check in British Pounds.

When a buyer pays for something through Western Union Auctionpayments.com, he pays for the money order online with a

FIGURE 7-1 This Auctionpayments.com graphic shows you how the service works. Notice the estimated cost calculator that makes it easy to get a clear idea of how much it will cost to pay for an item using Auctionpayments.com.

credit card. Western Union then sends you an e-mail confirming the payment and including the buyer's shipping address. From three to five business days later, you will receive a Western Union money order in the mail. That process can actually take as much as ten days, depending on your postal service, but the average is three to five days.

The only possible risk to a seller is if the buyer uses a stolen or fraudulent credit card to make the purchase, and here the risk is slight. If the card is bad, Western Union will send you an e-mail requesting you to destroy the money order. If you have not yet shipped the item, the sale is void, and you have only lost your listing fees. If you have cashed the money order but not shipped the item, Western Union will ask you not to send it, but if you have sent it, nothing more will happen. Typically, Western Union will honor the money order for you in spite of the bad credit card. Western Union Auctionpayments.com is a very popular choice for sellers who honor international sales. Buyers like them for their convenience and relatively low fees, as shown in Figure 7-2.

FIGURE 7-2 The fees for using Auctionpayments.com are clearly detailed.

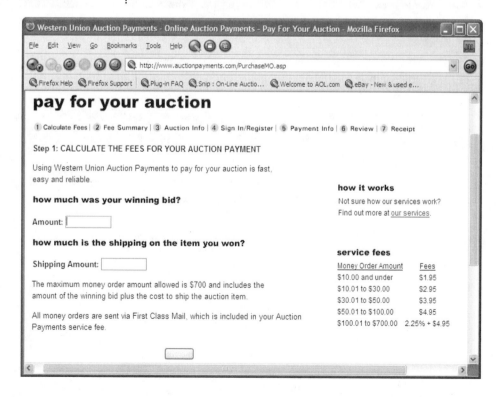

PayPal and Why It Really Is Your Friend

Among PowerSellers, you will hear a certain amount of grumbling about PayPal. Yes, it is an eBay-owned company, which means sellers pay fees twice, once to eBay and once to PayPal, also eBay. It's true PayPal's protection services are all heavily weighted in favor of the buyer, as you saw in Chapter 6. PowerSellers have legitimate complaints on these issues, but with that said, you still need to consider PayPal as your friend.

If you are already a PayPal user, you know how fast and easy it is to pay for something this way. While the auction is running, you'll see the PayPal logo. When you've won the auction, that logo becomes a Pay Now button and you simply click it to process your PayPal payment. Figure 7-3 is a screen from PayPal's web site that shows just how easy it is to do. Buyers like PayPal because it is so simple, and they also like the protection services PayPal offers. You *must* offer your buyers

FIGURE 7-3 The PayPal logo becomes a Pay Now button for the winning bidder. That makes paying for the item as easy as clicking this button.

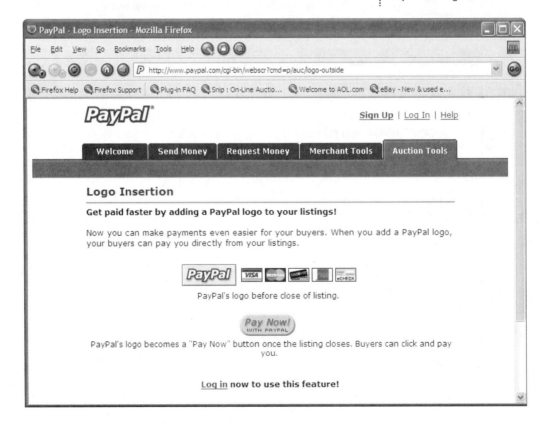

Register with Western Union's Auction Payments Service

PayPal if you are going for volume. It's all part of making it as easy as possible for people to shop with you. If you don't do this, your customers will have no trouble finding other sellers on eBay to buy from. Consider that by the end of the first quarter of 2004, there were more than 45 million PayPal accounts. The value of all PayPal payments processed during that time was $4.3 billion. Remember that although the greater advantage to the service is for the buyer, you also have the advantage of having a registered and confirmed customer base when you use PayPal. Don't concern yourself, just yet, with whatever grumbling you might find on the discussion boards about PayPal. Far more common than these grumblings are the many successful PayPal transactions that you never hear about.

PayPal Account Types

If you have spent most of your time buying on eBay, you most likely have a *Personal* PayPal account. This account is free of charges. It allows you to send money through funds kept on your PayPal account or through a registered credit card. The only time you will be charged a fee for using your Personal account is if you ask for an exchange of foreign funds. You can also receive funds as payment for sales on eBay, but you cannot receive payments funded by credit cards. You'll have to have funds sent by the buyer directly from his PayPal account.

The two other levels of PayPal accounts are the *Premier* and *Business* accounts. Both of these account types allow you to receive funds from a buyer's credit card. It is still free for you to pay for items from your own PayPal account, but now you will pay a fee every time you receive funds from a buyer. Figure 7-4 shows the PayPal fees screen that can be found as of this writing at http://www.paypal.com/cgi-bin/webscr?cmd=_display-fees-outside. The Premier account type is for sellers running small businesses, and that's the one you will be most likely to use. The Business account is for operations that are bigger than individual sellers. It offers services that allow businesses not only to use PayPal but also to have multiple logins, so that employees at a variety of levels can access the accounts. That way, a business owner can allow an employee who does shipping to have access to the portion of the account that includes shipping information, but still deny that employee access to the financial parts of the account history.

Register with Western Union's Auction Payments Service

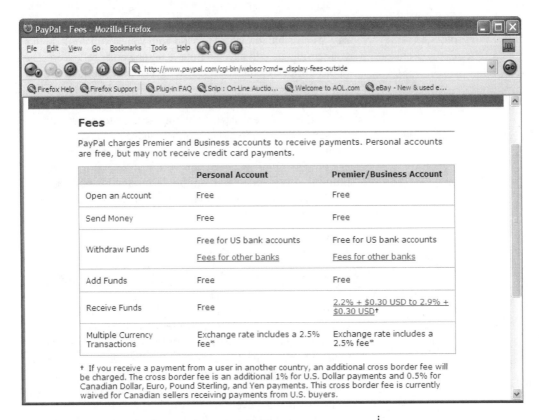

FIGURE 7-4 PayPal's fees for receiving funds from buyers

PayPal's fee structure recently changed. It's now performance-based, at least for Merchant accounts, so the higher your monthly sales volume, the lower your fee. The rate stayed the same though for Business and Premier accounts. The fee to receive payments funded by credit cards for both of these account types is either 2.9 percent or 3.9 percent plus $0.30 for each transaction. The 2.9 percent is the Standard rate and applies if you are accepting a PayPal payment from a U.S.-based customer. It increases to 3.9 percent (again plus $0.30) if you are accepting a PayPal payment from a *non-U.S.* buyer. This higher rate includes a cross-border fee of 1 percent of the sale for U.S. dollars and 0.5 percent of the sale for Canadian dollar, Euro, Pound Sterling, and Yen payments. As of this writing, Canadian sellers had the cross-border fee waived for U.S. buyers. If you accept funds involving a foreign currency, you will pay the retail foreign exchange rate at the time of the transaction. This retail rate includes a 2.5 percent spread above the wholesale exchange rate that PayPal uses to obtain foreign currency. PayPal keeps that 2.5 percent as a fee, and you will receive the exact exchange rate charges at the time the transaction is completed, since it varies and is adjusted regularly. Keep in mind, it is a violation of PayPal's user agreement for you to try to charge the buyer extra to cover these fees. You're stuck with them, but we do have some advice from PowerSellers about how to keep them as low as possible.

» Sign up for a Merchant rate as soon as possible

Again, the fees Premier and Business account holders pay are either 2.9 percent or 3.9 percent (plus $0.30) for each transaction.

The "Merchant" rate varies from 1.9 percent to 2.5 percent and it's available only for volume sellers. To qualify for the Merchant rate, your monthly volume must exceed $3,000 USD per month. The Merchant rate begins at 2.5 percent. If your monthly sales exceed $10,000 it drops to 2.2 percent. If they exceed $100,000 you're eligible for the lowest rate—1.9 percent. A separate transaction rate of $0.30 per transaction is added to each rate tier. As with the rates for Business and Premier accounts, Merchant rates are boosted by 1 percent for payments from non-U.S.-based buyers. Keep in mind that you must maintain this level of earnings. If your monthly volume drops below $3,000 for two consecutive months, you'll be bumped back to the Standard rate. Of course, you're not likely to let that happen.

It might surprise you to learn that some PowerSellers don't realize they are paying higher PayPal fees than they have to. That's understandable. When you first sign up for a Premier account, you can't have the Merchant rate. In the drive to build your business, it's easy to overlook a little detail like this, but this little detail can save you big money. So set your sights on achieving the volume you need to qualify, and then make the switch just as soon as you can.

» Get a PayPal ATM/debit card

PayPal offers its qualified users a PayPal MasterCard ATM/debit card that allows you to get cash withdrawals and earns 1.5 percent cashback rewards on purchases. The card is free from PayPal, and you can use it as an ATM card to withdraw funds from your PayPal account or from the bank account linked to

Get a PayPal ATM/debit card

your PayPal account. PayPal will charge you $1.00 for every ATM cash withdrawal, and you will also incur whatever fees the ATM terminal owner applies.

To qualify for the cashback rewards, you must use the card to make purchases that do not require a PIN number for processing. That includes most stores, restaurants, and other online and brick-and-mortar merchants. Just select the *credit card* option with the merchant (rather than the debit option), and it will be processed for the cashback rewards. Remember, funds will be immediately deducted from your account, because it is actually a debit card, but you must specify it as a credit transaction to get the rewards. "I save thousands of dollars a year by using this debit card as much as I do. I even pay my eBay fees with it," says one savvy PowerSeller from New York.

To qualify for the rewards program, PayPal users must meet eligibility requirements. First, the plan is offered only to U.S. PayPal users and a select group of non-U.S. users. As of this writing, these are the requirements for eligibility:

- You must have been a PayPal member for at least 60 days.

- You must have registered a credit card with a monthly statement that is sent to a physical address, not a P.O. box. PayPal will only mail the debit card to that address, and all statements and transaction information will be available only on the PayPal web site.

- You must have linked a bank account to your PayPal account and verified that you control that account.

- You must hold a Premier or Business account.

- You must be approved through PayPal's Account Review department as being an active member in good standing of PayPal.

To apply for a card, log in to your account. Then click the ATM/Debit card link at the bottom of any account-related page. If your application is accepted, it will take about two to four weeks for your account to be processed and your card mailed. Once you receive your card you must activate it by logging into www.paypal.com and following the instructions on the Activate Debit Card link of the Account Overview page. At this point, you will select your PIN and be ready to start earning your rewards.

To keep your rewards coming, you'll have to sell on eBay at a rate of at least one auction every three weeks, which, of course, isn't a problem. You will also have to confirm your eBay information with PayPal. Finally, you will have to list PayPal in *all* of your auctions as the only online payment option you accept.

PayPal Auction Management Tools

After reading Chapter 4, you're an expert in the field of auction management software. To make things simple for people who don't have all of your advantages, PayPal offers its users a set of auction management tools directly from their PayPal accounts. Through PayPal, you can get help from the time your auction begins to when you need to manage your PayPal fees.

As you saw in Figure 7-3, adding a PayPal logo to your auctions makes it easy for your buyers to click and pay immediately. PayPal also offers a free winning buyer notification e-mail. When your buyer wins the auction, PayPal guarantees to notify her within one hour of the auction's closing time. This e-mail will include a link to a secure PayPal payment page with all of the item details listed, including your shipping, handling, and payment instructions. You can also add a customized message to personalize the form and your logo and/or e-mail address.

Post-Sale Manager

PayPal's post-sale manager page displays all of the details you'll need to track for your closed auctions. Information on this page includes

- The Item number and title
- The end date
- The price you earned
- The quantity you sold
- The buyer's user ID
- Whether or not the buyer has paid
- If you need to send an invoice
- Your shipping status
- Whether or not you've left feedback
- Any memos you may have added to a particular transaction

Don't pay for your own purchases from PayPal's site

Now you can use one single display page to see exactly what's happening for all of your PayPal auctions.

Shipping Center

PayPal, in partnership with the USPS and UPS, has integrated some shipping services to make shipping your items easier. You can use PayPal to calculate your shipping costs and track your shipments online. You can also purchase and print your own shipping labels with this tool. Currently you cannot buy insurance through the USPS using PayPal, however.

Reporting Tools

The PayPal reporting tools can help you measure your sales by analyzing your revenue sources, automating some bookkeeping tasks, and reconciling your transactions. Monthly account statements give you a summary of the credits and debits to your account balance. Merchant sales reports track your weekly sales. A customizable history log can give you an online view of all your payments sent and received.

» Don't pay for your own purchases from PayPal's site

While you're spending so much time at PayPal's site, you may be tempted to just go ahead and pay for an item you bought on eBay. That's not your best option. Instead, you should make your PayPal purchases through your own My eBay page. Here's why: If you pay for your item directly on PayPal, that payment will show up in your PayPal records, but it will not be updated on My eBay. The item listed there, where you spend most of your time, will forever appear as not having been paid. When you're processing as many sales and purchases as you will as an active eBayer, it's too easy to overlook an item paid for on PayPal but not noted on My eBay. You don't want to accidentally pay for an item twice! So, always pay for your items through My eBay, not directly through PayPal.

Protect Yourself with PayPal's Seller Protection Policy

So, it's true, most of the protection from PayPal goes to the buyer. But, you should use what little protection is available to you as the seller, even if many PowerSellers think the amount is

Don't pay for your own purchases from PayPal's site

laughable. One of the things you can do is review the history of the person you are trading with before you accept a PayPal payment. From the My Account tab, choose the payment in question and select the status link in the status column, for example, Pending. Now you will be on the payment details page. You'll see the sender's name and her verification status. In order to be verified on PayPal, you have to confirm a bank account with the service. Verification is not the same as vouching for the honesty of the buyer, but it does prove that this buyer did provide PayPal with enough banking information to suggest that she isn't attempting to defraud anyone. You should also have *your* account verified to reassure your buyers that you are also a legitimate trading partner.

PayPal's seller protection takes the form of protecting a seller from chargebacks. As you saw in Chapter 6, it is not difficult for buyers to charge back items with PayPal. The focus of PayPal's seller protection is to protect the seller from out-and-out fraud by buyers, but you won't find much help if you just meet up with a buyer who wants to be difficult. How do you protect yourself? It's actually not easy, and you won't get much help from PayPal if the buyer claims he never received your item. Your only hope in getting protection through PayPal is to follow all of their seller's protection guidelines exactly, and doing that can sometimes conflict with your selling goals. Here's what you have to do to get any protection through PayPal:

- Have your account verified.
- Ship only to the address displayed on the Transaction Details page.
- Ship within seven days of payment.
- Keep all proof-of-shipment records that can be tracked online.
- Insist on delivery confirmation of items above $250.00.
- Remember, protection applies only to tangible goods.
- Accept only complete payments from a single PayPal account.
- Do not surcharge the buyer for your PayPal fees, except in the UK, where this is allowed.
- Respond immediately to PayPal's requests for information.
- Accept international payments from only approved countries.

Don't pay for your own purchases from PayPal's site

Let's focus on a particularly problematic requirement on this list and see what PowerSellers have to say. One of the problems in shipping only to the address displayed on the Transaction Details page has to do with an issue of fairness. PayPal will not back you up if you ship your item to an unconfirmed address. At the same time, they will allow a buyer to submit an unconfirmed address to the system. Why should that be allowed? This is a question PowerSellers ask on their discussion boards but are never completely able to answer. Just because a buyer lists an address, don't assume it's confirmed. Get the buyer's information page from PayPal and double-check. But when you're trying to build volume in your business, this is time you could be spending on more productive pursuits. You may consider stating in your listings that you will ship only to confirmed addresses. This may encourage your buyer to contact you if he wishes to have the item shipped to an address that is not confirmed.

The issue of unconfirmed addresses is a big problem for international sales. The reality is that no address outside of the United States can be confirmed. Every time you ship something through PayPal to an international customer, you are automatically giving up any right to the seller protection policy. Using the guidelines for accepting international payments only from approved countries is good advice, even if it doesn't help much with protection. Figure 7-5 shows the list as it was current at the time of this writing. We'll spend more time on international sales in just a little while, but for now, you're wise to stick just with these countries that PayPal has approved.

Protecting Yourself on eBay

In eBay's early days, it was often compared to the Wild West. Our image of that time in American history is of a freewheeling, lawless society where the smart, the quick, and the rugged survived. Figure 7-6 reminds us of just how rugged that time could be. Now that eBay has matured, some of that Wild West bravado has begun to fade. After all, the West never came complete with a Live Help feature! Still, when it comes to protecting yourself from fraud and loss, you should consider yourself to be your own best line of defense. As a company, eBay prides itself on providing a level playing field for all its participants. That's one of its great strengths and part of the reason so many people are able to come to eBay and operate their own businesses.

Don't pay for your own purchases from PayPal's site

PayPal®

Log Out | Help

My Account | Send Money | Request Money | Merchant Tools | Auction Tools

Non-U.S. Accounts

In addition to the U.S., PayPal is now available in the following countries:

- Anguilla†
- Argentina†
- Australia‡
- Austria‡
- Belgium‡
- Brazil
- Canada‡
- Chile
- China
- Costa Rica†
- Denmark‡
- Dominican Republic†
- Finland‡

- France‡
- Germany‡
- Greece
- Hong Kong‡
- Iceland
- India
- Ireland
- Israel
- Italy‡
- Jamaica†
- Japan‡
- Luxembourg
- Mexico‡

- Netherlands‡
- New Zealand‡
- Norway‡
- Portugal
- Singapore‡
- South Korea‡
- Spain‡
- Sweden‡
- Switzerland‡
- Taiwan‡
- United Kingdom‡

† Users in these countries are limited to sending money with their PayPal accounts. They may not receive payments.

‡ PayPal accepts withdrawals to local bank accounts in these countries. Users in any country may withdraw funds to a U.S. bank account.

FIGURE 7-5 The countries that are approved by PayPal for international trade

At the same time, that philosophy makes it difficult for eBay to police itself too closely. Yes, you will get support from eBay on issues of fraud and illegal activity, but for the day-to-day operations of your business, it's best to depend on yourself.

FIGURE 7-6 The Wild West, before eBay

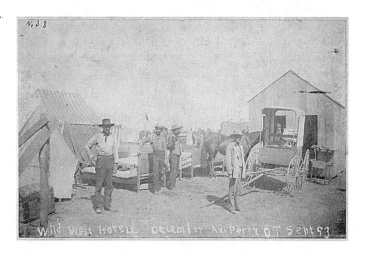

Don't pay for your own purchases from PayPal's site

The first thing you'll have to decide is how much risk you are willing to take. Each seller has to determine that individually. For example, you will find many PowerSellers who refuse to accept personal checks. They don't want to be bothered holding items for ten days, and they don't want to leave themselves open to the hassle of having to deal with returned checks. You'll find other sellers who won't even consider international sales. They consider them too risky and don't want to be hassled with the extra paperwork necessary for customs. On the other hand, you'll find other sellers who welcome personal checks. They may find that they rarely, if ever, have a returned check problem, and holding the item for ten days isn't such a big deal. Other sellers actually welcome international sales, figuring that the billions of people in the world who don't happen to live in the United States offer them a customer base that's worth an extra bit of trouble. All of these decisions are made individually, and we'll give you enough information here so that you can start considering them for yourself. We won't go so far as to recommend you make one choice or another. You'll have to decide for yourself what feels right once you find the balance between risk and security that will make you comfortable.

International Sales

Few running debates among PowerSellers are more heated than whether or not to offer international sales. It's easy enough to see why people shy away from them. They do require more effort. Each sale must be declared through customs, which requires extra forms and paperwork. It is difficult to track shipping across international borders. Dealing with foreign currency exchanges can be expensive and bothersome, and dealing with insurance claims for lost items is nothing but a hassle. Still, we spoke with PowerSellers who welcome international sales, and they have compelling reasons to do so.

Husband and wife eBayers Debnroo agree with Wegotthebeats even though they ship a great variety of items in many different shapes and sizes (see the following sidebar). "Yes, we are the most enthusiastic people we know about international sales, but it may be tantamount to masochism. It really can be a form of torture, in terms of shipping and customs forms, but in particular insurance claims. You can't even start an international claim with the USPS until 60 days after the shipment. And shipping times have suddenly jumped to about twice the normal on a fairly regular basis.

Selling Internationally

PowerSeller Wegotthebeats sells CDs and has very strong feelings about offering international sales. "There are sellers, like me, who make decisions based on 'what's good for the business' and what is the professional, customer service–oriented solution to a particular problem. We do not waiver from them even though we know that a small percentage of customers will exploit them to their advantage," he told us. "One basic issue with shipping overseas is simply fear of the unknown. 'Do I have to fill out lots of forms?' 'What if I can't speak German?' 'I've heard that people in Canada cause lots of problems and expect lower shipping rates.' 'What if they pay me in Euros?' The list goes on. Once you've shipped a few, it becomes old hat.

"There is a little bit more work involved, especially if you are selling many different-sized products, as many sellers do. I am fortunate that my merchandise is basically all one size, so I can clearly state up front and with total accuracy what the shipping rates will be for the United States and any other country in the world. Other sellers will have to either figure out the different shipping rates ahead of time and post them in their auction listing, or wait for e-mails from interested customers asking them to figure out what the exact shipping rate will be for their particular country.

"Fifty percent of my business is shipped overseas. I'd say 80 percent of that is paid for with PayPal. Every single one of those could file a claim of 'non-receipt' and PayPal would give them all instant refunds. It's never happened once." (He has a feedback number greater than 7,500!) "That said, I'm well aware of the possibility and am doing what I can to reduce the risk, namely encouraging payments using money orders through Auctionpayments.com or other methods of payment.

"For me, this is a calculated risk. Statistically, I have many more problems with domestic buyers than overseas. With so much of my business going overseas, the risk is clearly worth it. For others, it may not be worth it. Generally, I think it is important to leave yourself open to as many bids as possible. Sometimes the international bidders won't win, but they'll boost your final price while trying to win."

"Payment, on the other hand, has actually not been much of an issue. We get a significant number of international money orders sent through the postal system from Canada, and, to a small degree, the UK. The vast majority of international payments are now coming from PayPal. We find that Auctionpayments.com works as a good backup to PayPal.

"In our opinion, those who are not servicing international markets are more than welcome to continue their policies. It is making it far easier for those of us who want to get a leg up on our competition. Once USPS, UPS, and other international carriers adapt to the modern needs of international retailers, those of us with experience with this more difficult system will have a much easier time adapting than those who have turned a nose up to the other 5.8 billion people on the planet all this time. We are confident that existing shipping and payment barriers will continue to crumble and that the future for servicing the international markets just gets brighter."

Avoid these countries

You'll have to decide for yourself how risk-averse you are to the idea of international sales. That will be based largely on the products you sell, and your personal philosophy and hopes for your business. It may be too much to ask of yourself when you're just getting used to selling in volume, and you may decide to wait on international sales until you become more confident in yourself as an eBay seller. Overall, as you've heard before, it's best to keep your customer base as broad as possible when selling on eBay. Offering your items to all the citizens of the world is a way to do that.

» Avoid these countries

That said, there are some countries that have developed a reputation for having a high potential for credit card fraud. You're better able to offer international sales to the vast majority of people who want to honestly trade with you if you are armed with the information you'll need to protect yourself from the pockets known to be unreliable. PayPal has identified the following countries as being highly suspect in the field of credit card fraud:

- Russia
- Indonesia
- Ukraine
- Malaysia
- Romania
- Philippines
- Lithuania

International PowerSeller Wegotthebeats agrees. "It has become well-known that Indonesia is considered the 'credit card fraud capital of the world,'" he told us. "Don't take anything but an international money order in U.S. Dollars from there." Demanding the same for all of the countries on this list only makes good common sense.

» Consider the language barrier

PowerSellers who do accept international bidders have some advice for sellers when dealing with the language barrier between buyer and seller. One PowerSeller from south Florida recommends keeping your e-mails short and simple. "When you receive an e-mail from someone who is using broken English, keep your replies as simply written as possible. Do not use complex conjugations of verbs or unusual words," he advised. In dealing with people who are not fluent, it's very important to keep your communication simple.

Remember the cultural differences in communication too. For example, in the U.S., we generally sign our e-mails with "sincerely" or "best wishes." From England and Europe you are more likely to receive a "regards," a term that can sound a little snooty and off-putting to Americans. Don't take it the wrong way; it's nothing more than a different version of "sincerely," and the person writing it thinks no more of it than that. Be sure in your responses that you don't use slang. Think carefully about the things you take for granted because they are so familiar to your culture; your buyer may have no idea what you're talking about.

Eventually technology will make translation much simpler. "Can you imagine a future in which our eBay ads appear in Lithuanian or Maltese? Puts a smile on my face!" mused Debnroo. What is a barrier to your business now, in time will easily become a road to new opportunities. eBay itself owes its very existence to technological advancement. There's reason to stay optimistic about the ways these advancements will continue to bring us new opportunities.

Using Escrow Services

Buyers and sellers can agree to process their payments through an escrow service. If a seller agrees to this process, her auction listing will include escrow as a means of payment. She simply designates it as one of the payment choices when setting up her auction listing. The buyer may then elect to send his payment directly to the escrow service. That service will hold payment and notify the seller that her buyer has paid. The seller then ships the item to the buyer for inspection. If the buyer agrees that the item is just as the seller stated, he notifies the escrow service that he accepts the item, and the escrow service sends payment on to the seller. Escrow only makes sense for big-ticket

Consider the language barrier

items, because the escrow service will charge fees, and they cut even deeper into your profit margin. Figure 7-7 shows the fees Escrow.com charges, the calculator used to determine those fees, and the levels of service offered for both the Standard and the Premier escrow services available. If you are selling cars or luxury items such as jewelry, your buyers may insist on escrow.

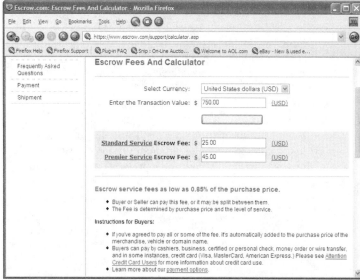

FIGURE 7-7 Here are the fees calculated for an imagined sale of an item priced at $750.00.

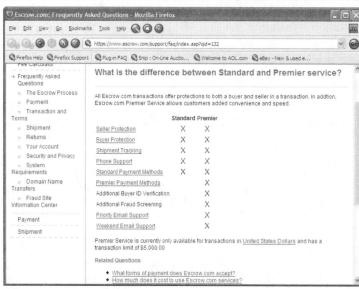

In order to use escrow, both parties must agree to the escrow service. Before any funds get transferred, both parties should also agree about who will pay the transaction fees, although it is customary for the buyer to pay the escrow fees. Other details of the escrow transaction to consider include

- Who will pay shipping?
- What will the shipping method be?
- What is the length of the inspection period?
- Will the shipping fees be refundable, and if so, under what circumstances?
- What are the terms under which the item can be returned?

All transactions between seller and buyer should include good, clear communications, but this is even more important with an escrow transaction. Don't assume the buyer and you agree on even the slightest detail. Make sure of it. Get everything worked out in writing, and be sure to save all of your e-mails related to the transfer.

The only online escrow service that eBay endorses for domestic escrow transactions is Escrow.com. If you are going to offer escrow services, do it through this company. Don't agree to go with any other, and if a buyer (or seller) insists on another, walk away from the deal and report that person to eBay. Escrow services, particularly online services, are fertile ground for fraud, and you can easily be taken in by offers from disreputable services. For international escrow services, eBay recommends the following:

- TradeSecure
- Escrow Europa
- Iloxx Safe Trade
- Triple Deal

One of the main sources of escrow fraud is e-mail. Never respond to e-mail from an escrow service other than Escrow.com. Also, don't click any links in e-mails you may get, even if they look like they've come from Escrow.com. Any time you need to conduct business with the escrow service or check on information, log on to the web site by typing in the complete URL. Don't use an auto-type feature from your browser; it's too easy to be diverted to a fraudulent site that way.

Consider the language barrier

Protect Yourself from Spoof E-Mails

Spoof e-mails are e-mails sent to tempt eBay users into revealing personal information. Now, you may think, "Who would actually do that?" But the fact is, the spoofers have gotten to be so good that you may get an e-mail that looks exactly like one generated by eBay or PayPal, the two biggest targets for fraud. If you're not careful, you can get caught. So, be vigilant and don't respond to any e-mail that requests you to click a link so you can give information about your accounts. Many of these e-mails will claim that your account is in danger, and you'll be shut out of the service, but don't fall for it.

If you get an e-mail with a link and a request to click that link, copy the address to your web browser and go to the site that way. eBay may send you an e-mail with a link in it, but that's only for your convenience. They will never send you an e-mail with a link that also requires you to submit information to the site by clicking that link. Be particularly careful with e-mails that include attachments. These are never legitimate, because eBay doesn't send e-mails with attachments.

When you are logging into eBay, make sure you are actually on an eBay page. All eBay sign-in pages will have addresses that begin with http://cgi.ebay.com/ or http://scgi.ebay.com/. All eBay sign-in addresses will include either .com or the letters that designate a particular country for international sites. If there are extra characters before the final forward slash, such as an @, it's definitely not from eBay. For a complete list of true eBay domestic and international sites, go to http://pages.ebay.com/help/account/mpi-account-theft-spoof.html.

PayPal is also the target of perpetrators of fraud. Be especially vigilant with your PayPal account, since it is likely to be a holding place for a significant amount of funds, and it is linked to your bank account and credit card information. One new eBay user reported that she received an e-mail from PayPal that requested her personal information. She went through with clicking the link. It took her to a site that looked exactly like PayPal, and she wasn't suspicious, because she recognized all the buttons and features of a PayPal page. Well, she completed the form and submitted the requested information, only then becoming suspicious when she didn't receive a "thank you" or a confirmation from PayPal. After calling PayPal and learning the sad truth, she got in touch with her bank and had to freeze her accounts. Ten days later, she had a new bank account and had to switch all of her passwords on all of her accounts all over the Internet. Fortunately, she didn't also lose money, but you don't want to spend your eBay time this way. You want to be building your business, and as anyone who has ever been a victim of identity theft will tell you, fixing it is simply a nightmare.

PayPal will never ask you for any of the following information or to take any of the following actions via e-mail:

- Credit card numbers
- Banking account numbers
- Social Security numbers
- Driver's license numbers
- For the user to download something to "fix" an account
- For the user to download something to have access to new features

If you receive a suspicious e-mail, forward it in its entirety to eBay and/or PayPal. Both sites are working hard to cut into the fraud perpetrated by spoof e-mails, and they need the help of the users who are the targets of these schemes. Be sure to forward the entire e-mail, including the header, so that eBay will have all of the information to help them track down the culprits. Send it to spoof@ebay.com. For updates on PayPal security issues, visit PayPal's Security Center (shown in Figure 7-8) at www.paypal.com/us/cgi-bin/webscr?cmd=_security-center.

Unpaid Items

Nothing gets the juices flowing among the PowerSellers quite like unpaid items, also known as non-paying bidders (NPBs). What are the reasons someone would bid on an item and then not pay for it? Well, there are actually quite a few reasons this happens:

- People often get caught up in the bidding and bid more than they actually want to spend on an item.
- Some inexperienced users may not have read eBay's terms of service closely enough to understand that a bid enters them into a binding contract, and they may then back out of their offer.

Consider the language barrier

FIGURE 7-8 The PayPal Security Center is a good place to keep current with PayPal security concerns.

- Some people may actually bid on an item to ruin the auction for the seller. If the highest bidder refuses to pay, the seller gets stuck. The best she can hope for is to make a second-chance offer to the next highest bidder, but she may well be stuck with the listing fees and the aggravation of filing a Final Value Fee refund. Plus she'll have to relist the item and do the auction all over again, hoping to get a price high enough to compensate for the extra time and trouble.

- There are some people who bid on items just for sport. They never actually intend to complete the sale; they just want to be part of the bidding action.

- Plain old buyer's remorse.

Non-paying bidders are a fact of life for PowerSellers. You have to decide if you're going to take them in your stride or fight them at every turn. The PowerSellers' discussion boards are filled with angry exchanges about NPBs, but most of the PowerSellers we spoke with said their energies were better directed toward getting the refund of their Final Value Fees and moving on with relisting the item for auction. Since there's really no way to avoid them, they noted, what's the point of expending too much energy being angry about them?

eBay has established the following procedure for dealing with Unpaid Items:

1. Sellers may file an "Unpaid Item reminder" seven days from the listing's close. This initiates a dialog between eBay and the buyer, whereby eBay reminds the buyer of his obligations, provides instructions on how to pay for the item, and offers a structured way for the buyer and seller to communicate.

2. Sellers may immediately file a "Mutual Agreement Not to Proceed." If this is done the buyer must confirm the understanding. After she does so, eBay will issue a Final Value Fee credit to the seller. Sellers will also receive a Final Value Fee credit should the buyer not respond within seven days. You can file an Unpaid Item notice by clicking on "File an Unpaid Item Dispute" in My eBay's selling area, or on the Services page, or related areas in eBay's help system.

It's important that you confirm the buyer's willingness to abide by this mutual agreement. If the buyer decides he does not wish to proceed with the agreement after all, the seller will lose the Final Value Fee credit. And the seller may not refile. So again, be certain of your understanding with the buyer before filing a mutual agreement.

» Always file for your Final Value Fee refunds

There is nothing you can do about your listing fees when you have a NPB, but hope that the item sells with your first relisting so that you can be reimbursed for them. As for your Final Value Fees, that's another story. Don't allow yourself to get so caught up in running your business that you neglect to file these. Once you file an Unpaid Item Dispute, the buyer has seven days to respond to eBay's attempts to convince him to pay. If after that seven-day period has passed, you still have not received payment, you can file for your Final Value Fee credit.

» Use Immediate Payment for fixed-price listings

As troublesome as NPBs are for your regular auctions, they are even more disastrous for your Fixed Price listings, your Buy It Now listings, and the things in your eBay store. At least in a regular auction, bidding doesn't end until the time you've specified. With luck, you'll have several bidders going for the same item, and you'll have a second-chance bidder to turn to if your highest bidder doesn't come through. But when you list a Fixed Price listing, the listing ends when the bidder makes the bid, and then it's over. If he then backs out, you don't have a backup customer to turn to. Fortunately, all may not be lost. eBay offers sellers a free feature for Fixed Price listings called the Immediate Payment option. This is an option through PayPal, and here's how it works.

A seller designates a Fixed Price auction to include the Immediate Payment option at the time of the listing. All shipping and handling fees must be included in the listing so that the bidder will know exactly how much he has to spend to purchase the item. When the bidder makes the Fixed Price offer, he must pay immediately for the item and he must use PayPal. There will not be the usual e-mail exchange between seller and buyer that marks the end of most auctions. The difference with this feature is that until the payment is actually processed, the listing does not end and the item is not sold. That way, if the buyer then backs out of the deal, his incomplete bid does not end the seller's auction, as it does without the Immediate Payment option. Since this is a free listing option, you should definitely take advantage of it for all your Fixed Price, Buy It Now, and eBay store listings. You have only to gain from the extra protection to your listing and nothing to lose.

» Learn to avoid problem bidders

Honestly speaking, you will encounter troublesome bidders and NPBs. All big sellers on eBay do, and if you generate the volume you'll need to become a PowerSeller, you will too. There simply isn't a way to protect yourself from every single possible bidder who is out to do harm to a seller. You could check on the feedback rating of every bidder, but then you wouldn't have the time you need to do everything else your eBay business requires. Plus, the cost-benefit equation simply doesn't support such paranoia, since most eBay transactions don't generate headaches and trouble.

You can get a feel for your trading partners through the e-mail communication you have with them, and if you spot a red flag, you certainly should do some checking. But, what constitutes a red flag? Some sellers stay away from new eBayers, who can easily be recognized by the icon shown in Figure 7-9. But weren't you once also a new eBayer? What's to be gained by shunning someone just because she has some learning to do? If you get a bid from a new user, send that person an e-mail. Introduce yourself, welcome her, and offer any help or guidance she may need. At the same time, reiterate your payment choices, and your shipping and customer service policies. You'll seem like a friendly neighbor. Not only will you reduce the chance that this bidder will make a new user's mistake, but you may just offer her a port in the storm of eBay that helps her to feel secure and makes her a regular customer.

FIGURE 7-9 The new user icon appears next to the username of someone who has just joined eBay. Here you see the icon and a complete description of who qualifies to have it listed as part of their eBay identity.

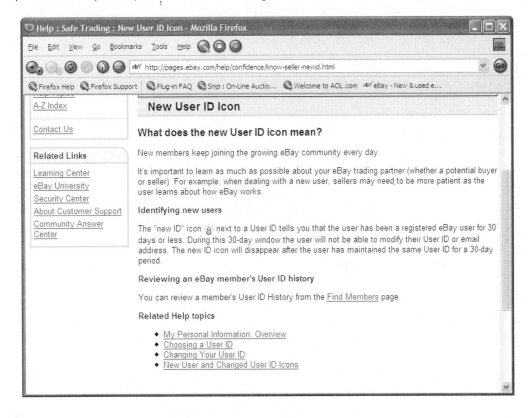

Learn to avoid problem bidders

You will learn a lot about problem bidders from spending time on the discussion boards. Sellers are happy to share the usernames of people who have caused them troubles, and you can be forewarned about them by learning from the bad experiences of others. Remember that eBay buyers have feedback ratings, too, and you can learn a lot about your bidders by checking on theirs. While you can't check out every bidder, it's a good idea to randomly check from time to time to see who is shopping with you. If you see negative feedbacks for a bidder, again be proactive. Send that bidder an e-mail to see if he has any questions or needs any support in making his offer. Be in touch with him before there is a problem and keep all of the e-mails you exchange with him, just in case.

With all of these warnings, keep in mind once burned, twice shy. When you do encounter a problem bidder, you can block that person from ever bidding in one of your auctions again. Simply go to http://offer.ebay.com/ws2/eBayISAPI.dll?BidderBlockLogin and click Add An eBay User To My Block Bidder/Buyer List. You'll see the form that appears in Figure 7-10. Now this person is blocked from all of your listings until you decide to let her back in. If you do ultimately resolve your issues, you can go back to this page to remove the block. But until you do, you are free of the problems she may have caused you.

Canceling a Bid

You won't have many reasons to cancel a bid and that's good, because canceling a bid isn't so easy. You may cancel a bid if a bidder contacts you with a reason he needs to back out. You don't have to let the bidder off the hook, but be reasonable. Bidders are human, and they sometimes have emergencies or other reasons why they can't follow through on a bid they've made. If you get a request to cancel a bid, consider it on an individual basis. Check out the bidder's feedback rating. Has he done this to other sellers? Are there negative comments that make you think this is more a habit than a single occurrence? If he has a good, solid feedback rating and he seems sincere in his request, why not go ahead and give him a break? Especially, if there's still plenty of time left in your auction and you have other bidders interested. On the other hand, if you suspect he's a deadbeat or you're out of time, go ahead and hold him to his bid. You'll most likely have to file an NPB report and pursue your Final Value Fee refund, but you will also bring him to eBay's

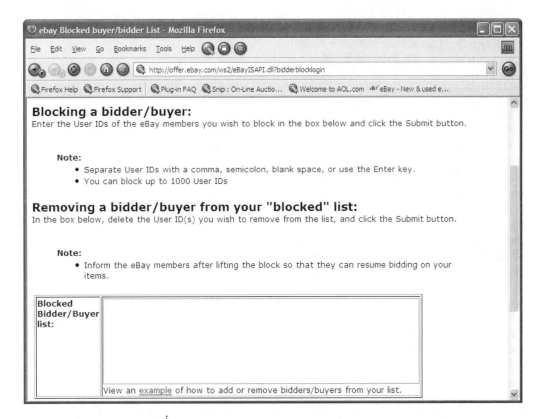

Blocking a bidder/buyer:

Enter the User IDs of the eBay members you wish to block in the box below and click the Submit button.

> **Note:**
> ♦ Separate User IDs with a comma, semicolon, blank space, or use the Enter key.
> ♦ You can block up to 1000 User IDs

Removing a bidder/buyer from your "blocked" list:

In the box below, delete the User ID(s) you wish to remove from the list, and click the Submit button.

> **Note:**
> ♦ Inform the eBay members after lifting the block so that they can resume bidding on your items.

Blocked Bidder/Buyer list:

View an example of how to add or remove bidders/buyers from your list.

FIGURE 7-10 Complete this form to block a bidder from all of your auctions. You can change it to include the bidder if you later decide to reinstate that person's rights to shop with you.

attention. Making bids and not honoring them violates eBay's terms of service and will ultimately lead to a bidder's suspension. So, add yourself to the list of sellers who noticed he doesn't operate in good faith. The number of retracted bids that have occurred over the previous six months becomes part of a member's profile.

You are free to cancel a bid if it comes from a person whose identity you cannot verify. If you've tried to find this person on eBay, and you've requested her contact information only to come up with a phone number that isn't connected, you don't have to take the risk. Just remember that once you've canceled a bid, it cannot be reinstated, so be sure you mean it when you do. The only other reason for canceling a bid is that you no longer have the item available for sale. In the rare event that something happens to the item between the time you list it and the time the auction ends—for example, a couple of kids, a game of catch in the house, and a vase—you must cancel all of the bids before you close the auction. Send an e-mail to each of the bidders explaining the unfortunate turn of events, and you shouldn't have any further trouble from the incident.

» Pre-approve your bidders

Just as you can block people from bidding on your listings, you can create auction listings that can be bid on only by a single individual or a small group of bidders. Now, why would you want to do this? In most cases, you won't. Your goal is to get as many bidders as possible so that your auction bidding can go ever higher, but in some instances, you may get a request from a potential customer to have a pre-approved auction. Suppose you list an item and it doesn't sell. You may get an e-mail from someone who was interested in the item, but never got the chance to make a bid. You can then negotiate a price for the item and relist the auction as a Buy It Now listing with this buyer as the only approved bidder. Now you will be guaranteed to sell the item, you will be refunded the second listing fees, and you won't be violating eBay's terms of service by selling a listed item outside of eBay.

Now suppose you have several identical items, but you list only one of them for sale on eBay. Then a buyer e-mails you after the auction ends to ask you if you have any other items like that one for sale. You are free to sell the other items to that buyer outside of eBay without violating eBay's terms of service. Your auction listing was for only one item like that, and as long as you've fulfilled that auction and paid your eBay fees for it, you are no longer under any obligation to sell the other identical items through eBay. This is a happy occurrence, because it turns your initial listing fee into free advertising by which you sell more products. Let's hope it happens!

Some Famous (or Infamous) Buyer's Scams

Once you spend some time on the discussion boards, you'll learn all about the many ways unscrupulous people have come up with to cheat sellers out of their earnings or goods. It can be astonishing to the non-criminal mind to discover how ingenious some of the schemes and scams are. Because sellers are so careful to guard their feedback ratings, they can sometimes be held hostage to a negative feedback. The feedback system actually makes sellers vulnerable. We are slightly less innocent than we were before we started researching this book, but we still have to agree, we never would have thought of most of these things. Thanks to PowerSeller Hessfine for providing us with some of the nastier things there are to know about eBay buyers. Read on.

"I really like it, but . . . "

Sometimes an unsavory buyer will receive the item and then contact the seller with a line that says, "I really like the item, but it's got, this, this, or this wrong with it. I don't want to send it back, but I'd like you to cut the price and refund some of my money." In this case, you can decide to take the hit and send a refund, or you can insist that the buyer send the item back to you, and you will refund the entire amount once you receive it and verify that it is still in the same condition it was when you sent it.

"I'll file an insurance claim"

In this variation, the buyer claims that the item has been damaged in shipping, but he still wants to keep it. He wants some of his money back because of the damage, but he'll take care of the insurance claim himself. Suggest that he send the item back to you and you'll take the insurance issue on for yourself or take the loss.

Contacting Your Winning Bidder

Sometimes you'll find that your winning bidder gets an e-mail from someone who claims to have exactly the same item. She'll offer to sell that item to your bidder for less money, and your winning bidder will be lured away to make the sale elsewhere. Whether or not that bidder ever gets his item, you'll still have to deal with this as an NPB and relist the item for auction.

Contacting Your Underbidders

Some experienced scammers will contact your underbidders and offer to sell them your item for less money off of eBay. They may even corrupt your e-mail address so that it seems you are contacting your own bidders. Often these e-mail addresses end in @juno or @hotmail, because addresses on these services are a little harder to trace. The unsuspecting underbidders may see the similar e-mail address and assume they are doing business with you. They'll send their payments on according to the

Pre-approve your bidders

directions in the e-mail, but of course, there is no item to be sold. Then they'll come back to you angry that you've not fulfilled your part of the "bargain." The best you can do here is to try to help them report the fraud and soothe their suffering.

Your Item Is a Fake

If you are selling something unique and of value, you may find someone is sending e-mails to your bidders warning them that the item is a fake. This person may also offer to sell your bidders the same authentic item off the eBay site. Hessfine told us of a German dagger he listed with no reserve. The auction reached $2,800 when people started to back out of their bids. He learned they were receiving e-mails from someone claiming that the dagger was fake. He got one of the e-mails and saw it had one of the suspicious endings we just mentioned. He pulled the auction listing and had the dagger appraised by three separate and independent appraisers. He then relisted the item with a guarantee of authenticity. It ultimately sold for $5,300, but he still had to cope with all of the aggravation it took to make this sale.

Credit Card Fraud

Some buyers may contact you and ask you to split the cost of the item between two credit cards. Then they'll go ahead and charge back on one of these charges and purchase your item for only a fraction of the closing auction price. The credit card company will automatically refund the sale, and you'll have a headache trying to prove that the charge was legitimate.

College Students and Bank Accounts

Perhaps this is the most chilling scam of all. People from outside of the country have contacted college students to appeal to their naiveté and their overall willingness to help. Such a criminal will contact a college student in a chat room and start up a friendship. Then he'll mention that he wants to sell things on eBay, but he can't get a bank account in the U.S. from his foreign location. He'll ask to have the money wired to the student's account, and he'll offer to pay the student 30 percent of what he earns as a reward for the help. Then, he'll go to your bidders and offer to sell them the identical item you are listing at a reduced price. He'll have them wire the money to the student's account, where he'll be free to access it. Of course, there is no item to sell, but the bidder doesn't know that and neither does the poor student who was only too willing to help. This is another example of why you should never trust a wire transfer outside of PayPal, and why you should continue to worry when your kids go off to college.

These are just a few of the many ingenious ways people have devised to cheat, lie, and steal in the electronic world. Consider them our contribution to the many you'll discover for yourself as you become a PowerSeller.

Meet a PowerSeller

Jeffrey Hess—One Half of Hess Fine Art

Hess Fine Art, Hessfine on eBay, is owned and operated by Jeffrey and Katrina Hess, who have been active on the site since 1998. Today, they have more than 13,500 feedbacks, so you can easily see that these are large-volume sellers. In addition to operating hessfine on eBay, the Hesses are Charter Master Dealers for Sothebys.com. They also operate a brick-and-mortar store in Florida. Jeffrey is a watch expert, and he and Katrina sell watches on eBay as well as other jewelry, fine art, silver, collectibles, and antiques.

When they started selling on eBay, they already owned their own store. The store supported five employees, including them. Today, they have 17 employees and they point to their online sales as their number one revenue stream. eBay has allowed them both to expand their market and to find interesting niches for their products.

"Before eBay," says Jeffrey, "all fine art dealers were beholden to the New York market. If New York shoppers wanted it, you could sell it, but if not, you were done for." Now, through eBay, the market is internationalized. The profit margins are tighter, but the potential customer base is so much broader that tighter margins are offset by the increased customer base, according to Jeffrey. At the same time, eBay has allowed the couple to make excellent use of tiny niche markets. Fraternity pins are just one example.

These small pins include a half-penny to a penny weight of gold. Most people have no real interest in them, and traditionally they were scrapped in the jewelry market. Through eBay, the market of former Fraternity members is so broad that these little pins sell easily. "I can get as much as $50 or $100 or even $1,500 for them now," reports Jeffery. "Just a small percentage of them brings the highest bid, but they rarely sell for less than scrap." This PowerSeller was surprised, but delighted, to discover the appeal of this small but sentimental niche market.

Jeffrey and Katrina start all of their auctions at less than $1.00 with no reserve. Yes, that's right. They start the auction there whether the item is for a single spoon or a jewel-encrusted pin. Search for them by bidder and take a look at their auction listings. When we stopped by at this writing, they had more than 300 items for sale. Prices ranged from $0.01 to $4,053.00. Jeffrey told us that he sells an average of one painting a month for five figures or more. The couple did $4 million dollars in sales during 2003, and they are expecting to do $6 million in 2004.

Today the couple's operation takes up 4,500 square feet. They have a 1,200–square foot showroom, and the rest is used for shipping and photographing eBay items and administering their online auction business. They use 18 computers in the office, all networked together, and they have four more at home. Their employees who do listings each have small light boxes on their desks, and they use both digital cameras and scanners to capture their images. They use Vendio auction management software.

The Hesses recommend that sellers do a little of everything to sell their items, including selling on eBay, owning a store, selling through wholesale outlets, mass marketing, and retail sales too. Within the last year, the couple has begun doing many more private auctions on eBay. In a private auction, only the seller knows who the bidders are, and only the seller will know who the winner is. This has helped reduce some of the issues with fraud and unscrupulous buyers that Jeffrey and Katrina were kind enough to share with us.

Chapter 8

You Sold It, Now Ship It

Continue to buy things on eBay

The ultimate test of your life as an eBay seller comes the moment your customer opens the package to get to the merchandise you sold. It is the most concrete way for a customer to know how you value his business, and it is the one thing your customers will remember about you long after they've forgotten everything else about their transactions. Your customer forms a clear expectation about the product she's getting from your photos and item description, but the package she receives remains a great unknown until the very end. Be sure your shipping procedures make your customers eager to shop with you again. Please them in this area, and you'll see them return to buy more.

Proper packaging and shipping is not just a matter of being nice to your customers. It's also a matter of protecting your business and keeping it moving smoothly. When you ship correctly, you eliminate customer complaints, damaged goods, and negative feedback remarks. Take a look at a PowerSeller's feedback history, and you'll see comments such as "fast shipping" and "great packaging," again and again. Trust us on this. It matters.

When you're planning your shipping operations, you'll need to develop procedures for packing your items, including sources for all the materials necessary to make a professional-looking finished package. You'll need to consider a fair and reasonable price to charge your customers for shipping and handling, and you'll need to choose your favorite shipping methods. All of these decisions combine to create your own particular shipping policies and procedures. There's also some psychology involved in setting your shipping and handling charges that can have a definite impact on the effectiveness of your overall marketing efforts. Fortunately, PowerSellers have been more than eager to share their tips and advice about shipping your products.

» Continue to buy things on eBay

"Continue to buy things on eBay," recommends a PowerSeller specializing in hobbies and crafts. "That way, you'll never forget what it feels like to open a package you've been waiting for. You'll always remember the difference between opening a well-packed package and a poorly packed one." This advice goes back to the old Golden Rule. Still, when you're busy and looking for fast turnaround of your products and inexpensive sources of packing materials, it's easy to lose sight of the final goal. You never want your customer to be disappointed by the package he receives. In this way, eBay shopping is very different from shopping offline. When you go into a store, you physically remove the product yourself, and the bag doesn't make much difference to you. But, eBay shopping has an element of surprise akin to receiving a present. That's part of the fun. Make sure you don't forget that when you send things on to your customers.

Packaging Your Items

How you package your items for shipping will depend, of course, on what you sell. Some lucky sellers, such as those who sell CDs or DVDs, hardly have any challenge at all. Their items are all the same size and shape. They determine the right packaging and how much each item will cost to ship just once, and then they can move on from there. Most sellers, however, are not that lucky. What you sell will determine which shipping method you choose and what types of materials you'll need to prepare your packages. But one thing will not change: it is your responsibility to protect your items and make every effort to get them to their destinations whole and undamaged. You can say whatever you want in your listing about your buyers needing to purchase insurance, and your not being responsible for damaged goods, but in the end, you are responsible. You enter a contract with your customer to deliver the product she purchased. If you deliver a broken product, she has every right to a refund. Not only will you lose any dispute with eBay or PayPal over this, but you'll also lose the customer. So, get it right from the very beginning.

» There's no such thing as too much packing material

"When I pack my items, I pretend someone is purposely going to try to damage the package." "I pack my items so they could potentially survive if a truck drove over them." "I double-box everything I ship." These are the voices of PowerSellers who told us how important it is to package everything carefully. We spoke with PowerSeller DavidK57, who was kind enough to share his packing techniques with us. When we asked about why he packages everything so carefully, he responded simply, "It's how I want to be perceived by others." Figures 8-1a and 8-1b show DavidK57's product before and after he's finished packing it. First he places the comic in a protective envelope and wraps it tightly. Next he wraps that package in a sleeve of bubble wrap. He then places the bundle between two pieces of foam board and tapes it all down securely. Finally, he places the whole thing in a Priority Mail box and fills the surrounding space with packing peanuts. A computer-printed label finishes the package neatly for an exceptional example of an eBay shipment.

On the other hand, you'll also see items sent out in packages like the one in Figure 8-2. Inside this discarded Blockbuster video box, we found a handful of packing peanuts and a bent and damaged vintage advertising card. Obviously, this seller was more interested in moving his merchandise and collecting his money than he was in making sure his customer was satisfied. That's not to say a seller shouldn't creatively use recycled materials. (At least we hope this video case was discarded and recycled!) We're all for that as you'll soon see. But if you use them, make them presentable. When we received this, we felt as though someone had mailed us his trash! Obviously, we will not be return customers.

» Spend less (or nothing) for packing materials

Getting the materials you'll need for packing your items is an opportunity for you to use your creativity. PowerSellers have discovered all types of sources for packing materials, including

FIGURE 8-1 (a) PowerSeller DavidK57 starts packing his comic book by wrapping it carefully to prevent the case from being scratched or damaged. (b) When packaging is complete, this comic book is so well protected that only a catastrophic event could damage it.

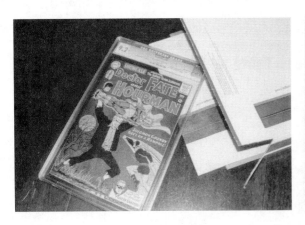 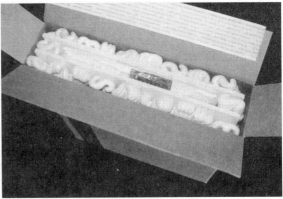

Spend less (or nothing) for packing materials

some that cost money and some that are free. Some of the best advice we heard follows:

- **Use the USPS Priority Mail** If you ship via Priority Mail, the box, tape, and labels are all available to you for free. Yes, the shipping rate is higher, but often if you factor in the cost of the materials and the faster shipment of your Priority Mail items, the additional cost is worth it. In the offing is a plan to make co-branded priority shipping boxes and tape available directly through eBay. The boxes and tape will have logos for both the USPS and eBay, and they will be available exclusively to eBay users. Check eBay's Shipping Page for updates.

Tip *At the time of this writing, the USPS had proposed a flat-rate pricing plan for boxes shipped by Priority Mail. Under this plan two different box shapes will be available for Priority Mail. The dimensions of the boxes are 14 inches by 12 inches by 3.5 inches or 11.25 inches by 8.75 inches by 6 inches. Either box will ship at a rate of $7.70 each no matter what the package weighs or what the destination is. This should make Priority Mail even more cost-effective.*

Spend less (or nothing) for packing materials

- **Buy boxes in bulk**   Once you determine the most useful size box for shipping your items, buy your boxes in bulk. "I buy my boxes from a local cardboard manufacturer," says one clothing manufacturer who is also a PowerSeller. "I buy boxes printed with my own logo," says a PowerSeller from the Southeast. "I just consider it one of my many business expenses, but it is also good advertising." If you shop in bulk, you'll be able to buy your boxes at a reduced rate. Explore your local resources to see if there is a good source of cardboard products nearby.

- **Reuse the boxes you receive**   eBay sellers are forever receiving packages in the mail, both from eBay purchases and from product sources such as wholesalers and manufacturers. Save all the clean boxes and all the packing materials you receive. A good sturdy box can be reused several times. When you do this, you get to use a product that someone else has already paid for!

- **Offer yourself as a recycler**   Think of the local businesses that may be receiving boxes routinely, and approach them with the offer of taking the used boxes off their hands. You'll want to get only clean boxes, so stay away from food stores and restaurants. Also, you don't want boxes that have been cut open with a razor. Approach local gift shops, for example. Unless they sell on eBay, they have no use for their discarded boxes. They'll be happy to have you stop by routinely and pick them up. This will save them the time an employee must spend breaking boxes down for recycling or the trash. You may also be able suggest they sign on as a consignment customer for eBay selling if you'd like!

- **Get free bubble wrap**   That gift shop is also a good place to pick up free bubble wrap, but the best source for free bubble wrap and plastic is your local furniture store. Furniture stores get huge quantities of bubble wrap, and they don't have a need to reuse it. It's more a nuisance to them than anything else, but to you it's clean, perfectly reusable packing material. Again, make a schedule to routinely pick up all the discards you need.

- **Use clean shredded paper**   With your office shredder you can create this excellent packing material. It's free, and you can produce as much of it as you need. What a great way to put that junk mail to work!

■ **Save those newspaper bags**   Clean plastic bags from your daily newspaper can easily be transformed into air-pocket cushions for packing your items. Just blow them up and tie the end. Now you have a cushion much like the ones other people are buying from the office supply store.

Labeling Your Packages

If packing your items carefully is the way to ensure they arrive at their destinations in good shape, labeling them carefully is the way to ensure that they arrive there at all. You can print labels using your auction management software, or you can print them online when you buy your postage (more about that in a minute). Either way, printing your labels on a printer makes them neater and more legible. If you must do it by hand, print them—don't write. "I always ask my customers to e-mail me their addresses, because I don't trust myself to type the address correctly," admits one PowerSeller from the Midwest. When he receives the e-mail, he simply cuts and pastes the address, and he doesn't need to worry about making a mistake. You may decide you don't want to take on this extra e-mail step, but just be certain you are careful when you make up the label, and then double-check it one more time. Once you have your label affixed to the box, cover it completely with a piece of clear packing tape. That way, nothing can smear if the box gets damp, and the label is much less likely to be damaged or lost.

❯❯ Include an invoice with every package

Including an invoice in every package leaves your customers with a sense that they are dealing with a professional seller. Every customer deserves a receipt, and your invoice will provide that. In addition, you can use your invoice to add a little note of thanks for the purchase, a greeting about your business, or a reminder that you plan to leave positive feedback for the buyer and hope for the same. Be friendly and you'll close your transaction on a happy, positive note. As a practical consideration, including an invoice protects you in the event that the package gets lost or damaged. Since the invoice will include both the buyer's name and address and your business's name and address, the carrier can open the box to investigate who owns the contents and where those contents belong should something happen to the label or to the box. And just to make it

Include an invoice with every package

simple, most auction management software programs have a built-in "print invoice" function.

Should You Use Delivery Confirmation?

PowerSellers are not of one mind on this question. Whether or not you should include delivery confirmation for your packages depends largely on what you sell. You don't need to bother with it if you sell items that are so inexpensive that you won't mind occasionally bearing the cost of replacing a shipment. For sellers of inexpensive items, for example, $5.00 to $10.00, it may not pay to spend the extra $0.45 or $0.55 (through the USPS) that delivery confirmation costs. For the random problem with delivery, it may be more cost-effective to just take the loss and replace the item. For most sellers, however, delivery confirmation is worth the cost.

For one thing, your customers appreciate being able to track their packages. It goes back to that feeling of getting a present we mentioned earlier. Once you ship your item, you can send an e-mail to your customer with the tracking numbers, and he can then watch the package travel toward its destination. Practically speaking, this is a good thing for you, too. Once you send that e-mail, you probably won't have any more correspondence with that customer. You certainly won't get further e-mails asking where the package is and when the customer can expect delivery.

One more benefit of delivery confirmation is that it helps make you less vulnerable to scam buyers. If a customer claims he never received an item you shipped, you'll have proof that he did. Usually it takes nothing more to get one of these dishonest buyers out of your life than just sending him an e-mail with the tracking numbers in it. Now he knows he won't get anywhere with you, and he's likely to just move on to his next victim.

Delivery confirmation is included with the price of some delivery services. Through the USPS you will have automatic delivery confirmation by purchasing the following services:

- Signature confirmation service
- Certified mail service
- Registered mail service
- International registered mail service

Tracking numbers are also available through services provided by UPS and FedEx.

Pricing Your Shipping and Handling

PowerSellers may not agree about delivery confirmation, but they do agree that you should not be using shipping and handling charges to generate profit and income for your eBay business. Your chance to make a profit is on the sale of the item; once it's sold, you are only being dishonest if you overcharge for the cost of shipping and handling.

» Pad the item, not the shipping charges

You don't want your customers to feel resentful about being overcharged for shipping fees. You also don't want to discourage potential customers by shipping charges that will easily send them on to your competitors' auction listings. "Don't pad your shipping costs. It makes your customers resent you, and you want them to come back to shop some more," advises a PowerSeller who deals in collectibles. At the same time, he advised, free shipping doesn't work either. "I tried free shipping, but I was just losing too much money that way."

How Much Is Too Much?

So how do you determine a fair rate of pay that covers your expenses but doesn't fleece your buyers? First keep in mind the term shipping and handling. Although this term can sometimes seem distasteful to a buyer (What's handling, anyway?), considering all its meanings helps you set pricing policy. Shipping and handling includes a good deal more than just postage.

In addition to paying for postage, your customer should expect to contribute toward your costs for preparing and sending the package. These are some of the costs:

- The materials you must purchase to prepare the package
- The time you spend getting the package ready
- The time you spend driving to drop off the package
- The time you spend waiting in line to mail the package
- The cost of the salary you pay someone to prepare your shipping

Time is money, and you deserve to be paid for the time it takes you to carefully send an item along to the customer. It's a service you provide, and you deserve to be paid for it. On the other hand, you may want to reconsider some of these charges in the light of your business practices. For example, if you claim your boxes as a business expense, is it fair to also charge your customers for them? If you have a daily pick-up arrangement with your postal carrier, is it fair to charge your customer as though you spent time in the post office? Be fair, but also be realistic about what you are actually spending and which parts of those expenditures you can honestly pass on to your customers.

» Don't disclose your postage costs

"I use Stamps.com and hide my postage costs," says one PowerSeller from New Jersey. "Shipping is more than just postage, and if my customer can't see the postage charge of $1.05, he can't get angry and ask me why I charged $2.50 for shipping." Stamps.com is not the only online postage service that will allow you to keep your postage charges private, but it's a good piece of advice to use one that will.

Flat-Rate Shipping Versus Variable-Rate Shipping

When you create your auction listing, you'll be asked to include shipping costs. You can handle this part of your listing in two different ways. You can calculate a flat rate for your shipping expenses and list that figure, which will apply to all your bidders. Or, you can include a rate calculator in the auction listing that will allow prospective bidders to calculate their specific shipping costs on the basis of their ZIP codes. You specify the weight and size of the package and the shipping service you wish to use. The bidder then inputs her ZIP code and a price for shipping appears, calculated to that specific location. This price will include the handling charge you specify and insurance, if you're offering that, too. You don't have to specifically itemize each of these fees, as the total price is all that the bidder will see. You can easily include a shipping calculator in your auctions. When you're creating your auction, you'll see it listed as an option from the Enter Payment & Shipping page.

Some sellers find it simpler to just create the flat rate price and then state it in the auction listing, leaving nothing further for the bidder to have to calculate. They may also use their shipping rates as sales incentives, keeping them as low as possible to attract buyers who watch their pennies in shipping charges. Sellers using this method prefer the simplicity, even if they occasionally charge slightly less than they should. Other sellers prefer the more precise estimates they get with the shipping calculators and expect their bidders to be willing to take that extra step in determining what their final costs will be. Try your shipping fees each way to determine which is right for your business.

» State your shipping charges clearly

Just be sure that when you list your item, you are very clear in stating your shipping charges and policies. Everyone who shops on eBay expects to pay shipping charges. If you clearly state what your charges are, the burden is completely on your customer. Customers who feel a seller's shipping charges are too high are free to move along and shop with someone else. But if you clearly state your charges and a buyer wins your auction, it's her responsibility to live up to the shipping charges you published in your listings. If she then gets back to you to ask you to adjust the shipping charges, you are within your rights to decline. She should have made that decision before bidding, and you are under no obligation to comply with her request.

At the same time, calculate your shipping fees carefully and then be prepared to live with them even if they turn out to be wrong. You'll get better at estimating your shipping fees with experience, but you must abide by your estimates from the very beginning. Every seller has sent out packages and taken a hit on the shipping fees. You can't go back to the buyer after the auction ends and explain that you made a mistake, and you'll need more money for shipping. That's just wrong. So be prepared to take one for the team. You'll be more accurate in your estimate the next time around.

Overall, PowerSellers clearly state their shipping and handling charges whether they choose to ship using variable rates or flat rates. Clearly stating all associated fees for each listing enables your customers to calculate exactly what they will have to spend to purchase and receive the items you've listed. From a psychological viewpoint, this will encourage them to take that final step and make the bid. If you leave it open-ended, requesting that buyers contact you for shipping and handling charges, you leave open a great unknown that will make your shoppers much more likely to move on to the next seller. They'll move on not only because they don't want

State your shipping charges clearly

to bother with that extra step, but also because, psychologically, it suggests that perhaps you have some reason not to be up front about the charge right in your listing.

On another note, you can use your shipping and handling charges as a marketing tool and an incentive to get your customers to bid on your items. Buyers appreciate low shipping charges, and eBay statistics prove that keeping your costs as low as possible makes it more likely for you to get increased bids on your auctions. Since you've already learned how to get free or very inexpensive shipping supplies, consider cutting your shipping and handling charges to the bone to entice customers to bid on your items. In this way, your shipping and handling charges will not only cover the expense of sending your items on their way, they will also become part of your overall marketing strategy. As a rising PowerSeller, you will work hard to distinguish yourself from the pack on every score, and shipping and handling is one more area where you can do that.

Shipping Oversized Items

If you're planning to deal in furniture, appliances, computers, or other large items, you'll have special shipping concerns that go beyond the scope of the average eBay seller. You'll need to do some research locally to determine your best shipping options. Very often you'll get the best price quotes from local shipping companies. Canadian-based PowerSeller Carrocel-antiques specializes in antique and restored furniture. Almost all of his shipping is via truck freight, and nearly 90 percent of his items get shipped to the continental United States. He does ship furniture to Europe, however, and when he does, he uses a combination of truck freight and ocean freight. His shipping fees are quite expensive, but that doesn't deter his customers from purchasing his beautiful furniture. Since he operates his own woodworking shop, he creates his own wooden customized crates for every piece he ships.

If your oversized items are less specialized than this, you'll want to explore freightquote.com. This company provides online business-to-business freight and logistics services and has entered into an agreement with eBay to market and provide freight services for eBayers who need to ship heavy items weighing more than 150 pounds. You can set up freight shipments directly from the eBay site and give your bidders precise shipping costs before they bid. Visit their web site at www.freightquote.com. You can use the estimating service free of charge, paying only for the shipping expenses.

Insuring Your Shipments

In almost all cases, the items you ship will arrive at their destinations without trouble. But in those very few cases when this is not true, insurance saves you and your buyer a huge headache. What type of insurance you choose will depend on what you sell, how you ship it, and how much risk you are willing to take. One collectibles PowerSeller told us he purchased a special collector's insurance policy for his inventory. This insurance covers his collection when it's stored at his site, when he travels to sell it at shows, and when he ships items from it to his customers. He has no worries about insuring anything, and the yearly premiums he pays for his insurance are less than he would pay if he insured every shipment. This might be a solution for you if you plan to deal in collectibles.

You certainly want to offer insurance to your bidders as an option with their shipping costs. Shipping via the USPS, you can purchase up to $50.00 worth of insurance for $1.30. Bumping that up to $100.00 of coverage will cost just $2.20. When you ship with UPS, you automatically receive up to $100.00 of insurance included in your shipping charges. An alternative to offering insurance to your bidders is to fold insurance charges into your total shipping costs and list your shipping fees as including insurance. This way, you are assured that the package will be covered from the time it leaves your hands until it arrives at your customer's location.

When you purchase insurance, you buy peace of mind, but you also buy simplicity in resolving problems if they arise. When you ship an item insured through the USPS, for example, you simply hold on to the insurance receipt. If your package doesn't arrive at its destination, you send the receipt onto your buyer, and he will then pursue it with the USPS on his end. Because you purchased insurance, the problem will now be resolved with no more input from you.

Scheduling Your Shipments

Once again, how frequently you send shipments out depends entirely on you. Some sellers ship every day. Others create a schedule of two or three shipping days a week. Neither approach is right or wrong, as long as you're up front with your customers about your policy. Obviously, from your buyer's viewpoint you should ship products every business day. But you may find your business works more efficiently if you set aside several days a week to send out your items. Make it clear in your auctions which days those are and include them again in your winning bidder e-mail. "I get my product out as soon as they pay. It's what my customers deserve," says a PowerSeller who ships every day. If you sell items that are more time sensitive, for example, gift items near the holidays, you may agree.

Your Carrier Options

We've all sent packages, so there's really not much mystery about the process of getting something sent to a distant destination. Which carrier you choose depends largely on what you ship and where you live. For some sellers, geography makes one carrier more convenient than another. For others, one carrier offers better rates for the oversized packages they ship. You'll have to make your choice for yourself, but we'll offer you a look at some of the most common options.

» Consider eBay's own shipping center

eBay makes it easy for you to pay for postage and print labels for both the USPS and UPS. You can buy postage through your PayPal account and print the labels directly from eBay's site. Then with the postage paid and the labels in place, you can take your packages to the post office or drop-off center and simply drop them off all ready to go. As an added benefit, when you use eBay's shipping center, your customer's address is automatically printed on the label from your eBay records. Then both you and your customer receive an automatically generated e-mail that includes the tracking information for the package. Go to http://pages.ebay.com/services/buyandsell/shippingcenter9.html for more information. Here's just a note of warning about using this service: At the time of this writing, it was not possible to purchase insurance through PayPal and eBay. This is a disadvantage to sellers who deal in valuable items or any seller who wants to offer insurance as an option for his customers.

The USPS

The USPS is a steady and reliable means of shipping your items. It also offers you a wide variety of options and prices for mailing your packages. If you sell books, magazines, CDs, or movies, you can use Media Mail, which is the least expensive way to send a package. Remember though, it also takes the longest to arrive, so be clear that this is the shipping method you will use when you list the item. Other choices range from Parcel Post all the way to Express Mail, which will give you overnight delivery. You can get a complete listing of fees and services by going to www.usps.com.

If you use Express Mail or Priority Mail, you can arrange to have your regular mail carrier stop by your house every day to pick up all your packages. If you choose not to ship every day, you can still arrange for free next-day carrier pickup by the USPS for Express Mail and Priority Mail. Simply go online to http://ebay.com/usps/usps_tools.html to arrange for your carrier to stop by on the next delivery day to pick up your packages. This new service, unveiled at eBay Live! 2004, shows you just how powerful the eBay selling community is! If you find yourself caught in a bind that requires you to ship an item even before your next delivery day, you can arrange for an on-demand pickup of an unlimited number of packages for $12.50. To use the on-demand pickup, you'll have to be shipping your packages via Express Mail, Priority Mail, Global Express Mail, or Parcel Post. Using Express Mail or Priority Mail also earns you free shipping supplies. Of course, you'll have to have already affixed the proper postage in order to use these services. You can do that through online postage services, Stamps.com among others.

» Use Stamps.com

"One of the best things I've learned is to use Stamps.com," said a PowerSeller in Florida. With Stamps.com you can purchase all your postage online using your credit card. You can print postage in any amount, including individual stamps and shipping labels, too. A rate calculator helps you ensure that your postage is correct, and you can purchase extras such as Delivery Confirmation. With the postage and labels already in place, all you need do is take your packages to the post office and drop them off. "I have an arrangement with my post office so that I can actually drive around back and just drop them off. No waiting in line at all," a PowerSeller from the Midwest told us. The software is easy to use. It has very modest hardware requirements, and it supports your QuickBooks 2004 address book. For more information, go to www.stamps.com.

» Consider Endícia.com

Another source of online postage is Endícia.com. Endícia Internet Postage is a service from Envelope Manager Software, a leading provider of desktop mail software for more than 15 years. Through Endícia.com's attractive and easy-to-use web site at www.endicia.com, you can sign up to purchase postage for all classes of mailings from Media Mail and Library Mail to Express Mail. Endícia.com offers three different pricing plans for users; each comes with a discount if you purchase a one-year subscription in advance. For the basic service known as the Windows Standard Plan, you'll pay $9.95 per month or $99.95 per year. You'll have access to all of the postage services plus an address book, free Internet address corrections, and interfaces to the Outlook and Act! e-mail programs. The Windows Premium Plan costs $15.95 per month or $174.95 per year. It gives you all the features of the Standard Plan, but it also allows you to hide your shipping and handling charges on your postage labels. It further allows you to search for packages from any computer, not just the one you used to create the shipping labels. You can search by name of recipient, address, company, ZIP code, reference ID, tracking number, and/or approximate shipping date. This feature could be very handy when you're trying to track down a missing package. Finally, Endícia.com offers a plan for Macintosh computer users. The MAC Premium Plan offers many of the same features as the Windows Premium Plan and costs $19.95 per month or $199.95 per year. All of these plans are available for a free one-month trial.

UPS

For the most part, UPS is somewhat more expensive than the USPS. Billing for UPS is based on zones, so calculating your shipping is a little more complicated and the final postage fees will vary depending on where your winning bidder lives. Still, you can do all the calculations online, and UPS has done its best to try to simplify the process. You can get complete rate information at www.ups.com. When you sign up on the web site, UPS will deliver a package to you with a tremendous amount of information to get you started. In that package you will receive some free UPS Express envelopes, shipping labels, and a map of the zones based on your own ZIP code.

Some advantages to using UPS are that the company has a higher weight limit than the USPS. UPS will ship packages up to 150 pounds, while the USPS won't go above 70 pounds. Also, when you ship UPS you receive automatic delivery confirmation and insurance of up to $100 per package at no extra charge. However, if you want to arrange for an on-demand pickup, you'll pay a fee for each package you send. You can offset that by arranging for a routine daily pick-up schedule. You will then be charged a weekly rate based on the total value of what you ship each week. You can get free shipping supplies, including boxes, tape, and envelope mailers, if you use UPS Express services.

FedEx

"We go with FedEx because for our oversized packages they are actually cheaper," says a PowerSeller who ships golf equipment. That may be so for his specialized shipping needs, but for the most part FedEx will be more expensive than either UPS or the USPS. Still, FedEx offers on-site pickup, and if you choose their two-day or overnight services, you'll also get the shipping supplies thrown in. Keep FedEx in the back of your mind for special shipping needs, but for the most part, the PowerSellers we spoke with chose either the USPS or UPS for the bulk of their shipping needs.

International Shipping

International shipping can seem intimidating, but more than anything it just involves extra paperwork. As you saw in Chapter 7, some PowerSellers believe the opportunities for selling to international markets far outweigh the challenges of arranging overseas shipping. If you do decide to go with international sales, be sure to clearly state that bidders from outside the United States must contact you for shipping costs—that the standard shipping offered for U.S. customers will not apply to those who live outside of the United States. Shipping internationally is far more expensive, and you don't want to be stuck with the difference coming directly from the profit you made on the sale.

To ship internationally, you should stick with the well-known shipping providers. Both UPS and the USPS handle international shipping. Sticking with the big names makes sense, because everything you ship internationally must clear

Consider Endícia.com

customs. The big name shipping providers are most experienced in getting packages through customs without a hitch.

When you ship internationally, you must complete customs forms for each package you send. These forms require you to declare both the contents and the value of the package. Most countries charge taxes and duty fees based on the value of the item you are shipping. It's very important for you to value the items carefully to avoid increasing these fees unnecessarily. The value of your item is the final price it brought on eBay. When you want to send a package that requires custom forms, you must take them directly to the post office or the UPS shipping center. These packages cannot be dropped off at a box or picked up by a carrier. To get more information about shipping internationally, stop by the International Trading Discussion Board on eBay. You'll find a lot of experienced sellers there willing to help you get started in the global market.

Meet a PowerSeller

Gary Neubert

You can find Gary Neubert on eBay with the username Gatorpack. Gary's family has been in the shipping supply business for many years. It was a natural extension for him to move part of that business onto eBay, and it's a move he's never had reason to regret. Not only does Gary have an automatic built-in source for his products,

but he also has a built-in market of return customers.

Gary first learned about eBay from his wife, who sells antiques. It didn't take long for him to see the business opportunities available to him through supplying online merchants with the necessities of life. When he first came to eBay in 1999, he was only the third seller handling shipping materials. Now he believes there are about two dozen such dealers. Gary sells everything you'd need for shipping whatever you might need to send, from bubble wrap to packing peanuts to bubble mailers and tape.

Today Gary operates Gatorpack from a 5,000-square-foot working space that includes a loading dock. He and his wife, Cheryl, are full-time employees in the operation, but he also employs four part-time workers. He says he could have kept his business small enough to operate without hiring employees, but adding part-time workers was not such a big expense. He said his operation as it stands makes his expenses for the additional help well worth the investment. His customers are primarily other eBay sellers, and he says the match is perfect. Other eBay sellers are generally too small to purchase the minimum order requirements for wholesalers or commercial dealers of shipping supplies. Yet, their need is great enough and constant enough to provide him with a strong, sustainable market.

Gary emphasizes service and quality over trying to offer the lowest price point of all his eBay competitors. "My customers really need what I sell, so I distinguish myself by providing great customer service and fast shipping," said Gary. "If I can't ship it out by 3:30 P.M. of the day my customer pays for the order, I refund all the shipping charges for that order. I get repeat business from people who care more about getting the product promptly than they do about saving a few pennies." Gary's feedback comments in his 100 percent positive feedback rating often include raves about the fast delivery of his products.

Gary's auction listings and store items also show his dedication to the needs of his customers. All of his photos of the bubble mailers are clearly marked with the dimensions of the mailer. This makes it very easy for his customers to see which mailers they'll need and avoid ordering the wrong size.

When we joked about the shipping demands of shipping his shipping supplies to customers, Gary told us how he overcame his biggest challenge. He said his biggest problem was trying to find a way to condense packing peanuts into a manageable size for shipping while still providing them in enough bulk. He went back to his high school math lessons and came up with a mathematical solution. He determined he could pack the most peanuts into a cylinder shape that measured 24 inches tall by 60 inches in diameter. The result is 4.5 cubic feet per parcel that he can then put into two vacuum-sealed poly bags for shipping. He uses a vacuum extractor to eliminate the air and compact the peanuts into a solid brick. Then he ships them off through the USPS. Now that he has this method worked out, shipping his shipping supplies is no problem.

Today, Gary is an active member of the eBay community. He works with eBay executives to address the concerns of eBay sellers. He has participated in eBay meetings in Washington, D.C., and he is a regular at the annual eBay Live! events held across the country. Look for him when you go to the next eBay Live! or just stop by his eBay store to get a good look at some great shipping products and the workings of a very successful eBayer.

Chapter 9

Your Customer Is Always Right (Even When He's Wrong)

Of all the subjects we discussed with PowerSellers, no other found the unanimous agreement that we saw on the subject of customer service. It didn't matter if the product they sold was a $3.00 CD or a painting that went for $20,000; all of them agreed that outstanding customer service is the hallmark of a PowerSeller's business. Providing great customer service may seem a daunting task when you're processing hundreds of orders a month, and the volume of e-mail from customers can feel overwhelming. But what can seem so complicated is really, at its core, fairly simple.

"It's funny how the most important thing we know about business is what we learned as children," noted a PowerSeller who specializes in collectibles. He was talking, of course, about the Golden Rule. Treat others as you would be treated yourself. It's so simple. It's so pure. It's so easy to lose track of when you're busy, hurried, and feeling hassled. You've already begun to live this rule, however, because you've gone into your eBay business with the intent to provide good-quality products. Since you are selling products you truly believe in, standing behind every sale will be easier. Starting from this position of strength will give you the solid foundation you need to handle whatever customer service challenges you may face.

The first thing to remember is not to be afraid of your customers. We've spoken before about the fact that ultimately every transaction on eBay comes down to a moment of trust. Your customer trusts that you will send the product that she expects to get, and you trust that your buyer has come to transact business with you in good faith. In the vast majority of cases, customer service will be no more difficult than fulfilling this commitment and leaving positive feedback. "PowerSellers meet all kinds of people; sincere, unreasonable, some you could never make happy in a million years. Out of 100 percent of my customers, 95 percent are people I want to deal with," says PowerSeller Jeralinc, who sells jewelry.

In this regard, great customer service on eBay isn't different from great customer service in a brick-and-mortar environment. If you dealt face-to-face with your customers, you'd have the opportunity to come to know them by face, personality, and preference. Most would come and go without much note, but there would be some who stuck in your memory for either pleasant reasons or unpleasant ones. While you'll find your eBay experience to be much the same, when you deal with your customers online, you do have some special challenges. It's easy to lose track of the person on the other side of the computer. Don't allow yourself to forget that most problems with customers are more a matter of miscommunication and misunderstanding rather than misdemeanor and misanthropy.

But, don't be intimidated. You've already gone a long way toward providing your customers with the service and support they deserve. When you write accurate descriptions of your products, that's customer service. When you state your policies clearly, that's customer service. When you provide your customers with a variety of payment options, you're providing great customer service. When you package your items carefully and arrange for them to be shipped properly, that's great customer service too. Even your About Me page is a step toward providing your customers the service they deserve. Look at all you've accomplished already! PowerSellers all agree that customer service is what distinguishes a great seller from a good one. They've shared their tips with us, and with those tips you'll find your own level of comfort. After all, you are the boss.

E-Mail: The Way Customer Service Is Done

Almost all of your customer service efforts will happen via e-mail. It is the medium through which you'll know your customers, but e-mail is a flawed method of communication. It is easy to misinterpret the intent and tone of a person's e-mail communication. Remember that when you receive e-mail from your customers, but never forget it when you send your own e-mails. "The most important, and time consuming, part of this job is answering e-mail," said a New England PowerSeller. You will have to respond to questions your customers pose about your items before the auction ends, and then you'll have a series of e-mails to swap as the auction ends and the transaction closes. Some of these can be automated, but don't ever let them seem automated. Don't forget that, although you may send out a dozen e-mail notifications of products shipped today, each of your customers is probably only receiving one. Don't let your e-mail feel processed to the point of removing the human touch. "Give them a personal touch," said our New England PowerSeller. "Let them see the person behind the e-mail."

» Your e-mail should be letter perfect

The first thing you want your customers to know is that the person on the other side of the e-mail is a professional,

Your e-mail should be letter perfect

committed to the business he operates. Your e-mails are the face you show your customers, and you want that face to represent you well. You don't have to be a great writer, but you do have to be sure your e-mails are grammatically correct and filled only with proper English; no slang here. You should also use your spell checker to ensure that you don't send e-mails off with misspellings or typos. That's really not excusable, because it's just too easy to prevent. Answer your e-mails promptly. Your goal is to respond to e-mail the same day you receive it, and when it comes to queries about your item before the auction closes, you must respond even more quickly. Don't keep your buyer waiting more than a few hours for a response to a query, because eBay buyers have short attention spans. In the time your customer waits for your answer, he may find just what he's looking for in some other seller's listings.

E-Mails Throughout the Transaction

Most of your transactions will happen with just a minimum of e-mails passed between you and the buyer. PowerSellers couldn't possibly process the volume of orders they do if each transaction required multiple e-mails. Some of these e-mail transactions can be automated, and that's a great time saver, as long as you don't allow your e-mails to seem too processed. You will surely send an e-mail when the auction ends, and you must send one when the item ships, but some PowerSellers go even further. "We send five e-mails for every transaction," reported PowerSeller Shoetime. "We send three end-of-auction e-mails, one payment-received e-mail, and one item-shipped e-mail." Certainly with more than 30,000 feedbacks, this PowerSeller has found a reliable method for automating these e-mails, but her customers still feel they are being tended through each step of the process.

You may find that you are able to combine some of these e-mails to cut down on your e-mail effort, but you still want to be certain that your customers feel you are taking good care of them through every step of the sale. We'll look at e-mails for each part of the transaction, so that you can see how PowerSellers keep their customers informed and interested. Remember that with each e-mail you send, your customer learns a little bit more about you. It doesn't take more time to be friendly and helpful, and your efforts are sure to pay off when your customer feels that shopping with you has been a pleasure. The first e-mail you receive is likely to come before your item is sold.

» Answer the query and add a little bit more

When a customer requests more information about your item, be friendly in your responses, but keep it professional. Answer the question directly, and then go on to add a bit about the product and how the person might use it, if appropriate. Use this e-mail as bait to make the person want the product just a little bit more than he did before he asked the question. You want him to actually see himself using your product and enjoying it. That's really not a difficult thing to do, especially since you're selling items you know about. Here's an example:

> Yes, I'm happy to say that the pattern book you're asking about does include instructions for both knitted and crocheted sweaters for children. You'll also find instructions for matching hats and mittens. I especially like this book, because there are instructions for using multiple colors for each project. The patterns can be adapted for either the beginner or the more experienced crafter. You'll be proud to give these finished projects as gifts or to enjoy seeing your own children dressed in your creations! Thank you for shopping with me.

The question has been answered, you've personalized the item, and you've given the customer a reason to see that she will enjoy owning this pattern book. You've also proved to her that her transaction is important to you, because you've given her a response that proves you value her interest in your item and you've thanked her. You may secretly be annoyed because your description clearly stated the patterns in the book included both crocheted and knitted projects, but your customer must never detect that annoyance. No matter how carefully you craft your auction listings, some customers just need to ask before they buy. They may actually view this as a way to "test" a seller before they bid. That can be frustrating, but think of it as the online equivalent of the smile you'd share with a customer who walked into your brick-and-mortar store.

» End the auction on a high note

When the auction ends and you have a winning bidder, you'll send an end-of-auction (EOA) e-mail. Here's your chance to set the stage for a smooth ending to your sale. This e-mail can be automated in that it includes standard policy information about payment and shipping, but again, don't forget the personal touch. First, send this e-mail out immediately after the auction

End the auction on a high note

closes. Chances are your customer is well aware of the auction's closing time, and sending out this e-mail quickly proves that you are right on top of your business details. Keep the tone friendly and upbeat. Remember this is a celebration. They don't call this person the "winning" bidder for nothing! Congratulate your winner and assure him that you're committed to his complete satisfaction with his new item. PowerSellers recommend that you include certain details in this e-mail to help ensure a smooth transfer of your item to its new owner:

- The item number should be both in the body of the e-mail and in the subject heading. This helps the buyer identify which auction item is yours if he's purchased more than one thing at a time. It also helps you quickly identify the e-mails you've sent and the responses you receive.

- Include your payment options. Yes, you included them before, but that doesn't mean this buyer was actually paying attention when paying you was a theoretical thing. Now that it's a reality, clearly state what your payment options are.

- Tell the customer when payment is due and provide your address.

- Detail your shipping options and how they will be affected by payment choices. If you hold personal checks for ten days or more, state that here. If you only ship twice a week, no matter what method of payment is used, be sure your customer knows that. Clearly state which days you ship. If you have not already calculated shipping charges and listed them in your auction, do it now before you send this e-mail. Make sure your customer knows everything he needs to know about completing the transaction before you hit Send.

- Ask the buyer to e-mail you in return stating his shipping preference, his intended method of payment, and his correct shipping address.

- Sign off with a hearty "thank you" and good wishes for the buyer with his new purchase.

This is not the time to ask for feedback. It's also not the time to be harsh and strict in detailing what the buyer must do and what will befall him if he doesn't do it. Remember, the tone is celebratory, co-operative, and upbeat. Here's a sample you can use as a template for your EOA e-mail:

Congratulations! You're the winning bidder for item #123456789! You've just purchased a great set of screwdrivers, and I'm sure you'll get many years of good service from them. I am committed to your 100 percent satisfaction with your item, and here are some details that will help us complete your transaction:

- You may pay for your purchase through PayPal; through Western Union Auctionpayments.com; or by money order, certified check, or personal check. If you send a personal check, I will hold it for ten business days before I ship your item.

- Please send payment to me within three business days to:

  1234 My Street
  Hometown, NY 23456

- I will gladly ship your item to you via USPS or UPS. The cost for first class mail will be $5.50. Priority mail will cost $7.75. UPS will cost $9.95. Your shipping costs include delivery confirmation, and I can add insurance for $1.30. I ship my products every Monday, Wednesday, and Friday.

- Please send me a return e-mail to let me know your preferred payment method and your shipping preference. Also, please include your correct shipping address.

Thank you for shopping with me. I look forward to completing this transaction with you. If you have any questions or concerns, please be in touch.

Sincerely,

Now you've made yourself clear. You've shown your buyer that you are partners in the transaction, and you've given him clear instructions for completing the sale. You've taken a big step toward completing your transaction with customer satisfaction and without any misunderstandings.

» Send the package and the e-mail too

Some PowerSellers choose to send an e-mail when they receive payment from the buyer. If your customer pays through the mail, it's good to let her know when her payment has arrived, but you can easily combine that communication with the shipping notice you send when you ship the item. Again, be sure to include the item number in the body and the subject heading of this e-mail.

Send the package and the e-mail too

Also send along any tracking numbers the customer can use to keep an eye on the delivery as it comes her way. Finally, thank your customer once again, and feel free to politely mention the subject of feedback. We'll talk about feedback in much greater detail soon, but when you broach the subject with your customer, be delicate. It's one thing to note feedback, it's another thing to solicit it outright. The latter is common, but also commonly considered tacky. Here are some examples of shipping e-mails you may use as templates if you like:

Hello! I am happy to tell you that I received your personal check today as payment for item #1234567. Thank you for sending this along so quickly. I plan to ship your item on the 23rd of this month, after the required time my bank needs to clear your check. I will be sending it via USPS priority mail, and I will send along all the tracking information once I've posted the item. Thank you again for your business.

Sincerely,

Hello! I received your PayPal payment today for item #1234567. I have already packaged your purchase and will send it out to you on my next shipping day, which will be Wednesday of this week. I will e-mail you then with all of the tracking information so that you can watch the progress of your item as it comes your way. Thank you again for your business.

Sincerely,

Hello! I sent your package for item #1234567 today via UPS. Your tracking number is 987654, and you can check on your package at http://www.ups.com. I am sure you will enjoy your new sunglasses. It has been a pleasure doing business with you, and I hope you share my enthusiasm for this transaction. I plan to leave positive feedback for you, and if you agree our transaction was successful, I would be pleased if you'd do the same. If you have any questions, concerns, or comments about my products and services, please e-mail me directly. I welcome the opportunity to address any issues you may have had and ensure your 100 percent satisfaction. Thank you, once again, for shopping with me.

Sincerely,

Hello! I sent item #1234567 to you today through the USPS with delivery confirmation and insurance. Your tracking number is 9876543. You can track your package at http://www.usps.com.

Please let me know that you've received your item and are completely satisfied either by sending an e-mail or leaving positive feedback. I plan to leave positive feedback for you, too. Thank you again for shopping with me.

Sincerely,

In the preceding e-mails, when you have reason to believe this will be your last interaction with your customer for this transaction, you have politely brought up the subject of feedback and informed your buyer that you'll be adding a positive feedback comment. But, you've been polite and positive and given your buyer every reason to think well of you. That will go a long way toward getting the positive feedback you would like.

Doing What's Right When Things Go Wrong

Despite all your best intentions and efforts, you will have customer service problems to deal with. In a way, that's not entirely a bad thing. It actually means you've attracted enough customers and sales to have some of them present you with problems. Sellers who aren't selling never have trouble with customers. By sheer percentages alone, you have to expect that some of your transactions will go sour. It's more important to know what to do when that happens than it is to worry about whether it will happen or not. It will.

» Think like the store manager, not the storeclerk

This advice comes from a PowerSeller who started his eBay business with nearly 15 years of experience in the offline retail world. He recommends that you keep in mind what happens when you have a problem in a brick-and-mortar store. If the clerk is not able to fix your problem, because of store rules or policies, you are likely to ask that clerk to get the manager. You know when you're dealing with the manager that this person has the authority to address your concerns. She also has the perspective to know that sometimes you must bend to your customer's needs if you're going to run a successful business. You are the store manager of your eBay business. You want to be as resourceful as you can in solving your customers' problems before they escalate into contentious issues that require mediation.

» Remember, it's business, not personal

You may get rude and insulting e-mails, and they will seem personal. Keep in mind that they can't be personal attacks, since your customer doesn't know you personally. They speak much more clearly about the sender of those e-mails than they do about you and your business practices. Bite your tongue, cross your fingers to prevent them from typing, step back from the situation, and keep your emotions out of the encounter. Acknowledge the customer's frustration, and calmly offer to do what you can to make the situation right, but don't allow this person to drag you into a nasty e-mail exchange. You cannot control what the other person says or does, but what you say and do is within your control. Always act in such a way that you can look back and note you did your best to satisfy the problem professionally and without rancor. Not only will it help keep the lid on your blood pressure, but these e-mail exchanges will also prove invaluable if you do ultimately go to mediation with a customer.

» Give your customer the benefit of the doubt

If you get an e-mail that seems insulting, give your customer the benefit of finding out what the problem is before you decide you're angry. This could be a person who doesn't have very good e-mail skills, and he may not have meant to come across negatively. Or, you could be dealing with a newcomer who is overly fearful of eBay trading. She may just need some reassurance, and her fear may make her seem overly defensive. Again, that's about her, not you, so don't allow yourself to be insulted. The first thing to do is respond in a professional and reassuring manner. Tell the person straight out that you are committed to your customer's complete satisfaction, and you will go out of your way to make sure the eBay shopping experience is pleasant. You may decide to ask the customer what he wants in order to make the sale seem right to him. Not only will you likely diffuse a potential problem, you'll go a long way as an ambassador to the world of online commerce. That's bound to benefit you and all the other eBay sellers, too.

Hello Sir!

I am dreadfully sorry about this! I will also give it my full attention to make you "whole" in this purchase.
We can do two things:

1. You ship the book back to me . . . I can re-submit it and return it to you, and I will pay all shipping costs, or

2. I can refund you in full the cost of the grading, and the extra shipping fees = $13.00 (my grading cost) plus $2.00 (extra shipping fee for graded book) = $15.00 by check or PayPal.

Please let me know which one you prefer. I am REALLY sorry about this…it has never happened before.

With true apologies,

» If the mistake is yours, own up to it

Everyone makes mistakes, and as a busy eBay seller, you won't be immune to the occasional blunder. If you've made a mistake, admit it right away and offer to fix the resulting problem. Don't spend time or energy trying to put a better face on a bad situation. Your buyer is human too, and you will be surprised to see how many eBay buyers will show understanding for your missteps. You'll gain more from being honest than you ever could by trying to pull one over on a buyer who may very well know that you goofed it up anyway. No customer can ask more from you than that you'll stand behind your actions and work to make them right. PowerSeller CarrerasComics shared this wonderful e-mail with us. He sent it out when a customer received his collectible comic with a cracked protective case that voided the grading guarantee.

Now, no one could stay angry with a seller who responded to a problem with an e-mail like that. The e-mail response was nearly immediate. This PowerSeller fixed the problem, and he even offered the buyer his choice of methods to correct the mistake. He also turned a disgruntled customer into a trading partner who respects his business ethics and plans to shop with him again. Yes, the seller had to pay $15.00, and that wasn't his first choice. But the buyer had expectations in this transaction that weren't met, too. The seller proved himself to be just the

kind of trading partner buyers can depend on, and that was
certainly worth the money he had to spend to make his accident
right. Not only did the customer understand completely how the
incident could happen and appreciate the seller's response, but
he also appreciated the honesty the seller showed in standing
behind his service. This type of customer service can often lead
to the best feedback a seller has. A buyer who has been treated
with this kind of consideration and respect is likely to speak
more specifically about the virtues of this seller's customer
service and honesty and less generically about fast shipping and
good products. Imagine how this transaction could have ended
if this seller instead suggested that maybe the customer himself
had cracked the case!

» When a problem comes up, know who you're dealing with

We don't want to suggest to you that PowerSellers should be
spineless individuals who fold at the sign of trouble and always
take the loss. We're just recommending that you enter into every
potential encounter with a positive attitude toward your trading
partners and a philosophy that says you'll go out of your way
to make a customer satisfied with your service. Armed with
that philosophy, you can take some steps to ensure your own
interests are protected. As soon as you get a problematic e-mail
from a customer, take some time to research who this person is.
Check his feedback rating, limiting it to feedback from sellers.
You'll soon see if other sellers have had problems with him. But
also go one step further and check the feedback this person left
for other trading partners. Simply click the "Left For Others"
tab from this person's feedback page, shown in Figure 9-1. Now
you'll see how he conducts himself with other sellers, and you'll
learn a lot about the personality he brings to your transaction.

If you see that you've gotten involved with a problem bidder,
offer to void the sale. Do what you must to cut your losses, and
move on. Don't fuel the fire. Don't send incendiary e-mails or
threaten this person with anything. If he's a problem already, he
can probably think of more things to do to damage you and your
reputation than you can think of to do to him. Once you've gotten
away from him, block him from all your future auctions, and
essentially, you've made him go away. You may remember this
from Chapter 7, but if not, go back and see just how it's done.

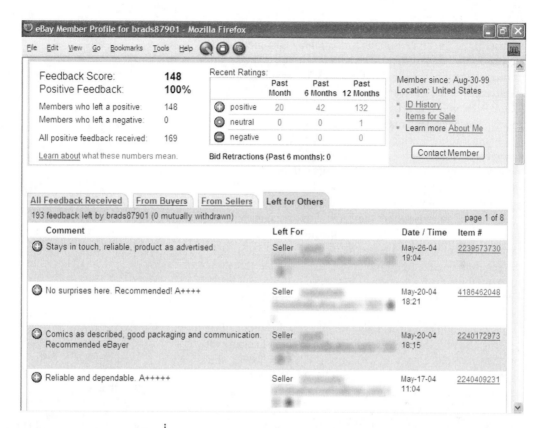

| Feedback Score: | **148** |
| Positive Feedback: | **100%** |

Members who left a positive: 148
Members who left a negative: 0
All positive feedback received: 169

Learn about what these numbers mean.

Recent Ratings:

	Past Month	Past 6 Months	Past 12 Months
positive	20	42	132
neutral	0	0	1
negative	0	0	0

Bid Retractions (Past 6 months): 0

Member since: Aug-30-99
Location: United States
• ID History
• Items for Sale
• Learn more About Me

Contact Member

| All Feedback Received | From Buyers | From Sellers | Left for Others |

193 feedback left by brads87901 (0 mutually withdrawn)   page 1 of 8

Comment	Left For	Date / Time	Item #
Stays in touch, reliable, product as advertised.	Seller	May-26-04 19:04	2239573730
No surprises here. Recommended! A++++	Seller	May-20-04 18:21	4186462048
Comics as described, good packaging and communication. Recommended eBayer	Seller	May-20-04 18:15	2240172973
Reliable and dependable. A+++++	Seller	May-17-04 11:04	2240409231

FIGURE 9-1 Here you can see all of the feedback this eBayer left for other trading partners.

If, on the other hand, you see the person in question has a clean feedback history and has not spent his time on eBay sending horrible feedback to other sellers, you know you're most likely dealing with someone who has a legitimate customer service problem. Now you can move ahead with confidence. You know that you have a reasonable trading partner who will appreciate your efforts to correct the problem and close the deal.

» Try the Negative/Neutral feedback tool

If you're searching through feedback comments from someone with many transactions, you must wade through page after page of comments to find the negatives and neutrals. eBay doesn't provide you with a simple way to call out only the ones you need. Fortunately, there's a clever little tool you can use for this job. You'll find the Negative/Neutral tool at http://auctiononlinedirectory.com/cgi-bin/negs. You can see from

Try the Negative/Neutral feedback tool

Figure 9-2a just how simple it is. Once you're at the site, enter the user ID of the eBayer you are researching and click either "Received By" or "Left By." The results will list every negative or neutral comment made about the user. We searched for our own records under the Received By link. As you can see in Figure 9-2b, you'll find the user's total feedback score, the positive feedback percentage, and the individual comments left by other users. Each comment comes with the complete statement by the party leaving the feedback, the reply left by the user who received it, the time and date of the comment, and the item number under discussion.

Using this tool will allow you to quickly see the person's history and evaluate whether the comments are consistent, indicative of a pattern, or reflective of a new user who may have needed some time to learn the ways of eBay. As you can see from our example, you could have found all three of our neutral feedbacks, but you would have had to scroll back through four years of eBay feedback records to get a complete look at all of them.

If you decide to use this little tool, please keep in mind that it's dangerous to view a seller's negative and neutral feedback all together and out of context. If a seller has 30,000 feedbacks, she's bound to have more than a few negatives. Taken in context of page after page of positives, you can view these feedbacks in a proper perspective. It's unlikely that any seller is going to please all buyers 100 percent of the time. Instead of paging through the list of negatives and neutrals with a growing sense of foreboding,

FIGURE 9-2 (a) The Negative/Neutral Feedback finder makes it simple to spot problematic eBayers. (b) Here you can see the results of the search for this user's negative and neutral feedback.

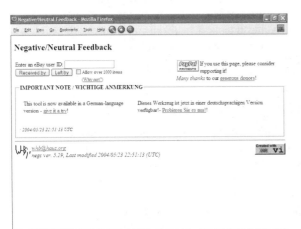

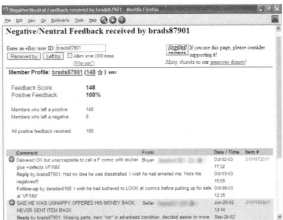

evaluate them for what they are. See how the seller may have responded to the comments. It could be the seller was a victim of a perpetually unhappy buyer. Also consider if the negatives all came within a certain period of time. That could mean the poor seller was caught in an emergency, whether medical, family, or economic. You can't know what was happening in this person's life that may have made their eBay performance slide, but they certainly deserve the benefit of the doubt if all their negatives occurred together. So, by all means, check out their negatives, but keep them in perspective too. This tool, like so many other ways of evaluating an eBayer, is part of the whole picture, not the whole picture itself.

The Negative/Neutral feedback tool works best with a high-speed connection. As you saw in Chapter 3, that's a requirement for your eBay shop, so you should be ready to use this tool. For those of you who are still working with dial-up connections, you'll find the tool can take quite a long time to complete the search and display the results. Still, as you may have noticed in Figure 9-2a, this tool, created by Win Bent, is free for you to use. If you use it, and like it, please support Win's great work by donating to his page through PayPal. And, be sure to bookmark this site so that you can get to it quickly.

What If Your Customer Is One of Those Scammers?

As you remember from Chapter 7, there are people who use eBay to scam legitimate sellers. They are a small minority of eBayers, but they can wreak havoc on the unsuspecting seller. Of course, you're no longer quite so unsuspecting, because PowerSellers have helped you to see what scams can happen. You're in a much better position to spot them than sellers who haven't taken advantage of the PowerSellers' secrets. Still, you may fall victim to a scam or a scheme, and if you do, be prepared to act quickly.

You'll know early in your interaction if the person you are dealing with is out to cheat you. If you find that's true, do everything you can to void the sale. That may mean you void the bid from this buyer. Or, you may have to actually end the entire auction. That will cost your listing fees, but if this is truly a scam in progress, you'll be better off losing those fees than losing the cost of the entire sale or the item itself.

If e-mail fails, pick up the phone

Archive every e-mail you send and receive. This will be your paper trail and will be valuable evidence if you end up in mediation. It will prove both what you did to resolve the issue and what the other person did to scam you. If you suspect this person is perpetrating fraud or crime, report it to eBay as soon as you realize it.

In the end, you'll have to face the harsh realities of being a victim of a thief. "Sometimes you just have to take one for the team" is a philosophy a PowerSeller and trading assistant from the Southwest shared with us. Accept that life isn't always fair and sometimes the bad guys really do win. But at the same time, keep in mind that any single encounter, no matter what the outcome, isn't going to make or break your business as an eBay seller. Keep your perspective, take your hit, and move on with the business of earning an income from the millions of honest eBay buyers who are still out there waiting.

» If e-mail fails, pick up the phone

If you are dealing with a customer who has already made a bid on your item, you can access that customer's contact information. Sellers can obtain contact information for any bidder participating in a current auction and for the winning bidder of a recently closed auction. You can't indiscriminately request contact information for eBayers who are not currently participating in a trade with you. That's only reasonable to protect the privacy of the community in general. Also, you may find it more difficult to get the contact information for someone from outside the U.S., but it is possible to obtain this information for some international traders.

To get to the form you'll complete to get contact information, go to http://cgi3.ebay.com/aw-cgi/eBayISAPI .dll?MemberSearchShow. The screen shown in Figure 9-3 will appear. You can get other information from this same screen, including the Feedback history of the user and her About Me page. But if you scroll down the form, you'll find the entry for requesting contact information that will include the user's phone number. Once you request the contact information, eBay will send an e-mail to that user notifying him that you've requested his contact information.

"If I can't get through with e-mail, I always pull the contact information and make that phone call," says PowerSeller

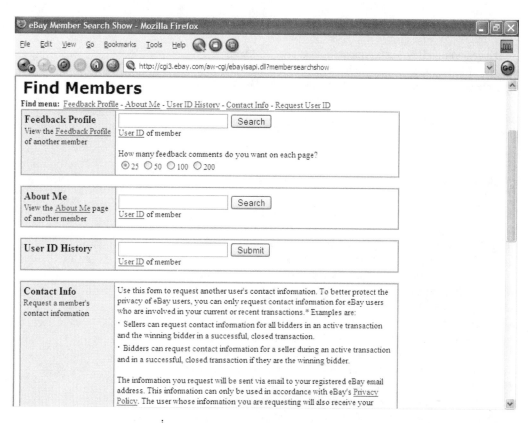

FIGURE 9-3 The Find Members form allows you access to an eBayer's phone number so that you can speak directly with a trading partner.

TraderNick. "Sometimes just that next level of person-to-person contact helps." Other PowerSellers agree with Nick. It's much more difficult to be ugly to a person on the phone, especially after this person willingly called to try and straighten out the problem between you. It shows your real commitment to making the situation right, and it personalizes you to your buyer in a way that e-mail can't.

That's especially true if you approach this as a chance to help instead of a chance to tell off someone who has angered you. If you send e-mails and the buyer never responds, it's possible that person is ignoring you, but it's also possible that person has an e-mail program with an overzealous spam filter. He may not even realize he's missing e-mail, and he may be wondering why you're not reaching out to him. Check your own filter periodically to ensure that it's not catching legitimate e-mails. If that's happening, adjust your e-mail software's settings to allow more e-mails to get through.

If e-mail fails, pick up the phone

What's the Word on Your Guarantee?

"In the beginning eBay was a typical Internet site. 'It is what it is. You get what you get, don't bother me. Too bad? So sad!'" remembers PowerSeller Hessfine. "Now it's almost like Macy's with returns for everything." Most PowerSellers offer their customers some form of guarantee on their purchases. It's important for them to do that to stay competitive with other sellers and safeguard their feedback ratings. These guarantees range from "Guaranteed to be as described" to "100 percent, guaranteed, no questions asked." You'll have to decide for yourself where you fit on this sliding scale of options. Much of that will depend on the type of product you sell and how confident you are with your products. Your policy may evolve as you gain more experience, and that means you could choose to become stricter just as easily as you could choose to become more lax.

Guaranteed to be as described is a sensible policy for sellers who are going to deal in used goods. If you choose it, also add a line to your policy statement telling the prospective bidders to ask questions *before* bidding. That, of course, doesn't mean he actually will. But in your effort to make your auction listings as clear as possible, this is a small step you can take toward your own protection. Unfortunately, as you know especially with new eBay users, it's easy for a bidder to get caught up and make a bid, not clearly understanding he is entering into a legally binding contract. Still, you will have done what you could to make your policies clear before a bid occurs.

If you handle used electronics or appliances, you might want to follow the advice of a trading assistant PowerSeller we spoke with who does the same. He guarantees his buyers that the item will not arrive "Dead on Arrival" (DOA). Beyond that he offers them a three-day review period to ensure that the product works to their satisfaction. Within those three days, they are free to return the item for a full refund, once he verifies that the item is returned in the same condition he sent it. Beyond the three-day period he is no longer obligated to accept the item for return. He makes this policy clear in his EOA e-mail and with his shipping statement, too. This reasonable policy assures customers that they won't be getting a box of broken junk without a return option. It also supports the PowerSeller, who knows that beyond the three-day review, he won't hear back from the buyer if the used item stops working.

PowerSeller Balkowitsch takes yet another approach. He offers his customers a 100 percent, no questions asked, satisfaction guaranteed return policy as long as the item is returned within ten days, with all of its original packaging. He even agrees to pay shipping for both sending the item to the customer and returning it to him. He uses his generous return policy within his auction listing to build bidder confidence in both his products and his services. This liberal return policy is a good way to go when it comes to returns. Your bidders are likely to pay a bit more if they know they can return an item, and they may be more likely to shop with you than with one of your competitors if they know you will honor their returns.

» Don't hesitate to offer a refund

"I hate giving money back, but I do it anyway," says a PowerSeller from Rhode Island. "Once they have a refund, or an offer of a refund, I have nothing more to prove about my willingness to support my products." Offering your bidder a refund is hard to do, especially when you're first starting out. But you need to be prepared to do it, and you need to be gracious about it when you do. It's the best way to turn a disappointed and potentially angry customer into a satisfied one. Once the buyer finds she'll be getting her money back, she'll be ready to move on, recognizing that the seller is professional and not out to cheat her. Of course, sometimes the buyer won't bother returning the item for a refund. But your offer goes a long way to diffusing misunderstandings.

"The first thing I do is refund their money. Then I work at getting my product back," says PowerSeller Carrocel Restorations. This Canadian-based PowerSeller deals in restored and antique furniture. He ships his products throughout the U.S. and Europe. Even so, when a customer is dissatisfied, he returns the money first and claims his product second. He told us he's never had a serious loss using this approach to customer service.

Tools That Support You While You Support Your Customers

PowerSellers have discovered some tools they've found useful in helping them provide great support for their customers. Some of these they recommend to you, and you might also find them useful. Others you'll want to keep in mind and bring into your business once you've grown big enough and busy enough to make them reasonable for you.

» Consider giving a telephone number and customer service hours

"You should offer a phone number for your customers to call," recommends a PowerSeller with more than 13,000 feedbacks and a 100 percent positive feedback rating. "I list a phone number in all my auctions and make it clear my customer service hours are from 8:00 A.M. until 10:00 P.M. Mountain time, Monday through Friday. In all the years I've been on eBay [and that's since 1999], no one has ever called outside of those hours. I've gotten international phone calls at 8:01! But, never before or after my official hours." Other PowerSellers agree, and it isn't at all unusual to find customer service telephone numbers listed in their auctions. This is a customer service feature that you can actually offer at little or no additional cost to you. If you decide to use your own phone number, you are adding a customer support feature to something you already pay for. Your customer will pay the long-distance charges to reach you. If you decide not to use your own number, you'll have the connection costs of a new phone line and the line's monthly charge.

You can also consider getting a cell phone to meet your customer service needs. Whether you choose to make your hours as flexible and convenient as our Rocky Mountain–based PowerSeller or decide instead to provide more limited access, it's definitely worth a try, since it seems such an effective tool for PowerSellers. Ultimately, you may be able to afford an 800-number, and then your customers will be even more likely to get in touch before they bid.

» Maybe you'll be ready for the thinkingVOICE Call Activator live callback application

In April 2004, thinkingVOICE of Mountain View, California, launched a sales and customer service platform designed just

Maybe you'll be ready for the thinkingVOICE Call Activator live callback application

for small to medium-sized e-commerce businesses. "The target audience for this new product is actually the eBay PowerSeller," said thinkingVOICE CEO, DC Cullinane. "Our goal was to give the small e-commerce owner the same type of call service functionality that much bigger companies can afford." Here's how it works: Call Activator is a hosted program. When you sign up, you receive a line of HTML code to include in your auctions. This becomes the "Click-to-Call" button that automatically puts your customer in touch with you. When your customer clicks the button, a form pops up asking for some basic information from the customer. She'll be asked

- The country from which she's calling
- Her telephone number
- Her e-mail address
- Her requested action, for example, call right now, respond via e-mail, call after 5:00 P.M. Eastern time.
- What type of information she's requesting

FIGURE 9-4 The button at the bottom of this form sends a pop-up to your computer screen to notify you that a customer wants to speak with you.

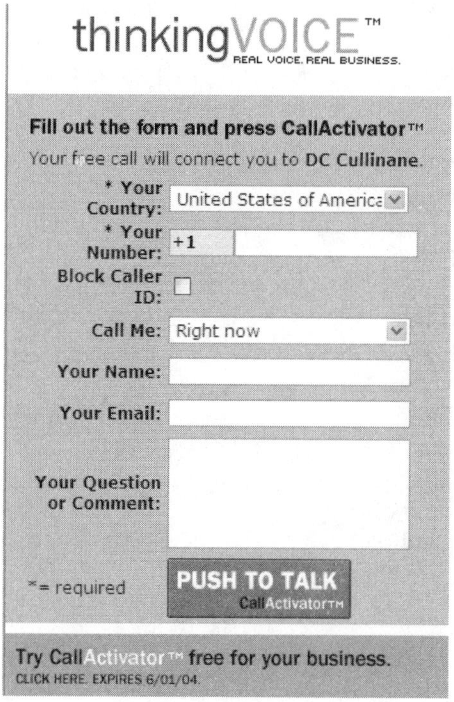

When she clicks the button at the bottom of the form, shown in Figure 9-4, the message will immediately be directed to you. She will see a graphic showing her that the call is being sent. You will then receive a pop-up notification at your computer that someone wants to speak with you. When you click that button, both your phone and the buyer's phone will ring, and you will be automatically connected. She has no cost in sending the message to you, but you will pay for the connect time to call her. Within seconds, you can be on the phone with a prospective customer. "Customers are usually blown away the first time they get the call back and are instantly speaking with me! But before they hang up they usually place a bid," reports PowerSeller Effordables.

For Call Activator users who also use Vendio (see Chapter 4), the service can provide much more information to the seller. When a buyer clicks the button in your auction listing, you will not only receive the request to speak to the buyer, but valuable information will come with the

Maybe you'll be ready for the thinkingVOICE Call Activator live callback application

request directly from Vendio. You will see the item in question, the number of bids currently on that item, and the highest bid. Before you even reach the buyer, you will be informed about the item in question and able to speak with authority about your product.

Even sellers who don't use Vendio can add requests for information to the form the buyer completes when he requests that you get in touch with him. You can customize that form and request information of your choosing in addition to the telephone number, e-mail address, and country of origin. For example, if you sell auto parts, you may want to add a request for the make and model the buyer is shopping for. If you sell apparel, you may want to add a request for the shopper's favorite color or the item he is currently interested in. Then as you answer your buyer's questions, you can also use this call as an opportunity to show him other products in your line that might be of interest. This turns a customer support service for your buyers into a new marketing tool for you.

If you don't wish to accept calls for a period of time, you can set Call Activator to go directly to e-mail. You can also set it to send requests to live chat, and then you can respond to your customer's requests live via the computer rather than on the phone. Diverting the Call Activator allows you to see quickly via e-mail that you have requests from customers. In future evolutions of this product you will be able to establish time-of-day routing that will simply record and list calls that arrive before or after your established business hours. "Future plans also include live video. Within a couple of years, you'll be able to hold up your item and show it to your customer from every angle while you talk about it together," said Cullinane.

For the time being, it costs $4.95 per month plus $0.10 per minute in usage charges to use the Call Activator. In the future, the company plans to move to a flat-rate monthly fee without the usage charge. Then the monthly fee will allow you unlimited access. "We're going for an all-you-can-eat approach," joked Cullinane. To learn more about the Call Activator and see what features are available to you now, you can go to www.thinkingVOICE.com, where you'll find the page shown in Figure 9-5.

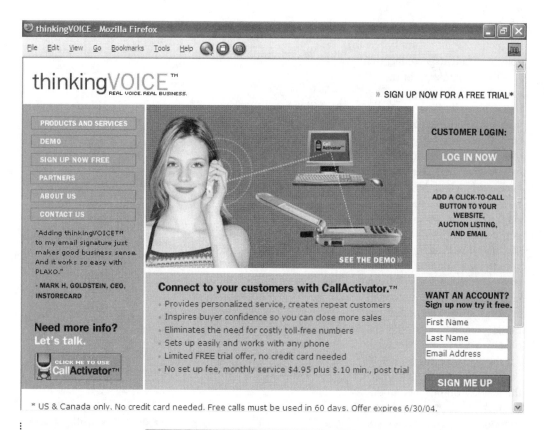

thinking**VOICE**™
REAL VOICE. REAL BUSINESS.

» SIGN UP NOW FOR A FREE TRIAL*

PRODUCTS AND SERVICES

DEMO

SIGN UP NOW FREE

PARTNERS

ABOUT US

CONTACT US

"Adding thinkingVOICE™ to my email signature just makes good business sense. And it works so easy with PLAXO."

- MARK H. GOLDSTEIN, CEO, INSTORECARD

Need more info?
Let's talk.

CLICK ME TO USE
Call**Activator**™

CUSTOMER LOGIN:

LOG IN NOW

ADD A CLICK-TO-CALL BUTTON TO YOUR WEBSITE, AUCTION LISTING, AND EMAIL

SEE THE DEMO»

Connect to your customers with CallActivator.™

• Provides personalized service, creates repeat customers
• Inspires buyer confidence so you can close more sales
• Eliminates the need for costly toll-free numbers
• Sets up easily and works with any phone
• Limited FREE trial offer, no credit card needed
• No set up fee, monthly service $4.95 plus $.10 min., post trial

WANT AN ACCOUNT?
Sign up now try it free.

First Name

Last Name

Email Address

SIGN ME UP

* US & Canada only. No credit card needed. Free calls must be used in 60 days. Offer expires 6/30/04.

FIGURE 9-5 The thinkingVOICE Call Activator makes it simple for your customers to get in touch with you.

» Try a Message Tag (MSGTAG)

You may have a tool to use if you come across the customer who claims "I never got your e-mail!" Message Tag is a little software tool you can add to your desktop. You'll find the company at www.messagetag.com. As you can see in Figure 9-6, you add a little capsule to your desktop that allows you to "tag" an e-mail. Once you do, you will receive an e-mail notifying you of the time that e-mail reached its destination and another message noting the time the recipient opened it. Now when you hear the old excuse, you can double-check for yourself and see if the problem might be a Spam filter, or if the problem is a bidder trying to dodge your e-mail. You surely won't want to tag every e-mail you send, but if

Try a Message Tag (MSGTAG)

you suspect that a customer interaction might get sticky, you'll be ready to get to the truth.

You can sign up for the basic Message Tag option for free. This will allow you to tag your e-mail, but the e-mail you tag will include a line at the end identifying it as being tagged by Message Tag. That's not necessarily a bad thing, but it does eliminate your element of surprise, if that's important to you. For $19.95 you can have Message Tag Plus. This gives you all the same features of the free version, but it also lets you personalize or hide the footer tag, and you get unlimited e-mail technical support, too. Finally, you can pay $59.95 for the Message Tag Status version, which includes all of the features of the other products but also gives you a "dashboard" monitor board from which you can see all the e-mails you send and the status of each one. You can also create groups of e-mail contacts, with different tagging rules for each one. If you have some concern about keeping in touch with your customers through e-mail, the free product offered by Message Tag seems like a good idea. At this point, the Cadillac service you'll get from Message Tag Status is very likely much more information than you need to concern yourself with. Stop by at www.messagetag.com to learn more about this tool.

MSGTAG : 3 Great Flavors

MSGTAG Free sends you notifications by email when your messages are opened at their destination. The eye-catching MSGTAG capsule sits on your desktop or in your system tray, allowing you to enable or disable tagging with one click. It doesn't hassle your friends with pop-up boxes, all they see is a small MSGTAG Footer at the end of your message. Best of all, MSGTAG Free is free!

free download → more info

Time to upgrade? MSGTAG Plus contains all the great features in MSGTAG Free as well as giving you the ability to personalize or hide the MSGTAG footer. Include your own signature or personal greeting — Or simply leave it blank!

FIGURE 9-6 With a click on this capsule, you can add a tag to your e-mail messages that will notify you when they have been opened by the recipient.

Feedback: A Human (and Therefore Imperfect) System

We all have eBay feedback ratings, and you probably know all about how feedback works. We saw in Chapter 1 what PowerSellers think about their feedback ratings and how they work to maintain as spotless a feedback rating as possible. As you progress from seller to PowerSeller, you'll develop a whole new perspective on the subject of feedback. This perspective will grow almost as quickly as your feedback rating itself as you sell more, buy more, and gain more experience in doing business on eBay.

Feedback is one of the main subjects of discussion among the PowerSellers. They debate when a seller should leave feedback. Is it when he receives payment from the buyer or when he learns the buyer is satisfied with the item she received? They discuss who should leave feedback first. Is it the buyer or the seller? They talk about whether you should leave feedback for someone who hasn't left feedback for you. And they even debate whether or not you should leave feedback at all. You probably have your own opinions about the feedback system already. These will grow and shift as you face some of the special challenges feedback presents to PowerSellers.

The feedback system is at once the heart of eBay ethics and a source of great injustice on eBay. For example, did you know that an NPB may leave negative feedback for a seller? That's something PowerSellers struggle with. Some eBayers even use feedback for extortion. Here's how it works. The buyer you've just completed a transaction with may leave you a negative feedback. Then he will contact you and offer to enter a mutual feedback withdrawal, if you refund a percentage of his purchase price. This is a complete violation of eBay's rules of trade, but while you do what's necessary to clear up the mess, you still have a negative feedback on the first page of your feedback comments. Also, you'll lose valuable time you could be spending listing and selling your products. Fortunately, the PowerSellers share lots of wisdom about navigating the feedback system with all of its flaws, and most of the time, your transactions will result in positive feedback or no feedback at all. We'll help you gain a good perspective on the whole subject, and we'll offer you some guidance about keeping your feedback rating solid.

» This is going on your permanent record

Oh no, that dreaded *permanent record*. It has kept many a middle-school student on the right track. Now that you've decided to join the upper echelon of the eBay world, your permanent record—your feedback rating—is more important than ever. When it's your turn to leave feedback, remember that what you say cannot be taken back. There are only a few instances when eBay will remove feedback, and then only the feedback score gets altered. In most cases the comments must remain. When you receive neutral or negative feedback, you have the opportunity to leave a comment in response to the one left by your trading partner. That comment also becomes part of your permanent feedback record, so watch yourself to make sure that your statement is worthy of being viewed in perpetuity. You're just like Charles Dickens' Jacob Marley in this case; you'll forever wear the chains you forge in life. Be conscious of how your actions might drag you down if you're not careful.

» Try for eBay's Mutual Feedback Withdrawal program

If you find yourself in a situation in which you've left negative feedback and so has your trading partner, you can mutually agree to withdraw both comments through eBay's Mutual Feedback Withdrawal (MFW) program. Now keep in mind that if you keep on reading and follow our advice, you will be much less likely to be in this situation, but just in case, it's good to know what to do if you need to undo the damage.

Let's suppose you've had a very contentious and difficult interaction with a buyer who flamed you with a negative feedback. You were so caught up in the event that you responded in kind. Now you both have a spot on your feedback rating. Let's further suppose that within a short while, you both calm down. You try one more time to make things better, and the buyer agrees. Now you can both go to the Mutual Feedback Withdraw page and begin to resolve the confrontation. You'll start the process by clicking the Services page. Next scroll down to the Feedback Forum hyperlink and click it. You'll see the form that appears in Figure 9-7. This is where your journey begins. Once you enter the item number of the contentious auction, you will be stepped through the form and finally the whole issue will be submitted to eBay for resolution.

Once both parties have agreed and worked together to remove the feedback, eBay will simultaneously remove both of the negative numbers from both of the parties' feedback scores at just the same moment. That way, neither party gets an advantage. The comments left cannot be removed, but they will be amended with a statement that the feedback score for this transaction was mutually withdrawn. Now you see, first

Try for eBay's Mutual Feedback Withdrawal program

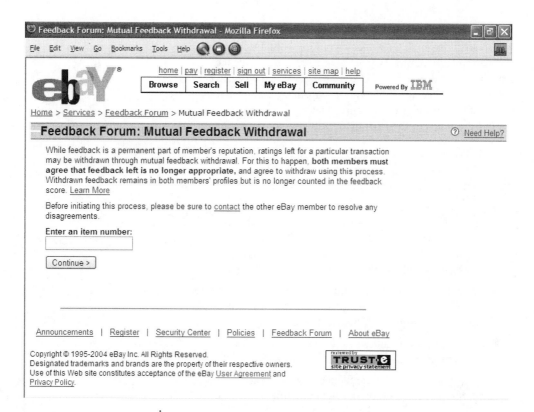

FIGURE 9-7 This Mutual Feedback Withdrawal form is your first step in resolving a bad interaction.

hand, why you must be so careful about what you say in your feedback comments.

The Mutual Feedback Withdrawal program is a fairly recent eBay offering. eBay introduced it to provide all trading partners with a forum for resolving conflict and removing negative feedback points. Before the MFW program, only those trading partners who were willing to go through Square Trade's mediation process, at the cost of $20.00 per incident, had a method for withdrawing a negative score. As a part of its effort to provide a level playing field for all traders, eBay introduced this program that allows for conflict resolution without a fee.

Sometimes, But Only Rarely, eBay Will Step In

eBay purposely leaves feedback up to the trading partners. You can't expect eBay to step in and fix an unfair feedback someone has left for you. eBay does, however, remove feedback for some very specific reasons. For example, if you accidentally leave feedback for the wrong customer, you can work to make that right.

Try for eBay's Mutual Feedback Withdrawal program

The first thing you must do is leave *exactly* the same comment for the correct person. It must match word for word. Once you've done that, you can inform eBay of the mistake and provide the usernames for both parties. Now, eBay will remove the negative from the score of the innocent buyer, but again the comment must remain with an amendment explaining that it was left by mistake.

Here are other reasons that eBay will step in:

- eBay receives a valid court order finding that the feedback in question is slanderous, libelous, defamatory, or otherwise illegal.

- The comment contains profane, vulgar, obscene, or racist language, or adult material. (On the other hand, although eBay discourages name-calling such as "fraud," "cheat," "liar," and "scam artist," these comments will not be removed.)

- Personal identifying information about another member is included in the comment, such as real name, address, telephone number, or e-mail address.

- The feedback includes references to a PayPal, eBay, or law enforcement organization investigation.

- The person who left the feedback was ineligible to participate in an eBay transaction at the time of the transaction or when the feedback was left.

- The person who left the feedback gave eBay false contact information and couldn't be reached. For the most part, the transaction period is considered to be 90 days from the end of the listing or 30 days from the date the feedback was left.

- Someone has bid on your item or purchases strictly to have the chance to leave negative feedback with no intention of completing the transaction.

This last reason is not the same as an NPB, because an NPB can claim that he *did* intend to complete the transaction at the time he made the bid or won the auction. It is difficult to prove intent. If you suspect that one of your feedbacks qualifies for removal for one of these reasons, you can contact eBay to get the process started. Remember, these are the only instances under which eBay will remove a negative feedback. In the meantime, you may want to make your feedback private while eBay is reviewing the matter. Generally, PowerSellers discourage you from making your feedback private. It suggests that you have something to hide from the legitimate trading community. But if you have a situation that is under review, you might want to make an exception during the review period.

» If all else fails, consider Square Trade

As you learned in Chapter 6, Square Trade can provide a feedback review and withdrawal service through a mediation process. At the cost of $20.00 per review, you will work with a Square Trade mediator to review the entire transaction and decide on the course of action. Even with this review, the negative comment can no longer be removed from your feedback, but you can have the negative point taken from your score. Consider how much you are willing to spend for the removal. Is it worth it to you to put out the money to remove the point?

Feedback Is Strictly Voluntary

Although the feedback system is the ethical backbone of eBay, participating in it is strictly voluntary. No one can force you to leave feedback, and there's nothing you can do to force someone else to leave it for you. Among the more experienced eBayers, actively soliciting feedback is considered quite tacky. So what can you do to encourage your partners to give you the positive feedback you deserve? First let's look at what you shouldn't do.

Don't send messages that say, "I'll leave good feedback for you after you leave good feedback for me." This reads a lot like a seventh-grader's diary. Also don't ask outright for positive feedback. It looks greedy and coercive.

Instead, frame your mention of feedback in the form of a thank-you note. You can include a phrase in your invoice, or you can attach a statement to your business card or giveaway that you slip into each of your packages. Here's a recommended statement that couldn't possibly offend anyone:

> It's been a pleasure to trade with you. I hope you're completely satisfied with your purchase. I plan to leave positive feedback for you. If you agree, I'd be pleased if you'd also leave it for me. If you have any questions or concerns with your purchase, please be in touch directly with me. I'll do my best to see you're satisfied.

Feedback is the last step in a transaction

Now all you can do is let it go. If the person doesn't leave a positive feedback for you, don't focus on it. You're right—that person who was completely satisfied should have left you a positive feedback. You earned it and you deserve it. But, we don't always get what we deserve in the world, and it isn't worth your time or energy to focus on each individual feedback.

» Feedback is the last step in a transaction

It's easy to know when you should leave feedback if you're the buyer. When you receive your package and inspect your item, if you're satisfied, go right to your computer and leave a feedback for the seller. If you're not satisfied, contact the seller and hold off on leaving the feedback. Give the person a chance to make the sale right. Remember that Golden Rule? You'd want one of your buyers to do the same for you. Either way, there's really no dispute. You can clearly see the point where feedback is called for.

As the seller, it's not so simple. Some sellers feel that the buyer's main responsibility is to pay for the item. They leave positive feedback for the buyer when they receive payment. If the payment is prompt and complies with the seller's policies, then these sellers believe the buyer completed his part of the transaction and has earned a positive. Other sellers disagree. They feel that the transaction isn't complete until the buyer has received the package and is satisfied with her purchase. Until you hear from that buyer, either via e-mail or through feedback, you can't be sure the transaction is complete.

Feedback is the final step in any eBay transaction. Any problems you may have with a transaction should be resolved long before you get to the feedback part. Leaving feedback before the transaction is complete and closed leaves you vulnerable. If you've already left feedback when the buyer paid, then you will have lost your chance to comment on the buyer's total behavior. You can't know how reliable a trading partner a buyer is just by judging how quickly she paid. After all, paying for an item she bids on is just complying with the legal contract she entered when she placed the bid. On the other hand, how this person handles a potential disappointment or problem speaks volumes about what she's like as a trading partner. So, wait until the transaction has actually ended with the buyer having received the product before you leave feedback.

Should You Ever Leave Negative Feedback?

"I have almost 6,000 feedbacks, and I can count on one hand the times I've left a negative feedback," says a PowerSeller who specializes in coins. This seller feels it just isn't worth the risk of retaliation and the aggravation negative feedback creates. You will find many PowerSellers agree. "It's just more important to me that I relist the item and get on with my business," says an Arizona PowerSeller. Indeed, you will find that the greatest percentage of Negative Feedbacks come from inexperienced eBay users. You can check on this yourself using the Negative/Neutral feedback finder we described earlier. The next time you come across a seller with a feedback rating ranging between 98 percent and 99 percent, enter that person's user ID into the finder and check your results. You are bound to find that most of the negatives come from people with fewer than 50 feedbacks of their own.

Other PowerSellers feel differently about leaving negative feedback. "Feedback is the way this community polices itself," says a PowerSeller from Georgia. "If I'm not willing to take a risk and make a statement against a bad eBayer, I'm only hurting other sellers who come along after me. That damages the whole community." This seller views it as her civic responsibility to accurately relate her experience so that others can learn from her misfortune. She doesn't view it as a burden to add to the feedback record of a bad eBayer, and she's willing to take the risk of retaliation.

» If your customer goes ballistic, don't go with him

Getting a negative feedback or dealing with a difficult customer will absolutely make you furious. In many of these instances, your anger is justified, and we're completely on your side. But, as we've said, never respond to a customer when you're caught in a fury. It's the same thing that keeps you from fighting it out on the highway with an aggressive driver. In the end, you're entering into a confrontation with a stranger. You are also dealing with someone who will be in your life for only a very brief period of time. Be angry, but also be smart. Never leave feedback when you're furious. We can guarantee you'll regret it, even if you will always believe the other party deserved it.

When it comes to a negative, stick to the facts

Any time you find yourself in a confrontation, the one who keeps cool has an automatic advantage. It's easy to get caught up in an escalating screaming match, and much more difficult to stay calm, but calm is what you need. When you're calm, the other guy starts to look ridiculous. He also starts to make mistakes, because he's allowed his emotions to take over his head. If you keep calm, you're much more likely to be thinking clearly, and you'll be more likely to see the solution to the confrontation. In the end, what you want is resolution, not vindication. You can be vindicated when you block this person from your auctions and make it impossible for him to ever bother you again.

» When it comes to a negative, stick to the facts

Just as you should never leave feedback when you're angry, you should never leave feedback that strays from the basic facts of the issue. You won't gain anything by name-calling, or by insulting or threatening an errant buyer. Also, don't use that Caps Lock. If you leave feedback in all caps, it makes you look like a hothead. Instead, make clear statements and include dates. For example,

> EOA sent 10/24; no payment r'cvd; filed NPB 11/15; FVF r'cvd 11/30.

Now, everyone viewing this person's feedback will see that he received a negative feedback because he didn't pay for your item, but you've conducted yourself in a business-like manner. You've also not invested the situation with more emotion than it deserves, and you've safeguarded your blood pressure, too!

Beyond these reasons for controlling yourself, you should never forget that the negative comments you leave for other people speak more about you than they do about the eBayer who receives the comment. If you flame this person or leave rude and insulting comments, your future buyers will see that when they check the feedback you've left for others. Savvy buyers will do that before they buy a relatively expensive item from you. You don't really want other customers to think of you as a loose cannon, just waiting to blow up at someone. You may know you're completely justified in calling this guy for what he is, but no one else is ever going to know the details of that deal that went wrong. They'll only be able to see how you conducted yourself, and you want that conduct to represent you well. Finally, remember that if you actually libel someone, you can be sued. Then, the single transaction that went bad will seem like a fond memory compared to the aggravation of a lawsuit.

» When the negative comes, let it go

Given everything you've learned, you'll probably go a long way without a negative feedback. When you're careful in your eBay business, you'll find it's much more likely that you'll be getting positives. Just keep your goals realistic. Getting your first negative feedback is much like getting that first scratch on your new car. It hurts, but at the same time, there's a bit of relief in the pain. Now that it's happened, the pressure to prevent it is off. A 100 percent positive feedback rating is a wonderful thing to have, but it isn't essential to a successful eBay business, and it isn't a requirement to guarantee your life as a PowerSeller.

You are bound to displease someone eventually, and that person may very well resort to a negative feedback without giving you the proper chance to make it right. Once you have the negative, you can amend it with a comment. If you add something like "buyer never told me she was unhappy. Would have refunded her money," the comment gains a bit of perspective. Now, you keep your perspective, too. It's not the end of the world.

During the first month or so, that negative comment will be right there on your first feedback page for all the world to see. As long as you stay busy and please more customers, that comment will get pushed further and further down your feedback comments. It won't be too long before it's off the first page completely. Anyone who bothers to scroll through your feedback comments is likely to understand that every seller can get a stray negative comment here and there. It won't dramatically alter your rating, and in time it will be subsumed in the sheer volume of your positive feedbacks. No reasonable buyer will wade through page after page of positive feedbacks to find the occasional neutral or negative, and even those buyers who use the Negative/Neutral feedback finder will keep the comment in context. So, pick yourself up, brush off your pride, and get back to the work of PowerSelling.

For this chapter, we decided to profile a professional mediator instead of a PowerSeller. Because this mediator's job requires complete anonymity, we're not going to reveal any details that could identify him or her. Instead we will call this person "Mediator" and switch pronouns between the feminine and masculine, so that no one will ever guess Mediator's true identity. From talking with Mediator, who currently works with Square Trade, we gained an interesting perspective that isn't tainted by this individual's personal experiences as either a buyer or a seller.

It's gratifying to learn that most of the mediations that come before Mediator have nothing at all to do with "outright fraud or malice." Most often, parties come to resolve disputes that began with miscommunication and escalated to rancor, creating a situation where neither party was able to step back far enough to see a resolution. A good many problems begin when the buyer simply doesn't read the auction listing. If he doesn't bother to read it, he may miss the fact that the item is used. He might not follow the seller's procedures for payment, and he may not get the shipping he thought he was going to get. Then he gets angry, because his expectations haven't been met. The seller is angry, because this buyer didn't have realistic expectations to begin with.

Another source of conflict is shipping. If an item gets damaged in shipping, the buyer is going to be disappointed. The seller must respond to this situation without blaming the buyer, but that doesn't always happen. If the seller responds to the buyer's complaint with suspicion or an accusation that the buyer may have caused the damage, the problem is likely to go to mediation.

Mediator recommends that before either party resorts to mediation, they try to resolve the issue between themselves through direct, calm, and reasoned communication. If that's not possible, the matter can be turned over to Square Trade, and Mediator or one of his associates will be assigned to intervene. eBay actually subsidizes the mediation, and one party, usually the seller, pays the fee of $20.00 to have the matter mediated. The first step is for Mediator to review all of the interactions between the buyer and seller, both through eBay and through e-mail outside of eBay, too. (Didn't we tell you to watch your e-mail tone and content?) Then she tries to see where the problem came about, and she attempts to suggest a reasonable resolution to the issue.

Mediator says that very often the issue is just getting everyone to stop blaming and shouting. He tries to get the aggrieved party to see that the other person meant no harm. Sometimes just an apology is enough to make the parties see each other more clearly and find a resolution. She reminds both parties that they want to be buyers and sellers on eBay for years to come, and that they are losing track of the big picture. She reports that she has seen a greater than 50 percent success rate with this approach.

Mediator makes some clear recommendations for preventing problems between buyers and sellers. These should all sound familiar to you by now:

1. Take clear photos that show the flaws, if there are any.

2. Be very careful in your descriptions.

3. Be rigorous in shipping your items.

4. Follow up with your customers to make sure they're happy.

5. Behave professionally.

Additionally, he recommends that you take certain things into consideration. Don't deal in products that are easily marked for fraud or misrepresentation. Mediator notes that Louis Vuitton bags are commonly mediated items. People sell them as genuine when they're not. They also sell them used and in excellent condition, only to find that the buyer detects a smell or marks on the bag that the seller didn't mention. Steer yourself away from things that could leave you vulnerable.

She also reminds you to be aware of your trading partner's feedback history. "With less than a 97 or 98 percent rating, get suspicious. Look at the individual comments, not just the numbers for these sellers, so you can see what the issues are. Remember that on eBay, a 91 percent does not mean this person is a good student."

Mediator further reminds us that participating in eBay is something of a game of chance. You take risks, and you reap rewards. When things go sour, do your best to fix it yourself, but if all else fails, turn to mediation. "It's a great alternative to lawyering up."

Chapter 10

Keeping Records—or Let's Have a Look at Those Books, Buddy

We hope that by now you've begun to think of yourself as a real businessperson. You've certainly been submerged in subjects that only businesspeople must consider. You've built yourself a PowerShop with all the tools necessary to operate a business. You've considered the best approaches to customer service. You've designed your own policies for receiving payments from customers and shipping your products to their final destinations. Now it's time to take a look at that other part of being a businessperson. Keeping your books and managing your records is a vital part of managing your own business. It's also the part where many new and small businesspeople begin to stumble.

To us it seems that record keeping is a lot like housework. Who among us really loves it? Yet, we all have to do it. Like housework, it's best done routinely and consistently, and we've all managed to find our own systems that work and our own schedules for getting the tasks done. Start managing your records and keeping your books from the very beginning. Do it right, right from the start. You'll reap the rewards of your efforts in the form of taxes that you can prepare without anguish, reports that will help you analyze your business growth, and nights of restful sleep knowing you've got everything in order.

Don't be hard on yourself if you're dreading this part of your business life. Many PowerSellers told us it's the part they dislike the most too. We'll help you to get started, and we'll make some recommendations that should lessen your load, but please remember we are not accountants or tax attorneys. We'll give you some guidelines, but you'll want to make sure you're complying with all of your state and local tax and business laws. We can't help you much with that. Not knowing what your local laws are will not excuse you if the regulating agencies in your area come calling. So, make sure you consult the proper professionals in your area to ensure that you are in compliance with zoning and licensing laws, and you are meeting the requirements of all local and state taxes.

Getting Off to a Good Start

That's not to say that keeping your business records and accounts is all challenge and no benefit. Yes, you have more work to do because you have these records to keep. But on the other hand, you now have business deductions that you were not eligible to take as an average taxpayer. Plus, it's never been easier to get help with having your own business than it is now, thanks to the Internet. Millions of others run successful businesses, and you can too. Now, let's get off to the right start.

» Visit SCORE

Since 1964 SCORE has been providing valuable support to people who want to start and build their own businesses. SCORE is a national nonprofit organization that works in partnership with the Small Business Administration. Its mission is to "provide professional guidance and information, accessible to all, to maximize the success of Americans' existing and emerging small businesses." You can visit SCORE online at www.SCORE.org, or you can arrange to meet in person with one of the 10,500 volunteers who work through 389 SCORE chapters across the country. These volunteers are local businesspeople who already operate successful businesses and want to help newcomers to the business world get started.

You will find that these businesspeople include accountants who are more than happy to answer your questions about how to get your business started. "The first thing I did was to schedule an appointment with an accountant through SCORE," said a PowerSeller specializing in gift items. "He sat with me and showed me all the records I'd need to keep, and how I might store and organize them." This PowerSeller isn't alone. In the last 40 years, SCORE has helped more than six million people who wanted to start businesses. Today you'll find that SCORE not only offers person-to-person meetings, but also low-priced local workshops, e-mail advice, and a toll-free number to help you find your local SCORE chapter.

The SCORE home page, shown in Figure 10-1, is a good place to start gathering information from professionals who are only there because they want to help you. You'll find a Reading Room with dozens of articles about every type of business concern from hiring employees to managing your office. You can also use SCORE's 60-Second Guides, quick tips on subjects as varied as cash flow, obtaining a loan, and writing a business plan. There is also an archive of business articles written by experts in fields as varied as Information Technology and Human Resources. Plus, you'll find specialized information for aspiring minority, women, veteran, and young entrepreneurs. Finally, sign up for SCORE's free e-mail newsletters. *SCORE*

Visit SCORE

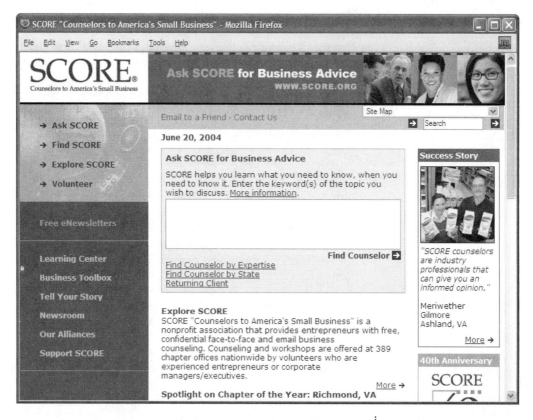

eNews is a monthly newsletter that discusses the latest trends and resources to help small business owners. *SCORE Expert Answers* discusses marketplace trends and provides advice from both small business experts and industry leaders.

FIGURE 10-1 The SCORE home page lets you easily see the resources available to you through this all-volunteer program.

You'll be able to find the SCORE volunteers closest to you by searching the site via ZIP code. Once you've selected a volunteer from those listed, you fill out a form in which you describe your business needs. Your SCORE volunteer will respond within 48 hours. E-mail exchanges are fine, but we recommend you arrange for a one-on-one meeting.

When you meet with your SCORE volunteer, prepare some questions in advance. Here are a few to get you started:

- What information should I be recording for each of my transactions?

- What records should I be keeping to document my expenses?

■ What are the local regulations for zoning, taxes, and licensing in our area?

■ Can you advise me about incorporating or registering my business?

■ Should I use cash-basis accounting or accrual-basis accounting? (Cash-basis accounting means you report income when you actually receive it and cost your expenses when you actually accrue them. Accrual-basis accounting is inventory based. When you sell an item from inventory, you report the earning even if you haven't yet been paid.)

■ How can I best depreciate my computer and office equipment?

■ Can you recommend an accountant and/or bookkeeper?

» Educate yourself

Your meeting will be more productive, and so will your business, if you educate yourself a bit about accounting. Even if you ultimately hire a bookkeeper and an accountant (more about that in a minute), you'll be better able to explain your needs and assess their work if you at least understand the vocabulary they use. You can, of course, get some great basic accounting books at the local library or invest in one for your own library. We recommend *Accounting and Finance for Small Business Made Easy* by Bob Low (McGraw-Hill, 2004). But you can also find some help online. BusinessTown.com, shown in Figure 10-2, is a valuable site you'll find at www.businesstown.com. The site offers a wealth of information about all types of business concerns, but it has a whole separate section for accounting information. Here you'll find easy-to-digest bits of information about accounting and very clear descriptions of accounting vocabulary terms. You will also learn how to read an income statement or a balance sheet, how to manage a general ledger, and the details of both amortization and depreciation. It's a great place to start your accounting education.

» Start with all new accounts

If you're going to run a legitimate and successful business, you must separate your personal banking from your business

Start with all new accounts

banking. This makes it so much easier to actually see how well your business is earning, how much you're spending, and where your money is going. You'll need a business checking account for paying bills, a business savings account for storing your profits with interest, and a business credit card. Once you open your business accounts, make sure all of your expenses are drawn directly from them and all of your earnings go directly into them. Your business credit card should be the one you use to register with PayPal and eBay. Now all of your monthly fees will come on a credit card statement that does not include the new sneakers your son needed last month and your spouse's charge for the dentist. When you're gathering your records for your tax returns, everything on the statements for this account will be for your business. That will make life easier for both you and your accountant.

FIGURE 10-2 BusinessTown.com makes it easy for you to quickly learn about all types of business issues.

Think Like a Business Now

In your regular life, it probably works for you to stick your receipts in your pocket or purse. You may have to uncrumple them and try to decipher what they once said. That's not going to work for you anymore. You'll need to come up with a system for keeping every receipt, bank statement, and canceled check. Your system should be both thorough and simple. If you make it too complicated, you're likely to sidestep it, and then you'll be missing valuable documents when it comes time to do your taxes or assess your actual business costs versus profits.

We've found the easiest way to keep paper records straight is to use an expandable accordion-like file folder. Ours comes with a little clasp that catches the fold-over top to keep things secure. Each tab inside the folder has an alphabetical label, but you can alter the label to suit your own needs. Every time you get a receipt or a statement from your accounts, slip the paper into this folder according to your own filing system. Resist the temptation to let them build up on your dresser or in your purse. Keep your records straight as they come in and you'll avoid those horrible hours of trying to re-create documentation that you received months earlier. When the time comes for you to use the information, just pull it out of its folder and you're ready to go.

» If it's deductible, don't forget to deduct it

To offset the aggravation keeping your books can bring, when you operate your own business, you acquire lots of deductible business expenses you may never have had before. Now that you're thinking like a business owner, don't forget to account for these. Using part of your home exclusively for operating your own business allows you to deduct a portion of your homeowner's expenses as business expenses. You'll want to figure the estimated square footage of your home that is used exclusively for your business. That percentage then becomes the percent of your home's expenses that you can attribute to your business. If, for example, your home office constitutes 10 percent of your total living space, then 10 percent of the cost of owning, heating, and insuring your home can go toward

If it's deductible, don't forget to deduct it

your business expense. Just remember, that means this part of your house is used exclusively for business. If the kids have been using your computer for homework, you'll have to get them one of their own.

All of the supplies and incidentals that you need to run your business count as expenses so long as you use them exclusively for that purpose. That includes all of your office supplies such as paper for your printer, labels and boxes for shipping your items, and postage too. But it also includes other things you may not have thought of. Your high-speed Internet connection is a business expense. So is all of your long distance calling for tracking down sources and working with your customers. The software you purchase is an expense, and so is the book you buy to teach yourself how to use the software. If you take a course to learn more, that's also deductible. If you subscribe to a newsletter that will help you educate yourself about your business, you can deduct the subscription fee. The same is true of the dues you pay to join an association or gain an accreditation in your particular field of expertise. You can even count the fees you pay your accountant when she does the taxes for your business.

Your travel expenses are deductible when you travel for business too. That includes the trip to the post office and the office supply store, or the trip you make to a trade show or to purchase inventory. Keep a small pad in the car and record the mileage for every trip you make for your business. It's not just your mileage that's deductible either. All of the tolls you pay, the meals you eat, and the lodging expenses you pay are deductions, as long as you made your trip on behalf of your business.

Now, you can't just claim you incurred these expenses. You have to prove it. You have to have paper documentation in the form of receipts, canceled checks, bill stubs, or credit card statements. For each expense you have to provide the date you incurred the expense, the person or company providing the service or product, and the business purpose of the expense. That's simple if you're buying a piece of software, but not quite so clear-cut if you're staying the weekend at a collector's show to build your inventory. Be sure to document the purpose of the expense when you incur it. That's so much easier than trying to figure it out months down the road. When you get home, file them all away into that simple, but thorough, filing system you devised.

For a much more complete list of business expenses, talk to your accountant. He'll know exactly what you can claim and how you can document everything you spend. Our suggestions are meant to get you started.

Uncle Sam May No Longer Want You, But He Does Want a Piece of Your Income

When you work for someone else, it's pretty clear what your tax liabilities will be. You complete a W4-form when you sign on telling your employer what to withhold for your tax bill. Every year your employer gives you a W2-form that states what you earned and how much federal income tax was withheld on your behalf. Those easy days are gone once you become your own boss. It will be up to you to estimate your tax bill for each year and pay estimated taxes quarterly toward your annual tax bill. Quarterly tax payments are due January 15, April 15, June 15, and September 15. If you fail to pay at least 90 percent of the tax you owe or an amount equivalent to your tax liability of the previous year, you could be facing penalties and interest charges. Work with your accountant to determine what your quarterly tax payment should be, and don't forget to make those payments on time.

When you complete your income tax return for your business, you will now have to use a Schedule C form along with your Form 1040. The Schedule C is the Profit or Loss from Business form. You'll use this form to itemize all of your business expenses for the year. Then you'll factor the cost of your operation against the profit you earned to determine your earnings and your tax liability.

He's Here to Help

Our only wish for you is that you'll have to pay a big tax bill next year. That's the best kind of problem to have, since only people who earn good money have to worry about big tax bills. While you make your transition from individual filer to business filer, you'll find the Internal Revenue Service hasn't left you all alone. Go to www.irs.ustreas.gov/businesses/small/index.html for the online resource center established by the IRS for the small business owner or the self-employed individual. You'll see the home page for this site in Figure 10-3. Here you'll find online workshops for helping you manage your taxes. You can also get

If it's deductible, don't forget to deduct it

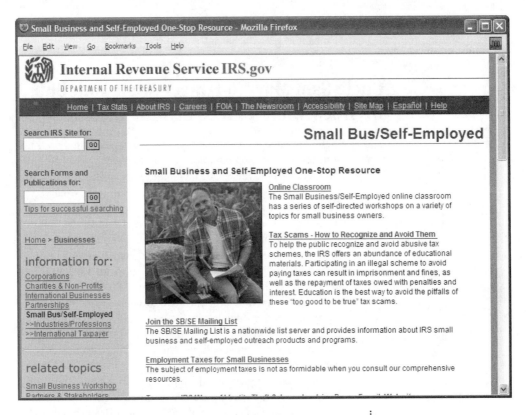

FIGURE 10-3 This online resource center from the Internal Revenue Service helps you learn about managing your records and preparing your taxes.

a Federal tax calendar here to help you track those estimated payments. A small business resource guide is available on CD-ROM to help you keep current with the changing tax laws.

Tax laws are very complicated, and only those who are well educated on the subject can claim to be completely up-to-date with huge and ever-changing codes. Educate yourself, of course, because you need to be an educated consumer, but never take the word of any book published about your individual taxes. The subject is too complicated. Each case is individual, and books about taxes, by virtue of their medium, can become inaccurate between the time their authors write them and the time you read them.

Social Security

Just in case you're already having too much fun with the subject of your income taxes, we'll spread a little more joy your way. You also have to pay for your own Social Security taxes while you're at it. The time was you paid part of it, which your employer deducted from your regular pay, and your employer paid part of it too. Now the entire bill is up to you. Plus, if you hire employees, you'll have to pay their Social Security taxes and withhold income tax from them too.

That's one reason why some people hire only independent contractors. If you want the fellow down the street to come into your home office twice a week to do some packing and shipping for you, you'll need to decide if he's your employee or if he's an independent contractor. If he's your employee, you'll be responsible for his Social Security and tax withholding. If he's a contractor, it will be his responsibility, but you'll need an invoice from him for all of the hours he works for you each week. Then he'll have to file the taxes on his return.

Sales Tax

Of course, by now, you've taken our advice from Chapter 2 and gotten yourself a tax ID number. That's good, because as soon as you start selling things, you'll have to start collecting state sales tax too. As of this writing, you only have to collect sales tax for items shipped to customers who live in your own state. That may change very soon, but it's been difficult for the states to agree on how to collect the taxes for items purchased and shipped across state lines. You are exempt from this only if you live in one of the five states that currently, as of this writing, doesn't have a state sales tax. Those lucky individuals already know who they are, but for the rest of us, those states are Alaska, Delaware, New Hampshire, Montana, and Oregon. All the rest of us have got to collect sales tax. There are no exceptions.

» Hire an accountant

This piece of advice probably doesn't come as a surprise to you, after you've read what we've had to say about setting up your accounts and dealing with your taxes. We'd tell you this even if it weren't the advice of countless PowerSellers. But, it is. PowerSeller after PowerSeller told us the same thing. Accountants earn their livelihoods by knowing all of the details of tax codes and money managing. Unless you are a trained accountant yourself, you couldn't possibly match the knowledge and expertise of a professional. Besides, we suspect that you'd

Hire an accountant

rather spend your energies staying current with the changes in your own market rather than staying current with the ever-changing tax codes. Find yourself a good Certified Public Accountant, and make friends. Begin your search by asking your friends or other small business owners for recommendations. You'll be glad you did, and so will your business.

The Tools You'll Use

Now, just because you're going to hire an accountant, that doesn't mean you're going to get away with not using any tools of your own. You don't want to pay an accountant's hourly rate to manage the day-to-day earnings and expenses of your business. You'll be going to your accountant for help with the big picture and to have someone do your taxes for you, but you'll be responsible for keeping track of the incidentals from one tax year to the next. Fortunately, when you built your PowerShop after reading Chapters 3 and 4, you included some important tools that will help.

Use Your Auction Management Software

As you saw in Chapter 4, your auction management software will track a great deal of information for you about what you spend, sell, and ship. You can use it as a vital part of your record-keeping toolbox. Most auction management software packages offer similar features and functions, whether the program you choose is Web-based or a desktop application. We'll discuss the features of eBay's own auction management software to serve as an example for you. As you will remember, Seller's Assistant Pro is desktop-based, and Selling Manager Pro is Web-based.

Both products allow you to tract your inventory. They both offer you automatic incrementing and decrementing of inventory items, so you don't have to manually add or subtract each item individually. They both offer you automatic restocking alerts to let you know when you're running low. And, they both allow you to create listings linked to a specific product.

Using either program, you can preview, edit, reschedule, or cancel scheduled listings online. You can also monitor active listings in real time. This allows you to quickly see what's happening with all of your auctions and make adjustments to your listings easily.

In addition, Selling Manager Pro, because it's a Web-based program, allows you to track your buyers' communications and note whether the items you've sold have been paid for and/or shipped. You can gather this information for both individual sales and those made in bulk. The communications features of Selling Manager Pro also allow you to record your buyer communication to help you with resolving issues with Non-Paying Bidders. You can also note and send automatic payment received notification e-mails and automatic item shipped notification e-mails. These help you keep track of the items that have actually sold and/or moved out of your inventory. Finally, Selling Manager Pro offers you the option of creating printer-friendly reports. This will ultimately save you some money on toner costs. But on the other hand, Selling Manager Pro will store your records for only 120 days, while Seller's Assistant Pro will allow you to keep them indefinitely, because they are all stored on your own computer.

PayPal Will Help

PayPal's Post-Sale Manager tracks all of your end-of-sale activities. Using it, you can view all of your information for the past 30 days. You can also view a log of your PayPal transactions for any time period you specify—even your entire PayPal history. You simply click the My Account tab along the top of any PayPal page, then the History subtab. From there you can specify the time period you're interested in viewing. You can download this History for use in your favorite spreadsheet, Quicken, or QuickBooks. Using PayPal's Post-Sale Manager gives you a central console for tracking all of your PayPal activities. The Post-Sale Manager will also give you access to records for transactions that have already been completed. Figure 10-4 shows you just what your page will look like. The data you can get through this page includes the following:

- **Item number**   The eBay item number and title for each of your listings.

- **End date**   The closing date for each of your listings. You can sort all your listings by end date if you wish.

- **Price**   The final price for each item sold.

- **Quantity**   How many items in a multiple listing sold.

- **Buyer's User ID**   The eBay ID for each winning bidder corresponding to the item purchased.

Hire an accountant

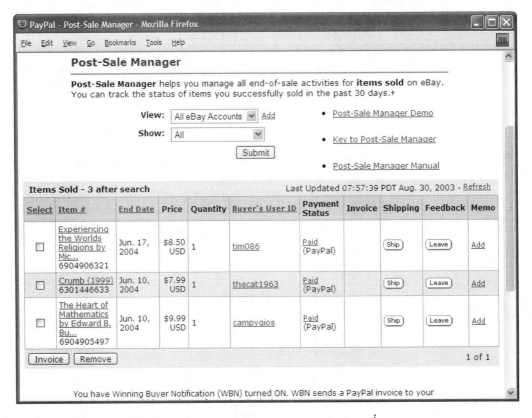

FIGURE 10-4 Here's a sample of PayPal's Post-Sale Manager. From this screen, you can easily track all of your PayPal activities.

- **Payment Status**   Whether or not the item has been paid for through PayPal. If you receive payment outside of PayPal, this will not automatically update.

- **Invoice**   Notification of whether or not you've invoiced your customer.

- **Shipping**   The status of items purchased, either shipped or yet to be shipped.

- **Feedback status**   Have you left feedback yet?

Tip   *PayPal offers you an online manual to help you learn all about using Post-Sale Manager. You'll find the link to the PDF file containing the manual at www.paypal.com/ cgi-bin/webscr?cmd=p/auc/auc_manager-outside. You'll need Adobe Acrobat to read the file.*

QuickBooks

"I used to recommend QuickBooks to my enemies," says CPA and QuickBooks Advisor Terry Lanier of LMGW Certified Public Accountants, based in California. That was before Intuit greatly improved their software. Now he says it's the easiest and most intuitive way to keep track of your business. An estimated 75 percent of LMGW's clients use the program to record their invoices and cash receipts, write checks, create financial statements, and prepare tax records for their accountants at the end of the year. Terry explains that the beauty of QuickBooks, its ease of use, is also its greatest disadvantage. Because nearly anyone can use the program, people often don't use it properly. The software, according to Terry, "was designed for people who don't know much about accounting, but who can follow rules." Problems occur when people *don't* follow the rules and either fill out the forms incorrectly or stray from the forms completely.

Terry has identified seven common mistakes that new QuickBooks users typically make:

1. **Initial set-up**   People often choose the wrong starting date. They don't properly enter bank account balances and outstanding checks or deposits. They don't properly enter amounts owed to the company by customers or amounts owed by their company to vendors. They select an inappropriate or incomplete chart of accounts.

2. **Use of the forms**   People often bypass the form for invoicing, check writing, and other functions and instead use journal entries for these activities.

3. **Receiving payments from customers**   Users often don't properly reduce their inventories when they receive payments. They also bypass the cash receipts form when processing their cash sales.

4. **Making payments to vendors**   Users often make mistakes when using the check writing function after entering a bill.

5. **Using credit cards**   Users commonly enter only the amount to be paid on a credit card bill, not the entire balance owed.

6. **Paying sales or payroll taxes**   People often neglect to use the "pay payroll taxes" or "pay sales taxes" functions.

7. **Setting up items and classes**   Users often improperly set up items to categorize sales and identify gross margins. They also improperly set up items for sales tax reporting, and they fail to use classes to separate profit or cost centers.

As long as you will be shopping around for an accountant anyway, why not look for one who is also a QuickBooks advisor? Your accountant can then help you establish your bookkeeping procedures, and you'll have someone to turn to when you have specific questions. You may also want to consider taking a QuickBooks course. Many local community colleges offer them.

Excel

We mentioned in Chapter 3 that you should also be using Excel, the spreadsheet program from Microsoft. If you're comfortable with Excel, you can download your PayPal account history directly into the spreadsheet software. Download My History is one of your options under PayPal's Reporting Tools. You'll reach these tools by clicking the My Accounts tab. You can customize the fields you're downloading and also specify a date range (up to one year). Of course, for working with your data within Excel, or any spreadsheet for that matter, you need to download that data as a comma-delimited file. You can also produce Excel-compatible reports with Selling Manager Pro, Seller's Assistant Pro, and many other auction management software programs.

» Hire a bookkeeper

"I used to do all my own books," says a PowerSeller from the Midwest. "Now I've hired a professional bookkeeping service, and I turn it all over to them." Many PowerSellers agree that their time is better spent in other parts of their businesses, and the money they spend for a professional bookkeeper is money well spent. You can easily hire a bookkeeper as an independent contractor and avoid having to pay all the payroll taxes and

Social Security taxes you'd pay an employee. That doesn't mean you can avoid learning about the bookkeeping aspects of your business, because you'll need to be educated in order to work with your bookkeeper, but you don't have to carry the entire burden of keeping your own records, once you've gotten yourself organized and under way.

Meet a PowerSeller

bidnow5—Glen and Diane Turner

Glen and Diane Turner have been dealing in antiques for many years. Before 1997, they sold mostly through antique shows and through their own store. In 1997, Glen began to believe that the future was going to be on the Internet. He bought a computer just for the purpose of selling his items online. In December of that year, he spoke with a friend who was selling Beanie Babies on eBay. The next morning he had his first auction listing. By 2000, he

had begun to work on his eBay business full time, and today he and Diane have a member profile that includes nearly 12,000 feedbacks with a positive rating of 99.9 percent. They've also expanded their inventory to include much more than antiques.

The couple found that it was just too difficult to generate enough income from selling only antiques. Plus, they found it labor intensive to have to create individual listings for each of the unique items they sold from their inventory. Glen happened to meet the manager of a company that sold new items, and that was the beginning of his working with wholesalers. Glen buys the fringes of the wholesaler's items, those small quantities of things that are left over when the larger orders are all filled.

According to Glen, he and Diane are professional shoppers. On Saturdays and Sundays they make their "house calls" at local garage, yard, and estate sales. During the week Glen visits wholesalers. They also regularly go to flea markets and the Salvation Army stores. Glen and Diane shop carefully because they have limited storage space for inventory, and they want to ensure that they'll quickly move the items they purchase.

Glen and Diane use four computers networked together to support their eBay business. They use Seller's Assistant Pro and have used it for years, even before eBay owned the product. They use Sellathon to analyze their sell-through and to determine how their customers found their auction listings. It also helps them see how many people are watching their items. Glen also uses counters, but now he uses them only when he's trying a new line of products. One of the couple's biggest technical challenges came when the house next door was struck by lightening. That blew out the phone lines and left Glen and Diane without a cable modem for about a week!

Glen offers free shipping with orders over $50.00. He operated a machine shop for 17 years before he entered his present life. He says when he prepares to ship his items, he imagines that someone is going to try to "drive a truck over them." With this image in mind, he's prepared to package everything so that it will arrive safely. He told us that he's shipped more than 50,000 items through the USPS and has had only one damage claim!

Providing customer service through his eBay business is "three times as hard" as it was in his brick-and-mortar store. Glen thinks that's because it's just so easy for people to take out their frustrations with someone when they only relate to them online. He deals with his customers by remembering that they are always right, and his feedback rating proves that his approach is successful. Glen recommends that people hoping to build successful eBay businesses remember this. He also suggests they use a digital camera from the very beginning and good software to support their business efforts. He, Diane, and their two daughters form a "collecting" family centered by a successful eBay business.

Chapter 11

Is It Time to Open an eBay Store?

Now that you've got your eBay business off to a great start, have you been thinking about opening an eBay store? Your eBay store will allow you to create your very own e-commerce site. You'll stock it yourself, and it will reflect your own personality and interests. If you're still thinking of eBay as a giant mall (the *real* Mall of America), your eBay store makes it easy for you to rent space in that mall, present your own store to the world, stock it with your items, and manage and promote it yourself. Topping it off, you'll create your eBay store using the same type of simple eBay templates you've used to create the listings you've already been running.

There are many reasons why you should have a store. Establishing yourself as an online retailer is much cheaper through eBay than it would be if you set out to do it on your own. Plus, through an eBay store, you have ready access to eBay's 100-million+ customer base.

Listing items is cheaper in your store than it is through regular eBay auctions outside of the special store environment. You determine how long your item remains for sale in your store, and as we'll explain, cross-merchandising (upselling) between your regular auctions and your store is simple. Having your own store gives you added credibility as an eBay seller. You'll also get your own static web address (www.stores.ebay.com/*your store name*) that you can use in any of your marketing materials both online and offline.

If you're still not convinced, eBay reports that sellers see a 25 percent boost in their revenues, on average, during the first three months after they've opened a store. Of course, that could just reflect the fact that overall, they have more items for sale once their stores open. Still, most of the PowerSellers we spoke with have stores and recommend them.

Even though you have an eBay store, you will still want to create regular auctions. Your auction listings will drive buyers to your store, because each of your auctions will include a direct link to your store. Once you've created your store, your regular eBay auctions will automatically appear in your store, too. In addition to your auction inventory, you'll also use the Store Inventory Format to list items for much less than you would through auctions outside of the store environment. Note that because of the reduced rates, Store Inventory Items only show up in regular eBay searches when there are ten or fewer results in auction or fixed-price format listings. These Store Inventory listings matching a search will appear after the "regular" search results list.

You can use your eBay auctions to direct buyers to the same items available in your store for the same price—either as an auction or in multiple quantities. Many storeowners also use their stores to sell add-ons, such as memory cards for digital cameras or other items that are normally purchased concurrently with an item if they are being purchased in a brick-and-mortar store.

Although a part of eBay, eBay Stores have their own set of guidelines dictating how they are "stocked," managed, and promoted. There's no reason at all to feel intimidated, because setting up an eBay store is simple. The rules about who can set up a store are quite broad—anyone can do so if they have a feedback rating of at least 20 or are ID verified. They must also already have a seller's account with eBay and have a credit card on file.

A Word about Fees

If you consider just listing fees, the question of whether or not to open an eBay store requires little thought. You're giving away money if you don't. For store items you can pay a listing fee of just $0.02 for every 30 days per item. As mentioned, these are for Store Inventory Items; they are not regular auctions. Listings can contain any quantity of items you want (e.g., a listing for 1,000 individual widgets, each separately for sale, still costs only $0.02). Also, listings can be set up as Good 'Til Cancelled (often referred to GTC), meaning the listing runs until the seller ends the sale or the item sells (or sells out, in the case of multiple items in a listing). In calculating your costs, you also have to figure in Final Value Fees, and the normal fees for listing upgrades.

In your eBay store, you'll be able to use listing upgrades at greatly reduced prices for store inventory items. You can add the Gallery feature, for example, for only $0.01 for each item. This feature will run for as long as you've listed your store item at the same low price. You can also choose an Item Subtitle upgrade for your store inventory items. This feature will cost only $0.02 for 60 days, $0.04 for 90 days, $0.06 for 120 days, or $0.08 for a Good 'Til Cancelled listing. As you can see, not only can you save money on your listings by placing your items in your store inventory, but you can make use of upgrades that you might not generally try in your regular auction listings.

When deciding about opening a store, you should factor in the subscription fees (the equivalent of rent) you must pay.

These vary depending on the complexity of your store and where eBay promotes it for you. The three categories are Basic ($9.95 per month), Featured ($49.95 per month), and Anchor ($499.95 per month).

Opening a Basic store is a great way to get started with your eBay store. With it you will receive five additional customizable store pages. When you're ready to upgrade, you can move up to the Featured store. This will give you 10 additional customizable pages for your store. You will also get a free subscription to Selling Manager Pro, which will definitely help offset the extra expense of the store, if you've chosen this as your auction management program. You will also gain additional traffic reporting tools that will help you analyze your store's performance and advanced sales data to help you determine your sales effectiveness. Your store will appear on eBay's Stores Pages, and you'll gain promotional dollars to spend on eBay's Keyword program. Finally, the Anchor stores will provide you with all of these features, but you will also gain 15 additional customizable pages and 24-hour dedicated live customer support services.

» Stick with a basic store until you've built up your feedback number

eBay buyers can be reluctant to buy from a new seller's store, so new storeowners may end up paying more in fees than they realize in sales revenue. You may want to stick with the Basic store subscription level until you have a healthy feedback number and rating. Then you can upgrade your store subscription level if you think it will help boost your sales. Of course, if you find that your store is doing well, then you may feel ready to move up to the next level sooner. With a step up in subscription level, you'll also have access to more marketing help through eBay through Featured stores or home page impressions (Anchor stores).

Getting Started

As with everything else on eBay, you should first look to eBay's online help pages for help in opening your store. From the site map follow the Services heading (the middle one) down to near the end of the page. Start by going to the Stores overview page, http://pages.ebay.com/storefronts/seller-landing.html, shown in

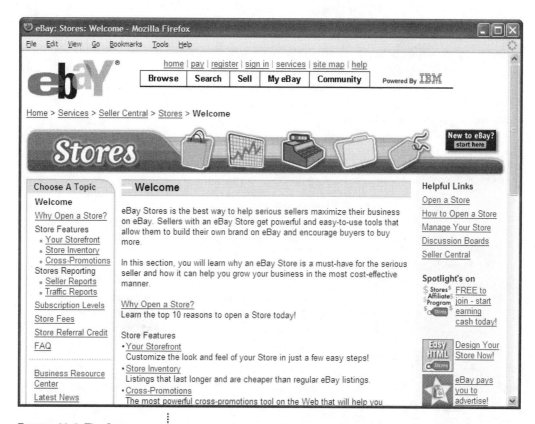

FIGURE 11-1 The Stores overview page is the place to start gathering information about opening your own eBay store.

Figure 11-1. From there you can find just about any information you need to explore the idea of opening a store, and then managing and promoting one.

» Take advantage of sales on eBay store subscriptions

eBay helps you promote your business by frequently running sales on its upgrade fees, listing fees, or advertising fees. You can also catch sales on the Subscription fees it charges for eBay Stores or explore free one-month store trials. When you're planning your eBay store, keep your eyes open for these deals. Have everything ready to go and launch your store to catch the reduced fees eBay offers during these promotions. Since you signed up for eBay's Newsflash after reading Chapter 1, you're sure not to miss the announcement.

Take advantage of sales on eBay store subscriptions

The eBay Stores Discussion Board

We think the eBay Stores Discussion Board is one of eBay's best boards. As a prospective and even current shop owner, you'll find many helpful discussions there. If your question hasn't yet been answered, the many experts who frequent that board will be glad to help you.

According to the eBay Stores Discussion Board, these are some of the top questions (with answers, of course) that people have about eBay stores.

Q: What must I do to open an eBay store?
A: You open a store by simply filling in the pertinent information in the Store Builder utility (http://cgi6.ebay.com/ws/eBayISAPI.dll?CreateYourStore).

Q: How do I list an item in my Store? (Store Inventory format)
A: There are many ways to list items in your store. The process resembles that for listing a regular auction. In the Sell Your Item form, choose "Sell in your eBay Store," and then select the Store Inventory option in the form. Or go to your store, click the Seller, Manage Store link, and choose the List Items for Sale in Your Store box.

Q: I want to change my store's appearance. How do I do this?
A: Manage just about anything you want by clicking the Seller, Manage Store link found at the bottom of your store home page. Also see the Manage/Edit My eBay Store link at the bottom of the Site Map.

Q: When someone conducts a regular search, will my store items appear among the results?
A: Your store items will not appear in regular eBay search results. However, when buyers search for something on eBay and there are ten or fewer results in auction or fixed-price formats, they will see additional Store Inventory listings matching their search. These will follow the "regular" search results list. If they get more than ten results from their search, they can click a link that says, "See additional Buy It Now items from eBay store sellers."

Q: Can I change a Store listing to a regular listing—and vice versa?
A: You cannot change the selling format of any live listing. But you can easily create a new listing and choose a new format then. Log into your My eBay page. Then click on the Sell Similar link under the Manage Listings column of your current listing. To end the original listing to avoid having duplicate listings running simultaneously, go to the Site Map and click the End My Listing link. Note: you can also end your store listings early through this link.

Take advantage of sales on eBay store subscriptions

Q: Why aren't my Store categories showing?
A: Only Store categories that you have listings in will show.

Q: How do I change my User ID to match my Store Name?
A: Take these steps:

1. Change your Store name temporarily to something else. (You can change it back later.)

2. Change your User ID. Be sure to check your spelling before submitting the change, as you can make User ID changes only once every 30 days.

3. When your User ID has been changed, go back and restore the name of your Storefront.

Q: What's the procedure for closing my eBay store?
A: From eBay's Home page click My eBay. Then click the All Selling link in the left-hand column, and the More... link under the Selling Links section. Click the Close Your eBay Store link in the eBay Stores section.

Driving Customer Traffic to Your Store

The help files and other information sources we have mentioned include all the information you need to manage your store. But a topic that's even more important is how you get customers in the "door." Your regular eBay auctions are the best tool you have for driving people to your store. That's because each one will contain a direct link to your storefront in the form of a red shopping tag that appears next to your username. As we've mentioned before, you can also add an HTML link to your listings that will take your shopper directly to your store for a great cross-marketing tool. Once you open your store, be sure to continue to have several auctions going at all times to promote your store as well as sell your products.

Another good way to direct customers to your store via regular auction listings is to use the Cross Merchandising tool that's part of the store seller package. It allows you to show additional items similar to the ones a buyer is viewing within your regular auctions. When buyers click the icons for these items, they'll be taken directly to the relevant page in your store. This tool can work on a "mega" level as well. You can also use it to promote related *categories,* not just items.

Finally, once you have a customer base, be sure they know about your eBay store! Include a link to it in all your electronic correspondence and discretely mention it in all your paper invoices and freebies you send along with purchases.

Of course, just because people have entered your store doesn't mean they will buy anything. Getting browsers to *buy* once they're in your store is another challenge. Strategies include making use of your store's customizable header to highlight certain items (e.g., NEW THIS WEEK). This header shows up on the storefront page and every other store page.

As with auctions, research tools can help here. You can put counters on your storefront, just as you can in your regular auctions. There is also a powerful new traffic reporting tool, which uses technology similar to the technology eBay uses to understand its own traffic. It's available to all store subscribers; you'll find the details at http://pages.ebay.com/storefronts/traffic-reports.html. Through these new "Traffic Reports" you'll receive *real-time* data on the number of times your eBay auctions or areas within your store are viewed, as well as the keywords buyers used to get to your listings. This tool is extremely powerful, and any PowerSeller could make excellent use of it!

» Create your own web site and link it to your eBay store

You've already seen some of the reasons why you should have your own web site. Here's another one: When you create your own site, you can link it directly to your eBay Store. This way, your store will get picked up in search engines outside of eBay. The idea is for your customers to visit you *first* before they even reach the eBay site. "I link my web site directly to my eBay store. That way, a customer comes to me first without ever stepping onto eBay," says a PowerSeller from the South. Why not completely bypass your competition too?

The 2004 Best in Store Winners

There are more than 100,000 eBay stores, so you'll have plenty of company in that great mall you're entering. In 2004, the eBay community selected the best three stores. You'll find the award winners at http://pages.ebay.com/storefronts/

Create your own web site and link it to your eBay store

bestinstores.html?ssPageName=CMDV:Boarin. The categories for which awards were granted, and the winning sellers, were

- **Best Looking Store**   The Frenchy Bee
- **Best Shopping Experience**   Glitz N Glamour Jewelry
- **Best Use of Custom Store Pages**   Cool Sneaks

We don't suppose this will come as a surprise to you, but two of these three stores are operated by PowerSellers. Perhaps one day your eBay store will be selected as one of eBay's best, too!

Meet a PowerSeller

Tony Cicalese

Tony Cicalese is better known on eBay as www.wegotthebeats.com. As you might guess, music is Tony's thing, and he knows what he's doing both musically and in his eBay business. Tony's been selling on eBay since 1999. He arrived on eBay through an accidental turn in his pursuit of his hobby rather than in pursuit of a business goal. You see, Tony is passionate about music and has been building his CD collection forever. He came to eBay to look for more and soon discovered that some of his own CDs were selling on the site for $20.00 or $30.00 more than he'd paid for them. So when he was shopping for CDs, he decided to look for things other people might want. At the same time, he bought ones he wouldn't mind keeping for himself if they didn't sell. In his first batch, he bought a Whitney Houston CD for $6.00 that he sold on eBay for $110.00! That was the beginning of Tony's incredible journey.

Today, Tony travels all over the United States shopping for inventory, but that wasn't always so. He started out living in Florida and making frequent trips from home to buy inventory. He was growing frustrated just thinking of how he was paying rent on his apartment, and he was also paying all of the travel expenses for his trips. Ultimately, he decided to let the apartment go, just for a little while, and live full-time in pursuit of his inventory. That was nearly two years ago, and Tony's traveling still, along with his faithful little feline companion. Together they visit record shops, wholesalers, some music shows, and they also buy from some smaller record labels. They maintain a well-stocked eBay music store.

Tony isn't just passionate about music. He's also smart about it. He seems to know not only what other people will want to buy, but also what will sell in international markets. That's very important because a lot of Tony's best customers are international. He does a great deal of business with people in both Japan and Germany. He has an uncanny sense of what musical styles will be popular there, honed from years of studying the music industry. He also studies his customers, researching their tastes and preferences. This allows him to shop with his customer base in mind. It also allows him to think in terms of niche markets, buying things here in the States that are not very popular (and therefore not expensive) and selling them overseas where they are.

Traveling has, for now, given Tony a fascinating life. He's gone to nine Mariah Carey concerts in the time he's been on the road. She's his favorite performer, and he even had the opportunity to meet her at one concert. He's met wonderful people and had incredible experiences. One afternoon while waiting in New York City for an evening Mariah concert, he happened into a large record store. He was browsing in the Mariah Carey listings, and as he reached for a particular CD, another hand came from the opposite direction and reached it first. Tony looked up to see a man in a Mariah Carey T-shirt holding the CD. They started talking about the concert, their shared admiration, and their collections. As it turns out, this other fan had purchased a rare Mariah Carey CD from one of Tony's own customers, who had purchased it from Tony. So two anonymous fans had an instant connection in a random meeting in the world's largest city.

Tony won't always be traveling around with his little cat. Eventually, he'll go back to his home in Florida and open a CD store in the real world to go along with his eBay business. Until then, you'll have to be satisfied meeting him on eBay. He's an active voice on the PowerSeller's Discussion Boards. You can almost always tell a "Tony" answer before you read the signature, because his opinions are fair, decent, kind, and smart. In the meantime, he's having an amazing adventure, sharing a world of music, and doing a world of good. Tony donates 10 percent of all of his profits from the sale of his CDs to the fight against AIDS. So as you can see, this is one PowerSeller with a great ear for music, a great brain for business, and a great heart for everything else.

Appendix

eBay's Top Sellers Ranked by Feedback Numbers

These are eBay's most experienced sellers, rated so because they have the greatest number of separate transactions. We've provided this list partly for inspiration—one day you may join their ranks. For now, search for these sellers' auctions by using their ID names (click Search at the top of any eBay page, then click the By Seller tab), and see what you can learn from them!

Novato Technology is the source of this data. Novato Technology is a software and web site design company that also provides eBay auction data to its customers' specifications. Novato updates this information monthly. For the latest information go to www.nortica.com/userArea/eBay500_14.asp.

Rank	ID	Feedback	Rank	ID	Feedback	Rank	ID	Feedback
1	jayandmarie	177296	31	techmedia-shop	64254	61	akku-king	53094
2	glacierbaydvd	144338	32	swedemom	63880	62	egameuniverse	53073
3	everydaysource	127539	33	vge007	62328	63	stadt7	52737
4	papier11	123698	34	casacaiman	61332	64	richieent	52121
5	restaurant.com	115417	35	ryanmcc	59838	65	wyomingben	51666
6	foto-walser	110754	36	customerone	59186	66	rgelber	51473
7	trade-company	96671	37	partyman1	59182	67	bargainland-liquidation	51447
8	justdeals.com	93139	38	jewelrybyezra	59180	68	www_boardbroker_de	51264
9	eforcity	92514	39	e-artikel	59096	69	elephantbooks-half	51015
10	alibris	91099	40	venize.de	58474	70	ebestdeal4u	49799
11	mr.mobile	88435	41	player004	57427	71	dotcom-sales	49643
12	fireflyfilmco	84994	42	xcceries	57036	72	hitmenowdotcom	49461
13	kmak333	79907	43	www.memoryworld.de	56778	73	jayhawkks	49304
14	accstation	78473	44	gothamcityonline	56703	74	wesellart	49211
15	itrimming	78352	45	goldngems1	56533	75	www.1aautomotive.com	49090
16	sell2all	77507	46	pugster888	56217	76	viccap99	48889
17	play_it	75620	47	olly_trading!	56117	77	skshop	48848
18	procarparts.com	74887	48	parrothead88	56018	78	inter-net	48656
19	totalcampus.com	74303	49	inetdvd	55993	79	www.csl-computer.com	48452
20	videoplanet	73749	50	grapevinehill	55942	80	bargainbuyers621	48295
21	hoots-loot	73355	51	directtoyou	55476	81	soundcitybeaches	48274
22	daniks-world	72915	52	crazyprices-half	55333	82	hdoutlet	47659
23	abebooks-half	72810	53	bookcloseouts	55081	83	aaka_de	47561
24	the_sharper_image	72395	54	budget-pc.de	54995	84	marsh-net	47227
25	bargains4less	70633	55	www.airbrushtower.de	54837	85	loreleijewelry	47056
26	buyessex	69941	56	foto-kontor	54445	86	47st.photo	46636
27	allshewants	68719	57	cametaauctions	54097	87	diageminc	46428
28	booksxpress	67549	58	art.com	54045	88	yescomusa	46330
29	www*save-it-smart*de	66942	59	megabuys.com	53720	89	omaha	46197
30	symmic	64747	60	cofan222	53475	90	pdg43y	46179

TABLE A-1   Top Sellers Ranked by Feedback, June 2004

Rank	ID	Feedback	Rank	ID	Feedback	Rank	ID	Feedback
91	member9ctb	45435	134	dsc33	38241	177	michael8c09	33393
92	potis-half	45212	135	pcpartusa*com	38174	178	mccomicscom	33265
93	dynamic-auction	45028	136	shippingsupply.com	37535	179	fitformobile-de	33244
94	beavinsons	44834	137	mjrsales	37439	180	kriete	33207
95	hpcb-online	44543	138	www-internetishop-com	37436	181	speedah	33094
96	lhobo	44227	139	(www.intercomsystems.de)	37173	182	milan354	33074
97	returnbuy	43451	140	sterlingtek.com	36682	183	penniesonthedollar!com	32952
98	copro-computer	43333	141	herko_de	36663	184	bargaindepot04	32897
99	5-stardeal	43230	142	familyfundist	36622	185	findingking	32730
100	www.cmttrading.com	43111	143	esmy	36443	186	dvds123dotcom	32604
101	mugsfrank	42882	144	posterden	36411	187	dealit*	32555
102	yang32096	42844	145	jesshopus	36252	188	genuine_oem	32527
103	doolicity	42544	146	budspencerseller	36218	189	shopwhileonline	32372
104	adeal.com	42442	147	evalueville	36183	190	okluge_de	32348
105	landofjewels	42396	148	weisbaden	36088	191	animecast	32330
106	jewelryauctioneer	42160	149	super-cover	36054	192	www-x-part-de	32144
107	closeoutvideo-half	42067	150	rjackson72	35952	193	jim.and.joyce	32109
108	rockbottomgolf	42054	151	www_bbt-shop_de	35865	194	yatchai	31937
109	theplace	41862	152	bargaincell	35833	195	nambca	31921
110	henrys.com	41653	153	daddyhog	35434	196	greatdeals00	31920
111	cdplusinc	41440	154	ediscountbike.com	35320	197	top-computer	31841
112	aboncom	41380	155	dealtree-auctions	35238	198	www.peanutscharms.com	31783
113	www.adko.de	41371	156	we-sell-2u	35214	199	cdfunshop	31607
114	all1euro	41145	157	simsclassicsports	35169	200	lazz2	31528
115	scala1	40911	158	cheapdiecast	35075	201	tommyway.com	31462
116	99volts.com	40900	159	worldsbestdeals	35012	202	globalgolfusa	31393
117	ravenb99	40600	160	media-distributors	34946	203	dallasgolf	31359
118	hitmenow.com	40550	161	addvision	34939	204	gkworld.com	31190
119	akkumann01	40520	162	gogamerscom	34660	205	oldwillknott--- (great-scales!)	31163
120	spoolmak	40499	163	trendline24	34648			
121	skinnyguy.com	40303	164	jdmadera	34624	206	firqual	31134
122	lars-369	39959	165	tele-zubehoer-de	34366	207	fountain_head-half	31125
123	powernetshop.de	39813	166	computermuething	34198	208	yourplanet	31064
124	mancon2	39604	167	shoetime	34108	209	www*celiko*de	30999
125	dvdlegacy	39583	168	oftimespast	34084	210	mr.barlow	30941
126	kokonuts!	39442	169	handyman67_de	33931	211	wirelesshut	30920
127	seedrack	39313	170	aaccessories	33773	212	zzl	30739
128	watchesrme	39232	171	postergiant	33727	213	barneysrubble	30722
129	www.5stardeal.com	38752	172	superbookdeals	33647	214	cd-discounters	30687
130	w.o.m	38720	173	wcg_auctions	33591	215	phoenix_trading_co	30644
131	patan01	38603	174	1busyman	33508	216	vc71	30508
132	williamady	38374	175	videojam-half	33479	217	superpawn	30456
133	movie*mars	38251	176	charmsalot	33456	218	h*a*s	30328

TABLE A-1 Top Sellers Ranked by Feedback, June 2004 *(continued)*

Rank	ID	Feedback	Rank	ID	Feedback	Rank	ID	Feedback
219	mwire	30300	263	live-guard	27829	307	videogameswholesale	25639
220	xinar	30201	264	ptron1	27809	308	cdi-wholesaler	25552
221	netclearances	30180	265	connect-comp	27726	309	encoreunlimited	25541
222	mermaidink	30126	266	shoebacca	27578	310	gold-pool	25525
223	vonderpalette_de	30011	267	edeals	27543	311	divotone	25493
224	astra1917	29842	268	gsprod2	27543	312	techmedia-shop2	25484
225	digitaldogpound	29740	269	lagasse	27495	313	cup-of-tea	25481
226	recordsurpluschi	29739	270	moviemagicusa	27494	314	buddentown	25368
227	toysbabyfachmarkt	29679	271	moviesunlimited.com	27453	315	discountwallpaper	25326
228	neoteric	29674	272	crazyape	27347	316	ludi-world	25290
229	supercards	29625	273	pcsurplusonline.com	27256	317	pda-heaven	25282
230	brentscard	29543	274	sandy810	27115	318	handytech24	25273
231	dvdntoys	29491	275	devotedreader	27026	319	cdsandsinglesstore	25256
232	der-grosshaendler	29477	276	rikkyboy69	27004	320	jeffsstuff8oqi	25200
233	shatzee	29419	277	orientalxpress	26989	321	doublejmusic2	25166
234	videogames.org	29396	278	theblueox	26972	322	twoladz	25127
235	edselbabe	29376	279	pfandhaus-hermann	26943	323	thaigem.com	25119
236	www_playdeluxe_de	29361	280	fabfreebird	26911	324	wwwinfinitymusicinstruments	25080
237	bookmarkthispage	29334	281	waxacar	26868	325	tt-netrade	25073
238	doulmite	29201	282	mikeward	26828	326	bookemporiumdotcom	24884
239	boing737	29035	283	richgu	26646	327	aj$	24877
240	wirelessproducts4u	29007	284	widget	26490	328	greatcatalogue	24871
241	olly_trading	28954	285	rcboyz	26232	329	mistyfallsemporium	24752
242	imicros	28946	286	faxbook	26230	330	mickdaniel	24660
243	cleonejr	28915	287	a1techbooks	26176	331	liquidationcenter	24536
244	terribas	28863	288	inovenda	26168	332	bookbyte_com	24530
245	mdgamesource	28848	289	ms-company	26156	333	daydeal.com	24430
246	efavormart	28806	290	kardkings	26154	334	softwarewholesaler	24411
247	stiller66aol	28797	291	galasports	26126	335	ebr01	24406
248	shopesales	28763	292	mytableware.com	26092	336	mrdiecastracing	24406
249	parob	28732	293	retrofacts	26081	337	ggiezgg	24358
250	moonlight-tech	28713	294	toys-to-treasures	26072	338	blueproton*com	24325
251	wherehousemusic	28685	295	money-savecom	26070	339	gold-chest	24277
252	inno-online	28585	296	esupplystore	26067	340	universalmusicgroup	24272
253	primevalue	28564	297	vcc113	26010	341	powerdealer2001	24260
254	kfzteile24-de	28524	298	tichnak	25969	342	gbayrob	24239
255	milde4	28468	299	intergalactic	25903	343	wildermuth-online.de	24237
256	proshopwarehouse	28376	300	seansky82	25895	344	makotoautotrends_com	24236
257	joeleighs	28338	301	vanzy	25845	345	opinionsrfun	24191
258	telko24	28267	302	diekamera	25822	346	globalpremier	24175
259	cat_from_mars	28221	303	ebatt_de	25746	347	seakap	24163
260	equiteric	28187	304	phonefever	25742	348	auctionbroker	24070
261	www.klema-com.de	28056	305	prime-star	25728	349	2myxcessories	24066
262	projectb_de	28049	306	mcx001	25712	350	bobmill	24032

TABLE A-1   Top Sellers Ranked by Feedback, June 2004 *(continued)*

Rank	ID	Feedback	Rank	ID	Feedback	Rank	ID	Feedback
351	rcorner	23994	393	ctideals	22785	436	jadgang	21852
352	mayet	23970	394	bargainthursday	22774	437	cashco1000	21843
353	www_alphamax_de	23941	395	cmhowell5	22774	438	antiquitybureau	21796
354	studioonellc	23888	396	vglq	22761	439	www_jerseystore2000_com	21778
355	onewikedclown	23882	397	dallasbob	22760	440	www.usedcomp.de!	21771
356	getitgotitgood-auctions	23865	398	fund	22721	441	flyposters	21730
357	actionstuff	23816	399	dackel-hamburg	22715	442	moviegoods.com	21720
358	dbsultan	23785	400	silverforless.com	22711	443	solfire2	21714
359	plegend2001	23777	401	ingopher	22696	444	melinda409	21708
360	gmtobra	23762	402	www.sjglew.com	22653	445	sim-buy	21705
361	www-mediaprofi24-de	23739	403	swapusa	22616	446	europhone	21691
362	click4life	23734	404	autobacs1	22610	447	fullhousedvd	21678
363	toynk	23707	405	davidscds-half	22582	448	xdr2	21634
364	goodies2001	23706	406	800watt	22580	449	discdiggers	21612
365	gotbaseballcards-com	23691	407	fairpricemedien	22533	450	blue-handy	21603
366	www_memoryworld_de	23597	408	pls	22523	451	spokanediscount	21594
367	bausihausi	23588	409	premium-cable	22496	452	mein-handyshop	21592
368	ctgdirect.com	23583	410	surefitoutletstore	22478	453	xenosales.com	21589
369	appleharbor	23544	411	proconnection	22417	454	palleyd	21585
370	oldtymecollectiblescom	23466	412	htdeels	22410	455	ctctct	21567
371	ecellphone	23401	413	dvdparty	22389	456	fastcashpawncom	21554
372	evaluecomp	23360	414	cook290	22387	457	tintensprinter	21494
373	auto4	23333	415	mydealsdirect	22369	458	(www.schnellelieferung.de)	21479
374	all-sports-superstore	23301	416	dm1968	22358	459	delroystreasures	21403
375	moneymartpawn	23270	417	dcbuys	22324	460	as-multimedia	21364
376	www.multimedia-rozanski.de	23235	418	great_service	22259	461	andreashartz	21342
			419	thegotoguy.com	22252	462	nyhunt	21317
377	trendycollectibles	23225	420	csnd69	22217	463	danazwerg	21305
378	interstatemusic	23214	421	books-galore	22211	464	somedudesstuff	21302
379	yumheart	23182	422	drstevew	22194	465	pastprs	21282
380	mymusiccom	23080	423	montana4me	22149	466	jamngems	21280
381	www.bestpricebusters.com	23055	424	laser-charm	22113	467	joelstoysntrains	21275
382	bart_capone	23052	425	royalbargains	22059	468	insidedevil	21269
383	computer-nation_de	23025	426	lyons233324hxb	22057	469	jcagney	21244
384	www.handyquelle.com	22965	427	tsn-cd.de	22053	470	hpcbonline-half	21215
385	ms.dusty	22955	428	doublebeez	21990	471	vette1986	21175
386	abacus24-7	22931	429	sacssales	21982	472	blsmartcom	21168
387	bunches_of_books	22904	430	memoryonly.com	21917	473	spun	21135
388	knackhartes_broetchen	22861	431	gentlegiraffe	21895	474	hirtsgreen	21095
389	ryanmcc2	22852	432	click2digital	21893	475	aracollectibles	21059
390	micksmuse	22850	433	sportscardzz	21890	476	bbcardconnection	21050
391	paylessauction	22816	434	goelecsa	21864	477	battlefield.store	21047
392	gyantzpod	22789	435	freedom-ky	21856	478	gotobidnow	21035

TABLE A-1 Top Sellers Ranked by Feedback, June 2004 *(continued)*

Rank	ID	Feedback	Rank	ID	Feedback	Rank	ID	Feedback
479	djbean	21028	486	99c.de_warenvertrieb	20957	495	digidepot	20864
480	cd-hammerpreise.de	21021	487	pcprintshop	20953	496	xullu0815	20858
481	scheerwholesale	21014	488	knallerpreis	20930	497	parrothead888	20857
482	www.bbtoystore.com	21001	489	fantastic_shopping	20911	498	www.abertek.com	20826
483	brough	20985	490	www-joysell-de	20902	499	recpools	20767
484	jayc	20979	493	posterplanet.net	20879	500	mjentertainment	20763
485	mister-five	20959	494	www.meuros.com	20870			

TABLE A-1   Top Sellers Ranked by Feedback, June 2004 *(continued)*

Index

INTERNATIONAL CONTACT INFORMATION

AUSTRALIA
McGraw-Hill Book Company
Australia Pty. Ltd.
TEL +61-2-9900-1800
FAX +61-2-9878-8881
http://www.mcgraw-hill.com.au
books-it_sydney@mcgraw-hill.com

CANADA
McGraw-Hill Ryerson Ltd.
TEL +905-430-5000
FAX +905-430-5020
http://www.mcgraw-hill.ca

GREECE, MIDDLE EAST, & AFRICA
(Excluding South Africa)
McGraw-Hill Hellas
TEL +30-210-6560-990
TEL +30-210-6560-993
TEL +30-210-6560-994
FAX +30-210-6545-525

MEXICO (Also serving Latin America)
McGraw-Hill Interamericana Editores
S.A. de C.V.
TEL +525-1500-5108
FAX +525-117-1589
http://www.mcgraw-hill.com.mx
carlos_ruiz@mcgraw-hill.com

SINGAPORE (Serving Asia)
McGraw-Hill Book Company
TEL +65-6863-1580
FAX +65-6862-3354
http://www.mcgraw-hill.com.sg
mghasia@mcgraw-hill.com

SOUTH AFRICA
McGraw-Hill South Africa
TEL +27-11-622-7512
FAX +27-11-622-9045
robyn_swanepoel@mcgraw-hill.com

SPAIN
McGraw-Hill/
Interamericana de España, S.A.U.
TEL +34-91-180-3000
FAX +34-91-372-8513
http://www.mcgraw-hill.es
professional@mcgraw-hill.es

UNITED KINGDOM, NORTHERN,
EASTERN, & CENTRAL EUROPE
McGraw-Hill Education Europe
TEL +44-1-628-502500
FAX +44-1-628-770224
http://www.mcgraw-hill.co.uk
emea_queries@mcgraw-hill.com

ALL OTHER INQUIRIES Contact:
McGraw-Hill/Osborne
TEL +1-510-420-7700
FAX +1-510-420-7703
http://www.osborne.com
omg_international@mcgraw-hill.com

Sound Off!

Visit us at **www.osborne.com/bookregistration** and let us know what you thought of this book. While you're online you'll have the opportunity to register for newsletters and special offers from McGraw-Hill/Osborne.

We want to hear from you!

Sneak Peek

Visit us today at **www.betabooks.com** and see what's coming from McGraw-Hill/Osborne tomorrow!

Based on the successful software paradigm, Bet@Books™ allows computing professionals to view partial and sometimes complete text versions of selected titles online. Bet@Books™ viewing is free, invites comments and feedback, and allows you to "test drive" books in progress on the subjects that interest you the most.

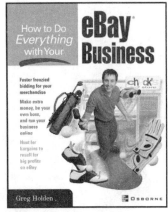